T. W. Allies

The Formation Of Christendom Vol. 2

The Christian Faith and Society

T. W. Allies

The Formation Of Christendom Vol. 2
The Christian Faith and Society

ISBN/EAN: 9783742835741

Manufactured in Europe, USA, Canada, Australia, Japa

Cover: Foto ©Lupo / pixelio.de

Manufactured and distributed by brebook publishing software (www.brebook.com)

T. W. Allies

The Formation Of Christendom Vol. 2

THE
FORMATION OF CHRISTENDOM

BY

T. W. ALLIES, K.C.S.G.

VOL. II

THE CHRISTIAN FAITH
AND SOCIETY

LONDON: BURNS & OATES, Limited
NEW YORK, CINCINNATI, CHICAGO: BENZIGER BROTHERS
1897

ADVERTISEMENT

In the six lectures forming the first volume of this work I was engaged in describing the operation of Christianity, as it took the individual human soul for its unit, purified it, and wrought in it a supernatural life. I began with the consummation of the old world in its state of the highest civilisation united with the utmost moral degeneracy; I proceeded thence to the new creation of individual man; compared heathen with Christian man in the persons of Cicero and St. Augustine; drew out certain effects upon the world around of Christian life, as seen in those professing it, and viewed Christian marriage as restoring the primary relation between man and woman, and thus remaking the basis of human society, while the Virginal Life exhibited the crown and efflorescence of the most distinctive Christian grace in the soul.

I had thus, beginning with the stones of which the building is formed, reached the building itself; and the next thing was to consider the Christian Church in its historical development as the Kingdom of Truth and Grace: for while the soul of man is the unit with which it works, the word "Christendom" betokens a society founded in Christ, made by Christ, stamped with the image of Christ. It is the first great epoch of such a Kingdom of Truth and Grace, proceeding from the Person of its Founder, which I here attempt to delineate.

ADVERTISEMENT

But not merely is the volume which I now publish a part only of a projected design; even as a part it is incomplete. It was my wish to finish this portion of my subject in one volume, which should reach to the great Nicene Council. But the treatment of the Greek Philosophy was too large for my limits, and so the last two chapters serve but as an introduction to the actual contact of that Philosophy with the Christian Church, which remains to be considered before I can complete my view of the Formation of Christendom in the ante-Nicene period.

CONTENTS

LECTURE VII
THE GODS OF THE NATIONS WHEN CHRIST APPEARED

	PAGE
The imperial unity how advantageous to the provinces	1
I. Transition to the polytheistic idolatry	3
1. Its multiplicity	3
Specimen of the worship at Athens	5
Greek worship encompassing all nature	7
Roman worship	7
Oriental religions	9
Effect of conquest on these idolatries	9
Exception of Jewish Monotheism	10
2. Universality of Polytheism	10
3. Its grasp on daily life by means of institutions	11
And still more by the belief in invisible agency	13
4. Moral influence of Polytheism	16
Varro's fabulous and civil theology identical	16
Corruption of the theatre image of corruption in the temples	17
Absence of any moral teaching on divine warrant	19
Prayers not for moral objects	20
Corruption arising from the sensual relation attributed to the deities	20
Idea of sanctification absent from religion	21
Moral corruption the source of polytheistic idolatry on man's part	21
5. Further, a consummating cause for it outside of man	23
Its unity consists in its worship of the fallen Angels	23
And it is directed by one Sovereign	24

CONTENTS

	PAGE
Statements of Scripture corroborated by historical facts	25
1. Its injuriousness to man's happiness here and hereafter	25
2. Its illogical character	26
3. The superhuman power shown in it	27
Witness of its victims to this	28
Witness of its opponents in facts, in the prayers and rites of the Church, and in Christian writers	29
Cumulative force of this evidence	31
6. Relation of Polytheism : 1. to civilisation	31
2. to the political constitution of the empire	33
3. to the national feelings of the provinces	36
4. to despotism and slavery	37
Prospects of Polytheism in the last twenty years of Augustus	38
II. Truth in the judgment-hall of Pilate	40
Truth the second Person in the Godhead	42
The restoration of truth His proper work	43
The restoration of man springs from the eternal relations in the Godhead	45

LECTURE VIII

THE FIRST AND THE SECOND MAN

Introduction : Universality of false worship in the most diverse nations the summing up of man's whole history	47
Fact of man's corruption hence proved	48
I. Solution of this fact given by the Christian Faith	49
Man a race	49
Creation of man : 1. The ideal state of pure nature	49
2. The state of integrity	50
3. The state of original justice or innocence	51
Great elevation of this state	52
One of its conditions, Adam's headship	52
His disobedience and its consequences	54
Condition of Adam and his race after the Fall	55

CONTENTS

	PAGE
The captivity to the devil	57
Heathenism the result of this state	58
Adam's headship shown in the communication of guilt to his race	58
The force of man's social nature	59
Summary of the preceding	60
The counterpart of the First Man as an individual Person, as Head, and as one Body with his race	63
II. How the action of Christ in His Headship is permanent as that of Adam	66
1. The Kingdom of Truth	67
2. The House or Temple of Christ	71
3. The Body of Christ	73
4. The Bride of Christ	75
5. The Mother of the race	76
The various loves of Christ shown in the titles of Kingdom, Temple, Body, Bride, and Mother.	76
What the union of these terms imports	78
Parallel in the formation of the natural and mystical Body of Christ	79
The Church "the Power of the Holy Ghost coming upon men"	80
Five analogies between the natural and the mystical Body	80
The Holy Ghost the soul of the Church: St. Augustine	81
The power of the Holy Ghost the whole treasure of Truth and Grace	83
The five titles indicate that the fruits of the Incarnation come through the Church	83
The first communication of the divine life in Baptism	84
Coherence of the natural and mystical Body in the Eucharist: St. Augustine	85
Universal sense in Christians that the mystical Body of Christ is imperishable and incorruptible	86
Imputation of falsehood to this Body the denial of all Christian belief	86
The force of corporate unity	89
And that in the Body of Christ	91
The ultimate result	92

LECTURE IX

THE SECOND MAN VERIFIED IN HISTORY

I. The giving of the Spirit the result of the Dispensation of the Son	95
So set forth by our Lord at His resurrection, His ascension, and in the discourse preceding His passion	96
Its generic character the communication of Truth and Grace	99
Its differential marks: 1. that it is to be perpetual; 2. that it is to come upon a Body of men	101
Four gifts bestowed upon this Body, that is the joint-possession: 1. of Unity; 2. of Truth; 3. of Charity; 4. of Sanctity	103
These gifts co-exist in this Body in their completeness, and there alone	105
Qualities bestowed on the individual by incorporation with the body: 1. The forgiveness of sins	106
2. The illumination of faith	106
3. The adoption of sonship	107
4. Sanctification by charity	107
These qualities not irrevocable in the individual	108
The complete pentecostal gift of the Spirit	108
Analogy between it and the relation of man's soul and body	110
Again, between it and the human commonwealth	110
And, again, between it and the natural unity of the race	111
II. Historical fulfilment of the above statement	114
Actual creation of the divine Society by the descent of the Holy Ghost	114
The fruits of the Incarnation received by admission into it	118
Its unity through the unity of its jurisdiction	120
Transmission of the Truth in the Church at first by personal oral teaching alone	122
Secondly, by writings also, the subject of which was taken out of this oral teaching	124
These writings, the mode in which they were given, and the persons to whom they were addressed, like the use of oral teaching alone at first, a direction of the Holy Ghost	126

CONTENTS xi

	PAGE
Relation of the Church to the Scriptures	127
Further, the Truth itself committed for its propagation to a Society invested with Grace	128
The transmission of the Truth conveyed in this Society by a triple succession, first, of men	129
Secondly, of the doctrines taught by them	130
Thirdly, of the institutions established in it.	132
Instances of the force of this union in maintaining doctrine, first, the forgiveness of sins	133
Secondly, the Real Presence	134
Thirdly, Episcopacy	135
Fourthly, the Primacy	135
Instance of a doctrine preserved without the Written Word	136
This mode of transmitting the Truth enjoined by our Lord in His concluding words as given by St. Matthew	137
Development of the Truth in its various relations the proper work of such a Body	139
The result a divine life, embracing the intellect and the will of man, produced over against the corrupt life of heathenism	140
Statement of St. Augustine to this effect	142

LECTURE X

THE FIRST AGE OF THE MARTYR CHURCH

The Heathendom reigned over by Augustus and Tiberius unconscious that there was an order of moral truth of infinite value	145
That this truth is bound up with a Person the subject of the last two chapters	147
Its recognition, as being so bound up with a Person, by the Roman empire the present subject	148
The principle of persecution lay precisely in this union of the Truth with the Person of the God-man	149
The Christian Church for the first ten generations a special witness to this union	151
Picture of the result of the Apostolic age, the first seventy years	152
How the empire treated the Christian Faith	154

xii   CONTENTS

	PAGE
Importance of Nero's act for the subsequent status of Christians	156
The end of the reign of Antoninus Pius a fit time for estimating the progress of the Church	160
Its material extension	161
Its internal growth	162
Picture of it in the epistles of St. Ignatius, as the seat of authority and tradition, having one Faith in one Communion	163
The rise of heresies, and the power by which it resisted them	167
Clearness of the testimony of St. Ignatius to this power	169
Attitude of Trajan towards the Christians	171
Pliny's report to him, and his answer	172
What state of things these prove	174
Trajan's own conduct: Martyrdom of St. Ignatius	176
His special mention of the Roman Church	179
St. Chrysostom's notice of his power of intercession	180
Conduct of Hadrian, and state of Christians in his reign	181
His rescript to Minucius Fundanus	182
His persecution of St. Symphorosa	184
State of Christians under Antoninus Pius	185
First Apology of Justin	186
Statements by Celsus in corroboration	189
Rescript of Antoninus Pius to the Province of Asia	190
Highest point of toleration in the first 130 years	191
A Roman emperor's view of Christianity at the conclusion of this period	191

LECTURE XI

THE SECOND AGE OF THE MARTYR CHURCH

I. Grandeur of Hadrian's position in his imperial progresses	198
Altered position of Marcus Aurelius	199
Septimius Severus and his successors	200
Alexander Severus	201
Lesson taught by the rule of Commodus and those who followed	203
Morality and civil liberty at Rome from 180 to 222	204

CONTENTS

	PAGE
II. Internal history of Christian Faith and Church	206–240
Great numerical increase of Christians in this period	206
First mode of their increase	208
What constituted a Church in each place	208
Second mode of increase	210
Dying out of the personal disciples of the Apostles	212
First assault of heresy	213
Opposition of Gnosticism to Christian doctrine and institutions	213
It may represent the principle of heresy	215
How the danger was met by Irenæus	217
He appeals to the unity of belief in the Church over against the diversity of error	218
He appeals to the tradition in the principal churches, and specially that which has the superior principate	219
He sets forth the Church absolutely as the treasure-house of all truth	221
He distinguishes the perpetual teaching office set up in her	221
He contrasts the certainty of one truth in her with the uncertainty of ever-varying error without her	222
The main idea in Irenæus, and that which is subsidiary to it	223
Tertullian in like manner rejects the appeal of heretics to Scripture, and puts forward the possession of the truth by the Church throughout the world	226
Clement of Alexandria does the same	229
And Origen appeals to the like rule on the same ground	231
Effects produced by heresy	232
1. The enucleation of doctrine	232
2. Determining of the Canon of the New Testament	234
3. Statement of the principle of Tradition	236
Union of Scripture and Tradition in the teaching office	236
4. Extension and corroboration of the hierarchy	237
Summary of the internal history in 161–235	237
First movement towards the formation of Theology	239

CONTENTS

	PAGE
III. Treatment of Christianity by the empire in 161–235	240
The bearing of Marcus Aurelius to it	241
Junius Rusticus and his sentiments as expressed by Maximus of Tyre	241
Judgment of Justin and his companions by Rusticus	242
This judgment expresses the mind of Marcus Aurelius towards Christians	246
The martyrdom of Polycarp at Smyrna	247
The persecution at Lyons in 177, and the Emperor's approval	247
Position of Christians in the reign of Commodus	249
Persecution of Severus	249
Review of the period	251

LECTURE XII

THE THIRD AGE OF THE MARTYR CHURCH

I. In the third century the Christian Church is taking possession of society	254
Three great contrasts to it	254
1. The empire in a state of apparent dissolution	255
2. The unstable barbarism beyond	257
3. The sects which fought around the Church	259
Christians drawn from every tribe and religion in the empire form one society	261
Testimony of the author of the letter to Diognetus	262
Of Justin Martyr	263
Of Origen, who distinguishes the work of Christ in the individual, in the local Churches, and in the whole Church which is His Body	264
Time of peace in which Origen wrote succeeded by a great storm	266
Testimony of St. Cyprian on occasion of the first Antipope	268
He develops from many texts with many illustrations the idea of organic unity founded on the Primacy given by Christ to Peter	269
Origen and Cyprian give us the mind of the third century	276

CONTENTS

Causes of this belief: 1. The catechetical instruction of every convert in the article, "the Holy Catholic Church" 276
    2. The moral change which accompanied conversion 276
    3. The persecution which marked them out as one Body 279
    4. The historic origin of the Church on the day of Pentecost 280
The Christian society in its moral character, in its priesthood, and in its government, expresses that connection with its Founder to which Cyprian and Origen bear witness 281
Historical sequence of this fact 285
    In the first generation, A.D. 29 to 67 . . . 285
    St. Paul's testimony, about 66 286
    That of St. Ignatius, about 110 287
    That of St. Irenæus, about 180 288
    Crowned by that of St. Cyprian in 251 . . . 288
Chief events of the third century which bring out the unity of the Church, and the Primacy as its instrument 289
    The doctrine and practice of penance . . 290
    The question of rebaptizing heretics . . . 291
    The time of keeping Easter 292
II. The empire's treatment of the Church, A.D. 235–313 . 293
Persecution of Decius 293
State of relaxation among Christians preceding it . 296
Persecutions of Valerian and Aurelian . . . 297
Persecution of Diocletian 298
Termination of the state of persecution . . . 305
Roman law in the matter of Christianity from A.D. 64 to 313 306

LECTURE XIII

THE CHRISTIAN CHURCH AND THE GREEK PHILOSOPHY

PART I

	PAGE
The encounter of the Heathen mind with the Christian	308
Rise of Greek Philosophy	309
The Greek race and its language	310
Standing-point of the Greek mind	313
Human reason left more to itself in this race than in any other	314
The Pre-Socratic Philosophy	317
The second period of Philosophy: Socrates	318
The special principle which he gave to Philosophy	320
His view of the gods and the godhead	323
He halts between unity and plurality in his conception of the godhead	326
Xenophon and Plato as his disciples	328
Plato embodies in a system the Socratic principle of induction and definition	329
His philosophy and his idea of God	330
This idea only stated incidentally, and combined with polytheism	335
His God not absolutely personal, nor free, nor a creator	336
His ethical system	338
Plato's conception of the method of teaching	339
The example herein of Pythagoras	340
Writing viewed as a means of imparting doctrine, as set forth in the Phædrus	341
Plato carried this conception out in his life	345
Aristotle's conception of teaching the same	346
It was the Greek idea	348
Zeno and Epicurus pursued the same plan	349
Oral teaching the great work in their schools to the end of Greek philosophy	350

LECTURE XIV

THE CHRISTIAN CHURCH AND THE GREEK PHILOSOPHY

PART II

	PAGE
Aristotle's character as a philosopher	354
His view of the soul	355
Relation of his philosophy to religion	357
New political era begins with Alexander	359
Four great schools at Athens	360
Zeno sets up the Stoic school : his conception of God and of the soul	361
Epicurus and his doctrine	365
The Sceptic school of the Middle Academy . . .	368
The rise of Eclecticism	370
Cicero its chief representative : the sources of his philosophical treatises	371
Review of the effect produced on the mind of the cultured classes by Philosophy at the beginning of the reign of Claudius	374
Two great external events, the conquest of Alexander .	375
And the establishment of the Roman empire . . .	376
Negative effect of Philosophy	378
Its positive effect : 1. As to belief in the unity and personality of the Godhead	380
2. As to the belief in the human personality . .	384
3. As to the duties owed by man to God . .	385
4. As to the duties of man to man, and the conception of human society	388
Failure of Philosophy to construct a society impregnated with its principles	394
Importance of considering what human reason had done up to the time that the Christian religion was published .	397

THE FORMATION OF CHRISTENDOM

LECTURE VII

THE GODS OF THE NATIONS WHEN CHRIST APPEARED

"Emmanuel, Rex et Legifer noster, Expectatio gentium, et Salvator earum, veni ad salvandum nos, Domine Deus noster."

UNDER the sceptre of the imperial unity were brought together a hundred different lands occupied by as many different races. That rule of Rome which had grown for many centuries without, as it seemed, any presiding thought, by the casual accretions of conquest, may be said to assume under the hands of Augustus, about the year of Rome 750, certain definite and deliberately chosen limits, and to be governed by a fixed Idea, more and more developed in the imperial policy. The limits which the most fortunate of Roman emperors, nay the creator of the empire itself, put to it, were the Rhine and Danube, with the Euxine Sea, on the north; the deserts of Africa on the south; the Euphrates on the east; the ocean on the west. The Idea, which may indeed have been conceived by Julius, but was certainly first embodied by Augustus, was to change the constitution of a conquering city, ruled by an aristocratic senate, into a commonwealth governed by one man, the representative of the whole people; and the effect of this change, an effect no doubt unforeseen, at least in its extent, by its framer, was gradually to absorb the manifold races inhabiting these vast regions into the majesty of the Roman law, order, and citizenship. The three centuries which follow Augustus are occupied in working out the drama of this unity. During this time the provinces appear to come out more and more as parts of one whole. Some which at its commencement had only just entered the circle of Roman power and thought, as Gaul, become entirely interpenetrated with the law, language, customs, and civilisation of the sovereign city. Spain was nearly as much, and Northern Africa perhaps even more Latinised: in all, local inequalities, and the dissimilarity arising from conflicting races, customs, and languages, are more and more softened down, though never entirely removed; and while throughout this period the great city continues the head, yet the body assumes an ever-increasing importance, until at length its members engage the equal solicitude of that central potentate to whom all equally belong. In the times of so-called Roman liberty, the plunder of lands which received pro-consuls for their annual rulers, served to replenish the fortunes of nobles exhausted by the corruption requisite to gain high office; but if the dominion of one at Rome seemed an evil exchange to a nobility which deemed itself born to enjoy a conquered world, at least it served as a protection to those many millions for whom the equality of law and order, the fair administration of justice, and the undisturbed possession of property constituted the chief goods of life. Cicero and his peers might grieve over the extinction of what they termed liberty, but Gaul, Spain, Africa, and Asia exulted in deliverance from the oppression of a Verres, a Fonteius, a Gabinius, a Piso, or a Clodius, in the communication of citizenship, and in the peace of a common civilisation.

I. With a passing glance at the progress of this unity, which, great and magnificent as it is, is yet external, let us turn to an object filling the whole of this vast empire with its varied manifestations: for this object leads us to the consideration of another unity, wholly internal, without which that of government, law, and order must be apparent rather than real, or at best, however seemingly imposing, be deprived of the greater part of its efficacy.

1. It has been said that the empire contained in it many lands and many races, but these likewise worshipped their own distinct gods, which were acknowledged and sanctioned as national divinities for the several countries wherein they were locally established. Had Augustus ordered an enrolment not only of the numbers, the landed property, and the wealth of his subjects, but of their gods, his public register, or Breviarium, would have included at least ten distinct systems of idolatrous worship. First of all, there would be the proper gods of Rome, then those of the Hellenic race; and these, though the most similar to each other, yet refused a complete amalgamation. But besides these there were on the west the Etrurian, the Iberian, the Gallic, and the Germanic gods; on the east, the Carian and Phrygian, the Syrian, the Assyrian, the Arabian; on the south, the Phœnician, Libyan, and Egyptian. All these different races, inasmuch as they were subjects of the empire, enjoyed undisturbed the right of worshipping their ancestral gods,[1] who, so long as they did not overstep their local

---

[1] Tertull. *Apolog.* xxiv. "Ideo et Ægyptiis permissa est tam

boundaries, were recognised; they possessed priests, rites, temples, estates, and self-government; they held the soil, and their worship was legal. It was a matter of Roman policy not to interfere with them. Nay, their several worshippers could carry their rites along with them in their various sojourns and settlements, and even in Rome build altars, and adore Egyptian, Asiatic, African, or Gallic gods. These various systems agreed all in one point, that they were systems of polytheistic idolatry: they all divided the attributes of the godhead, assigning them to more or fewer objects, and worshipping all these by visible symbols which the power worshipped was deemed to inhabit;[1] but they did not make the same division with a mere difference of name; on the contrary, they ran into and across each other with the most bewildering multiplicity, variation, and contradiction. Even in the same system, if we may give this name to any of the various mythologies, the several divinities were perpetually interfering with each other's province. When the Roman made vows for the removal of his ailments, in his uncertainty to which god the ailment belonged, or who was most proper to remove it, he addressed his vow to several together; or in public supplications, being often uncertain to whom exactly the prayer or offering should be made, he cautiously expressed himself, "whether it be a god or a goddess." And the various Hellenic, Asiatic, or Egyptian cities often possessed local gods, whose worship was supreme there,

vanæ superstitionis potestas, avibus et bestiis consecrandis, et capite damnandis qui aliquem hujusmodi Deum occiderint. Unicuique etiam provinciæ et civitati suus Deus est, ut Syriæ Astartes, ut Arabiæ Disares, ut Noricis Belenus, ut Africæ Cælestis, ut Mauritaniæ Reguli sui," &c.; and Minucius Felix, Octavius vi., in like manner.

[1] See Aug. *de Civ. Dei*, l. viii. 24.

while they exercised far less influence, or were even scarcely known elsewhere.[1]

Now, merely as a specimen of what this worship was all over the Roman empire, let us take the brilliant Athens, Greece's eye, the world's university. First of all ruled in her the worship of Pallas-Athené: she was the lady of the land, who had won it for her own after a hard contest with Poseidon. Her chief sanctuaries were the temple of Athené, guardian of the city, with its old statue fallen down from heaven on the Acropolis. On the Acropolis likewise the Parthenon, built expressly for the gorgeous Panathenaic festival; and in the lower city the Palladium with the statue of the goddess supposed to have been brought from Troy. Yet the worship of the "high goddesses," Demeter and Persephoné, was also richly endowed with shrines and festivals, and affected scarcely less the feelings of the Athenians. Then Jupiter, as "supreme," was honoured with unbloody offering before the Erechtheium, dedicated to Athené; whilst as "Olympian" he had the colossal temple begun by Peisistratus and finished after many hundred years by Hadrian, and as "guardian of the city" distinct festivals. Yet more manifold was the invocation of Apollo, as the Pythian, the Delphic, the Lycian, as the ancestral god of the Ionians. The multiform Artemis had her temples and worshippers as the Tauric, by the name Brauronia; as the port-goddess, by the name Munychia; as the goddess of the hunt, by the name Agrotera, who had the credit of the victory won at Marathon; as presiding over birth, she was called Chitone, while Themistocles had built a temple to her as the Counsellor. Heré had only a

---

[1] Döllinger, *Heidenthum und Judenthum*, pp. 528, 529.

doorless and roofless temple on the road to Phalerum; but the god of fire was worshipped in Athens abundantly. Hermes had his peculiar statues in every street, irreverence to which might be fatal even to an Alcibiades, the city's darling; while Aphrodité had a crowd of temples and shrines, whose unchaste worship found but too many frequenters. Poseidon had to content himself with a single altar in his rival's city, and with games in its harbour; but Dionysos had three temples, with brilliant festivals; Mars was not without one; Hestia was throned in the Prytaneum; the Earth, Kronos, and Rhea had their temples and festivals, as also the Erinnyes, who were worshipped only in two other places in Greece. Here alone in Greece was a sanctuary and a rite to Prometheus; while the Asiatic mother of the gods had a splendid temple where the archives of the state were kept. Besides, there was the worship of the Hours and the Graces, of Eileithyia, goddess of victory and of birth, of Æsculapius and Themis, of the Kabirian Anakes, the Arcadian Pan, the Thracian Cotytto and Bendis, the Egyptian Serapis. Mercy and Shame, Fame and Endeavour had their altars; and the hero-worship numbered Theseus, Codrus, Academus, Solon, the tyrant-slayers Harmodius and Aristogeiton; and Hercules, originally a hero, but here and elsewhere widely honoured as a god.[1]

Athens, if the most superstitious as well as the most intellectual of cities, may be taken as the type of a thousand others of Hellenic race scattered over the Roman empire from Marseilles to Antioch. Say that she had twice as many deities and festivals as her sister cities, enough will remain for them where-

[1] From *Heidenthum und Judenthum*, pp. 101-2.

with to occupy the soil with their temples and to fill the year's cycle with their rites.

The lively Grecian imagination impregnated not with stern notions of duty, nor with reverential devotion to those whom it worshipped, but regarding them as objects of æsthetical satisfaction,[1] and yearning for a serene and confidential exchange of relations with them, had in process of time spun out a complete web of idolatrous worship which encompassed heaven and earth, the whole domain of nature, every state and act of human life. Rain and sunshine and the weather stood under the ordering of Zeus; the fruitfulness of the soil was Demeter's care; countless nymphs of field, of fountain, and of river, offered to men their gifts; the vine and its juice was under the protection of Dionysos, and Poseidon was lord of the sea. The flocks had their defenders in Hermes and Pan; the Fates ruled the lot of men. Kings and magistrates had in Zeus their prototype and guardian. Athené held her shield over cities; the hearth of each private home and the public hearth of the city were in Hestia's charge. Marriage was secure under Heré's care. Demeter was entrusted with legislation; the pains of childbirth were recommended to Eileithyia, or Artemis. Music, archery, divination, were Apollo's attributes; the art of healing claimed him and his son Æsculapius as patrons. Athené and Ares swayed the issue of war; the chase was the domain of Artemis; smiths and all workers in fire saw in Hephæstus their patron; whilst Athené the Worker protected the gentler trades, and Hecate watched over the roads.[2]

Yet Rome itself, whose own Capitoline Jupiter

---

[1] *Heidenthum und Judenthum*, p. 480.
[2] *Ibid.* p. 107.

claimed a certain superiority over all these gods, would scarcely have yielded to any Grecian city, even were it Athens, in the number or variety of her deities, the frequency and solemnity of her festivals; while in the costliness of victims offered to her gods, and in the strictness of her ceremonies, she probably far surpassed that and all other cities. Her sterner worship of originally shapeless gods, presiding over the labours of a simple agricultural life, had long yielded to the seductions of her dangerous Grecian captive. The rude block Terminus, and Jupiter the Stone, ceased to satisfy those who had beheld the majesty of the father of gods and men embodied by the genius of a Phidias; and she had ended by going further in breaking up the conception of one god, and in the personification of particular powers, operations, physical functions, and qualities than any nation of antiquity.[1] But though the beautiful forms of the Hellenic gods, as expressed by the skill of unrivalled sculptors, had carried her away, yet the nature of her worship was in strong contrast with that of Greece. Her religion had rested originally on two ideas, the might of the gods friendly to Rome, and the force of ceremonial over these gods;[2] and still when she accepted the gods of conquered nations for her own, it was to secure the possession of their might, and to have them for friends instead of foes; while her own worship was a matter of routine and habit jealously guarded by unchanging ceremonies, and prosecuted not out of affection, but for the material security of daily life, which, according to the deeply-rooted feeling of the people, could not go on without it.

[1] *Heidenthum und Judenthum*, p. 469.
[2] *Ibid.* pp. 468, 480.

The individualised and humanised Latin and Hellenic gods, if they had much in common, still could not be thoroughly amalgamated; but Rome, as the mistress of Western Asia and Egypt, came upon Oriental religions of a very different stamp. Instead of this wide Pantheon of gods, each of whom had his occupation, these Asiatics generally regarded the deity in a sexual relationship, as one male and one female god, representing the active and passive forms of nature,[1] and worshipped with a mixture of fear and voluptuousness. Such were Bel and Mylitta, Moloch and Astarte, and by whatever different names the same idea was presented. The worship of the great mother Cybele, so widely spread through Asia Minor, approached in many respects in character to that of this female goddess. But it is needless to go further into the specific differences of these various idolatries; only bear in mind that they in their several countries occupied the domain of public and private life, as the worship of which I have given the details did at Athens. So it was before the influence of external conquerors reached them. After this a certain change ensues. The Roman empire was accomplishing in the west as well as in the east what the progress of Grecian rule and thought had commenced three hundred years before[2] under Alexander and his successors, the bringing together and in some sort fusing the multiform and often contradictory worship of the nations surrounding the Mediterranean Sea. Not merely in Rome, but in all the chief cities of the empire, the Asiatic, the Egyptian, the Libyan deities, and many others of subject nations under the Roman sway, were worshipped side

---

[1] *Heidenthum und Judenthum*, p. 344.
[2] *Ibid.* p. 312.

by side. Accordingly, in the time of Augustus, and at the year of Rome 750, where we are taking our stand, there prevailed all over the hundred millions of men ruled by him a polytheistic idolatry bewildering by its multiplicity, internal contradictions, fluctuations, and mixtures, yet imposing by its universal extent and prevalence. The only exception seems to have been the Jewish worship of one God, whether in its chief seat, the small province of Judæa, or as it was seen in the lives of Jewish settlers scattered throughout the empire. It must be remarked that this Jewish worship of the true God was sanctioned as that of a national god belonging to the Jews, and sacrifice was perpetually offered for Augustus in the temple at Jerusalem. But the Jews did not, as a rule, make efforts to convert the Gentiles to their religion, nor seek to exhibit it as antagonistic to the prevailing idolatry, and as claiming to subdue and cast it out. They were content to keep their own worship to themselves, and with the toleration which the Roman law thus allowed them. Yet even so in every place where they dwelt in any numbers some of the better heathens were found to be attracted to their worship by the intrinsic beauty of their belief in one God.

2. But such an exception as this hardly made a perceptible break in that continuous mass of evil and falsehood which then surrounded young and old, learned and ignorant, rich and poor in its grasp. The sea stands in Holy Writ as the well-known image of the world's disobedience to the divine promptings, of its impetuosity and lawlessness. What image is there in nature so striking and awful as the long waves of the Atlantic bearing down in storm upon a helpless ship, and sweeping it upon an iron-

bound coast! So broke that wild sea of human error over the individual mind of man. The observer looked round upon all the nations, and it was everywhere the same—a multiplicity of gods filling up the whole circle of human life, many-named, many-natured, but all without truth, purity, and justice; full of violent and sensual deeds, and still viler imaginations. What stay was there for the spirit of man against that universal flood? Its vastness was everywhere. Who was strong enough, who wise enough, to resist what all his fellows accepted? And the struggle of a single soul against it might seem like that of "some strong swimmer in his agony" alone at night amid the waste of waters.

3. For this polytheism was no dormant, otiose power withdrawn into the background and crouching apart from the actions and feelings of daily life. Its presence was indicated in every home by the little images of the Lares; homage was done to it at every table by libations; every house had its consecrated emblems; every street its statues of Hermes and serpents; in the forum there were feasts in honour of the gods; the shops, taverns, and manufactories had little altars on which wine and incense were offered to them; there were idolatrous emblems on the foreheads of the dead, on their funeral pyre, on their tombs. The places of amusement were specially dedicated to the gods; the theatres had representations in honour of them; the circus had their images, chairs, carriages, robes borne in procession; the amphitheatre was consecrated to them, and as being so Tertullian called it "the temple of all demons." So much for private and social life. But not only so. All political acts were bound up with a crowd of religious formalities and outward signs of divine concurrence, and were

carried on with a ceremonial, every part of which was prescribed as having an exact inward meaning. Then there were continually recurring vows to the gods made for the great, made for private individuals, made for the emperor and his family. Three special ceremonies were used to obtain favours from them or to deprecate calamities, feasts, the solemnly bearing their images on cushions, processions with naked feet.[1] To this we must add the priestly colleges, pontifices, flamines, augurs, and magistrates, whether distinct or co-ordinated. Then, besides, consider the magical character of the prayers, and the strict use of formularies without mistake, omission, or addition, which were supposed to ensure success apart from the intention of those offering them. Thus the whole life of the Romans was filled with invocations, propitiations, purifications, and even in any small matter a whole string of gods had prayer and service offered to them, and no one of their names might be omitted. Consider again the great frequency of the offerings, whether propitiative or consultatory; and, further, how particular beasts belonged to particular gods. The mere expense of victims was felt as a great burden. It was reckoned that on the accession of Caligula 160,000 animals, chiefly oxen and calves, were sacrificed in the Roman empire in token of the general joy; and Augustus and Marcus Aurelius devoted such a multitude of beasts to their sacrifices that what had been said of the former was repeated as to the latter, how the white oxen had written to him, saying, "If you conquer, we are lost." Indications of the will of the gods were to be taken on all occasions; nothing was to be done in public or private without consulting

[1] "Epulæ, lectisternia, nudipedalia."

the auspices. Then there was the institution of the Haruspices, in its two branches of examining the entrails of the victims, and divining the meaning of all prodigies. One is still amazed at the ever-untiring solicitude which the senate showed to have all these things carefully watched—eclipses, rainbows of unusual colours, shooting-stars, misbirths, human or bestial; showers of earth, stones, chalk, or ashes; mice gnawing the golden vessels of a temple; bees swarming on a public place, but especially a shrine touched by lightning. Such things struck senate and people with consternation; special supplications were ordered to appease the causers of them.[1]

These are the external manifestations of polytheism which struck every eye, and affected the mind by their constant recurrence. But if we go beneath the surface and examine the root, we shall find an universal sense in the minds of all men in that day of unseen power over and above the material operations of nature. It was too strong as well as too general and invariable to be called an opinion, and it so acted on the nerves and feelings of men that I term it not so much a logical conviction as a sense of the close contact between man and nature, or rather an unseen power behind the veil of nature and working through it. Various as the forms of idolatry were—Egyptian, Asiatic, Libyan, Greek, or Roman; or again, Iberian, Gallic, German—all teemed with this sense. To the adherents of these religions, one and all, the world was very far from being a mere system of nature governed by general laws,[2] it may rather be said that

---

[1] These incidents are taken from various places in *Heidenthum und Judenthum*, pp. 531, 549, 550, &c.
[2] Champagny, *Les Antonins*, liv. v. c. 3.

this was precisely what it was not. They looked upon nature in all its forms as an expression of the divine will, and therefore the unusual productions of nature became to them intimations respecting that will. And having lost the guidance of a fixed moral and religious teaching, they were ruled by an ever-watchful anxiety to gain acquaintance with that will. On this sense rested the universal belief that it was in man's power to hold intercourse by means of charms, spells, adjurations, with spirits of greater might and knowledge than his own—that is, magic or witchcraft. Hence the evocation of the spirits of the dead to reveal secrets of their prison-house, or necromancy. Hence the recurrence to oracles, running through all pagan history, of which there were many scattered through the Roman world, and which, after a temporary discredit, rose again into name in the time of Hadrian. Not less general was the belief that men and women might be possessed by spirits who ruled their words and actions according to an overmastering will. Then divination existed in endlessly various forms; and of its force we can gather a notion by Cicero's remark that it lay like an oppressive burden on the minds of men, so that even sleep, which should be the refuge from anxieties, became through the meaning attached to dreams the cause of a multitude of cares.[1] To this must be added the use of sortileges, amulets, and talismans in countless number and variety; and the belief that the actions and fortune of men were swayed by the course of the stars—that is, astrology. It was not the vulgar and ignorant merely whose minds were filled with these things. Scarcely a philosopher, scarcely a statesman, scarcely a ruler can be found

[1] *De Divinat.* ii. 72.

whose mind, even if proof against a genuine devotion to a divine providence, was not open to one or more manifestations of the dark mysterious power pressing upon the confines of human life, and every now and then breaking through the veil of visible things with evidences of malignant might. A more determined and unscrupulous conqueror than Sylla, a more genuine philosopher than Marcus Aurelius, a more sagacious user of religion than Augustus, we shall not easily find; yet each of these, like their ordinary countrymen, had this sense of the supernatural and intangible above, beneath, and around them. Sylla, on the eve of any battle, would, in the sight of his soldiers, embrace a small statue of Apollo, which he had taken from Delphi, and entreat it to give an early fulfilment of its promises.[1] Marcus Aurelius, in his war with the Marcomanni, collected priests from all quarters to Rome, and was so long occupied in offering rites to their various foreign gods that he kept his army waiting for him. And Augustus watched carefully the most trivial signs, and was distressed if in the morning his left shoe was given to him for his right. Even that Julius before whose genius all men quailed, and whose disbelief of a future state stands recorded at a notable point of Roman history, never mounted a chariot without uttering certain words for good luck and preservation against calamity.[2] We shall therefore judge most inadequately of the force which the innumerable rites, temples, festivals, pomps, ceremonies, prayers, invocations, priesthoods, sodalities, initiations, and mysteries of polytheism exercised upon the minds of men, unless we take into full account that remark-

---

[1] Valerius Max. i. c. 2, 3.
[2] Merivale's *History of the Romans*, ii. 447.

able sense of contact and sympathy between the external world and man—of invisible power betraying itself through palpable agents, whether in reasoning or unreasoning productions, whether in the animal or vegetable world—which served as its basis. The line between religion and superstition in paganism no eye can trace; but at least the foundation of true worship plunged deep out of sight into the secret recesses of abject fear.

4. But what was the moral influence of this multiform, universal, all-embracing, and all-penetrating worship?

Varro, whom Cicero calls the most acute and learned of writers, and whose great work in forty-one books he praises as containing the names, classes, offices, and causes of all divine and human things, divided theology into the fabulous, the natural, and the civil. In the first, he said, are many fictions unworthy of the nature and dignity of immortal beings: such as that one god sprung from the head, another from the thigh, another from drops of blood; such, again, as that gods were thieves or adulterers, or became slaves to men. In fact, this fabulous theology attributed everything to them which might happen not merely to a man, but to the most contemptible of men.[1] Let us leave what he calls natural theology, which is the discussion of philosophers concerning the physical nature of the gods, and proceed to the third, which he calls civil, and which is that which the citizens, and especially the priests of human communities, are bound to know and administer. This treats of what gods are to be worshipped, and with what rites and sacrifices. The first theology, he says, belongs to the theatre, the

[1] See Varro, quoted by St. Aug. *de Civ. Dei*, lib. vi. 5.

second to the universe, the third to the city. S. Augustine, commenting at length upon his division, proves that the first and the third, the fabulous and the civil, are, in fact, identical, since the universe is a divine work, but the theatre and the city works of men. The theatre is indeed made for the city, and the very same gods are ridiculed on the stage who are adored in the temple; the same have games exhibited in their honour and victims sacrificed to them. The images, features, ages, sexes, bearing of the gods in the one and in the other are the same. Thus this fabulous, theatrical, and scenic theology, full of everything vile and criminal, is actually a part of the civil, cohering with it as limb with limb in the same body.[1]

Conceive, then, every revolting detail of adultery, prostitution, incest, or of dishonesty, or of violence, which the perverted invention of modern writers has ever dressed up for the theatres of great cities in this and other countries. They will perhaps yield in turpitude to that which the theatres of the Roman empire exhibited. But what these theatres represented in mimic action was the exact image, as reflected in a mirror, of what was transacted at the solemn service of the gods in unnumbered temples.[2] The exact image, so far as it went, yet stopping short in some respects, for our eye-witness above cited declares that gratitude was due to the actors, inasmuch as they spared the eyes of men, and did not lay bare upon the theatre all that was hidden within the walls of temples. It was not enough, then, that all the many

---

[1] *De Civ. Dei*, l. vi. 5, 6, 7.
[2] "Illam theatricam et fabulosam theologiam ab ista civili pendere noverunt, et ei de carminibus poetarum tanquam de speculo resultare: et ideo ista exposita, quam damnare non audent, illam ejus imaginem liberius arguunt." *De Civ. Dei*, vi. 9; id. vi. 7.

games and spectacles in which such things were represented were dedicated to the gods, acted under their especial sanction, even enjoined by them as means of gaining their favour or averting their wrath, which alone would have made them answerable for the immorality so portrayed; not enough, even, that actions of this quality were in the theatres ascribed to the gods who presided over them; but these acts of immorality were not the fictions of poets or the acting of players, but the very substance of the theology itself in which the worship of all these nations was embodied. Priapus appeared to make a laugh on the stage exactly in the costume in which he was worshipped in the temples, or in which he entered into the rites of marriage; a costume of indescribable turpitude, the shame of our human nature. The players on the stage and the statues in the temples equally exhibited Jove bearded and Mercury beardless, Saturn in decrepitude and Apollo in youthful beauty. In the rites of Juno, of Ceres, of Venus, of the mother of the gods, words were uttered and scenes acted such as no decent person would suffer to be spoken or acted before his own mother; or rather they contained, as a portion of themselves, the worst crimes which the theatres represented; nay, crimes which they stopped short of acting, and persons so infamous that they were not tolerated even on the stage, where yet to take part was a civil dishonour. What, then, was the nature of those rites wherein those were chosen to take part whom the utmost license of the stage banished from its boards?[1] Let us conceive—if such a conception can be adequately

[1] "Quæ sunt ergo illa sacra quibus agendis tales elegit sanctitas quales nec thymelica in se admittit obscœnitas." *De Civ. Dei*, vi. 7.

represented to the mind—that the vilest drama ever acted upon a modern theatre was being daily carried on in all the churches of Christendom by troops of priests and priestesses, with all the paraphernalia of costliest worship, with prayers, invocation, and sacrifices, as a service acceptable to the Ruler of man's lot, and as an account of what that Ruler had Himself done, and of what He loved to be imitated by others. That would be a picture of heathen worship in the time of Augustus; that would be the moral food on which was nurtured that crowd of nations which acknowledged Cæsar's sway; that the conception of divine things wrought into the minds of the hundred millions of men who formed the Roman empire.

Was it surprising that all worshippers of the gods should look for their example rather in Jupiter's actions than in Plato's teaching or the moral judgments of Cato?[1] A nature subject in itself to the sway of passion was stimulated by an authority supposed to be divine to the commission of every criminal excess; and herein lay a strong proof of the malignant and impure character of these gods.

On the other hand, the same eye-witness challenges the defenders of the pagan gods to produce a single instance wherein moral precepts of living were delivered to their worshippers upon divine authority. True, indeed, there were here and there whispers of secret rites in which a pure and chaste life was recommended, but where were the buildings dedicated to the public preaching of such truths? Places there were in abundance consecrated to the celebration of

---

[1] "Omnes cultores talium deorum—magis intuentur quid Jupiter fecerit, quam quid docuerit Plato vel censuerit Cato." *De Civ. Dei*, ii. 7.

infamous games, rightly termed "Fugalia," since they put modesty and decency to flight, but none where the people might listen to divine commands repressing avarice, ambition, or unchaste desire. Thus with the positive inculcation of all evil, under cover of their own example, was united the negative absence of all moral teaching.[1]

For even the prayers which accompanied these sacrifices and this ceremonial, and this lavish exhibition of every human wickedness under divine names, were not addressed for moral goods, but for wealth, bodily strength, temporal prosperity. Horace but expresses the general mind when he says:

"Sed satis est orare Jovem quæ donat et aufert;
Det vitam, det opes, æquum mi animum ipse parabo."
—*Epist.* i. 18, 111.

They were moreover viewed as carrying with them a sort of physical force, not as prevailing through purity of intention in those who offered them. In fact, the gods to whom they were addressed were powers of nature, or malignant and impure powers, but in neither case beings who looked for a moral service from rational creatures.

One other turpitude the Asiatic idolatry added to the Greek and Roman forms. By consecrating the sexual relations themselves in one male and one female god, they effected this crowning connection of idolatry with immorality, that unchaste acts became themselves acts of sacrifice, and so of worship.[2] This is the strange perversion borne witness to by Herodo-

---

[1] *De Civ. Dei,* ii. 6. "Demonstrentur vel commemorentur loca— ubi populi audirent quid dii præciperent de cohibenda avaritia, ambitione frangenda, luxuria refrænanda." See also sec. 28.

[2] See *Heidenthum und Judenthum,* p. 398. Herodotus, i. 199. Baruch, vi. 42-3.

tus, and corroborated by the prophet Jeremiah. A great seat of this worship was the city of Hierapolis, in Syria, where was one of the most magnificent temples of the ancient world, dedicated to Derketo, and rich with the offerings of Arabians, Babylonians, Assyrians, Phœnicians, Cilicians, Cappadocians, and all nations of the Semitic tongue. Nor was this worship confined to the East, for hence, as from a centre, the adherents of the Syrian goddess spread themselves in begging troops over the provinces of the empire. And the worship of Venus at Eryx, and other places in the West, with the thousands of female priestesses dedicated to it, reproduced the same abomination.

As the great result of all that we have said, we find the notion of sanctifying the human will absent from the religious rites of the polytheistic idolatry in all its forms. To this corresponded the absence of the notion of holiness in the gods. And this leads us finally to the remarkable character which defines it as a whole. This worship was throughout a corruption,[1] the spoiling, that is, of something good; a turning away from the better to the worse. The worship itself had been originally good. The corruption lay in the alteration of the quality and the object of the worship. Worship had been implanted in man, and prescribed to him. It was at once the need of his nature and the command of Him who gave that nature. It had for it, first, positive institution, and then tradition and custom, and throughout, the conscience, the reason, and the heart of man. The reason of man ever bore powerful witness to the unity of the Godhead; the breaking

[1] See S. Athan. *con. Gentes*, 5–9. In like manner S. Theophilus lib. i. ad Autolyc. c. 2.

up of that unity, as exhibited by this idolatrous polytheism, in contradiction to the original prompting and continued witness of the reason, is a very strong proof of that moral corruption in the will which first generated it, which continued its existence, and which, while multiplying, degraded its forms from age to age. But man was free to decline from the good in which he had been placed. The corruption which was left in his power he exerted; he changed the quality of the service, and the person served. The productive cause of idolatry on the part of man was the soul of man turning away from the notion of a good and holy Creator, the contemplation of whom was its present support and future reward, to visible things. Of these things the chief were bodily pleasures. Thus this corruption of the soul, in process of time, and continually becoming worse, produced this whole pantheon of gods, originally the creation of its own lusts, and subsisting as a perpetual food and support of those lusts. For this cause it had broken up the one perfect idea of God the Creator and Ruler of all persons and things into a multitude of gods, whose functions became more and more divided, until the ether, the air, the earth, and the water swarmed with these supposed beings, which took possession even of wood and stone, dwelling in the statues erected to them; and every desire which the soul in its corruption could entertain had its corresponding patron, helper, and exemplar. In this descending course cause and effect were perpetually reacting on each other, and as the corruption of the human soul had generated these gods, so their multiplication and degradation intensified its corruption from age to age.[1]

[1] In order to form a notion how far this division of gods could

5. But this was not all. If corrupt affection in man himself, if the charm of representing the unseen objects of worship in visible characters of wood or stone, if, finally, the ignorance of the true God, together with the beauty of the creature substituted for Him,[1] were the disposing causes within man to idolatry, there was a cause outside of him which must not be forgotten. When we look upon this idolatry, occupying not one country or race, but all; not merely bewildering savage or uncivilised man, but throned in the chief seats of the world's choicest civilisation; when we look upon its endlessly divergent forms, its palpable contradictions, its cherished or commanded immoralities, its crowd of debasing, irrational, heterogeneous superstitions, its cruelty, sensuality, and fearfulness, all these being no less an insult to man's reason than a derogation from God's majesty, who is there that does not feel this to be the strangest and most astonishing sight which history presents to man? And yet there is a unity which runs through it all, and stamps it with a double mark. Not only is it a service due from man to God, which is paid by him to the creature rather than to the Creator,[2] but more especially it is that service paid by man to God's enemies, the fallen angels. These it is who have assumed the mask of dead men; these it is who, within the sculptured forms of Jupiter, Juno, Mars, and Venus, of Baal and

descend, and what an incredible depth of turpitude it reached, see *De Civ. Dei*, l. vi. c. 9, de officiis singulorum deorum. Its foulness prevents any adequate representation of it.

[1] See S. Thomas, *Summa*, 2, 2, q. 94, a. 4.
[2] Of this whole polytheism in the mass S. Paul pronounces the judgment: Οἵτινες μετήλλαξαν τὴν ἀλήθειαν τοῦ Θεοῦ ἐν τῷ ψεύδει, καὶ ἐσεβάσθησαν καὶ ἐλάτρευσαν τῇ κτίσει παρὰ τὸν κτίσαντα. Rom. i. 25. And the Psalmist adds: Ὅτι πάντες οἱ θεοὶ τῶν ἐθνῶν δαιμόνια· ὁ δὲ Κύριος τοὺς οὐρανοὺς ἐποίησεν. Sept. xcv. 5. See also Ps. cv. 37.

Derketo and Mylitta, of Anubis and Serapis, of Thor and Woden, and so many more, receive man's adoration, and rejoice above all things in possessing his heart. These it is who have seduced him by exhibitions of visible beauty, have lain in wait for him by fountain, forest, and field, and filled the groves and high places with the charms which best pleased him under the name of worship; or have promised to disclose future things to him; or, again, have harrowed his soul with phantasms and terrors of the unseen world. These incoherent systems; these deities, whose functions ran into and athwart each other; these investings of human passions, and even unnatural and monstrous vices, with immortality and terrible power; these rivals ever quarrelling with each other, and jealous for the possession of man's homage, all serve the purpose of those behind the scenes, are puppets under their command, and have a common end and result in the captivity of their victim. More even than this; while they seem disunited and contradictory, they are really one, marshalled by the power, directed by the mind, held in the hand of him who is called "the ruler of this world," "the power of darkness," "the might of the enemy," who "holds the power of death," "the ancient serpent, who leads into error the whole world," "that malignant one in whom the whole world is lying," "the prince of the power of the air, the spirit who now works in the children of disobedience," who musters "the principalities, the powers, the world-rulers of this life's darkness, the spirits of wickedness in ethereal places," to serve him in his conflict with man's flesh and blood; in fine, for S. Paul's language goes one point even beyond that of his Master, and terms him not merely the ruler, but "the god of this world;"[1] that is to say, this manifold idolatry is the establishment of his kingdom, the enthronement of his godhead over men, the mark of their captivity and prostration before him.

The statements of our Lord and His apostles being so express and definite as to the existence of this diabolic kingdom, and as to the personal sway of a sovereign over it, let us look once more at this idolatry itself by the light thus shed upon it.

And first, whether we regard men as made to be members of a well-ordered society, enjoying temporal prosperity in this life, or as further intended for happiness in a future life, resulting from their present actions,[2] the condition in which the heathen nations are actually found at our Lord's coming is quite unintelligible unless we suppose the reality of a diabolic power exercised upon them. The polytheism which we have witnessed holding all human life in its grasp, while it did not teach and uphold the great laws of morality, did, on the other hand, actively inculcate the violation of those laws by continually representing to the minds and eyes of men such a violation in the acts of the deities worshipped. It was a perpetual incitement of men to crimes, as well against social order as against all the sanctities of private life; it fostered the savageness of slavery, and the utmost cruelty in carrying on war, because its deities, being diverse for every nation, and belonging exclusively to the nation, had obliterated the idea that all men were of one blood, and thus delivered over the captive and

---

[1] See John xii. 31; xiv. 30; xvi. 11; Luke xxii. 53; x. 19; Apoc. xii. 9; Heb. ii. 14; 1 John v. 18; Ephes. vi. 12; ii. 2; 2 Cor. iv. 3.
[2] These two subjects occupy respectively the first five and the second five books of S. Augustine's *City of God*, where the argument is carried out in great detail.

the slave to the pitiless hatred or equally pitiless luxury of their fellow-men. So much for its action on human society as terminating with this life, while for a life to come it had no doctrine and made no preparation, but had suffered the earlier teaching of a future retribution to be considered as a fable fit for children and old women. Looking at such a condition of human society from the moral point of view, we may conclude with certainty that man would never, if left to himself, have devised it.

Secondly, regarding this polytheism as an object presented to the human intellect, nothing more unreasonable and monstrous than this crowd of deities can even be conceived. The human reason demands imperatively the unity of the Godhead, since infinite power at least enters into the conception of the Godhead, and to divide or limit infinity is an unreason. All the great works and order of the world bore witness likewise to this unity of the Godhead, and were sufficient to prove it;[1] and even in the worst times of paganism we find this proof exhibited with a force and lucidity to which even now little can be added. And in the worst times, again, we find the natural witness of the human soul breaking out in moments of sudden trial or great anguish, and calling upon the one God for help.[2] Yet in spite of this we see whole nations renowned for their intellectual productions, and men among them in whom the force of reason has rarely or never been surpassed, bowing their necks to this yoke of polytheism, and accepting this tissue of monstrous error, paying homage to it in their life, and dying with

---

[1] Rom. i. 20. See the Stoical argument for the unity of the deity in Cic. *de Nat. Deor.* 2.
[2] Tertullian *de Testimonio Animæ*, 2.

it on their lips; as Socrates offering the cock to Æsculapius, and Seneca the libation to Jove the liberator. We know not how to account for this, were man's reason left alone. We can see an adequate ground for it only in "men having been made unreasonable, and in the demoniacal error overshadowing the earth, and concealing the knowledge of the true God.[1]

Let us take a third view of it, neither the moral nor the logical, but the view of it as an existing fact, as something which for many hundred years occupied the earth, ruled nations, moulded the institutions and characters of men. Here we do not speak merely of the multitude of temples, of priests or priestesses serving in them, of sacrifices offered by these, of prayers, vows, festivals in honour of the gods—because all these enter into the notion of a service rendered by man to the power superior to him, and in their utmost perversion there is nothing which may not be accounted for by a simply human corruption stealing into and spoiling an originally good institution; but all these in the actual condition of paganism were mixed up with and penetrated by other elements, and accompanied by effects not to be so accounted for. Let us take the universal persuasion that the statues of the gods were inhabited by the deities which they represented, as bodies by souls.[2] Here was the notion of a spiritual power taking possession of material forms. But how was this notion introduced, propagated, and maintained in men's minds? By certain visible

---

[1] Οὕτω τοίνυν ἀλογωθέντων τῶν ἀνθρώπων, καὶ οὕτω τῆς δαιμονικῆς πλάνης ἐπισκιαζούσης τὰ πανταχοῦ, καὶ κρυπτούσης τὴν περὶ τοῦ ἀληθινοῦ Θεοῦ γνῶσιν. S. Athan. de Incar. 13.

[2] See S. August, de Civ. Dei, viii. 24. "Immundi spiritus, eisdem simulacris arte illa nefaria colligati, cultorum suorum animas in suam societatem redigendo miserabiliter captivaverant."

and palpable effects,[1] of which those who were eye-witnesses give us many details. Take again the oracles which existed throughout the heathen world, and, as dealing with the same subject-matter, divination in all its forms. However much of deceit there might be here, was there not also, in many instances, an exhibition of power and knowledge beyond that of man, which no mere deceit could produce? Take again magic, the invocation, adjuration, and compacting with spirits, which ran through heathen society in numberless shapes; and take lastly the fact of spirits seizing upon and possessing the bodies of men, speaking by their voice, and controlling their minds. The four classes which we have just given, comprehend in themselves an innumerable multitude of facts which are apparent in pagan history, in all which the corruption of the human soul is an agent or patient, but for which that corruption by itself supplies no adequate cause. A spiritual power is behind, laying hold of and acting upon this corruption, and by fault of the human will making an inroad into the visible world, and partially mastering it, bending it to an evil purpose, and making it serve as an agent to man's captivity. Let us briefly cite as to the reality of this spiritual power the witness of its victims and the witness of its opponents.

First, as to its victims. Scarcely a writer, whether poet, historian, philosopher, or biographer, can be found among the heathens of Greece and Rome who does not attest facts belonging to one or more of these four

[1] Called by S. Athan. ἡ τῶν δαιμόνων ἀπάτη — μανία — φαντασίαι. Thus, *De Inc.* 47. πάλαι μὲν δαίμονες ἐφαντασιασκόπουν τοὺς ἀνθρώπους, προκαταλαμβάνοντες πηγὰς ἢ ποταμοὺς, ἢ ξύλα, ἢ λίθους, καὶ οὕτω ταῖς μαγγανείαις ἐξέπληττον τοὺς ἄφρονας. Νῦν δὲ τῆς θείας ἐπιφανείας τοῦ Λόγου γεγενημένης, πέπαυται τούτων ἡ φαντασία.

classes which surpass human power, and suggest an invisible spiritual agency. The poet who writes expressly to deny such an agency speaks of the whole world as bowed beneath the fear of it; another poet,[1] referring tacitly to this very passage, felicitates the man not who has a pure conscience, but who through knowledge of natural things has trampled these fears under his feet. Nor is such a belief confined to the vulgar; but scarcely a man of eminence, a soldier, or a statesman can be cited who does not in his life and actions acknowledge it, shrink from it, or cower beneath it. It is too powerful for Alexander or even Julius to escape; and the philosophers who affect to deny it in their systems exhibit it in their conduct. They have all the conviction of an evil power beyond and above nature, but taking hold of natural forms, and ever lying in wait to burst forth from them upon human life. The Greek name for superstition is fear of the demons; and what S. Paul said of the Athenians, that he found them in all things too fearful of the demons, might be applied to the whole circle of nations surrounding the midland sea.

Secondly, as to the opponents of this power. Now they offer a triple witness to its existence. The first of these is in the facts mentioned in the New Testament. The strongest, most terrible, and most inexplicable instance of this power lies in those diabolical possessions with which so many of our Lord's miracles are concerned. Again, as to the reality of divining

---

[1] "Humana ante oculos fœde quam vita jaceret
  In terris, oppressa, gravi sub religione," &c.   Lucret. i. 63.

"Felix qui potuit rerum cognoscere causas,
Atque metus omnes et inexorabile fatum
Subjecit pedibus, strepitumque Acherontis avari."
                                —Virg. *Geo.* ii. 491.

powers arising from the presence of a demon in a human form, we have the evil spirit in the girl at Philippi acknowledging in S. Paul a servant of the most high God, and, when cast out by the Apostle in the name of Christ, leaving his victim destitute of those powers which had brought gain to her masters, who forthwith try to avenge themselves for their loss by exciting a persecution against the Apostle.[1]

A second witness is found in the rites and offices of the very power set up to dethrone and abolish this other power. The Church called upon every one who was received into her bosom to begin by renouncing the usurpation of this great enemy, which was thus declared to be universal. She provided forms for exorcising him. One of her Apostles warned those to whom he wrote that men could not partake at once of the Christian sacrifice and the heathen; for as truly as one was the chalice of the Lord, the other was the chalice of devils; as one was the table of the Lord, the other was the table of devils.[2]

A third witness is found in the unanimous testimony of all Christian writers as to the reality of the demoniacal powers with which they were waging war; as to their perpetual interference with human life; as to the open and palpable effects which they produced; as to their unwilling retirement in the face of that Stronger One who was come upon them. It was not merely the fervid Tertullian who offered to rest the truth of Christianity and the life of any ordinary Christian upon his power publicly to expel a demon. Athanasius, who weighs every word he utters, says also, "Let him who will, try the truth of what we have said, and in the very presence of the spectral

---

[1] Acts xvi. 16.   [2] 1 Cor. x. 21.

illusion of the demons, of the deceit of oracles and the wonders of magic, let him use the sign of the cross derided by them, only naming the name of Christ, and he shall see how by Him the demons fly, the oracles cease, and every sort of magic and witchcraft is annulled." No less express is S. Augustine in acknowledging the reality of these dark powers, and the wonders worked by them.[1]

Resuming then for a moment our view of heathenism as a whole, with regard to the exhibition of diabolic power in it, let us bear in mind, joined to the absence of moral teaching, its flagrantly immoral disposition; secondly, its illogical character, by which it is an insult to human reason while yet accepted by the human will; and thirdly, the superhuman effects noted in it and attached to its rites, ceremonies, and practices, attested by many generations alike of its victims as of its opponents. These proofs have each their own separate force, but they have likewise as to our conclusion a cumulative force; and its result is, that the existence of a diabolic kingdom and sovereign throned in heathenism, pervading its rites and directing its operations, which is so expressly declared in Holy Writ, is no less strongly proved by the facts of history.

6. Now, having sketched in four main points the substance of this polytheism, its multiplicity, its universality, its hold upon daily life, and its moral cor-

---

[1] Tertullian, *Apologeticus*, 23; St. Athanas. *de Inc.* 48; St. Aug. *de Civ. Dei*, xxi. 6, who says, "Ut autem demones illiciantur ab hominibus, prius eos ipsi astutissima calliditate seducunt, vel inspirando eorum cordibus virus occultum, vel etiam fallacibus amicitiis apparendo, eorumque paucos discipulos suos faciunt, plurimorumque doctores. Neque enim potuit, nisi primum ipsis docentibus, disci quid quisque illorum appetat, quid exhorreat, quo invitetur nomine, quo cogatur, unde magicæ artes earumque artifices exstiterunt."

ruption, to all which a consummating force is added by the indwelling of diabolic power, it remains to give a glance at certain conditions and circumstances under which it was acting on the minds of men. We have here taken it and examined it by itself, abstracting it from those circumstances, but it never so appeared to those who lived under it. The wonderful error which so enfolded these widespread nations never exhibited itself to them bare and naked. On the contrary, it came to them interwoven with the dearest claims of the family, the city, the country, with the force of habit and tradition, with the dread of change, with the past history and future hopes of their fatherland, coloured moreover with the radiant dress of a rich and ever-advancing civilisation.

To judge of its power, vitality, and chance of permanence, we must look at it under these conditions. And if, when we regard this idolatrous polytheism in itself, one is lost in wonder at its ever having arisen, at its existence, at its continuance, so, when one regards it as throned in the customs, feelings, convictions, and interests of society, one wonders how any moral force could ever overthrow it. At the present time not only are there religions outside of Christianity, but there are also sects within it, so irrational, so devoid of the witness given by internal truth and harmony, so unable to render any account of themselves and their claims which will satisfy a mind looking for consistency, that, regarding them merely as facts, one cannot account for them, yet notwithstanding they may have existed for several hundred years, and had a large share in forming national habits of thought, or even national character; nay, perhaps their secret strength lies in some fold of this character itself. And because they are never seen by themselves, their intrinsic absurdity does not come before their adherents, and the last thing which these think of examining is the foundation of their sect, inasmuch as in fact it has never approached them otherwise than as a condition of their daily life. So we shall understand paganism better by considering it as interwoven with civilisation, polity, and national feelings. We will treat of it briefly under these three heads.

1. First, the whole eastern part of the Roman empire was made up of many various nations having a long and sometimes renowned history, kingdoms and polities much anterior to Rome herself, of which the Romans had taken violent possession, but wherein remained still the fruits of a rich and undisturbed civilisation. And this word comprehends all the natural life of man, all the discoveries gained by his invention or experience, and accumulated by wealth descending from age to age, all the manifold ties of social intercourse, all the pleasures of the intellect, united, moreover, in their case with an art even now unrivalled in portraying the beauty of the human figure, and in the elegance with which it adapted material forms to the conveniences of life. So rich and varied an inheritance unfolded itself in a thousand Hellenic cities studding the shores of the Mediterranean. The culture itself since the time of Alexander might be termed Hellenic, but it embraced Egypt, and Syria, and all Western Asia. And so completely was idolatrous polytheism interwoven with culture, so inextricably was it blended with the bulk, so gradually had it grown with the growth, and wound its fibres about the tree and the branches, that

the worship might be absolutely identified with the civilisation. The gods of Greece were the heads of the most illustrious Grecian families; their hero-worship consecrated every city, every grove, every field. The gods of Egypt were blended with the long renown of the Nile-land, with every Egyptian custom, with the beginning and the end of life. Not less had the gods of Syria and Western Asia occupied their respective lands. These deities struck their root into the home of man, into the union of the sexes, into the loves of parent and child, of brother and sister. They had their mementos in every street of busy traffic; they watched over the Acropolis; not a fountain but laid claim to their patronage, nor a field which was fruitful but by their supposed influence. These countries had lost their political independence, but the material ease of life under the majesty of the Roman name they retained. There was a passionate love for this world's goods, comforts, and enjoyments in the Greek, Syrian, Asiatic, Egyptian, and Libyan races, all of them more or less worn, and effete, and deeply sensualised; but their glory was this great Hellenic civilisation, with which polytheism might be termed one and the same thing.

2. When we turn to the West, the seat of the sovereign city and of the empire itself, we find that from the very beginning and through many centuries the political constitution of the city had been indissolubly blended with the worship of the Roman gods. The religion of Rome was much more than national; her polity seemed only another name for her worship. Her temples were as much a part of her political life as her forum. So far at least she had embodied in her whole structure the legend of her Etruscan teacher,

wherein the dwarf Tages sprung from the soil to communicate the worship claimed by the gods.[1] Her soil and her worship were indivisible. And even after seven centuries, when the city was embracing the world in its arms, this union practically existed. Rome indeed admitted, as we have said, the gods of the conquered nations into her pantheon, but it was on the same tenure as the nations themselves shared her civic rights. Jupiter Capitolinus was a sort of suzerain not only to the gods of the Grecian Olympus, but to the dark forms of the Nile deities, to the Syrian, the Libyan, the Gallic, the Germanic, the Sarmatian Valhalla. When the greatest of her poets would express unending duration, he joins together the race of Æneas enthroned on the Capitol with the god who dwelt there:

> "Nulla dies unquam memori vos eximet ævo,
> Dum domus Æneæ Capitoli immobile saxum
> Accolet, imperiumque Pater Romanus habebit."

The Roman father is the Capitoline Jupiter. "I am not a king; the only king of the Romans is Jupiter," said the most royal of the race, and the founder of her empire, when, seeing all prostrate at his feet, he put away reluctantly the diadem offered by his creature. Thus even he who had seized the reality of power, who would have omens when he pleased, and whose will was his law, left the crown on the head of Jupiter. In Rome, all through her history "piety and patriotism were the same feeling."[2] When her empire became world-wide, this sort of devotion did not cease. Rome had long been deified; and the

---
[1] Merivale, iii. 496.
[2] Beugnot, *Destruction du Paganisme*, i. 8.

double import of her name [1] expressed strength against the foe without, and nourishment to the child within. She was at once a warrior-goddess clothed in mail to meet the enemy, and a mother offering her bosom to her citizens clustered around her. And so in her new constitution, adapted for the world, her emperor too was deified, as the first of her children, her living representative, the embodiment of her force and love, the visible wielder of her unseen power. All that is sacred in home and country to us the Roman signified when he swore by the genius of the emperor. Nothing could be more tolerant than this polytheism, if the innovation extended only to the borrowing or creating a new divinity, to reforming a rite or a ceremony,[2] or to suchlike modifications of worship which admitted that on which it rested; but nothing more intolerant than the same polytheism when the worship itself was attacked. A movement against the Capitoline Jupiter would be not only sacrilege but high treason, and the refusal to call to witness the emperor's genius was in fact to deny his imperial authority. The worship of the gods was as much identified with the empire of Rome in the West as with the civilisation of Greece throughout the East.

3. But as if these two powers were not ties sufficiently strong to hold polytheism together, there was another feeling distinct from both, which formed its last bulwark. The iron hand which held in its grasp these vast countries, many of them so large that by themselves they might have been empires, was strong enough to prevent or crush insurrection, but provided only the majesty of the Roman peace was accepted,

---

[1] ῥώμη, strength; *ruma*, a mother's breast.
[2] Beugnot, i. 17.

did not seek to disturb a large remnant of local feeling and interest still representing the former life and polity of the several provinces. Now whatever of national, tribe, or race feeling existed, was grouped everywhere about the worship of the native gods.[1] The Nile-land had ceased to be a royal seat, and was governed by a simple Roman knight as prefect of the emperor; but not for this had the Nile gods abdicated their dark sway over their votaries. In them the Egyptians still felt that they had something which was their own. Thus, whatever force of patriotism still lurked in the several parts of the empire was nurtured by its own form of polytheism, which it in turn invested with the memories dearest and most ineradicable in man, of past independence or renown. Not only the Egyptians, but the various Asiatic and Libyan races, the Gauls and Germans under Roman sway, were thus attached to their native gods with a feeling no doubt akin to that of the English towards "Old England," or the Russians towards "Holy Russia."

Two more conditions of society throughout the whole empire we have yet to consider in their bearing on the maintenance of polytheism: first, the concentration of the vast power of the state—in itself an acknowledged omnipotence, without the restriction or reservation of individual rights—in one hand, the hand of the emperor, the sole representative of the people. By this it would seem that all the upper classes of society, the classes at ease as to their maintenance, the classes who have leisure to think and will to act in political matters, were deprived of so much of their freedom, and such deprivation would tend to

[1] Οἱ ἐγχώριοι θεοί.

support an existing institution. Secondly, the despotism above was met by a corresponding despotism below. The rights of the slaveholder over the human labourer left as little margin of freedom to daily toil as the right of the imperial autocrat to the freedom of conscience in the rich. The servants throughout the world of Rome being slaves, were as much in the hand of their masters as those masters were in the hand of the prince.

We can now take a prospect of human society in reference to the polytheism of the empire from the standing-point of Augustus in the last twenty years of his reign. The worship of her gods was so intertwined with the political constitution of Rome from her birth through seven centuries and a half, that it might be said to be one thing with it. Almost as close was the identification of the several religious systems of the East with the enjoyments of civilised life which they prized so highly, and which the empire of Rome secured to them. Further in the background the national gods of the many races included in the empire were the last inheritance of their former independent life. Again, not only was the emperor as Pontifex Maximus the official head of this polytheism, but as representing the whole power of the state he was its guardian, and whatever assailed it was an insult to the majesty which he embodied; while the slavery in which the masses were lying seemed to represent in human society the chances of war, which had all ended in the dominion of Rome and the subjection of the whole pantheon of incongruous gods to the sovereignty of the Capitoline Jupiter. These were general conditions to that multifarious whole of nations and races. Then if Augustus sought to examine more narrowly the society of Roman citizens spread through his empire, he would find it divided very unequally as to numbers into two classes. The vast majority were those who take things as they find them, and who belonged with more or less fidelity and heartiness to the idolatrous polytheism. The worship which came to them as part and parcel of the empire, of civilised and of national life, they accepted without thought. To all these an indefinite number of immoral gods was throned in possession of Olympus; to all these the result of such worship was, as we have seen described by St. Augustine, the utter perversion of morality, the consecration of fables equalling in turpitude the utmost license of the theatres. But everywhere among the educated classes were to be found a small number of sceptical minds: philosophers they termed themselves: it was fashionable to follow some philosophic system or sect, and these fell mainly into two. Now the Epicureans and the Stoics, while they left the existing polytheism in practical possession, as a matter of custom and state religion, and so delivered themselves from any unpleasant consequences of denying the prevailing worship, concurred entirely in this, that the one by the way of atheism, the other by that of pantheism, destroyed all religion of the heart and inner conduct; because they equally removed the notion of a personal God, and its corresponding notion of a personal being in man outliving the body and the world of sense, and meeting with a personal retribution. Whether the power they acknowledge be nature, as in Lucretius, or a hidden physical force running through all nature, which might be called Jupiter, Juno, Hercules, or the name of any other god, as in Marcus Aurelius, the notion of a personal Creator, provident and rewarding, was equally destroyed. Nor before the preaching of the Gospel does there appear a single individual who drew out of the existing polytheism such a conclusion. On the contrary, in Augustus and his successors the imperial idea of unity in religion was to make out that all these systems of polytheism, running into and athwart each other, came practically to the same thing, differing in name only. Their obedience to Jupiter of the Capitol was the only bond of unity, and pledge of the empire's duration, conceived by the Roman rulers.

II. Thus in the time of Augustus no human eye, whether we look at the mass of mankind or the thinking few, could see any sign either that the dominant polytheism was about to fall, or that the lost doctrine of the divine Unity and Personality could be extricated from the bewildering mass of error and superstition which had grown over, disguised, and distorted it. Darker still, if possible, became the prospect under his successor, Tiberius, whose reign had reached the climax of moral debasement, when Sejanus was all-powerful at Rome. Hope for the human race there appeared none, when such an emperor devolved his omnipotence on such a prime minister. Then in the judgment-hall of a procurator in a small and distant eastern province, there passed the following dialogue between an accused criminal and his judge:—"Pilate went into the prætorium again, and called Jesus, and said to Him, 'Art thou the king of the Jews?' Jesus answered him, 'Sayest thou this thing of thyself, or have others told it thee of me?' Pilate answered, 'Am I a Jew? Thine own nation and the chief priests have delivered thee up to me: what hast thou done?' Jesus answered, 'My kingdom is not of this world. If my kingdom were of this world, my servants would strive that I should not be delivered to the Jews; but now my kingdom is not from hence.' Pilate therefore said to Him, 'Art thou a king, then?' Jesus answered, 'Thou sayest that I am a king. For this was I born, and for this came I into the world, that I should bear witness to the truth. Every one that is of the truth heareth my voice.' Pilate saith to Him, 'What is truth?'" He who thus declared Himself to be a king, the cause of whose birth and advent into the world, the function of whose royalty, was to bear witness to the truth, received from the power which then ruled the world the punishment allotted to the slave who was worthy of death. For many ages a false worship had overshadowed the earth, hiding the true God from men, and setting up instead a multitude of demons for gods. And during this time the thinkers of Greek and Roman society had been asking, What is truth? And now the officer who asked that question of the Truth Himself, replied to it by crucifying Him. And when the body of that Crucified One was the same day taken down from the cross and laid in its sepulchre, the power which reigned in polytheism and spoke by the mouth of the judge, seemed to have given the final answer of triumphant force to its question, What is truth? and falsehood might be thought to reign supreme and victorious in the world.

It was with the resurrection of that Body, in which Truth was enshrined, that the resurrection of truth among men began. He had said to His disciples a few hours before, not "I show the truth," but "I am the Truth." His birth and His advent took place that His witness might be given to it, the witness to it being that very birth and advent, His appearance among men, and the reception He would meet with. The crucifixion itself—the reply of triumphant force to its own unanswered question—was the witness which, first in Him, and then in His followers, should make itself heard over the earth, now held in captivity by falsehood. And since Truth is His proper Name and His personal Being from eternity, and by being the Truth He who spoke is the second Person in the Godhead, the perfect Image of all Truth, let us consider the import of His Name as the summing-up of the great antagonism which He then planted on the earth.

For He named Himself the Truth because He is the Son and the Word of the Father. "Thus the Father, as it were uttering Himself, begot His Word, equal to Himself in all things. For He would not fully and perfectly have uttered Himself, if there were anything less or anything more in His Word than in Himself. . . . And therefore this Word is truly the Truth; inasmuch as whatever is in that knowledge of which He is begotten, is also in Himself; and whatsoever is not in it, is not in Himself. . . . The Father and the Son know each other, the one by generating, the other by being generated."[1] Thus it is that He is the perfect Word, the absolute Image of God; and being the Image of God He created man in the beginning a copy of that Image, and according to its resemblance, in that He created him in the indivisible unity of a soul intelligent and willing—a created copy of the Trinity in Unity. But though by the original constitution of the soul this copy could not be destroyed, being the very essence of the soul, yet the resemblance might be marred, and the harmony which reigned in

[1] St. Aug. *de Trin.* l. xv. c. 14, tom. viii. 984.

the original man between the soul, its intellect, and will, through the indwelling of God's Spirit, was broken by the act of sin; whereupon that Spirit withdrew from him, and left the copy of the divine Image defaced and disordered. All the heathenism we have been considering is the sequence of that disorder, part of which is the grievous obscuration of truth, that is, of the whole relation between God and man, of which idolatrous polytheism is the perversion. It was the exact representation of the soul's own disorder, being the distortion but not the extinction of worship; the fear of many demons, instead of the fear of one God; slavish instead of filial fear.

But as the Truth of the Father is beheld and expressed in generating His Son, His Word, His perfect Image, so truth to man is the resemblance of created things to the archetypal idea of them in God; the resemblance of the works of the divine art to the Artificer's intention. In this long act of heathenism we see the work of the divine Artificer marred and obscured, and the marring and obscuration seem to have gone as far as was possible without touching the essence of the soul. Who, then, should restore, but He who had first created? Who should give back to the copy the lost harmony, and reimprint the defaced resemblance, save the perfect Image of God? Thus, when the corruption had run its course, and the original disobedience had reproduced itself all over the earth in a harvest of evil and disorder, the time for the work of reparation was come, and the Divine Word, the Image of the Father, took flesh.

Magnificent as had been the dower of the First Man, and wonderful the grace which held his soul in harmony with itself, and his bodily affections in obedience to his soul, incomparably more magnificent was the dower of human nature in its reparation, inconceivably grander the grace which ruled the Soul and Body of the Restorer. For whereas the first man's person had been simply human, the Person of the Second Man was the Divine Word Himself, the perfect Image of the Father; and whereas the grace of the first man was such that he was able not to sin, the grace which had assumed the nature of the Second Man was a Person who could not sin, the fountain of grace itself, measureless, absolute, and personal. The Image of God Himself came to restore the copy of that Image in Man; his appearance as man among men was the reconveying of the Truth to them, because He was the Truth Himself. The Truth in all its extent; the Truth in the whole moral order and every relation which belongs to it; the Truth by which all the rational creation of God corresponds to the Idea of its Creator, was the gift which He brought to man in His Incarnation.

But this truth is not merely external to man. In order to be received and appropriated by him, he must become capable of it. The Restorer works his restoration by an inward act upon the soul, its intellect and will. The Image of God sets up His seat within His work, the copy. Man is sealed by the Holy Spirit with the likeness and resemblance of the Father's Face, the Son; and having the Son within him, and giving a home within the soul to the divine character, and making this his treasure, man is formed after God.[1] The supreme likeness, which is beyond all others, is impressed on human souls by the Spirit of the Father and the Son. As the defacing of the

---

[1] St. Cyril. Alex. tom. v. 1, pp. 544, 557 a.

likeness, the result of the original fall, caused the obscuring of the Truth, so its restoration was itself the recovery of the Truth.

And this restoration is itself the witness to the Truth of which He spoke before Pilate as the object of His birth and advent. But to make the witness operative and fruitful, the greatest wonder in this list of wonders is required, the suffering of the Truth Himself. He said of the corn of wheat, which was to bear fruit in unnumbered hearts, that it would remain alone unless it fell into the ground and died. And so His crucifixion in the nature which He had assumed was the act from which the renewal of truth went forth; and not only in His Person, but likewise in His chosen witnesses this special mode of vivifying the truth, and making it fruitful, should be repeated. Not only must the absolute Truth of God appear in our nature itself in order to be accepted, but the nature in which it appeared should offer the sacrifice of itself; and this particular mode of propagating the truth should be observed in that chosen band whom He termed specially His witnesses. Their witness should be their suffering; in them too the Truth should be crucified, and so become fruitful.

And as man in his original creation had been a copy, however faint, of the eternal relations of the Godhead in itself, so his restoration springs from those same eternal relations. In it the Father, the Son, and the Holy Spirit are seen working.[1] It springs from the Father, in that He is the Father of the only-begotten Son, the Original of the Image, and so the Father of all those who are the copies of that Image. It springs from the Son, in that He is the perfect

---

[1] St. Cyril. Alex. *in Joh.* x. p. 858 b.

Image of the Father, and by dwelling in a created nature has raised it to the dignity of His Person, from which the grace of Sonship comes. It springs from the Holy Spirit, whose work as the Spirit of the Father and the Son is to imprint the copy of the Son on man. He performs in every one of the redeemed by communicating to them a participation of the divine nature, by dwelling in them, by contact and coherence with them, a work infinitely less in degree, but yet of the same order with that work of His whereby all the fulness of the Godhead dwelt by personal unity in our Lord's Manhood.[1]

But we left our Lord before Pilate, bearing witness to the truth. It remains to see how that truth became impressed on the world.

[1] Petav. *de Trin.* lib. viii. c. 7.

LECTURE VIII

THE FIRST AND THE SECOND MAN

"Totus Christus caput et corpus est. Caput unigenitus Dei Filius, et corpus ejus Ecclesia, Sponsus et Sponsa, duo in carne una." St. Aug. *De Unitate Ecc.* tom. ix. 341.

"Totus Christus, id est, caput et membra." St. Thomas, Prolog. ad 1 Sentent. art. 4.

LET us look back on the space which we have traversed, and gather up in a few words the sight which it presents to us. We have man before us as far as history will carry us back, as far as reasoning, planting itself on the scanty traces of history, will penetrate into the cloudland of prehistoric times : and the result stands before us exhibited in the manifold records still remaining of the most renowned ancient civilisation. Here, then, we see nations whose genius, whether in history, poetry, and literature, or in works of art, or in civil government, we still admire, comprising men in many of whom the powers of reason reached their utmost limit; nations inhabiting the most varied climates and countries, and amongst them the fairest in the world, nations formed under the most different circumstances and pursuing the most distinct employments, some agricultural, some commercial, some inland, some nautical, but alike in this, that they were enthralled by systems of a false worship, of which it is hard to say whether it was the more revolting to the reason by its absurdity, or to the conscience of man by its foulness. And this false worship does not lie distinct and apart from the concerns of daily civil and domestic life, but is intertwined with all the public and private actions of men, forming their habits and ruling their affections. Moreover, the polytheistic idolatry described above as existing at the time of Augustus in every province of his empire except one, in almost[1] every country which touched upon it, or was known to it, is the result, the summing-up, the embodiment of man's whole history up to that time, so far as we know it: it is that into which this history had run out, its palpable, it almost seemed its irresistible, form. And it amounts to a complete corruption, first of the relation between man and his Creator, secondly of the relation between man and his fellow, thirdly of the relations of man in civil government, that is, of states and political communities, to each other.

Now, looking at this polytheistic idolatry simply as a fact, without for the moment any attempt to give a solution of it from authority, looking at it just as modern science would regard the facts of geology or astronomy, there is one thing, we may suppose, which it proves with a superabundance of evidence not found to belong to any other fact of history; and that is, the intrinsic corruption of man as a moral being. That which in theological language is called the Fall of man is, apart from all revealed doctrine on the subject, brought in upon the mind with irresistible force by the mere enumeration of the gods which heathendom worshipped, and of the worship paid by it to them; a force which is indefinitely increased by every inquiry into the moral and religious state of man as he lived under this worship.

[1] An exception must be made in favour of Persia, where the original monotheism was preserved with more or less corruption.

THE FIRST AND THE SECOND MAN 49

Now, then, let us consider what solution the Christian faith does give of this fact, which exists, be it remembered, independently of this solution, and would exist with all its force undiminished, if this were rejected.

I. The Christian faith, as a solution of this wonderful maze of polytheistic idolatry, with all its accompaniments and consequences, carries us back to the first father of the race, whose development we have been following in it. This, it says, is nothing else [1] but the body of Adam carried out through thousands of years, the body of Adam fallen under a terrible captivity. Not only does the Christian faith set before us man as one race descended from one, but because he is this one race, descended from one, it represents him as having come into such a state. To understand this we must contemplate the original creation, the fall of man, and its consequences, in their several bearings on each other, which will then lead us on to the nature and mode of the restoration.

In speaking of the creation of man we may first consider the union of the soul and body simply by themselves; that is, in order to obtain a clear view of our subject, we may form to ourselves a purely ideal state of simple nature. Such a state would include two things; one positive, the other negative.[2] Positively, human nature in this condition would have all natural faculties in their essential perfection, and the assistance and providence of God naturally due to it: negatively, it would have nothing superadded to nature, nothing not due to it, whether evil or good, that is,

---

[1] "Das Heidenthum ist nichts anderes als der gefallene und nicht wiedergeborne Mensch im Grossen." Möhler, *Kirchengeschichte*, i. 169.
[2] Suarez, *de Gratia*, Proleg. 4, cap. i. sec. 3.

neither sin on the one hand, and what follows sin, the guilt which entails punishment, nor on the other hand any gifts of grace, or perfections not due to nature.

Human nature, if created in such a state, would have no supernatural end; its end would be to love God with a natural love, as the Author and Ruler of the world.

Of such a state it is requisite for our present purpose to say only two things further. The first, that it is not contrary to any attribute of God to have created human nature in such a state. The gift of eternal beatitude, arising from the vision of God, which such a creature would not have had for its end, is simply and absolutely a gratuitous gift of the divine bounty, which God is not bound to bestow on any creature as such. Secondly, God did not in fact so create man.

Going on from this state of simple nature, we may consider another state in man, in which, beyond all his natural faculties,[1] he would have a certain special perfection, consisting in the absence of immoderate concupiscence, or in the perfect subjection of the sensitive to the rational appetite, so that the inferior appetite should not be allowed to set itself in motion against the superior, or to anticipate reason. For human nature, regarded in itself as the union of a spirit and a body, is as it were divided in its natural affections, which tend in diverse directions, and thus totters, so to say, in its gait; when, therefore, it receives an inward peace in its own proper faculties, it is said to be supplemented, or to receive its integrity.

Now it is much to be noted that this special gift of

[1] Saurez, *de Gratia*, Proleg. cap. ii. sec. 3.

integrity would not be connatural to man, that is, not given to him by force of his nature itself. It is true indeed that as such a gift perfects nature in regard to all natural acts, and supplies a sort of natural deficiency arising out of the combination of a spiritual with a material substance, wherein a conflict is engendered, in such a sense it may be called natural: but strictly speaking it is a gift superadded to nature.

It must further be noted that this state of nature in its integrity, however high and beautiful, is not only entirely distinct from but of an inferior order to the state of human nature raised to the gift of Divine Sonship. Between human nature in this condition and human nature raised to the gift of sonship, there would be more than the difference [1] that with us exists between the kindly-treated servant and the adopted son: for human nature in this integrity would still not by virtue of it possess sanctifying grace, or, in consequence, have God and His vision for its supernatural end.

But, thirdly, it was not merely in this state that God created man, but in a state which not only included this, but had grace for its basis,[2] that is to say, every perfection which it had sprang out of this, that it was united to God by grace. This is a state of far superior order, absolutely gratuitous, and beyond anything which is due to nature. The first man, Adam, then, was not only a union of soul and body, not only did he possess this nature in its integrity, but he was created in grace, so that there was a union of the Holy Spirit with him, whereby he was exalted to the condition of a supernatural end and adopted sonship,

---
[1] Kleutgen, *die Theologie der Vorzeit*, ii. p. 559.
[2] Suarez, *de Grat.* Proleg. 4, cap. v. sec. 3.

and in this union was rooted the integrity of his nature, and the supernatural power of so ruling all the lower faculties of his soul that the higher could mount undisturbedly to God: and certain other gifts over and above, such as immunity from error or deception, so long as he did not sin, immunity from even venial fault, immunity from death, and from all pain or sorrow. Such was the original condition which grace bestowed on human nature, wherein man had not only a supernatural end, but the power to attain it easily.[1]

Now it is evident that man, by being created in grace, was raised to an astonishing height of dignity, to which not only his nature, but any created nature whatsoever had no claim. All that the justice and goodness of God required him to do in creating such a being as man of two substances, soul and body, was to bestow on the compound being so united such perfections as made the several substances complete in their own order. Such would be the ideal state of simple nature as delineated above. It was a gift beyond nature, such as nature in its first beginning could not claim, to bestow on it the integrity which in the second place we considered. But how far beyond this, passing it by an unmeasured chasm, was that dower of sonship rooted in sanctifying grace which God actually bestowed on His favoured child? It is obvious at first sight that the divine gift here intended, being in Adam's actual creation the root of all which was over and above the natural faculties of body and soul in their union, was bestowed absolutely by the pure goodness of God, and therefore could be bestowed with such conditions attached to it as pleased

[1] Kleutgen, *die Theologie der Vorzeit*, vol. ii. 650.

the Giver. In all that is beyond the mere faculties and needs of nature—in forming which God's own being is a sort of rule to Him—He is absolutely free to give as pleases Himself, to what degree He pleases, on what terms He pleases. What, then, were the conditions on which He invested Adam with the gift of sonship, and created him in grace as its foundation? He created him, not only as the individual Adam, but as the Head of his race, so that his race was summed up in him, and a unity was founded in him attaching his whole race as members to his body, in such manner that the supernatural gift of sonship bestowed on him was to descend from him by virtue of natural propagation to every member of that body, which thus became a supernatural race from a supernatural father. So absolute was this unity that the order maintained in the case of every other creature put under the dominion of the man so formed was not followed in his case. For whereas they were created with the difference of sex, each a male and a female, he was created alone, as the Head, and then she, by whose co-operation the race was to be continued, was formed out of him. It was not a second man who was so formed from the first, but one made with reference to him, in dependence on him, to be a help meet for him, not for herself, with an independent being, but for him. This formation of Eve from Adam, which has a meaning of unfathomable depth in the development of the race, is an essential part of the original design. "Therefore," says Adam, speaking in an ecstasy sent upon him by God, the words of God, "this is now bone of my bone and flesh of my flesh: she shall be called woman, because she was taken out of man. Therefore shall a man leave his father and his mother, and shall cleave unto his wife, and they shall be one flesh." First, the Eve so formed from him is one flesh with him; secondly, the race springing from both is one flesh likewise with him. The consequence intended by that one flesh was the transmission of that magnificent inheritance in which Adam was standing when he so spoke. In this he was Father and Head, for this created alone, then Eve built up from him, from whom afterwards was to issue their joint race. On the further condition of his personal obedience to God and fidelity to His grace, he held the whole supernatural gift of grace conferring sonship, both for himself and for his race: on these terms it was bestowed by the charter of God, the original Giver. Thus, the greatness of his Headship was visible in two things, the power of transmitting his quality of divine sonship to his race by propagation, and the dependence of that quality, in them as well as in himself, on his personal fidelity to God.

But the First Man, the Father and Head of the race, did not stand in his inheritance. He broke the divine command, and lost the gift of sonship, and with it all the prerogatives attendant on that gift, which were above nature and rooted in grace, and which the eminent goodness of God had bestowed upon him: and by the terms of the original charter lost the gift, not only for himself, but for his race. But he did not, therefore, destroy that ralation between the Head and the Race, which was part of the original foundation of God. This continued; but whereas it had been intended to communicate the blessing of adoption, it now served to communicate the demerit of adoption lost, the guilt, and with it the punishment incurred by that loss.

THE FIRST AND THE SECOND MAN 55

This is the original sin, the sin of the nature, not of the person, inherited by the members of Adam's body; and as there can be no sin without free-will, the sin of the whole nature included in Adam as its Root and Head, which sinned by Adam's abuse of his free-will.

Let us try to determine as accurately as we can the position into which Adam and his race fell.

Did, then, Adam simply lose with the forfeiture of sanctifying grace the gift of sonship, the supernatural inheritance, all which God had bestowed on him beyond that ideal state of pure nature which we described in the first instance? God, we said, might have created man originally in this condition, and man so created, that is, in virtue of this creation, would not have been under any sin, nor exposed to the anger of God. Did man, by Adam's sin, fall back into it? Not so. His state after his fall differed from such a state of pure nature in that he had upon him the guilt of lost adoption, of adoption lost by the first Adam's fault, and in proportion to the greatness of the loss, and the gratuitousness of the gift originally bestowed, was the anger with which, on the donor's part, the loss was regarded. How would a king, a man like ourselves, regard one whom he had raised out of the dust to be his adopted child, and who had been unfaithful to the parent who had so chosen him with more than natural affection? Such an anger we can indeed understand when felt against the person sinning; but we fail to enter into it as resting on the race, because the secret tie which binds the head and the 'race into one is not discerned by us; because too the greatness of the divine majesty, the awfulness of His sovereignty, and the wrath of that majesty slighted, are feebly appreciated by us. But this image may at least give us some notion of the nature of that divine anger which pressed upon Adam and his race after the fall. Not only, therefore, was the gift of sonship and the prerogatives attending it withdrawn, but this withdrawal was a punishment, which their absence in the presumed case of an original state of simple nature would not have been. Thus death was a punishment to Adam and his race; the body's weakness and disease, the soul's sorrows and pains, the disobedience of the inferior appetites to the reason, the resistance of the reason to the law of God, were all punishments, and a remarkable point of the punishment is to be seen in this. Adam, as the head of his race, was in virtue of natural propagation to have bestowed on the children of his flesh, the members of his body, his own supernatural inheritance. Thus a singular honour was conferred on the fathership of Adam. But now when, in virtue of this natural propagation, he, continuing to be the head of his race, transmitted to it the guilt of adoption lost instead of the blessing of adoption conferred, a peculiar shame was set by God upon this fathership of Adam, and upon all the circumstances attending it: so that henceforth in the disinherited race the bride veiled her head, and the act of being a father became an act of shame.

The condition, therefore, of Adam and his posterity after his fall differed from the condition which would have been that of simple nature by the whole extent of the guilt incurred by the nature in its fall from sonship.

And herein lies one peculiarity, and one strangely

distressing condition of his state, in that while he
lost by the fall the grace in which, as an indwelling
gift, his whole supernatural state had been rooted,
he yet did not lose that condition of being formed
and intended for a supernatural end which grace
alone could enable him to attain. For the supernatural vision and love of God he had been created,
and in his fall he did not sink to be merely a natural
man; but his original end was still held out before
him as that which he might reach supported by that
grace the aids of which were in a different measure
promised to him in order to lead a life of penance,
and as the earnest of a future restoration.

This, however, is far from being a complete statement of his case, and we must go back to the circumstances of his fall in order to add that further still
more peculiar and remarkable condition which, added
to the one just described, made up the whole of
his fall.

Adam had not disobeyed the divine command, and
so broken the covenant of his sonship, by the simple
promptings of his own will. Another had intervened;
had suggested to the woman doubts against her Maker
and Father. She had yielded to these doubts, and
disobeyed; and then Adam had suffered himself to be
drawn with her in her disobedience. Who was this
other? He was the prince and leader of spirits
created good, but fallen into enmity with God. Thus,
the favourite son of God had listened to the persuasion
of God's chief enemy, and his fall from sonship had been,
by the judgment of the offended Parent, not a simple
fall from his supernatural estate, but a fall likewise
into servitude to that enemy. This servitude also,
with the guilt of the nature in which he had sinned,

Adam transmitted to the members of his body in and by their nature. Adam with his race was the captive taken in war by the enemy of God, and the life which he was allowed to live had the condition of this servitude impressed on it, with this alleviation only, that the assistance of the divine grace offered to him by the mercy of God in his state of penance could protect those who accepted it from the effects of this servitude, and ultimately deliver them.

Here, then, is the condition of Adam's posterity in consequence of his fall; members of a Head who had broken his allegiance to his Creator and Father, and so inheriting with their nature the disinherited state into which he had cast himself; captives, moreover, of that powerful spirit, God's antagonist, who had tempted Adam, seduced him, and led him to his fall.

Now the heathenism which we have been contemplating is the carrying out in time and space of this body of Adam in those who, by their personal fault, fell away from the aids of grace which were accorded to man after his fall—aids given first to Adam for the whole race, and then renewed to Noah for the whole race; and the false worship, so blent and mingled with heathenism, which seemed as if it were the soul of its body, is the sign and stamp of that captivity to the evil spirit which the first man's sin inaugurated.

How powerful was the bond between Adam and his race, how great and influential the headship which the Divine choice had vested in him, we see in that mysterious transmission of guilt which passed from him to his children. And it must be expressly noted that it was not a transmission of punishment alone. Rather, the divine justice cannot punish where there is no guilt; and as in this case Adam's fall, and that of his posterity with him, was not merely a loss but a punishment, so it had the special nature of guilt, not only in him but in his posterity, and was a sin both of the person and of the nature in him, of the nature only in them. We see the force and range of the divine endowment of Adam here, though it be in the tenacity of the calamity which ensued to his race; but it must be remembered that such in this respect as the punishment was, the blessing would have been. Adam was created both an individual and a race. In him were two things—the single man and the head; but of these two things the headship was peculiar to himself, while such as the individual Adam was, his race was to be. He had it in his power to break the covenant of his sonship with God, but not the tie between himself and his race.

And this sheds a light upon the darkest part of that terrible picture which collected heathenism presents to us. Man, as a social animal, is incessant in his action on his fellow-man; the parent and the family form the child; the companion and the neighbourhood lead forth the child into manhood. This work is perpetually going on in all its parts, and society is the joint result. When, therefore, we see this society once fallen into the possession of a false worship, which perverts the very foundations of morality, and instils deadly error into the child with the mother's milk, no thoughtful mind can gaze without horror upon beings involved in such a maze,[1] yet intended for an eternal duration. Man's nature, as a race, seems turned against him; and in addition to the guilt under which each individual of the race is born,

---

[1] This is called by St. Peter, 1. i. 18, ἡ ματαία ἀναστροφὴ πατροπαράδοτος.

and the nature which each inherits, wherein the internal harmony of peace is broken, and neither the appetites obey the reason nor the reason is obedient to God, comes the force of habit, of education, of culture, of companionship, of man's business and leisure, his play and his earnest, the force of his language, the expression of his thoughts upon himself and others, the whole force, in fact, of man's social being when it is put under possession of an evil power, man's adversary. But this social nature was to have been to him the means of the greatest good. As by his natural descent from Adam unfallen would have come the grace of sonship, so the whole brotherhood of those who shared that gift would have helped and supported each in the maintenance of it. The human family would have had a beauty and a unity of its own as such; an order and a lustre would have rested on the whole body, confirming each member in the possession of his own particular gift. The concatenation of evil in the corrupt society is the most striking contrast to the fellowship of good in the upright; and while it is distinct from that guilt which descends to man as the sin of his nature, yet springs like it from the original constitution of that nature as a race. It is the invasion of evil upon good carried to its utmost point, wherein we discern most plainly "the prince of this world" wielding that "power of darkness" by which the Apostle described the whole state of the world, out of which these nations, which made the empire of Augustus, were a part.

We have thus contemplated four distinct pictures. The first of these was human nature bare and naked by itself, a merely ideal view of man, as a being compounded of soul and body, each possessing only the faculties which belong to them as spiritual and corporeal natures, the result of which is a substantial union, because the spiritual substance becomes the form of the corporeal, not by making the body, when already animated by another principle, to participate of spiritual life, but by becoming itself the principle first animating it. And we set forth this condition of human nature in order to throw light upon our second picture—the first man as he was actually created, possessing, as a gift superadded by the purest divine bounty to this his natural constitution, a divine sonship founded in grace; which transcendent union of the Holy Spirit with his soul kept the soul with all its faculties in a loving obedience to God, and the body in obedience to the soul; and added even to this state the further gratuitous prerogatives of immunity from error, fault, pain, distress, and death. Our third picture was man in this same state, but constituted besides by the divine will, whose good pleasure was the sole source of all this state of sonship, to be father of a race like to himself, receiving from him, with its natural generation, the transmitted gift of sonship; that is, from our view of him as an individual person we went on to consider him as the head of a body—the root of a tree. Fourthly, we have looked on the same man stripped by a fault, personal to himself but natural to his race, of this divine sonship—reduced to a state like that which the first would have been, but altered from it by two grave conditions, one of guilt lying on himself and his race on account of this gratuitous gift of sonship lost, another of captivity to that enemy of his Creator and Father who had seduced him to fall. And this picture included in it the double effect of guilt transmitted through a whole race from its head and father, and of the personal sins of each individual of the race: which, moreover, had a tendency to be perpetually heightened by the social nature of man— that part of his original condition which, as it would have supported his highest good in the state of innocence, so came to make his corruption intense and more complicated in the state of fall. It has not been our purpose in this sketch to dwell upon those who, like Adam himself after his fall, accepted the divine assistance offered to them, and the promise of a future Restorer, and who, living a life of penance, kept their faith in God. Such an assistance was offered not only to Adam but to his whole race, and such a line of men there always was; of whom Abel was the type in the world before the flood; Noah after the flood, as the second father of the whole race; Abraham, the friend of God and father of the faithful, in whose son Isaac a people was to be formed, which, as the nations in their apostasy fell more and more away from the faith and knowledge of the true God, should maintain still the seed of promise out of which the Restorer should spring. But before that Restorer came, the heathenism—of which we have been speaking in the former chapter, and of which we have been giving the solution above —was in possession of all but the whole earth, and the captivity of man to his spiritual foe, on account of which that foe is called "the ruler" and "the god" "of this world," which is said "to lie in the malignant one,"[1]

---

[1] The Apostle speaks here not of "wickedness," but of a personal agent, "the wicked or malignant one;" as the context shows. "He who is born of God keeps himself, and the malignant one touches him not. We know that we are of God, and the whole world lies in the malignant one." 1 John v. 18, 19.

was all but universal. This universality denoted that the fulness of the time[1] marked out in the providence of God was come.

For Adam, in his first creation, and in the splendour of that robe of sonship[2] in which he was invested, had been the figure of One to come: his figure as an individual person, his figure as father and head of a race; his figure likewise, when the race itself is viewed as summed up in one, as one body. Let us take each of these in their order.

What was the counterpart of Adam, as an individual person, in the new creation? It was the Eternal Son Himself assuming a human soul and body, and bearing our nature in His divine personality. Over against the creature invested with sonship stood the uncreated Son, invested with a created nature. For the grace of the Holy Spirit given by measure, and depending for its continuance on the obedience of the creature, was the Fountain of Grace Himself ruling the creature by a union indefeasible and eternal; for grace communicated grace immanent in its source. For the son gratuitously adopted was the Son by nature, making, by an inconceivable grace, the created nature assumed to be that not of the adopted but of the natural Son. In a word, the figure was man united to God; the counterpart, the God-man.

What, again, is Adam's counterpart as Father and Head of his race? It was human nature itself, which the Word of God espoused in the bridal chamber of the Virginal Womb, and so is become the Second Adam, the Father of a new race, the Head of a mystical

---

[1] Gal. iv. 4. τὸ πλήρωμα τοῦ χρόνου.
[2] τύπος τοῦ μέλλοντος. Rom. v. 14. "Forma futuri e contrario Christus ostenditur." St. Aug. tom. x. 1335.

Body, which corresponds to Adam's original Headship, but as far transcends it as the grace of the Incarnate Word transcends the grace bestowed on the first man. As Adam, had he stood in his original state of son, would have transmitted the gift of a like sonship to his whole race—as, falling, he did actually transmit to that race the guilt of adoption lost, so the Second Adam, out of His own uncreated Sonship, but through the nature which He had assumed, bestowed the dower of adopted sons and the gift of justice on His race. From the one there was punishment generating through the flesh,[1] from the other, grace regenerating through the Spirit. From the one, nature stripped and wounded, yet still bound to its head by an indissoluble tie; by the other, the Spirit of the Head, the Spirit of Truth, Charity, Unity, and Sanctity, ruling His Body and animating it, as the natural soul animates the natural body. Precisely where the mystery was darkest and the misery greatest, the divine grace is most conspicuous, and the divine power most triumphant. The very point which brings out Adam's connection with his race has an exact counterpart in Christ's Headship of His people, and an inscrutable judgment serves to illustrate an unspeakable gift. In exact accordance with the doctrine that the sin of Adam is man's sin, and the guilt of Adam man's guilt, is that boundless and unimaginable grace that the Incarnate Word did not merely assume an individual human nature, but espoused in that assumption the whole nature; that on the cross He paid the debt of the whole nature, whether for original or actual sin; that

---

[1] "Adam unus est, in quo omnes peccaverunt, quia non solum ejus imitatio peccatores facit, sed per carnem generans pœna : Christus unus est, in quo omnes justificentur, quia non solum ejus imitatio justos facit, sed per spiritum regenerans gratia." St. Aug. tom. x. p. 12 c.

His resurrection is our collective justification; that the gift of sonship is bestowed on men not as individual persons, but as members of His Body, before they have personally merited anything, just as the guilt came on them, as members of Adam, before they demerited anything personally. Exactly where the obscurity of the fall was the deepest, the light of the restoration is brightest; and where the sentence was most severe, the grace most wonderful. But to deny the first Adam would entail the loss of the Second; and he who declines the inheritance of the father stripped and wounded cannot enter into the Body of the Word made flesh.

But thirdly, as in that terrible corruption of heathenism, wherein immorality was based on false worship, we saw the body of Adam run out through time and space into the most afflicting form which evil can assume in the individual and social life of man, so in that Body which is ruled by the Divine Headship we see the counterpart, the triumph of grace, individual man taken out of that state of fallen nature, and invested with a membership answering to the dignity of the Head. The one great Christian people, the Kingdom of Christ, stands over against that kingdom of violence, disorder, impurity, and false worship. As there is a unity of the fallen Adam, a force of evil which impact only gives, so much more is there a unity of the Second Adam, which is not a collection of individuals, but a Body with its Head. The first unity consists in the reasonable soul, informing the flesh which was moulded once for all from the clay and descended to the whole race; and the race so descending was polluted by a common guilt, on which, as an ever-fertile root, grew the whole trunk of man's personal sins, of falsehood, enmity, corruption of morals, division, having the common quality of egotism. The second unity consists in the Holy Spirit of the Head communicated to the soul and body of the faithful people, both being restored by that grace of which truth and charity, unity and sanctity, are the tokens, the full virtue being planted in the cross of the Head, and from the cross diffusing itself to His Body.

II. And so we are brought again to Him who stood before Pilate to make the good confession, and who declared that the cause of His coming into the world was to bear witness to the truth. In what form was that witness to be made, and how was it to be efficacious? This is that point which we have now to illustrate. Adam's disobedience was a single act, the power of which, springing out of his headship, extended through the whole line of his race; through the consequences of this act the truth was obscured to them, and human life involved in manifold error. What was that action on the part of Christ, the purpose, as He declares, of His Incarnation, which had an equally enduring effect? If the guilt communicated was not transitory, then should the corresponding grace be perpetual. And how was it so? The Son of God, as the Head of His race, does not stand at disadvantage with Adam, but rather, we are told His grace is superabundant in its results over the other's sin: and He Himself declared that He had completely finished the work given Him to do.[1] But here He describes this work to be the bearing witness to the truth. For, indeed, it was worthy of the eternal wisdom to clothe Himself in flesh[2] in order that truth,

---

[1] John xvii. 4.
[2] St. Thomas, *Summa contra Gentiles*, l. i. c. 1.

the good of the intellect, and the end of the whole universe, might stand forth revealed to His rational creatures: and He who made all things in truth would Himself restore truth, when it had been obscured by the traducer.

1. Let us take the character which He acknowledged and claimed before Pilate: His character of King, and the kingdom in which it is exercised.

The Person of Christ, as that of the eternal Word, is the Truth itself. But He has assumed a body, and in that body He declares that He is a king, and that the exercise of His royalty is the bearing witness to the truth.[1] His words therefore indicate no less than the creation of a kingdom to which the truth should be the principle of subsistence. But what in the material or temporal kingdom is that by force of which it subsists? Plainly power. A kingdom may be larger or smaller in population, wealth, extent, stronger or weaker in the quality of its people; but as long as it retains in itself that in which power culminates, sovereignty, it will be a kingdom. If this power departs from it, if it falls into subjection to a foreign authority, or if its own subjects successfully rebel against its power, it ceases to be. In the kingdom, therefore, of which Christ speaks, the maintenance of truth corresponds to what the maintenance of power is in a material kingdom.

But power in the material kingdom moves men to the natural end of society; it preserves order, administers justice, allows and assists all natural forces to develop themselves, and it must be in its supreme

---

[1] John xviii. 37. "Thou sayest that I am a king. To this end was I born, and for this cause came I into the world, to bear witness unto the truth."

exercise one and indisputable: that is, it culminates in sovereignty. So in the spiritual kingdom truth, the corresponding power, moves men to the supernatural end, and truth culminates in infallibility. But where is this power seated, and how does the King wield it?

The same who here calls Himself King and declares it to be the function of His royalty to bear witness to the truth, in describing elsewhere the very creation of His kingdom says to His apostles, "You shall receive power by the Holy Ghost coming upon you," bidding them also to remain in Jerusalem "until they were endued with power from on high."[1] But a few hours before that scene in the hall of Pilate He had told them also that He would send them the Spirit of Truth, who should abide with them for ever, and should lead them into all truth. He creates therefore the kingdom of the truth by sending down the Spirit of the Truth to dwell for ever with those to whom He is sent; and this Spirit of the Truth is His own Spirit, whom He Himself will send as the token of His ascension and session; the Spirit who dwelt in the Body which He had assumed, and in which He spoke before Pilate, should be sent by Him when that Body had taken its place at the right hand of God, should invest with His own power those to whom He was sent, and should never cease to be with them in His character of the Spirit of Truth. Here, then, is that power in the kingdom of the Truth which enables it to bear a true and a perpetual witness. It is the power of the King, for it is His Spirit: it is the power of the kingdom, for it remains in it, is throned in it, and makes it to be what it is.

[1] Acts i. 8; Luke xxiv. 49.

But to create a kingdom of the truth, and to bear perpetual witness in that kingdom to the truth, is not only to state what is true. These expressions mark out an organisation in and by means of which truth is perpetuated. And further, the spirit in man is both reason and will; and that man may act, the intellect which has truth for its object must work on the will which has good for its object. And so the witness which our Lord speaks of is that action of the truth upon the will which produces a life in accordance with it: it is truth not left to itself, but supported by grace. This power of the Spirit of Truth is therefore double, as intended to work on the two powers of the soul, the reason and the will: it is the double gift of Truth and Grace; as He is the Spirit of Grace no less than the Spirit of Truth, and all grace is His immediate gift.

Thus the Word made flesh, being full of Truth and Grace from His own Person, communicated that Truth and Grace as the power which should form His kingdom for ever, abide in it, and constitute its being a kingdom; the gift of truth and grace being the very presence of His own Spirit, who took possession of His kingdom on the day of Pentecost and holds it for ever.

This whole possession of Truth and Grace dwelling in a visible body is the work of the eternal Word, who assumed a body for that purpose. It is the counter-creation to the kingdom of falsehood which commenced with the sin of the first man believing a falsehood against his Maker, and which spread itself with his lineage into all lands.[1] And as in the natural creation He not only created but maintained—for He did not make His creatures and then depart from them, but

[1] See St. Aug. tom. iv. 1039 e. "Ipse ergo Adam," &c.

from that time they exist in Him—so in the supernatural the act of maintaining is equivalent to the act of creating, it is a continued creation. As the guilt had a force which was fruitful, which continued and propagated itself, and produced a widespread reign of falsehood, how much more should that mighty and astonishing grace of a Divine Person assuming a created nature be fruitful, continue, and propagate itself in the maintenance of a visible kingdom, whose distinctive character and its very life should be the possession and communication of the truth! Should the Creator of man in His greatest work be less powerful than His seduced creature in his fall? and if the fall, pregnant with falsehood, bore fruit through ages in a whole race, should not the recovery likewise have its visible dominion, and stand over against the ruin as the kingdom of truth?

It is as King ruling in the kingdom of truth that the Divine Word incarnate redeems man from captivity, which began in a revolt from the truth, and in becoming subject to falsehood. All who are outside His kingdom lie in this captivity;[1] the life which He gave voluntarily is the price paid for their liberation; and as age after age, so long as the natural body of Adam lasts, the captivity endures, so age after age the liberation takes effect by entering into His kingdom. And this is the most general name, the name of predilection,

---

[1] Οἴδαμεν ὅτι ἐκ τοῦ Θεοῦ ἐσμὲν, καὶ ὁ κόσμος ὅλος ἐν τῷ πονηρῷ κεῖται· οἴδαμεν δὲ ὅτι ὁ υἱὸς τοῦ Θεοῦ ἥκει, καὶ δέδωκεν ἡμῖν διάνοιαν ἵνα γινώσκωμεν τὸν ἀληθινόν· καὶ ἐσμὲν ἐν τῷ ἀληθινῷ, ἐν τῷ υἱῷ αὐτοῦ Ἰησοῦ Χριστῷ. 1 John v. 19. Two persons are here opposed to each other, ὁ πονηρός and ὁ ἀληθινός. Compare the Lord's Prayer, ῥῦσαι ἡμᾶς ἀπὸ τοῦ πονηροῦ. Matt. vi. 13, and John xvii. 14, 15. ἐγὼ δέδωκα αὐτοῖς τὸν λόγον σου, καὶ ὁ κόσμος ἐμίσησεν αὐτοὺς, ὅτι οὐκ εἰσὶν ἐκ τοῦ κόσμου, καθὼς ἐγὼ οὐκ εἰμὶ ἐκ τοῦ κόσμου. οὐκ ἐρωτῶ ἵνα ἄρῃς αὐτοὺς ἐκ τοῦ κόσμου, ἀλλ' ἵνα τηρήσῃς αὐτοὺς ἐκ τοῦ πονηροῦ.

which both in prophecy marked the time of Messiah the King, and was announced by His precursor, and taken by our Lord to indicate His having come. The eternal duration of this kingdom may be said to be the substance of all prophecy, and it was precisely in the interpretation of a vision describing under the image of a great statue the four world-kingdoms, that is, the whole structure, course, and issue of the heathenism which we have been contemplating, that Daniel contrasts these kingdoms with another. "In the days of these kings shall the God of heaven set up a kingdom which shall never be destroyed; and the kingdom shall not be delivered to another. people, but it shall break in pieces and consume all these kingdoms, and shall stand itself for ever." As King in this kingdom through all the generations of men from the moment that He stood in Pilate's hall until He comes to judge the world, our Lord bears witness to the truth, His witness and His royalty being contemporaneous and conterminous to each other.

2. This perpetual possession and announcement of the truth is indicated by another image which is of constant recurrence,[1] wherein Christ is the Inhabitant, His people the Inhabited, while both are the House or Temple, for that in which God dwells is at once His House and Temple. Thus Moses is said to have been "faithful in all his house as a servant, but Christ as a Son over His own house, whose house are we." Here the King who bears witness to the truth is the God who sanctifies the faithful people by dwelling in them and building them in the truth.

[1] Heb. iii. 1-6; Ephes. ii. 19-22; 1 Cor. iii. 9, 10-15; 2 Cor. vi. 16; 1 Pet. ii. 4, 5.

It is not merely the individual believer, but the whole mass of the faithful which grows up to be a holy temple; and the ever-abiding Spirit of truth, whose presence is the guarantee of truth, is the equally abiding Spirit of sanctity, whose presence imparts holiness. The Son dwells in His own house by His Spirit for ever: as He ceases not to be incarnate, He ceases not to dwell in His house, and could falsehood be worshipped in His temple, it would cease to be His. That was the work of heathenism, when a false spirit had caused error to be worshipped for truth; the specific victory of the Word incarnate was to set up a temple in which the truth should be worshipped for ever, "the inhabitation of God in the Spirit." But living stones make up this temple, that is, individual spirits, endued with their own reason and will, yet no less fitted in and cemented together by His grace, and so forming a structure which has an organic unity of its own, being the House and Temple of One. It is in virtue of this inhabitation that the Church is termed the House of God, the pillar and ground of the truth, inasmuch as it contains, as between walls,[1] the faith and its announcement and proclamation, that is, the law of the King of Truth declared by His heralds. "We speculate," says S. Augustine, "that we may attain to vision; yet even the most studious speculation would fall into error unless the Lord inhabited the Church herself that now is."[2] And again: "In earthly possessions a benefit is given to the proprietor when he is given possession; not so is the posses-

---

[1] Τοῦτο γάρ ἐστὶ τὸ συνέχον τὴν πίστιν καὶ τὸ κήρυγμα. S. Chrys. in loc. Compare S. Irenæus, lib. i. c. 10. Τοῦτο τὸ κήρυγμα παρειληφυῖα, καὶ ταύτην τὴν πίστιν, ὡς προέφαμεν, ἡ Ἐκκλησία, καίπερ ἐν ὅλῳ τῷ κόσμῳ διεσπαρμένη, ἐπιμελῶς φυλάσσει, ὡς ἕνα οἶκον οἰκοῦσα.
[2] St. Aug. in Ps. ix. tom. iv. 51.

sion which is the Church. The benefit here lies in being possessed by such a one."—" Christ's Body is both Temple and House and City, and He who is Head of the Body is Inhabiter of the House, and Sanctifier of the Temple, and King of the City.— What can we say more acceptable to Him than this, Possess us?"[1]

3. Again, to take another image, which is the greatest of realities. What a wonderful production of divine skill is the structure of the human body! Even its outward beauty is such as to sway our feelings with a force which reason has at times a hard combat to overcome, so keen is the delight which it conveys. But the inward distribution of its parts is so marvellous that those who have spent their lives in the study of its anatomy can find in a single member, for instance, in the hand, enough out of which to fill a volume with the wise adaptation of means to ends which it reveals. There are parts of it the structure of which is so minute and subtle that the most persevering science has not yet attained fully to unravel their use. In all this arrangement of nerves and muscles, machines of every sort, meeting all manner of difficulties, and supplying all kinds of uses, what an endless storehouse of wisdom and forethought! And all these are permeated by a common life, which binds every part, whatever its several importance, into one whole, and all these, in the state of health, work together with so perfect an ease that the living actor, the bearer of so marvellous a structure, is unconscious of an effort, and exults in the life so simple and yet so manifold poured out on such a multitude of members, a life so tender that the smallest prick is felt over

[1] *Ibid.* in Ps. cxxxi. tom. iv. 1473.

the whole body, and yet so strong that a wound may transfix the whole structure, leaving the life untouched. And, in addition to this physical marvel, the incorporeal mind, which has its seat in this material structure, and whose presence is itself its life, rules like an absolute monarch with undisputed sway over his whole dominion, so that the least movement of volition carries with it a willing obedience in the whole frame, and for it instantaneously the eye gazes, the ear listens, the tongue speaks, the feet walk, the hands work, and the brain feels with an incomparable unity. The marvel of the body is that things so many and various by the rule of the artificer impressed upon them are yet one, concur to one end, and produce one whole, from which no part can be taken, and to which none can be added without injury, the least and the greatest replete with one life, which so entirely belongs to the whole body that what is severed from the body at once dies. "Now, as the body is one, and has many members, but all the members of this one body, being many, are one body, so also," says S. Paul, "is Christ," giving the name of the Head to the whole Body. What the human head is to its own body, that our Lord is to His Church. Perhaps no other image in the whole realm of nature would convey with such force the three relations [1] which constitute spiritual headship, an inseparable union, by which the head and the body form one whole, an unceasing government, including every sort of provision and care, and a perpetual influx of grace. This is on the part of the head, while as to the body perhaps no other image but this could equally convey the conjunction of many different members with various functions, whose union makes

[1] Petavius on the Headship of Christ.

the structure, and whose unity is something entirely distinct from that which all the parts in their several state, or even in their collocation and arrangement, make up, for it is the life which makes them one. Thus it is an unfathomed depth of doctrine, which is conveyed in the words, "God gave Him to be Head over all things to the Church, who is His Body, the fulness of Him who fills all things in all." For though no language could exhaust or duly exhibit the meaning of the kingdom or the temple in which the abiding work of our Lord is indicated, we have in this title yet more strikingly portrayed the intimate union and common life of His people with Christ, and His tender affection for them, since the King of Truth who redeems and the God of Truth who sanctifies, is at the same time the Head who by His own Spirit of the truth rules and vivifies His own Body. If it be possible to dissociate the idea of the King from His kingdom, or that of God from the temple of living souls in whom He is worshipped, and whose worship of Him makes them one, yet in the human frame to dissever the head from the body is to destroy the propriety of both terms, and it is as a whole human body that the apostle represents Christ and His people to us.

4. Yet, as if this were not enough, S. Paul goes on to delineate Him as the Bridegroom, whose love after redeeming sanctifies one who shall be His bride for ever, one who obeys Him with the fidelity of conjugal love, one whose preservation of His faith unstained is not the dry fulfilment of a command, but the prompting of wedded affection. The image seems chosen to convey intensity of love, first on the part of the Bridegroom as originating it, and then on the part of the Bride as responding to it. But no less does

the unity of person in the Bride, given by St. John as well as by S. Paul, indicate in the Church something quite distinct from the individuals who compose her. For she is the pattern of the faithful wife in that she is subject to Christ; and in these words a fact is stated,[1] a fact without limit of place or time, which therefore marks that she who is so described can never at any time be separated from the fidelity and love due from her to her Head and Husband. And this is not true of the individual souls belonging to her, for they, having been once faithful members of the body, may fall away and be finally lost. The Bride alone is subject to Christ with a never-failing subjection. And He on His part loves her as His own flesh, a union of the two loves of the Head for the Body, and of the Bridegroom for the Bride, which is true with regard to Him of the Church alone, since individuals within her He may cast off, but her alone He cherishes and fosters for ever. It is indefectible union and unbroken charity with Him which her quality of Bride conveys.

5. And out of this wedded union by that great sacrament concerning Christ and the Church, of which in the same passage St. Paul speaks, that they two shall be one flesh, springs the whole race, in the generation of whom is most completely verified his title of the Second Adam. From the womb of the Church, become from a Bride the Mother of all living, the Father of the age to come bears that chosen race, and royal priesthood, and holy nation, and purchased people. And here we see expressed with great force the truth that all who belong to the Father's supernatural race must come by the Mother. Her office of

[1] Passaglia, *de Ecclesia*.

parent is here set forth; as her fidelity and intense affection shine in the title of the Bride, as her union, submission, and unfailing reception of life in her title of Body, so in the title of Mother all the saved are borne to Christ by her, as St. Cyprian[1] drew the conclusion, "he cannot have God for his father who has not the Church for his mother."

In all this we see the five[2] great loves first shown by God to man, then returned by man to God; the love of the Saviour, redeeming captives, and out of these forming His kingdom; the love of the friend, who is God, sanctifying those whom He redeems into one temple; the love which He has implanted in man for self-preservation, since that which He so redeems and sanctifies He has made His own body; the love which He has given to the bridegroom for the bride, since it is the Bride of the Lamb who is so adorned; and the love of the Father for his race, since it is his wife who bears every child to him. Why is the whole force of human language exhausted, and the whole strength of the several human affections accumulated, in this manner? It is to express the super-eminent work of God made flesh, who, when He took a human body, created in correspondence to it that among men and out of men in which the virtue of His Incarnation is stored up, the mystical Kingdom, Temple, Body, Bride, and Mother. No one of these titles could convey the full riches of His work, or the variously-wrought splendour of His wisdom, which the angels desire to look into; therefore He searched through human nature and society in all its depth and height

---

[1] St. Cyprian, *de Unitate*, 5.
[2] All these five relations between Christ and the Church are mentioned in one passage of St. Paul, Ephes. v. 22-33.

for images whose union might express a work so unexampled and unique. Rather, it is truer to say that these natural affections themselves, the gift of that most bountiful giver, were created by Him originally to be types, foreshadowings, and partial copies of that more excellent supernatural love which He had decreed to show to man, since first of all things in the order of the divine design must the Incarnation have been. The whole structure of the family, and the affections which it contains, must spring out of this root, for nature was anticipated by grace in man's creation, and must ever have been subordinate to it. And now, when the full time of grace is come, these titles of things which by His mercy have lasted through the fall, serve to illustrate the greatness of the restoration. For this, which has many names, all precious and dear, is but one creation, having the manifold qualities of redemption and sanctification, of organic unity in one body, wherein many members conspire to a corporate life, which life itself is charity, and in which is the production of the holy race. As we gaze on the Kingdom, Temple, Body, Spouse, and Family, one seems to melt and change into the other. The Kingdom is deepened and enlarged by the thought that the King is the eternal Truth who is worshipped therein; and the worship passes on into the love of the Incarnate God for the members of His own Body, whom He first saves, then fosters and cherishes as His own flesh: and here again is blended that tenderest love of the Bridegroom for the bride, which further issues into the crowning love of the Father for His race. The mode of the salvation seems to spring from the nature of God Himself, since all paternity in heaven and earth springs from that whereby He is

Father of the only-begotten Son, who, descending from heaven with the love of the Bridegroom for the bride, binds together in sonship derived from his own the members of His body, the bride of His heart, the subjects of His kingdom, who are built up as living stones into that unimaginable temple raised in the unity of worshipping hearts to the ever-blessed Trinity. To this grows out, as the fulness of Him who fills all in all, that body of the Second Adam, of which in the body of the first Adam He had Himself deposited the germ.

When the angel described to the Blessed Virgin herself that miracle of miracles which was to take place in her, the assumption of human flesh by the Son of God, he used these terms: "The Holy Ghost shall come upon thee, and the power of the Most High shall overshadow thee." When the Son of God, at the moment of His Ascension, declared to His Apostles the creation of His mystical body, by using similar words, He referred them back to His own conception: "You shall receive power, the Holy Ghost coming upon you:" having already on the day of His Resurrection told them, " I send the promise of My Father upon you; but wait you in the city until you be indued with power from on high."[1] Our Lord Himself thus suggests to us the remarkable parallel between the formation of His natural and His mystical body. He who framed the one and the other is the same, the Holy Ghost: the Head precedes, the Body follows; because of the first descent, that Holy Thing which was to be born should be called the Son of God; because of the

---

[1] Luke i. 35. Πνεῦμα ἅγιον ἐπελεύσεται ἐπὶ σε, καὶ δύναμις ὑψίστου ἐπισκιάσει σοι. Acts i. 8. λήψεσθε δύναμιν, ἐπελθόντος τοῦ ἁγίου Πνεύματος ἐφ' ὑμᾶς. Luke xxiv. 49. ἕως οὗ ἐνδύσησθε δύναμιν ἐξ ὕψους.

second, " you shall be my witnesses in Jerusalem, and in all Judea, and Samaria, and to the farthest part of the earth;" and this is said in answer to their question whether He would then restore the kingdom to Israel: that is, the second descent of the Holy Ghost forms the kingdom whose witness to Christ is perpetual; forms the body with which and in which He will be for ever by this power of His Spirit dwelling in it to the end of the world. We have therefore here all the various functions and qualities which, under the five great titles of Kingdom, Temple, Body, Spouse, and Mother, delineate His Church, gathered up into that unity which comprehends them all, and from which, as a source, they all flow, " The Power of the Holy Ghost coming upon men."[1] This creation is as absolutely His, and His alone, as the forming of our Lord's own Body in the Virginal Womb; it is the sequel of it; the fulfilment among men of those divine purposes for which God became Incarnate; in one word, the Body of the Head perpetually quickened by His Spirit. And here we may remark those striking resemblances between the natural and mystical Body which this " power of the Holy Ghost," the former of them both, indicates. For in the first the manhood[2] cannot be severed from the Person of the Word, nor in the second can the body of the Church be severed from Christ the Head and His Spirit. Secondly, in the first the Person of the Word and His manhood make one Christ, and in the second Christ the Head and the Church the Body made one complete Body. Thirdly, in the first the manhood has its own will, but

[1] The Church is so called by St. Augustine.
[2] These five are taken from Passaglia, *de Ecclesia*, lib. i. cap. 3, p. 34, 5.

through union with the Godhead is impeccable and indefeasible; and in the second the Body of the Church, though possessing its own liberty, is so ruled by Christ and guided by His Spirit, that it cannot fail in truth or in charity. Fourthly, in the first there is an influx of celestial gifts from the Person of the Word into the manhood, and in the second there is a like influx from Christ the Head into His Body the Church, so that he who hears the Church hears Christ, and he who persecutes the Church, as Saul before the gate of Damascus, persecutes Christ. Fifthly, in the first the Head, through the manhood as His instrument, fulfilled all the economy of redemption, dwelt among men, taught them, redeemed them, bestowed on them the gifts of holiness and the friendship of God; and in the second, what He began in His manhood He continues through the Church as His own Body,[1] and bestows on men what He merited in His flesh, showing in and by the Church His presence among men, teaching them holiness, preserving them from error, and leading them to the eternal inheritance.

It is also by this one "power of the Holy Ghost coming upon men" that we learn how the Head and the Body make one Christ. As in the human frame the presence of the soul gives it life and unity, binding together every member by that secret indivisible force, from the least to the greatest, from the heart and brain to the minutest portion of the outward skin, so

---

[1] Compare St. Athanasius *cont. Arian. de Incarn.* p. 877 c. —καὶ ὅταν λέγῃ ὁ Πέτρος, ἀσφαλῶς οὖν γινωσκέτω πᾶς οἶκος Ἰσραὴλ ὅτι καὶ Κύριον καὶ Χριστὸν αὐτὸν ἐποίησεν ὁ Θεὸς τοῦτον τὸν Ἰησοῦν ὃν ὑμεῖς ἐσταυρώσατε, οὐ περὶ τῆς Θεότητος αὐτοῦ λέγει, ὅτι καὶ Κύριον αὐτὸν καὶ Χριστὸν ἐποίησεν, ἀλλὰ περὶ τῆς ἀνθρωπότητος αὐτοῦ, ἥτις ἐστὶ πᾶσα ἡ ἐκκλησία, ἡ ἐν αὐτῷ κυριεύουσα καὶ βασιλεύουσα, μετὰ τὸ αὐτὸν σταυρωθῆναι· καὶ χριομένη εἰς βασιλείαν οὐρανῶν, ἵνα συμβασιλεύσῃ αὐτῷ τῷ δι' αὐτὴν ἑαυτὸν κενώσαντι, καὶ ἀναλαβόντι αὐτὴν διὰ τῆς δουλικῆς μορφῆς.

in this divine Body, which makes the whole Christ, it is the presence of the Holy Ghost, as of the soul, which gives it unity and life. The conclusion was drawn by a great Saint, and no less great a genius, fourteen hundred years ago, and I prefer St. Augustine's words to any which I can use myself: "Our spirit by which the whole race of man lives is called the soul; our spirit, too, by which each man in particular lives is called the soul; and you see what the soul does in the body. It quickens all the limbs: through the eyes it sees, through the ears it hears, through the nostrils smells, through the tongue speaks, through the hands works, through the feet walks; it is present at once in all the limbs that they may live; life it gives to all, their functions to each. The eye does not hear, nor the ear nor the tongue see, nor the ear nor the eye speak, but both live; the functions are diverse, the life common. So is the Church of God. In some saints it works miracles; in others gives voice to the truth; in others again, maintains the virginal life; in others keeps conjugal fidelity; in these one thing, in those another; each have their proper work, but all alike live. Now, what the soul is to the human body, that is the Holy Spirit to the body of Christ, which is the Church: what the soul does in all the limbs of an individual body, that does the Holy Spirit in the whole Church. But see what you have to avoid, what to observe, and what to fear. It happens that, in the human body, or in any other body, some member may be cut off, hand, finger, or foot. Does the soul follow it when cut off? As long as it was in the body it lived: when cut off, it loses life. So too the Christian man is a Catholic while he lives in the body; when cut off, he becomes a heretic; the Spirit does not follow the amputated limb."[1]

But what is this "power of the Holy Ghost coming upon men"? It is the whole treasure of truth and grace, which dwelt first in the natural body of Christ, which He came to bestow on men, which He withdrew not when He ascended, but of which He promised the continuance in the Person of the Holy Ghost, and fulfils by that Person indwelling in the Church. It was the imparting the whole treasure of truth and grace by such an indwelling which made it expedient for Him to go, which made His bodily departure not a loss, but a gain, which was "the promise" of which He spoke on that last night, and which was expressly declared to be a perpetual presence, leading, as it were, by the hand[2] into all truth—an all-powerful, all-completing, all-compensating presence, such as that alone is or can be which maintains the intellect of man in truth, because it maintains his will in grace: and, instead of the two wild horses of which the great heathen[3] spoke, guides the soul in her course as borne aloft on those twin divine yoke-fellows,[4] faith and charity.

Correlative, therefore, to the Person of Him who is at once King, and God, and Head, and Bridegroom, and Father, is that singular creation of His Spirit, by which, in the Kingdom, Temple, Body, Spouse, and Mother, He deposited the treasure of the truth and

---

[1] St. Aug. serm. 267, tom. v. p. 1090 e.
[2] Luke xxiv. 49 and John xvi. 13. $\dot{\epsilon}\kappa\epsilon\hat{\iota}\nu$os, τὸ πνεῦμα τῆς ἀληθείας, ὁδηγήσει ὑμᾶς εἰς πᾶσαν τὴν ἀλήθειαν· and 14, 15. ἐγὼ ἐρωτήσω τὸν Πατέρα, καὶ ἄλλον παράκλητον δώσει ὑμῖν, ἵνα μένῃ μεθ' ὑμῶν εἰς τὸν αἰῶνα, τὸ πνεῦμα τῆς ἀληθείας.
[3] Plato.
[4] πανταχοῦ συνάπτει καὶ συγκολλᾷ τὴν πίστιν καὶ τὴν ἀγάπην, θαυμαστήν τινα ξυνωρίδα. St. Chrys. 3rd Hom. on Ephes. tom. xi. p. 16.

grace which He became man to communicate. It was not as individual men, living a life apart, but as common children of one race, joint members of one body, that the guilt of the first father fell upon them; it is only on them as children of a higher race and members of a far greater body, that the grace of the Deliverer is bestowed. The distinctions of race and the divisions of condition drop away as they are baptized into one body, and made to drink of one spirit. The new and supernatural life cannot be communicated save by this act of engrafting into a new body. As Eve from the side of Adam sleeping, so the Church from the side of Christ suffering; as Eve bears still to Adam the children of men, so the Church to Christ the children of Christ. These are not two mysteries, but one, unfathomable in both its parts, of justice and of mercy; but the whole history of the human race bears witness to the first, and the whole history of the Christian people to the second. It would be amply sufficient to prove what we have been saying, that the first communication of the supernatural life is conferred by being baptized into one body and made to drink into one spirit. But this is not all. There is a yet dearer and more precious gift, which maintains and increases the life so given. Our Lord stands in the midst of His Church visibly forming from day to day and from age to age that Body of His which reaches through the ages; He takes from Himself and gives to us. He incorporates Himself in His children. He grows up in us, and by visible streams from His heart maintains the life first given. Here, above all, is the one Christ, the Head and the Body. This is but an elemental truth of Christian faith, though it is the highest joy of the Christian heart. It was in an instruction to catechumens that St. Augustine said, "Would you understand the Body of Christ? Hear the Apostle saying to the faithful, 'But you are the Body and the members of Christ.' If, then, you are Christ's Body and His members, it is your own mystery which is placed on the Lord's table; it is your own mystery which you receive. It is to what you are that you reply amen, and by replying subscribe. For you are told, 'the Body of Christ,' and you reply, amen. Be a member of the Body of Christ, and let your amen be true. Why, then, in bread? Let us bring here nothing of our own, but listen to the Apostle himself again and again, for in speaking of that sacrament he says, 'We that are many are one bread, one body.' Understand and rejoice. Here is unity, verity, piety, charity. One bread. Who is that one bread? We being many are one bread. Remember that the bread is not made of one, but of many grains. When you were exorcised, it was as if you were ground; when baptized, as if you were kneaded together with water; when you received the fire of the Holy Ghost, it was your baking. Be what you see, and receive what you are. This the Apostle said of the bread. Of the chalice what we should understand is clear enough even unsaid. For as to make the visible species of bread many grains are kneaded with water into one, as if that were taking place which Holy Scripture records of the faithful, 'they had one mind and one heart in God,' so also in the case of the wine. Many grapes hang on the bunch, but their juice is poured together into one. So too Christ the Lord signified us; willed us to belong to Himself; consecrated on His own table the mystery of our peace and unity. He who receives the mystery of unity and holds not the bond of peace receives not a mystery for himself, but a witness against himself."[1]

Thus the coherence of the natural and mystical Body of Christ was at once exhibited and effected in the great central act of Christian worship, and the whole fruit of the Incarnation was seen springing from the Person of Christ, and bestowed on men as His members in the unity of one Body. Thus were they taken out of the isolation, distraction, and enmity —that state of mutual strife and disorder which heathendom expresses—and made into the one divine commonwealth; and thus the Body of Christ grows to its full stature and perfect form through all the ages of Christendom.

And if there be one conviction which, together with the belief in the Incarnation itself of the Word, is common to all the Fathers, Doctors, Saints, and Martyrs of the Church—which together with that belief and as part of it is the ground of their confidence in trouble, of their perseverance in enduring, of their undoubting faith in times of persecution, of their assurance of final victory, it is the sense which encompassed their whole life, that they were members of one Body, which, in virtue of an organic unity in itself and with its Head, was to last for ever. The notion that this Body, as such, could fail, that it could cease to be the treasure-house of the divine truth and grace, would have struck them with as much horror as the notion that Christ had not become incarnate, and was not their Redeemer. The Body which the Holy Ghost animated on the day of Pentecost never ceased to be conscious of its existence—conscious that the

[1] St. Aug. serm. 272, tom. v. p. 1104 c.

power of its Head, the Eternal Truth, was in it, and would be in it for ever. Confidence in himself as an individual member of the Body, the Christian had not, for he knew that through his personal sinfulness grace might be withdrawn from him, and that he might fall away; confidence he did not place either in his own learning, knowledge, and sanctity, or in these gifts as belonging to any individual Christian; his confidence lay in the King who reigned in an everlasting Kingdom, in the Head who animated an incorruptible Body. To sever these two would have been to decapitate Christ.[1] The thought that the Bride of Christ could herself become an adulteress, and teach her children the very falsehoods of that idol-worship which she was created to overthrow, would have appeared to him the denial of all Christian belief. And such a denial indeed it is to any mind which, receiving the Christian truth as a divine gift, looks for it also to have a logical cohesion with itself, to be consistent and complete, to be a body of truth, not a bundle of opinions. Let us take once more St. Augustine as expressing, not a private feeling, but the universal Christian sense, when he thus reprehended the Donatist pretension, that truth had deserted the Body of the Church to dwell in the province of Africa. "But, they say, that Church which was the Church of all nations exists no longer. She has perished. This they say who are not in her. O shameless word! The Church is not, because thou art not in her. See, lest therefore thou be not, for though thou be not, she will be. This

---

[1] "Quid tibi fecit Ecclesia, ut eam velis quodammodo decollare? Tollere vis Ecclesiæ caput et capiti credere, corpus relinquere, quasi exanime corpus. Sine caussa capiti quasi famulus devotus blandiris. Qui decollare vult, et caput et corpus conatur occidere." St. Aug. tom. v. p. 636.

word, abominable, detestable, full of presumption and falsehood, supported by no truth, illuminated by no wisdom, seasoned with no sense, vain, rash, precipitate, and pernicious—this it was which the Spirit of God foresaw, and as against these very men, when He foretold unity in that saying, 'To announce the name of the Lord in Zion, and his worship in Jerusalem, when the peoples and kingdoms join together in one that they may serve the Lord.'"[1]

Now, to suppose that anything which is false has been, or is, or can be taught by the Church of God, is to overthrow the one idea which runs through the titles of the Kingdom, Temple, Body, and Spouse of Christ; it is to make the Mother of His children an adulteress, to deny that power of the Holy Ghost coming down on the day of Pentecost, and abiding for ever, with His special function of leading into all truth, that presence of the Comforter in virtue of which the Apostles said for themselves and for the Church through all time, "It has seemed good to the Holy Ghost and to us." With all men who reason, such a supposition is equivalent to the statement that Christ has failed in what He came on earth to do, for "the Word was made flesh, that He might become the Head of the Church."[2] Next, therefore, in atrocity to that blasphemy which assaults the blessed Trinity in Unity upon His throne is the miserable and heartless blasphemy which, by imputing corruption of the truth to the very Kingdom and Temple, the very Body and Spouse of the Truth Himself, the Incarnate God, would declare the frus-

---

[1] St. Aug. in Ps. ci. tom. iv. p. 1105 d.
[2] St. Augustine, tom. iv. p. 1677. "Elegit hic sibi thalamum castum, ubi conjungeretur Sponsus Sponsæ. Verbum caro factum est, ut fieret caput Ecclesiæ."

tration of that purpose which He became man to execute, the falsifying of that witness of which He spoke in the hall of Pilate, and would so annihilate that glory to God in the highest, and on earth peace to men of good-will, which was the angelic song on the morning of His birth, and is daily [1] in the mouth of His Bride. The truth can as little cease out of the House and Temple of God as the Father and Son can cease sending the Spirit to dwell in it: the truth can as little cease to be proclaimed and taught in its own kingdom as the King can cease to reign in it. The conjugal faith of the Bride of Christ cannot fail, because He remains her Bridegroom. The power of the Head, the double power of truth and grace, cannot cease to rule and vivify His Body, because He is its Head for ever. The Mother cannot deceive her children, because she is of one flesh with the Son of Man, in the union of an unbroken wedlock.

It has been said above that the power of that bond which from the origin of man united the race to its head was shown not only in the guilt which the act of that head was able to inflict on the body, not only in the exact transmission of the same nature, thus stained, from age to age, but likewise in that social character of the race in virtue of which such a thing as a man entirely independent of his fellowmen, neither acting upon them, nor acted upon by them, never has existed nor can exist. It was in that connected mass which this social nature creates, that corporate unity of human society, that heathenism appeared most terrible, because corruption seemed to propagate itself, and evil by this force of cohesion to become almost impregnable. But it was especially

[1] By the "Gloria in excelsis," &c., in the Mass.

in creating a corporate unity which should show the force of our social nature for good, as the corruption had shown it for evil, that the power of the Restorer shines forth. The true Head of our race came to redeem and sanctify not so many individuals, but His Body. Surely there is no distinction more important to bear in mind.[1] "No single member by itself can make a body; each of them fails in this; co-operation is required, for when many become one, there is one body. The being or not being a body depends on being united or not united into one." And, again, beautiful as the individual member, the hand or the eye, may be in itself, far higher is the beauty which belongs to the body as the whole in which these members coalesce and are one. Each member too has a double energy, its own proper work, and that which it contributes to the body's unity, for this is a higher work which the co-operation of all produces; each a double beauty, its beauty as a part, and that which it adds to the whole: and these two, which seem to be separate, have the closest connection, for a maimed limb impairs the whole body's force, and as to its beauty, as it is incomparably finer than the beauty of any part, so is it marred by a slight defect in one part, as the fairest face would be spoilt by the absence of eyebrows, the fairest eyes lose their lustre, and the countenance its light, by the want of eyelashes. It is, then, in the beauty of the Body of Christ that the

---

[1] Οὐδὲν γὰρ αὐτῶν καθ' ἑαυτὸ σῶμα δύναται ποιεῖν, ἀλλ' ὁμοίως ἕκαστον λείπεται εἰς τὸ ποιεῖν σῶμα, καὶ δεῖ τῆς συνόδου· ὅταν γὰρ τὰ πολλὰ ἓν γίνηται, τότε ἐστὶν ἓν σῶμα . . . . τὸ γὰρ εἶναι ἢ μὴ εἶναι σῶμα ἐκ τοῦ ἡνῶσθαι ἢ μὴ ἡνῶσθαι γίνεται. . . . τῶν γὰρ μελῶν ἡμῶν ἕκαστον καὶ ἰδίαν ἐνέργειαν ἔχει καὶ κοινήν· καὶ κάλλος ὁμοίως καὶ ἴδιον καὶ κοινόν ἐστιν ἐν ἡμῖν, καὶ δοκεῖ μὲν διῃρῆσθαι ταῦτα, συμπέπλεκται δὲ ἀκριβῶς, καὶ θατέρου διαφθαρέντος καὶ τὸ ἕτερον συναπόλλυται. St. Chrys. on I Cor. xii. tom. x. pp. 269, 271, 273.

Christian mind would exult, not merely in the several graces of those who are its members, but in that corporate unity which they present. We see in the course of the world that great image of the prophet, lofty in stature and terrible to behold, whose head is of gold, whose breast and arms of silver, the thighs of brass, the legs of iron, the toes mixed of iron and clay. This is the form of the first Adam, seen in his race; and over against it likewise is the one man Christ, forming through the ages, gathering His members in a mightier unity. This is the Word made flesh, the Second Adam, "so that the whole human race is, as it were, two men, the First and the Second."[1]

So much, then, is the creation of the Church superior to the creation of a single Christian as the creation of a body is superior to that of a single bone or muscle. This superiority belongs to the nature of a body as such. It is another thought, which we only suggest here, *whose* body it is. And here it appears in two very different conditions, the one as it is seen by us now, the other as it will be seen hereafter. There is, I conceive, no subject in all human history comparable in interest to that which the divine commonwealth as such, when traced through the eighteen centuries which it has hitherto run, presents. What nation can be compared to this nation? what people to this people? what labours to its labours? what sufferings to its sufferings? what conflicts to those which it has endured? what triumphs to those which it has gained? what duration to that portion only of its years which is as yet run out? what promise to its future? what performance to its past? What is

---

[1] St. Aug. *Op. imp. contr. Julian.* lib. ii. tom. x. p. 1018 d.

the courage and self-denial, what is the patience and generosity, what the genius, the learning, the sustained devotion to any work, shown by any human race, compared to those which are to be found in this race of the Divine Mother? How do those who are enamoured of nationalities fail to see the glories of this nation, before which all others pale their ineffectual fires? How do those with whom industry is a chief virtue, and stubborn perseverance the crowning praise, not acknowledge her whose work is undying and whose endurance never fails? These men admire greatness and worship success. Let them look back fourteen hundred years, when that great world-statue seemed to be breaking up into the iron and clay which ran through its feet. Then this kingdom was already great and glorious, and crowned with victory, and filled the earth. The toes of that statue have meanwhile run out into ten kingdoms, and the islands which were forest and swamp when this kingdom commenced have become the head of a dominion which can be mentioned beside that of old Rome; but still in undiminished grandeur the great divine republic stands over against all these kingdoms, penetrates through them, stretches beyond them, and while they grow, mature, and decay, and power passes from one to the other, her power ceases not, declines not, changes not, but shows the beauty of youth upon the brow of age, and amid the confusion of Babel her pentecostal unity. If success be worshipful, worship it here; if power be venerable, bow before its holiest shrine.

But if this be the Body of Christ here in its state of humiliation, during which it repeats the passion of its Head, if these be the grains of wheat now scattered among the chaff,[1] what is that one mass to be which these shall make when the threshing-floor is winnowed out? We see the Body in its preliminary state of suffering, where it has a grandeur, a duration, and a beauty like nothing else on earth. What it shall be in its future state St. John saw when he called it the great City invested with the glory of God, the Bride adorned for her husband; and St. Paul hints, when he speaks of the perfect man compacted and fitly framed together by what every joint supplies, and grown up to full stature in the Head. There is in the redeemed, not only the exceeding greatness of the quality of their salvation, that is, the gift of divine sonship; nor, again, that this gift is heightened by its being the purchase of the Son of God, so that He is not ashamed to call those brethren whom He has first washed in His own blood: but over and above all this, one thing more, that the whole mass of the redeemed and adopted are not so many souls, but the Body of Christ. Faint shadows, indeed, to our earthly senses are House and Temple, Kingdom and City paved with precious stones of that mighty unity of all rational natures, powers, and virtues, each with the perfection of his individual being, each with the superadded lustre of membership in a marvellous whole, under the Headship of Christ. The exceeding glory of this creation, which will be the wonder of all creation through eternity, is that God the Word made flesh, the Head and His Body, make one thing, not an inorganic, but an organised unity, the glorified Body of a glorified Head.

---

[1] "Grana illa quæ modo gemunt iuter paleas, quæ massam unam factura sunt, quando area in fine fuerit ventilata." St. Aug. in Ps. cxxvi. tom. iv. p. 1429.

Once more let us note the consistency and unbroken evolution of the divine plan.

In the first creation of the human race the Body of Christ is not only foretold but prefigured, not only prefigured but expressed in the very words uttered by Adam in his ecstasy, the words of God delineating that act of God, the greatest of all His acts of power, wisdom, and goodness, whereby becoming man, and leaving His Father and His Mother,[1] He would cleave to the wife He so took, the human nature which in redeeming He espoused. This, and no other, was the reason why Eve was formed out of Adam. It is the beginning of the divine plan, which is coherent throughout, which was designed in the state of innocency, which remains intended through the state of guilt, which is unfolded in the state of grace, which is completed in the state of glory, when what that forming of Eve from the side of Adam, and of the Church from the side of her Lord, what that growth through thousands of years, through multitudinous conflicts, through unspeakable sorrows, through immeasurable triumphs, shall finally issue in, shall be seen by those whom the Second Adam has made worthy of that vision, and by whom it is seen enjoyed.

[1] See Origen on Matt. xiv. 17. καὶ ὁ κτίσας γε ἀπ' ἀρχῆς τὸν κατ' εἰκόνα ὃς ἐν μορφῇ Θεοῦ ὑπάρχων ἄρρεν αὐτὸν ἐποίησε, καὶ θῆλυ τὴν ἐκκλησίαν, ἐν τὸ κατ' εἰκόνα ἀμφοτέροις χαρισάμενος· καὶ καταλέλοιπέ γε διὰ τὴν ἐκκλησίαν κύριος ὁ ἀνὴρ πατέρα ὃν ἑώρα, ὅτε ἐν μορφῇ Θεοῦ ὑπῆρχε, καταλέλοιπε δὲ καὶ τὴν μητέρα καὶ αὐτὸς υἱὸς ὢν τῆς ἄνω Ἱερουσαλήμ, καὶ ἐκολλήθη τῇ ἐνταῦθα καταπεσούσῃ γυναικὶ αὐτοῦ, καὶ γεγόνασιν ἐνθάδε οἱ δύο εἰς σάρκα μίαν. διὰ γὰρ αὐτὴν γέγονε καὶ αὐτὸς σάρξ, ὅτε ὁ λόγος σὰρξ ἐγένετο καὶ ἐσκήνωσεν ἐν ἡμῖν, καὶ οὐκέτι γέ εἰσι δύο, ἀλλὰ νῦν μία γέ ἐστι σάρξ, ἐπεὶ τῇ γυναικὶ λέγεται τό, ὑμεῖς δέ ἐστε σῶμα Χριστοῦ καὶ μέλη ἐκ μέρους, οὐ γάρ ἐστί τι ἰδίᾳ Χριστοῦ σῶμα ἕτερον παρὰ τὴν ἐκκλησίαν οὖσαν σῶμα αὐτοῦ, καὶ μέλη ἐκ μέρους. καὶ ὁ Θεός γε τούτους τοὺς μὴ δύο ἀλλὰ γεγομένους σάρκα μίαν συνέζευξεν, ἐντελλόμενος ἵνα ἄνθρωπος μὴ χωρίζῃ τὴν ἐκκλησίαν ἀπὸ τοῦ κυρίου.

LECTURE IX

THE SECOND MAN VERIFIED IN HISTORY

"Magnum principium, et regni ejus non erit finis. Deus fortis, dominator, princeps pacis."

IN order to complete the view taken in the preceding lecture of the work of Christ as the second Adam over against the work of the first Adam, it is necessary to dwell at greater length upon a point of which only cursory mention was made therein. It was our object there to bring out the relation of Christ to the Church, but this cannot be done without fully exhibiting the relation to the same Church of the Holy Spirit. To the Incarnation the Fathers in general give the title of the Dispensation of the Son, and as the equivalent, the result, the complement and crown of this Dispensation, they put the Giving of the Spirit.[1] This Giving of the Spirit occupies the whole region of grace, and is co-extensive with the whole action of the Incarnate God upon men whom He has taken to be His brethren. The Holy Spirit in this Giving is He who represents the Redeemer, and executes His will, not as an instru-

---

[1] As St. Irenæus, v. 20. "Omnibus unum et eundem Deum Patrem præcipientibus, et eamdem dispositionem incarnationis Filii Dei credentibus, et eamdem donationem Spiritus scientibus;" and St. Aug. tom. v. app. p. 307 f. "Ecce iterum humanis divina miscentur, id est, Vicarius Redemtoris: ut beneficia quæ Salvator Dominus inchoavit peculiari Spiritus Sancti virtute consummet, et quod ille redemit, iste sanctificet, quod ille acquisivit, iste custodiat." This striking sermon is quoted by Petavius as genuine, but placed by the Benedictines in the appendix.

ment, not as one subordinate, but as the very mind of Christ between whom and Christ there can far less enter any notion of division or separation than between a man and his own spirit. He is that other Paraclete, abiding for ever, who replaces to the disciples the visible absence of the first Paraclete, the Redeemer Himself: He is the Power constituting the Kingdom of Christ; the Godhead inhabiting His Temple; the Soul animating His mystical Body; the Charity, kindling into a living flame the heart of His Bride; the Creator and Father of His Race.

This connection between the Dispensation of the Son and the Giving of the Spirit was delineated by our Lord Himself when He first appeared to His assembled disciples after His resurrection. As they were gazing in wonder and trembling joy on that Body which had undergone His awful passion, as He showed them the wounds in His hands and His feet, He told them how His sufferings were the fulfilment of all that in the Law, the Prophets, and the Psalms had been written concerning Him. And thereupon it is said, He opened their mind to the understanding of these Scriptures. It was thus that the Christ was to suffer, it was thus that He was to rise again on the third day. Hitherto He has dwelt upon His own dispensation, as the fulfilment of all prophecy, now He proceeds to its fruit: that in the name of this Christ repentance and remission of sins should be proclaimed to all nations, beginning at Jerusalem. "And you," He says, "are the witnesses of these things. And, behold, I send the promise of my Father upon you: but stay you in the city of Jerusalem until you be endued with power from on high." Again, at another occasion of equal solemnity, when He was with His assembled disciples in visible form for the last time, at the moment preceding His ascension, He uses the same emphatic words, charging them not to depart from the city, but to await there that promise of the Father, the baptism in the Holy Ghost, which they were to receive in common together, which was to be the power in virtue of which they should be His witnesses for all time unto the ends of the earth: the power which instead of restoring a local kingdom to Israel, as was in their thoughts when they questioned Him, was to create an universal kingdom to Him in the hearts of men. It is then as the result of His passion, and the token of His resurrection, that the Son sends down upon His disciples the promise of the Father, that is, the perpetual presence of the Spirit of the Father and the Son, the Spirit of Truth and Grace, that permanent and immanent power from on high, who, dwelling for ever in the disciples, makes the Church.

But these words, so singular and so forcible, which He uses on these two occasions, at His resurrection and His ascension, are themselves a reference to the long discourse which He had held with His apostles on the night of His passion. It is in this discourse, from the moment that Judas left them to the conclusion of the divine prayer—and if we can make any distinction in His words, surely these are the most solemn which were ever put together in human language, since they are the prayer not of a creature to the Creator, but the prayer of One divine Person to Another—it is in this discourse that He describes the power from on high with which, as the promise of the Father, He, the Son, would invest His disciples. It is here He says that He would ask the Father, who should give them another Paraclete, the Spirit of truth, to abide with them for ever: whom the world would not receive, nor see, nor know, but whom they should know, because He should abide with them and be in them. This other Paraclete, co-equal therefore with Himself, whom the Father should send in His name, and whom He should send from the Father, the Spirit of holiness as well as the Spirit of truth, should teach them all things, and remind them of all His teaching. And His coming, though invisible, should profit them more than His own visible presence. For while He declared Himself to be the Way, the Truth, and the Life,[1] He revealed to them here that it was by that very way that the Spirit of truth should lead them by the hand into all truth. It was in this Truth, that is, in Himself, that they should be sanctified, and that they should be one, the glory of the Incarnation, which had been given to Him, passing on to them as the members of His Body, by the joint possession of the spirit of truth and holiness, whose presence was the gage that the Father loved them, as He loved Christ, the Body being identified with the Head. In all this He was describing to them the work of that other Paraclete, His own Spirit, "who was to sanctify what He had redeemed, and to guard and maintain possession of what He had acquired."[2] This is but a small portion of that abundant revelation, which our Lord then communicated to His apostles, concerning the Power from on high with which they were to be invested.

[1] There is in the original words here something which is lost both in the Vulgate and in the English translation. First, c. xiv. 6. ἐγώ εἰμι ἡ ὁδὸς, καὶ ἡ ἀλήθεια, καὶ ἡ ζωή· then c. xvi. 13. ὅταν δὲ ἔλθῃ ἐκεῖνος τὸ Πνεῦμα τῆς ἀληθείας, ὁδηγήσει ὑμᾶς εἰς πᾶσαν τὴν ἀλήθειαν. As Christ is the ὁδὸς, so His Spirit is the ὁδηγῶν. "Ego sum via et veritas; ille vos docebit omnem veritatem," does not render this: and as little, "I am *the way*, the truth, and the life; He shall *lead* you into all truth."

[2] St. Aug., quoted above in note.

The words of our Lord to His apostles at the three great points of His passion, His resurrection, and His ascension, stand out beyond the rest in their appeal to our affections. The last words of a friend are the dearest, and these are the last words of the Bridegroom, and they are concerning His Bride. When He was Himself quitting His disciples He dwells upon the Power which was to create and maintain His Church, upon the gift of His Spirit, His other self, in which gift lay the formation of His kingdom. It is thus He expresses to us the point with which we started, that the Giving of His Spirit is the fulfilment of all that Dispensation wherein the eternal Word took human flesh.

It is not only then the unanimous voice of the Fathers which sets the Giving of the Spirit over against the Incarnation of the Son. They are but carrying on that which our Lord so markedly taught; their tradition was but the echo of His voice, as their life was the fulfilment of it.

But it was a double malady in man which God the Word became man to cure. It was the whole nature which was affected with a taint, and the soul through the whole race touched in both its powers of the intellect[1] and the will. That false worship which we have seen spreading through the earth, and that deep corruption of manners which was interlaced with it, were the symptoms of this malady. The perversion of the truth concerning the being of God, and all the duties of man which grow out of this being, was inextricably blended with the disregard of these duties in the actual conduct of man. It was in vain to set the

[1] This word is used as the equivalent of λόγος, *ratio*, *Vernunft*, in man.

truth before man's intellect without a corresponding power to act upon his will. Therefore the apostle described the glory of the only-begotten Son, when He dwelt as man among us, by the double expression that He was "full of grace and truth." Viewed as the Head of human nature, its Father and new beginning, He is the perpetual fountain to it of these two, which no law, not even one divinely given, could bestow. For the law could make nothing perfect, because it could not touch the will; and the law gave the shadow, but not the very truth of things. But when that unspeakable union of the divine nature with the human had taken effect in the unity of one Person, Truth and Grace had an everlasting human fountain in the created nature of the Incarnate Word. Now was the fountain to pour forth a perpetual stream upon the race assumed. And this it does by the descent of the Spirit. In this descent upon the assembled Church the Grace and Truth of the divine Head, with which His Flesh, carried by the Godhead, overstreams, find themselves a human dwelling in the race. Such an operation belongs only to the Divine Spirit, for God alone can so act upon the intellect and will of creatures as to penetrate them with His gifts of Truth and Grace, while He leaves them their free-will, their full individuality, as creatures. This, then, was the range of that power with which our Lord foretold to His apostles that they should be invested, and for which He bade them wait. The whole field of truth as it respects the relation of God to His creatures as moral beings, and the whole extent of grace, as it touches the human will, for the performance of every act which a reasonable creature can execute, made up the extent of that divine indwelling in men which the Spirit of Christ assumed upon the day of Pentecost. This was the power of the Holy Ghost which then came down upon men. Through the whole divine discourse which preceded His passion, our Lord dwells upon this double power, referring to Himself as the Truth, to His Spirit as the Spirit of the Truth, to Himself as the Vine, and so that root of grace which should communicate its sap to the branches, and to His Spirit, who should take of His and give it to them; uniting both ideas of Truth and Grace in that one word, " Sanctify them in Thy Truth," that is by incorporation with Me, who am the Truth, in My Spirit, who is the Truth. And so the eternal Word, having assumed a human Body, when He withdraws His corporal presence, proceeds to form that other human Body, the dwelling-place of His Spirit, in which His Truth and Grace are to become visible.

Thus the transfusion of Truth and Grace from the Incarnate Word to His mystical Body is the generic character of the Giving of the Spirit.

Two differential marks distinguish this giving from any which preceded the coming of our Lord.

First, the Spirit should come upon them, but should never depart from them. " He shall give you another Comforter, to abide with you for ever, the Spirit of Truth." This giving was not an intermittent operation, whether extraordinary, such as had shown itself in Moses and the Prophets, for their inspiration in writing, or their guidance in particular trials, nor that ordinary one whereby from the beginning He had enabled all the good and just to lead a life acceptable to Him. It was a far higher gift,[1] wherein, as

[1] See Petavius *de Trin.* vii. 7, where he states it to be the general belief of the ancient writers that a new and *substantial* presence of the Holy Ghost began at the day of Pentecost.

St. Augustine says, by the very presence of His majesty no longer the mere odour of the balsam, but the substance itself of the sacred unguent was poured into those vessels, making them His temple, and conveying that adoption in virtue of which they should not be left orphans, but have their Father invisibly with them for ever. No intermittent operation, and no presence less than that of His substance, would reach the force of the words used by our Lord, "I will ask the Father, and He shall send you another Paraclete, the Spirit of Truth, to abide with you for ever;" for that word "other" conveys a comparison with Himself, from whom they had never been separated since He had called them, in whose continuance with them alone was their strength, their unity, their joint existence and mission, without whom they could do nothing. All this to them that "other" Paraclete was to be, in order that the departure of the Former Paraclete should be expedient for them. For in this continuity of His presence was involved the further gift that the Paraclete was to come to them as a Body, and because of this manner of coming He replaced the Former. Had He come to them only as individuals, they would have suffered a grievous loss, the loss of the Head who had made them one. But He came to them as the Body of Christ, and by coming made them that Body, being the Spirit of the Head. That rushing mighty wind filled the whole house in which they were sitting, and they all were filled together with the presence; and as a sign that the old confusion and separation of mankind were in them to be done away, speaking in one tongue the one truth which was evermore to dwell with them, they were heard in all the various languages of the nations present at the feast. "The society by which men are made the one Body of the only Son of God belongs to the Spirit,"[1] and He came upon all together in one House to indicate, as He made, that one Body. "The mode of giving," says St. Augustine, "was such as never before appeared. Nowhere do we read before that men congregated together had by receiving the Holy Ghost spoken with the tongues of all nations."[2] "Therefore He came upon Pentecost as upon His birthday."[3]

It is His presence alone which confers four gifts upon the body which He vivifies.

It was the will, says St. Augustine,[4] of the Father and the Son that we should have communion with each other and with Them by means of that which is common to Them, and by that gift to collect us into one, which, being one, They both have; that is to say, by the Holy Ghost, who is God, and the gift of God. For, says St. Thomas,[5] the unity of the Holy Spirit makes unity in the Church. It is not by similarity, or by juxtaposition, or by agreement, how much less by concessions and compromises, that unity exists in the body of Christ, but because the Spirit is one, because all gifts, however various, all functions, however distinct, are distributed by this One.

For the same reason truth dwells in this Body, because He is the Spirit of Truth. Our Lord Himself has defined His great function in this particular, to lead His disciples by the hand[6] into all truth, to teach all things, and remind of all things which made up His own teaching. This function began on the

[1] St. Aug. tom. v. 398 g.   [2] St. Aug. tom. iii. pp. 2, 527.
[3] Ib. tom. v. 47.   [4] Ib. tom. v. 392 e.
[5] St. Thomas in Joh. i. lec. 10: "Nam unitas Spiritus Sancti facit in Ecclesia unitatem."   [6] ὁδηγεῖν.

day of Pentecost, and lasts to the day of judgment, and belongs to the Body of Christ, and to it alone, and belongs to it because it is animated by the Spirit of Truth. And this animation is like the Head, the same yesterday, to-day, and for ever. It is not of any past time more or less than of the present or the future. It is the illumination which belongs to that whole last day, through which the Body of Christ grows, teaches, labours, and suffers, until the mortal day break into the light of eternity.

His third gift to the Body is that of charity, and for the same reason, because He is this Himself. He who is not only the Unity of the Father and the Son, but their mutual Love, coming as the gift of that Divine love which redeemed the world by the sacrifice of its Maker, and as the Spirit of that Love, who invested Himself with human flesh, creates in this human dwelling-place that one charity which bears His name, and is of His nature, and which in that one body joins the wills of men together as His Truth joins their intellects. If the Body of Christ has one prevailing charity, which reaches to all its members, and encompasses the least as well as the greatest, it is because the heart is divine.

The fourth gift which He bestows upon the Body is sanctification, and it may be said to be the result of the other three. This, again, is His own name and nature, and many have thought and said, His personal attribute, to make holy; and that, as Fathership indicates the First Person, and Sonship the Second, so the making holy names the Third, the bond of the most blessed Trinity. But this, at least, may be said to be the final cause of the body which He animates, the imparting of holiness. In virtue of

this gift, all the means and aids and rules of holiness
are stored up in the Body. And this does not mean
that there is not a continual falling away from the
rule and practice of holiness in particular members,
but it means that while these, in spite of the Body's
nurture and solicitude, fall away from it and perish,
the Body lasts for ever, the rules and aids and means
of holiness lasting for ever within it, because it is the
Body of the Spirit of holiness.

Now these four gifts, Unity, Verity, Charity, and
Sanctity, can none of them exist in the Body without
the other, and all of them exist together there, because
they have one divine root, that indwelling of the
Holy Spirit which is the fruit of the Incarnation, and
whereby the mystical Body of Christ corresponds to
His natural Body. Of this Body the beginning is
Unity, the substance Truth, the bond Charity, the end
Sanctity. Countless heresies and schisms have sought
to break up the co-inherence of these gifts, but in vain.
The only success which the indwelling Spirit allows
them is to detach from the Body those who are unworthy to remain in it, and to prolong for a time
their maimed existence by some portion of some of
His gifts. Truth, for instance, has such a vitality
that many a heresy will live for ages on that frag-
ment which it has detached from the mass; unity
and charity have such force that even their shadow,
that is, the joint possession of a fragmentary truth,
and the good-will thence proceeding, will prolong for
a time a sort of corporate existence. Holiness has so
attractive a power, that zeal and self-denial, which
present the seeming of it, will make the fortune of a
sect for a time. But in the union and the completeness of these four gifts, the great Body of Christ

stands out through all the ages inimitable and unapproachable. Alone it dares to claim them thus united and complete, for alone it can present their realisation.

These four gifts, then, dwell in the Body in a higher degree than that in which they adorn the members of the Body, as in it, by force of the Spirit's indwelling, they ever exist together. Let us now see the qualities which the Spirit imparts to the members of the Body, by virtue of their incorporation into it.

First of all is the forgiveness of sins. The Spirit takes them out of that state of alienation in which they are born, and unites them to His Body; and in so doing He effaces both the birth-sin and every actual sin which they may have committed. This is that plenary forgiveness of sins, the pure gift of God unpreceded by any merit on man's part, which greets the new-comer out of Adam's body of sin into the Body of Christ. It is imparted by and from the Body, and to its members alone.

The second quality is that illumination of the mind, irradiated by the truth, the whole compass of which exists in the Body. This illumination is the root of the virtue of faith, by means of which the individual mind appropriates the divine truth presented to it. The force of the virtue differs in the individual as the keenness of sight in the natural man, but the visual power is the same in quality in all. By it the mind of the believer lays hold in ever-varying degree, one more and one less, of that great harmony of truth which is held in its completeness, its manifold applications, and all but infinite relations, only by the Body. For the truth with which we deal is not unlocalised and scattered, the prey, as it were, of the individual mind, which can hunt it down and take it as a spoil, but it is a divine gift, orbed in the sphere which was created for it, the Body of that Word who is the Truth. Hence the first question to the applicant for baptism: What askest thou of the Church of God? and the answer is, Faith.

The third quality is the adoption of Sonship, which flows directly from incorporation into the Body of Christ, and to which man has no sort of title in himself or from his own nature, but which comes to him only by kindred with Him who, on the morning of His resurrection, greeted that great penitent who bore the figure of the Church with that paschal salutation of the Second Adam, "Go to My brethren, and say, I ascend to My Father and to your Father, to My God and to your God." And the divine virtue of hope well corresponds to this quality, the effects of which in a state of trial and conflict are to so great a degree future and unseen. It seems, moreover, to be as a special link and tie between the virtue which purifies the intellect, and that which corrects the will and makes it obedient. Thus through it we pass on to the fourth quality of Sanctification, which is the completion of the other three and their end, the harmony of each individual will with the divine will, the work of charity. That divine virtue is the special fruit of the passion of Christ, which was to gather up into one what sin had disunited and torn away, first from its Author, and then from the order by Him created, which was to heal the animosities thus introduced, and to change the world from a conflict wherein each sought to better himself at the expense of his neighbour, into a community cemented together with mutual affection. It was with reason, therefore, that St. Augustine would not allow the possession of charity, save in the unity of that one Body which Christ had created,[1] and without charity there is no sanctification.

The four qualities thus slightly sketched, forgiveness of sins, illumination of faith, adoption to sonship, and sanctification by charity, which come to the individual by and with incorporation into the Body, are not given to him irrevocably, but are conditional upon his perseverance. They are portions and derivations of that vast treasure of Truth and Grace which the Body holds in their entireness and for ever, because of the perpetual indwelling of the Spirit who makes its life, but which He dispenses as it pleases Him to the members, and which He may withdraw from them in default of their co-operation. Vast are the losses thereby incurred, not to the treasure-house, which remains inexhaustible, but to those who fall out of it back into the world, or rather that body of Adam from which they were taken. But these losses touch not the beauty and the glory of that Body of Christ, which goes on through the ages, and takes up its own, fulfils its appointed work, and reaches its intended end.

Thus on the day of Pentecost a new Power, the Spirit of the Incarnate God, descended not upon single men, but upon an assembly of men, binding it in a unity, conveying to it a truth, kindling in it a charity,

---

[1] Epist. 185, tom. ii. p. 663. "Proinde Ecclesia Catholica sola corpus est Christi, cujus ille caput est, Salvator corporis sui. Extra hoc corpus neminem vivificat Spiritus Sanctus, quia sicut ipse dicit Apostolus: Caritas Dei diffusa est in cordibus nostris per Spiritum Sanctum, qui datus est nobis. Non est autem particeps divinæ caritatis, qui hostis est unitatis. Non habent itaque Spiritum Sanctum qui sunt extra Ecclesiam."

and working through these a sanctification never before known; which Power, thenceforth dwelling in that Body, was to collect and draw into itself out of all nations and ranks of men those who should form the Church, that is, the Kingdom and Temple, and House, and Body, and Family of Christ. In it was to work and from it to go forth henceforward to all time the virtue of Him who had assumed our flesh, not transiently, but for ever; in the Head and the Body, through the life of His Spirit, Christ should teach and bear for ever that witness to the truth of which He spoke in the hall of Pilate, and concerning which He said that "this gospel of the kingdom should be proclaimed through the whole world, for a witness to all nations, and then that the end should come."[1] To the continuance, the indissolubility, the purity of this power He has pledged His word in such a way that they who deny it must in doing so deny Him. He has even made the unity of this Body the special mark to men of the truth of His mission, beseeching His Father in that last prayer, " Neither pray I for these alone, but for those also who through their word shall believe in Me, that they all may be one, as Thou, Father, art in Me, and I in Thee, that they also may be one in Us, that the world may believe that Thou hast sent Me."

There are three analogies[2] which illustrate this creation of our Lord—a creation in itself as singular as His assumption of man's nature.

[1] Matt. xxiv. 14.
[2] See Möhler, *Die Einheit in der Kirche*, p. 176. "Der Körper des Menschen ist eine Offenbarung des Geistes, der in ihm sein Dasein bekundet, und sich entwickelt. Der Staat ist eine nothwendige Erscheinung, eine Bildung und Gestaltung des von Gott gegebenen κοινωνικόν."

First, that of the relation between the soul and body. The soul is the life of the body; the body, as it were, the mansion and home of the soul, its bearer. Through the body the qualities of the soul become visible and known; its powers exercise themselves, and personal unity so binds the two together that we love or hate, admire or despise, the one for the sake of the other; the grief of the soul acts upon the body, the sickness of the body depresses the soul. Through the acts of the body we learn the very existence of the soul, and in these acts it portrays itself. Human nature has been so made by its Creator that the qualities of soul and body, of spirit and matter, are imputed in the individual man to each other. Now to the Body we have been considering the Spirit of Christ is, as it were, the soul. It is nothing strange, then, if it was His will to create such a Body, if it be the result of His Incarnation, that the like effects which exist in the case of every human soul and body should take place here. To this Body also the power and virtue of its soul are communicated; and, since Christ by His Spirit animates it, in honouring it He is honoured; in despising it, He is despised. There is an imparting to it of the qualities which He has; and thus it is that unity and sanctity, truth and charity dwell in it as the operation of His mind. Thus every man contains in himself, in the union of soul and body, an image of that tie by which Christ and His Church are one.

Secondly, because God has created man for society, He has implanted in him an irrepressible instinct of communion with his brother men. This instinct it is which, under circumstances of every possible variety, results in one end, the State. The human commonwealth, whatever external shape it wear, whatever division of its powers it make, springs from this. In virtue of this original formation of man, that he is made to live together, and gregariously, not separately, the supreme power of government, the power of life and death, dwells in the community, and obedience to it has a divine sanction. Thus, the commonwealth has a variety of powers which the individual has not, and not only so, but it also has powers which do not arise from the mere aggregation of individuals, rather which belong to it as a community, as a whole, for instance, sovereignty in all the details of its exercise. But now the very object for which Christ became Incarnate was to constitute a divine commonwealth. He is the King: it is the tenderness of a God Incarnate that He calls and makes His Kingdom His Body. The powers, then, which belong to the earthly commonwealth belong, with the changes which the change of subject carries, to the Divine. They who have so great a reverence for human government, who respect in the nation an ultimate irresponsible power, ought, if they were consistent, when they acknowledge Christ as having come in the flesh, to acknowledge His government in the kingdom which He has set up. All that his country is to the patriot, the Church is to the Christian, but in so much higher a degree, as the object for which Christ came is above the needs and cares of this present life. Has the City of God, then, less claim upon Christians than the City of Romulus had upon Romans? Thus, in the natural duty of the citizen, as well as in the compound nature of man, is contained a reminder of the Christian's relation to the Church, and a picture and ensample of the Church's authority.

Thirdly, there is the analogy presented by the transmission of natural life[1] through the one flesh of Adam to all his race. As the breath of natural life, once given to Adam, is continued on to all those sprung from his body, the power of the Creator never starting anew, but working in and through the trunk of human nature; so the supernatural life springing from our Lord, as the gift of His Incarnation, is breathed on the day of Pentecost into the whole Body of the Church to be communicated from that Body for ever. Christ is to the one exactly what Adam is to the other. As the Word of God, creating, joined to the inheritance of the flesh of Adam from generation to generation the communication of a spirit such as Adam's, by which double action we have the unity of race, so the Word of God, redeeming, when He had taken our flesh as the first-fruits of human nature, breathed forth from that flesh the communication of His Spirit to the Body of the Church, by which we belong to the race of the Incarnate God, and are become His family, and make His house. Thus that which the body of Adam is naturally, the Body of Christ is spiritually, and the descent of human nature in its unity a picture of the Holy Spirit's unity working through the Body which He has chosen. And this analogy is made the more striking by the statement so often repeated in the Greek Fathers, that with the natural life, as first given to Adam, was conjoined the gift of the Holy Ghost, forfeited afterwards by his sin, and withdrawn from him and his race, and now restored as the special

---

[1] Möhler, *Einheit*, &c. p. 8. "Wie das Leben des sinnlichen Menschen nur einmal unmittelbar aus der Hand des Schöpfers kam, und wo nun sinnliches Leben werden soll, es durch die Mittheilung der Lebenskraft eines schon Lebenden bedingt ist, so sollte das neue göttliche Leben ein Ausströmen aus den schon Belebten, die Erzeugung desselben sollte ein Ueberzeugung sein."

gift of the Incarnate God.¹ Thus the descent of the Spirit at Pentecost is a true and real counterpart of the creation of man in Eden; but they who share it are become kindred of God through His flesh, and by so sharing it together, they form that society which failed through Adam's sin. In the first creation, the Omnipotent Creator, in His bounty towards His favourite child, as foreseeing the assumption of that nature by Himself, attached to the gift of natural life the Spirit of sanctification; in the second, having assumed that nature, He gave through His own Body, first taken out of us, then crucified, now risen and exalted, the gift of the Spirit, Who, with all the endowments springing from Him, as the Inspirer of truth and charity, of unity and holiness, dwells in that Body for ever.

Thus in the union of the soul and body, in the constitution and authority of the human commonwealth, and in the race's natural unity, God holds before us three analogies, which each in some respect, and altogether very largely, illustrate His finished work, to which all natural productions of His providence are subordinate, His work of predilection, His work of unbounded love and sovereign magnificence, the creation of that which is at once the Body, the Kingdom, and the Family of the Incarnate Word.

From all that has gone before we gather this conclusion, that to become a Christian was to enter into a spiritual and physical ² unity with Christ by incor-

---

¹ For instance, two passages on the Incarnation in St. Cyril of Alexandria, tom. iv. pp. 819-824 and 918-920, set forth the whole sequence of the Fall and the Restoration, and how wonderfully the gift of the Spirit replaces what was lost in Adam.

² See St. Cyril. Alex. in Joan. p. 997 e. ἐν δὲ τούτοις ἤδη πως καὶ φυσικὴν τὴν ἑνότητα δεικνύναι σπουδάζομεν, καθ' ἣν ἡμεῖς τε ἀλλήλοις καὶ οἱ πάντες Θεῷ συνδούμεθα· κ.τ.λ.; and p. 998. τίς γὰρ ἂν καὶ διέλοι καὶ

poration into that Body which He had created as the result of his becoming man. This it was for the individual to become a Christian. But Christianity itself was neither a mere system of belief, nor an outward order representing that belief, but "the great and glorious Body of Christ,"[1] possessing and exhibiting the whole truth of doctrine, possessing and distributing all the means of grace, and presenting together to God those whom it had reconciled with Him, and made one, as the members of the Son by the indwelling of the Spirit.

Let us now trace the exact correspondence of the historical fact with the dogmatic statement just given.

The Acts of the Apostles exhibit to us the creation of the divine society by the descent of the Holy Ghost on the day of Pentecost. When they were all together, the sound as of a rushing mighty wind was heard, which filled the whole house wherein they were sitting, and tongues as of fire were seen, the tongues apportioned severally, but the fire one,[2] which rested upon each, to kindle in all that eternal flame of charity which was to draw into one the hearts of men, the fire of which our Lord had spoken as being that which He was come to light upon the earth. Fire, whose inward nature it is at once to illuminate and warm, to purify and unite, was thus appropriately

τῆς εἰς ἀλλήλους φυσικῆς ἑνώσεως ἐξοικέοι τοὺς δι' ἑνὸς τοῦ ἁγίου σώματος πρὸς ἑνότητα τὴν εἰς Χριστὸν ἀναδεσμουμένους;

[1] St. Iren. iv. c. 33, 7. ἀνακρινεῖ τοὺς τὰ σχίσματα ἐργαζομένους, κενοὺς ὄντας τῆς τοῦ Θεοῦ ἀγάπης, καὶ τὸ ἴδιον λυσιτελὲς σκοποῦντας, ἀλλὰ μὴ τὴν ἕνωσιν τῆς ἐκκλησίας· καὶ διὰ μικρὰς καὶ τὰς ὑψούσας αἰτίας τὸ μέγα καὶ ἔνδοξον σῶμα τοῦ Χριστοῦ τέμνοντας καὶ διαιροῦντας, καὶ ὅσον τὸ ἐπ' αὐτοῖς ἀναιροῦντας, τοὺς εἰρήνην λαλοῦντας καὶ πόλεμον ἐργαζομένους, ἀληθῶς διυλίζοντας τὸν κώνωπα, καὶ τὸν κάμηλον καταπίνοντας.

[2] Acts ii. 3. ὤφθησαν αὐτοῖς διαμεριζόμεναι γλῶσσαι ὡσεὶ πυρός, ἐκάθισέ τε ἐφ' ἕνα ἕκαστον αὐτῶν, καὶ ἐπλήσθησαν ἅπαντες Πνεύματος ἁγίου.

selected as the outward sign, both expressing and conveying the fourfold office of the Comforter, who came to be "no longer an occasional visitant, but a perpetual Consoler and eternal Inhabitant[1] of this His chosen Home. As each in that assembly spoke in the one tongue of the country, he was heard by those present in the several tongues of all the nations of the earth represented at that great feast by the Jews who dwelt in them. And this was the mark, says St. Augustine,[2] of the Church which was to be through all nations, and that no one should receive the Holy Spirit, save he who should be jointed into the framework of its unity; the mark which signified that the confusion of Babel, dividing the race into nationalities jealous of each other and perpetual enemies, was to be reversed and overcome by the one Power whose force to unite should be greater than the force of sin to sever; who should gather out of all nations the City of God, fed by the exulting and abounding river of His Spirit, the fountain proper and peculiar to the Church of Christ: the mark of that one truth,[3] which

[1] Non jam visitator subitus, sed perpetuus consolator et habitator æternus." St. Aug. tom. v. d. app. p. 307.

[2] Con Crescon. lib. ii. c. 14, tom ix. p. 418. "Hic Spiritus sanctus veniens in eos tale signum primitus dedit, ut qui eum acciperent linguis omnium gentium loquerentur, quia portendebat Ecclesiam per omnes gentes futuram, nec quemquam accepturum Spiritum sanctum nisi qui ejus unitati copularetur. Hujus fontis largo atque invisibili flumine lætificat Deus civitatem suam, quia Propheta dixit: Fluminis impetus lætificat civitatem Dei. Ad hunc enim fontem nullus extraneus, quia nullus nisi vita æterna dignus accedit. Hic est proprius Ecclesiæ Christi."

[3] Ἡ ἀλήθεια: there seems to be no one word in the New Testament of more pregnant signification than this, which in a great number of instances bears the sense of *the whole body of the divine revelation*. The root of this meaning would seem to lie in Christ Himself, who as the Divine Word is the αὐτοαλήθεια, the εἰκών of the Father; on which title St. Athanasius and St. Cyril of Alexandria specially dwell, while St. Hilary expresses the Blessed Trinity by "Æternitas in Patre, Species in Imagine, Usus in Munere," on which see St. Augustine's magnificent

conveys and harmonises and works out into all its details the whole revelation of God, and so is the utterance of one voice, the voice of Christ; speaking to all nations, not in the broken languages of their division, but in the Unity of His Person, carried by His Body. We have then in the one Fire the one inward power; in the one language its outward expression, in the assembly its receptacle, the House of God. This Body appears at once as formed and complete. In it sits and prays in her silent tenderness and unap-

comment, *de Trin.* l. vi. 10, p. 850; and as our Lord is from eternity the Truth, so in and by His Incarnation He becomes in a special sense the Truth to man: ἐγώ εἰμι ἡ ὁδὸς, καὶ ἡ ἀλήθεια, καὶ ἡ ζωή: and so the Spirit who proceeds from the Father and the Son, "ille ineffabilis quidam complexus Patris et Imaginis" (St. Aug.), is τὸ Πνεῦμα τῆς ἀληθείας, who ὁδηγήσει ὑμᾶς εἰς πᾶσαν τὴν ἀλήθειαν: and again, 1 John v. 6, τὸ Πνεῦμά ἐστι τὸ μαρτυροῦν, ὅτι τὸ Πνεῦμά ἐστιν ἡ ἀλήθεια. This is the first meaning. Secondly, as derived from it, the Truth is the whole body of the divine revelation. In this sense it is used in a great many places of St. John's Gospel and the Apostolic Epistles, *e.g.*, John i. 14, 17; viii. 31; xvi. 13; xvii. 17; xviii. 37; 1 John ii. 21; iii. 19; 2 John i. 1-3; 3 John 3, 4, 8, 12; 1 Tim. iii. 15, where, because this whole body of truth dwells in the Church of Christ and there alone, it is emphatically called the "House of God, which is the Church of the living God, the pillar and ground of the Truth;" 1 Tim. ii. 3; Rom. xv. 8; 2 Cor. iv. 2; xiii. 8; Gal. iii. 1; v. 7; Ephes. i. 13; iv. 21-24 (in which passage the Apostle contrasts heathen man with Christian, the one, τὸν φθειρόμενον κατὰ τὰς ἐπιθυμίας τῆς ἀπάτης; the other, τὸν κατὰ Θεὸν κτισθέντα ἐν δικαιοσύνῃ καὶ ὁσιότητι τῆς ἀληθείας, and again, the mass of the Gentiles, as τὰ ἔθνη περιπατεῖ ἐν ματαιότητι τοῦ νοὸς αὐτῶν, ἐσκοτισμένοι τῇ διανοίᾳ, while Christians ἐν αὐτῷ ἐδιδάχθητε, καθώς ἐστιν ἀλήθεια ἐν τῷ Ἰησοῦ); 2 Thess. ii. 8-13; 1 Tim. iii. 3; vi. 5; 2 Tim. ii. 15, 25; iii. 7, 8; iv. 4; Titus i. 1 and 14; Heb x. 26; Jac. v. 19; 1 Pet. i. 22; 2 Pet. ii. 2. In this second sense, as signifying the whole body of the divine revelation, the expression has been searched for, but without success, in the Gospels of St. Matthew, St. Mark, and St. Luke, and in the Acts.

Thirdly, as the effect of this revelation to man, the Truth signifies uprightness, as equivalent to justice or sanctity, in the individual.

Fourthly, it means sincerity, absence of hypocrisy: and

Fifthly, correspondence to fact.

In the Apocalypse our Lord is designated "the holy, the true," "the Amen, the Witness faithful and true," the rider of the white horse, "called faithful and true," "whose name is the Word of God," iii. 7, 14; xix. 11.

proachable grandeur, as the Mother of the risen Lord and Head, and the Mother too of His race, the most beloved, the most lovable, and the most loving of creatures,[1] whose great function in the Church for ever is to pray for the members of her Son, and to solicit the graces of His Spirit, which as the Mother of the sacred race she gains and distributes to all and each that belong to it, a Second Eve who corresponds to the Second Adam, as the First Eve in the divine plan corresponded to the First Adam. In it the Apostles, so long before chosen and designated by their Lord, and having already received from Him portions of their supernatural power on the day of His resurrection and during the forty days of His secret instruction, teach and govern; in it Peter at their head exercises that primacy, which, imaged out by a new name imposed at his first calling, promised at his great confession, and confirmed and conveyed on the sea-shore of the lake of Galilee, is exhibited with such grandeur, as he stood with the eleven and lifted up his voice, to describe to the men of Judea and the inhabitants of Jerusalem the nature of the event which they were witnessing, and the fulfilment of all the promises made through their prophets concerning that presence of God in the pouring out of His Spirit among men in the last days. That first discourse of his at the head of his brethren is the summary as it were of his perpetual office of teaching and promulgating the dispensation of the Christ in the midst of the Church. Its immediate effect was the aggregation of three thousand persons to the Body, who were told that this was the way in which they should receive remission of

---

[1] "La creatura, la più amabile, la più amata, e la più amante di Dio." St. Alfonso, *Gran Mezzo della Preghiera*, p. 280.

sins and the gift of the Holy Ghost.[1] The subsequent teaching of Peter and the Apostles, accompanied with miraculous cures, produced further aggregations among all ranks of the people. And the mode of salvation for all time is pointedly marked out by the words, "the Lord was adding to the Church day by day such as should be saved."

We have only to repeat the process which is thus described as having taken place at Jerusalem in the first months after the day of Pentecost, by carrying it through the various cities of the Roman empire, Damascus, Antioch, Rome, Alexandria, and between these all round the shores of the Mediterranean, to have a just picture of the mode in which the Divine Society grew and gathered into itself more and more of those who listened to the truth which it announced. What is important to dwell upon is that men uniformly became Christians in one way, by being received into the Divine Body, through which reception forgiveness of sins and the gift of the Holy Ghost were conveyed to them. From the whole account contained in the sacred Scriptures, and from all that remains to us of history, the great fact is established for us that Christianity came into the world at its first beginning a society created by the Holy Ghost, and held together and informed by Him as its soul, who is sent down upon it as the Promise of the Father from the Incarnate Son.

Further, it was in and by their reception into this society that men received all the fruits of the Incarnation; it was in it that all the gifts of the Holy Ghost dwelt, and through it that they were dispensed. By hearing the truth announced by its ministry peni-

[1] Acts ii. 38.

tence was engendered in the listeners, itself a preventing grace of the Holy Ghost, which gave inward effect to the outward word. As a working of this penitence they came, according to the instruction of the teachers, to be baptized. By and in the act of baptism they were received into the divine society, and made partakers of the full operation of the Spirit who dwelt in it. They had the supernatural virtues of faith, hope, and charity infused into them, each according to the measure of the grace accorded to him, and to help the exercise of these virtues, that they might be borne as it were with the wings of a Spirit, the sevenfold gifts of wisdom, understanding, counsel, fortitude, knowledge, piety, and fear, were added to the soul. None of these virtues and gifts were possessed by believers as individuals; all of them came to men as members of her who was dowered with the blood of Christ,[1] and whose bridal quality imparted to her children all which that blood had purchased. In her was stored up that great, inexhaustible source of abiding life, the Body and Blood of her Lord and Husband: in her the redeeming Word gave direct from His heart the vivifying stream. In her was the gift of teaching which illumined the understanding, and not only drew from without, as we have seen, those who should be saved from the ignorance of the pagan or the carnalism of the Jew, but which erected in the world the Chair of Truth,[2] that is, the

---

[1] "Non te fefellit sponsus tuus: non te fefellit qui suo sanguine te dotavit." St. Aug. tom. v. 1090 b.

[2] "Quod tunc faciebat unus homo accepto Spiritu sancto, ut unus homo linguis omnium loqueretur, hoc modo ipsa unitas facit, linguis omnibus loquitur. Et modo unus homo in omnibus gentibus linguis omnibus loquitur, unus homo, caput et corpus, unus homo, Christus et Ecclesia, vir perfectus, ille sponsus, illa sponsa. Sed erunt, inquit, duo in carne una; judicia Dei vera, justificata in idipsum: propter unitatem." St. Aug. in Ps. xviii. 2, tom. iv. 85 f.

rule and standard of right belief, which was the continuance of the pentecostal gift, the illuminating and kindling fire, and the speaking tongue of unity, which the Body of Christ possesses for ever. It was by enjoying these endowments together in her bosom, by the actions of a life pervaded with these principles, by the joint possession and exercise of these supernatural powers which at once opened to the intellect a new field of knowledge and strengthened the will to acts above its inborn force, that men were Christians. And those who remembered what they had been as Jews, and what they had been as heathens, had no difficulty in recognising such a life as the effect of a divine grace, and no temptation to refer it to anything which belonged to them as individuals, since its commencement coincided with their entrance into a divine society, its growth depended on their membership in that Body. Their union with Christ in this Body was something direct and palpable; to them the several degrees of that one ministry constituted by Christ were the joints and articulations of the structure; the teaching thence proceeding as it were the current of life; by their being parts of the structure they were saved from the confusion of errors which swept freely round them without, through the craft of men and the seduction of deceit.[1] "Possessing the truth in charity," or "sanctified in the truth," was the expression of that divine life in common whereby they were to grow up into one, and be called by the name of their Lord,[2] because inseparably united to Him by the nerves and ligaments of one Body.

And this makes manifest to us how Christians,

---
[1] Ephes. iv. 11-16. ἀληθεύοντες ἐν ἀγάπῃ. Joh. xvii. 19. ἡγιασμένοι ἐν ἀληθείᾳ.
[2] 1 Cor. xii. 12. οὕτω καὶ ὁ Χριστός.

while scattered through every city of the great Roman empire, formed one Body. It was by virtue of the unity of spiritual jurisdiction which directed the whole ministry of that Body. The command of our Lord was, " Go, and make disciples all nations," " proclaim the gospel to every creature ; " the Body assembled and empowered at Pentecost was to carry out this command. How did it do so? The teaching and ruling power was distributed through a ministry wherein those of a particular order were equal as holding that order : bishops as bishops were equal, priests as priests. But not the less by the distribution of the places where the ministry was to be fulfilled, subordination was maintained through the whole Body. Had it been otherwise, as each Bishop had the completeness of the priesthood in himself, his sphere of action, that is, his diocese, would have constituted a distinct body. But no such thing was ever imagined in the Church of those first centuries. The Bishops were, on the contrary, joint possessors of one power, only to be exercised in unity.[1] The unity was provided for in the Apostolic body by the creation of the Primacy, without which the Body never acted, the Primate being designated before the Body was made ; the Primate invested with his functions on the seashore of the lake of Galilee before the Ascension, the Body on which he was to exercise them animated on the day of Pentecost. Spiritual jurisdiction being nothing else but the grant to exercise all spiritual powers, two jurisdictions would make two bodies; a thousand would make a thousand; so that the more

---

[1] So says the great maintainer of episcopal power, St. Cyprian, in his famous aphorism : " Episcopatus unus est, cujus a singulis in solidum pars tenetur."

the Church grew, the more it would be divided, were it not that the root of all its powers in their exercise is one. A spiritual kingdom is absolutely impossible without this unity of jurisdiction; and in virtue of it the whole Church, from north to south and from east to west, was and is one Body in its teaching and its rule; that is, in the administration of all those gifts which were bestowed at the day of Pentecost, and which have never ceased to be exercised from that day to this, and which shall never cease to the end of the world. Thus as it is through the Body that men are made and kept Christians, so the Primacy is that principle of cohesion and subordination without which the Body cannot exist.

Let us carry on the history of the divine Body to another point. How was the Truth transmitted in it?

Peter and his brethren having received through the great forty days from our Lord the complement of His teaching concerning His Kingdom, were empowered by the descent of the Holy Ghost to commence its propagation. And for this work they use the same instrument which their Lord had used— the living spoken word. They labour together for some time; after several years they divide the world between them; but in both these periods they found communities and supply them with everything needful for complete organisation and future increase and progress by their spoken teaching, which therefore contained the whole deposit of the truth. The gospel of which St. Paul so repeatedly speaks was that which he communicated by word of mouth, and St. Peter and all the rest did the same. Communities were planted by Apostolic zeal over a great part of the Roman empire before as yet anything was written by their founders. The whole administration of the sacraments, and the order and matter of the divine service, were arranged by this personal teaching of the living word. All that concerned the Person of our Lord, all that He had taught, done, and suffered, was so communicated. One reason of this is plain. It was not the bare gospel, but the "gospel of the kingdom,"[1] which was to be proclaimed to all nations. It was not a naked intellectual truth of which they were the bearers, but a kingdom which they were to build. They were not disseminating a sect of philosophy, but founding an empire. They were a King's heralds, and every king has a realm. Thus the Kingdom of the Word was proclaimed by the word spoken through many voices, but as the outpouring of one Spirit given on the day of Pentecost. This whole body of their teaching, therefore, was one Tradition; that is, a delivery over of the truth to them by inspiration of the Spirit, as the Truth who had become incarnate taught it, and a delivery of this truth from them to the communities which they set up. The first communication of the Christian faith to the individual was never made by writing. How, said the Apostle, should they invoke one whom they did not believe, but how believe in one of whom they had not heard, and how hear without a preacher, and how preach except they were sent?[2] It did not occur to him to ask how should they believe in one of whom they had not read. On the contrary, he gives in these few words the whole order of the truth's transmission. He conceived not heralds without a commission, any more than faith without trust in the

[1] Matt. xxiv. 14.   [2] Rom. x. 15.

word of the heralds. But here is the great sending, at and from the day of Pentecost, the root of perpetual mission from which the heralds derive their commission; they are sent, they proclaim, they are heard, they are believed, and this faith opens the door for the admission of subjects into the kingdom, according to the law which they proclaim. Thus are described to us at some length the acts of that wise masterbuilder whose words we have just cited; but though he laboured more abundantly than all, all acted after the same manner. The Church was founded by personal teaching, of which the living word was the instrument, and the whole truth which was thus communicated was termed the Tradition[1] or Delivery.

We now come to the second step. Before the Apostles were taken to their reward, the same Spirit, who had instructed them that they were to found the spiritual kingdom by means of the living word, inspired them to commit to writing a portion of that great tradition which they had already taught by mouth.[2] But they never delivered these writings to men not already Christians. One evangelist expressly says that he drew up a narrative in order that his disciple might know the certainty of what he had already been instructed in catechetically, that is, that by that great system of oral teaching by question and

---

[1] ἡ παράδοσις. It will be shown hereafter that the four great writers, Irenæus, Tertullian, Clement of Alexandria, and Origen, unanimously refer to Tradition in this sense.

[2] See St. Irenæus, ii. 1, expressly stating this of St. Mark's and St. Luke's Gospel, and of the Apostles generally: "quod (Evangelium) quidem tunc præconaverunt, postea vero per Dei voluntatem in Scripturis nobis tradiderunt;" which is repeated by Euseb. *Hist.* ii. 15, who declares that the Roman Christians, not content τῇ ἀγράφῳ τοῦ θείου κηρύγματος διδασκαλίᾳ, besought Mark with many prayers ὡς ἂν καὶ διὰ γραφῆς ὑπόμνημα τῆς διὰ λόγου παραδοθείσης αὐτοῖς καταλείψοι διδασκαλίας, which St. Peter afterwards approved.

answer, that grounding of the truth in the memory, intellect, and will, which Christianity had inaugurated, and that he wrote after the pattern of those who had delivered over the word to us, having been its original eye-witnesses and servants.[1] A second evangelist declares that what he was putting into writing was a very small portion indeed of what his Lord had done.[2] Another very remarkable thing is that the Apostles are not recorded to have put together what they had written themselves, or others by their direction, so as to make it one whole; far less that they ever declared what was so written to contain the complete tradition of what they had received. But what they did was to leave these writings in the hands of particular churches, having in every case addressed them to those who were already instructed as Christians, and not having left among them any document whatever intended to impart the Christian faith to those who were ignorant of it. These writings were in the strictest sense Scriptures of the Church, which sometimes stated, and always in their form and construction showed that they were adapted to those who had been taught the Christian faith by word of mouth. Moreover, it was left to the Church to gather them together, and make them into one book, which thenceforward should be *the Book;* it was left to the Church to determine which were to be received as inspired writings, and in accordance with the teaching already diffused in her, and which were not. And this collection of the several writings from the particular Churches to which they were addressed into one mass would seem not to have taken place until at least three or four generations after the whole order

---

[1] Luke i. 2-4.   [2] John xx. 30.

and institutions of the Church had been established by oral teaching, which filled as with a flood the whole Christian people. Then, finally, the authority of the Church alone established the canon of Scripture, and separated it off from all other writings.

Now as the planting of the Church by oral teaching was a direction of the Holy Spirit, from whom the whole work of mission proceeded, so all these particulars concerning the degree in which writing was to be employed, and the manner in which that writing was to be attested, and the persons to whom it was to be addressed, were a direction of the same Spirit. That a spiritual kingdom could not have been established save by oral teaching Christians may infer with certainty, because, in fact, that method was pursued. That a portion of the great Tradition should be committed to writing they may for the same reason infer to have been necessary for the maintenance of the truth, because it was so done. That these writings were the property of the Church—her Scriptures—may be inferred with no less truth, because they were addressed only to her children, and presupposed a system of instruction already received by those who were to read them. And, finally, that they were to be understood in their right sense only by the aid of the Spirit who dictated them, is, their being given in this manner once admitted, an inference of just reasoning. It is plain, when once these things are stated, that these writings were not intended to stand alone, as ordinary books, and to be understood by themselves. Not only were they part of a great body of teaching, but a portion of a great institution, to which they incessantly alluded and bore witness. They would speak very differently to those without and to those within the kingdom of which they were documents. They would remind the instructed at every turn of doctrines which they had been taught, corroborating these and themselves explained by them. Some of them indeed were letters, and we all know how different is the meaning of letters to those who know the writer and his allusions, and to those who do not. A word of reference in these documents to a great practice of Christian life would kindle into a flame the affection of those who possessed that practice, while it would pass as a dead letter to those who had it not.[1] Such word, therefore, would be absolute proof of the practice to the former, while it would seem vague and indeterminate and no proof at all to the latter.

From what has been said we may determine the relation of the Church to the Scriptures. She having been planted everywhere by the personal oral teaching of the apostles and their disciples, being in full possession of her worship and her sacraments, filled by that word which they had spoken to her, and ruled by that Spirit in whom they had spoken, accepted these writings which they left as conformable to that teaching which they had delivered by word of mouth, esteemed them, moreover, as sacred, because proceeding from the dictation of the one Spirit, and finally put them together and severed them off from all other books, as forming, in conjunction with that unwritten

---

[1] As one instance out of many take the words of St. Paul, 2 Cor. i. 22: "He that *confirms* us with you is Christ, and that has *anointed* us is God; who has also *sealed* us, and given the pledge of the Spirit in our hearts." How differently would this passage appear to one who had received the confirming chrism, with the words conveying it, "*Signo* te signo crucis, et *confirmo* te *chrismate* salutis;" and to one who had lost the possession of this Sacrament. Those who have deserted the ecclesiastical tradition and practice read the Scriptures with a negative mind, and so fail to draw out the truth which is in them.

word in possession of which she passed this judgment upon them, her own canon or rule of faith. Thenceforth they were to be for all ages a necessary portion of the divine Tradition which was her inheritance from the Incarnate Word, distributed by His Spirit. They were to be in her and of her. To her belonged, first, the understanding of them; secondly, the interpreting them to her children, out of the fund of that whole Tradition lodged in her, and by virtue of that indwelling Spirit, who, as He had created, maintained her; as part and parcel, moreover, of that whole kingdom, of that body of worship and sacraments, which she is.

And this brings us to a further point of the utmost importance. For the Truth, which is the subject matter of all this divine Tradition or Delivery from the Incarnate Word, in order to be efficacious and permanent, approached men in the shape of a society invested with grace.[1] It was not proposed as a theory which is presented simply to the reason, and accepted or rejected by it. True, it was addressed to the reason, but only when illuminated by faith could the reason accept it. Here, again, it showed itself manifestly as "the gospel *of the kingdom.*" It was the good tidings proclaimed, not simply and nakedly to man's intellect, but as the gift and at the same time the law of that kingdom which accompanied its publication by the bestowal of power to accept it, and to make it the rule of conduct. There were many whom the word, though proclaimed to them as to others, did not help, because it was not mixed with faith in those who heard it. St. Paul preached to many when the heart of one Lydia was opened to receive what he

[1] Eine Gnadenanstalt: our language does not supply the expression.

THE SECOND MAN VERIFIED IN HISTORY 129

announced.[1] Thus with the first hearing of the message coincided the beginning of grace to accept it. But so likewise the Church supplied a storehouse of grace for the continuance of the truth in those who had once received it. Truth and grace, as they come together in her, so they remain together inseparable. Wisdom, understanding, counsel, and knowledge, which perfect the intellect, are linked in her with fortitude, piety, and fear, which perfect the will. And this which is true of the individual is true of the mass. In the Body, as well as in each single member of it, and the more because the Body is an incomparably grander creation, it is the sanctified intellect which must receive, harmonise, and develop the truth. If the sevenfold fountain of the Spirit's gifts is one in the individual, much more is it one in that Body out of whose plenitude the individual receives. Thus wherever the Apostles preached the word, if faith made it fruitful, they bestowed the sacraments.

We shall see, if we observe it closely, that it is a triple cord through which the Holy Spirit conveys His life perpetually to the Body; and in His life is the Truth.

First, there is the succession of men. As the Word Incarnate taught, so men bear on His teaching. Personal labours, intercourse from mouth to mouth, the action of men on men, the suffering of men for men, this was from the beginning, this is to be for ever, the mode of spreading His kingdom. It is not a paper kingdom, it cannot be printed off and disseminated by the post. But from His own Person it passed to Peter and the Apostles, and from them to a perpetual succession of men, whose special work it

[1] Heb. iv. 2; Acts xvi. 14.

is to continue on this line by a chain never to be broken. These are the messengers, or heralds, or stewards, or ministers, or teachers, or shepherds. They are all and each of these according to the manifoldness of the gift which they carry. Through the unbrokenness of this line the continuity of the gift is secured. Through it the Redeemer, King, and Head touches, as it were, each point of time and space, and with a personal ministry lays hold of each individual through the vast extent of His kingdom in time and space. And the gift is as living and as near to Him now as it was when St. Paul spoke of it as communicated by the imposition of his hands to his disciple; nay, as it was when He Himself breathed on His Apostles together assembled, and said, "Receive the Holy Ghost;" and will be equally living and direct from Him to the last who shall receive it to the end of time. And all this because these men who are taken up into this succession are the nerves of His mystical Body, through which runs the supply to all the members. This is the indestructible framework which He has wrought for carrying on to men His own teaching, until the whole mass grow up to that fulness of the perfect stature which He has foreseen and determined.

The second succession is that of the Truth itself committed to these men. For that plenitude of teaching which the Apostles delivered orally to the Church has never ceased to rest in her, and out of it she dispenses to all the ages her divine message. But part of this teaching by the further ordering of the Spirit of Truth has been incorporated in writing. And no one can doubt that this incorporation has given a firmness and stability to the teaching which we do not see how it could otherwise have possessed. Thus the great Tradition of the Truth poured out upon the Church has been partly written and partly unwritten; not as if there were two teachings separable from each other, but one and the same which runs in a perpetual blending. Through the written teaching we receive the very words consecrated by our Lord's use: we have the priceless privilege of knowing how He spoke; of catching the accents of His voice, and the look of His eyes, and the gestures of His body, portrayed in that narrative. The words of Him who spake as never man spake live and sound for ever in our ears; and we recognise in the structure of His sentences, which convey in a clause principles of endless application, forces on which a universe can be built, the Father's Word, and the world's Creator, and the Church's Head. Parable and apophthegm and answer, metaphor and plain speech, when used by Him, are all impregnated with this power. And now that we possess this peculiar language of the Word Incarnate, embodied and fixed for ever to our senses as well as our affections, it seems as if we could not have done without it. Then the mode in which His own Apostles apply and illustrate His doctrines, and exhibit to us the formation of the society which He came to institute, possesses a value only subordinate to His own words. The written word, it has been said,[1] gives to the whole Church through all times a sense of the truth and consistency of her teaching like that which the sense of personal identity gives to the individual respecting his own being. And again, what memory is to the single man, such is the whole tradition of the Truth in the

[1] By Möhler.

bosom of the Church. But it is through the unwritten teaching deposited in her by the Apostles that she possesses the key to the true understanding of that which is written. The one in her practice has never been severed from the other. So dear has the written word been to her that almost the blackest epithet in language, "traitor," is derived from the name which she gave to those who, under fear of persecution, surrendered to the heathen her sacred books. With these in her hand, or rather in her heart, she has directed and carried out that great system of instruction which the Apostles laid down and established by their acts. For to her what they did was as sacred as what they said, or what they wrote; and numberless acts of theirs constituted her teaching originally, and have prolonged and continued it on since.

For, besides the succession of men and the succession of doctrine, there is in her likewise the succession of institutions. As chief of these, but involving a number of subordinate rites, the Apostles with their first oral teaching delivered likewise to the Church sacraments, instituted, not by them, but by their Lord Himself, which at once embodied the truth taught by them, and conveyed the grace by which that truth was to find a home in men's heart and mind. No sooner was the first teaching of Peter at the head of the Apostles uttered, and the gift of forgiveness of sins and of adoption disclosed, than three thousand persons received the double gift by the baptism which followed. Thus they established in the Church seven great rites, encompassing the whole of human life. The regenerating power which was the beginning of the whole change that they sought to work in man was stored up in one; the confirming and developing it in a second; the feeding and increasing it in a third; the removal of obstacles to it in a fourth; the supporting and restoring the human nature so elevated, when under pressure of sickness and in fear of death, in a fifth; the blessing and consecrating the union of the species in a sixth; and, finally, the conferring that distinctive power which transmitted through all ages her Lord's gift to the Church in a seventh. This is that great and marvellous sacramental system by which the Church, dowered, as we have said, in her quality of Bride with her Lord's blood, applies that blood to His members, according to their needs. This is the perpetual consecration of matter to a supernatural end, of which the highest example is found in the Body of the Head Himself, and so it is an enfolding of human nature with the Incarnation, and a transforming it into the image of its Head. But such, likewise, is the summary of the whole written and unwritten teaching of the Church; such also, in few and brief words, the perpetual work of the succession of men whom we have described.

Thus the three successions, of men, of doctrines, and of institutions, are woven by the Holy Spirit together as three strands of a rope which cannot be broken: in the union of these three His perpetual presence dwells; and this is the spinal cord whereby He joins the Body with the Head.

Let us take instances wherein the force of this union is seen.

The first gift He bestowed upon men when the gospel of the kingdom approached them was the forgiveness of sins. This is a power belonging to God alone, as sin is an offence against His majesty. The conferring of this power upon the Apostles by our Lord Himself is explicitly recorded. But then two sacraments exhibit the application of this power, first, that of baptism, where it is given plenarily; secondly, that of penance, where it is given under restriction. And further, an order of men is instituted for this perpetual application. Here, then, we see the force of the triple cord carrying on through all ages this great truth of the forgiveness of sins in and by the Church of God. The very definite mention of the grant of this power in the written tradition is not left exposed by itself to the action of unbelieving reason. It has a double bulwark in the two institutions which assert its perpetual exercise as a matter of history, and in the order of men established to carry it out.

Take again the doctrine of the Real Presence, upon which infidelity falls as being a proof charge of human credulity,[1] on which faith and love rest as the sovereign gift of God. The recorded words of our Lord Himself express it distinctly and emphatically; further words of His in the sixth chapter of St. John allude to it with equal force, and St. Paul repeatedly refers to it. But this is not enough for the solicitude with which the Holy Spirit has guarded it against all attack. As the great central rite of Christian worship it is presented day after day, in myriads of churches, from age to age, to the eyes and hearts of men. The act in which Christians assemble, in which they offer up at once their repentance and their requests, their thanksgivings and their praises, to Him who has formed them into one Body, lives upon this truth. And further, the order of men which is the backbone of the Church, the great Christian priesthood, made

[1] See Macaulay's Essays.

by our Lord in instituting the rite and conferring the gift, exists for its continuance. Against such a truth, defended with such bulwarks, both infidelity and heresy dash themselves with impotent rage in vain.

Thirdly, we have in the epistles of St. Paul a mention of the bishop's office and the duties belonging to it. The mention is incidental, and the words not so determinate as in the former instances given. Those who are outside the Body, in their attack upon the necessity of episcopacy, thought that they could cut through these words so as to make it doubtful whether the office of bishop, as distinguished from that of priest, was of original institution. But then history disclosed the fact that when the last apostle was taken from the earth not a church existed which was not under episcopal jurisdiction, and through the whole world, by the institution of bishops, was fulfilled the prediction, "Instead of thy fathers thou shalt have children, whom thou mayest make princes in all lands." Thus, while the written record was interpreted, the unwritten teaching of the Church found a plain and unanswerable proof in her invariable practice. All through her long history she is seen to be governed by bishops; and the words of St. Paul, flanked by the institution and the practice, are more than sufficient to maintain the truth.

Once more let us take the primacy of St. Peter's see in the Church. This, as is well known, rests in the written word mainly on three great passages of St. Matthew, St. Luke, and St. John. These, indeed, are so specific and definite that they convey the dignity intended as clearly as the passages above referred to convey the forgiveness of sins or the Real Presence. But over and above these, what an overwhelming proof in the unbroken succession of those who exercised the primacy from the beginning, and are referred to from age to age by the doctors, fathers, and historians of the Church! Beside the charter of institution stands the long record of the work wrought in virtue of it, the witness of the Church to it in councils, the obedience to it in fact. As the priesthood exists in attestation of the Real Presence, so the primacy stands beside our Lord's words, first promising and then conferring it, like the comment of eighteen hundred years, uniform and consistent.

What we have here applied in the case of the forgiveness of sins, the Real Presence, episcopacy, and the primacy of the Church, might be carried out in the case of many more doctrines forming a part of the great deposit. But it may be well to cite one instance of a truth not contained in the written word at all, which through the unwritten teaching of the Church has passed into universal practice. This is not the abolition only of the Jewish Sabbath, constituted as it was by the most express divine command, for to that abolition there is a passing reference in an epistle of St. Paul, but the further substitution of the day of the resurrection, the first day of the week for the seventh, with a modified observance. This rests solely upon the deposit of the Church's unwritten teaching, corroborated by universal practice from the apostolic times.

Viewing, then, the transmission of the Truth as a whole, and the creation of the mystical Body of Christ as its home, and the Holy Spirit as the perpetual Indweller who fills that treasure-house of Truth and Grace, we may consider its maintenance as secured by the triple succession or tradition of men, of doctrine, and of institutions which are inseparably joined together in that its home. But there are some words of our Lord so distinctly and translucently expressing all this statement respecting the mode in which His Truth was first and is ever to be transmitted, and the conditions to which His perpetual presence is attached, that we cannot forbear to adduce them.

His parting instructions to His Apostles on the Mountain of Galilee given by St. Matthew run thus: "Jesus approached them and said unto them, All power has been given unto Me in heaven and on earth. Go therefore, and make disciples all nations, baptizing them in the name of the Father and of the Son and of the Holy Ghost, teaching them to observe all things whatsoever I have commanded you; and behold I am with you all days even to the end of the world." We shall here note six things. First, there is the root and foundation of all mission, the power bestowed upon Christ as man, in virtue of the Incarnation: "all power has been given to Me in heaven and on earth." Secondly, there is the derivation of this power from Christ to His Apostles, in virtue of which sent by Him, as He by His Father, they were to go forth: "Go ye therefore." Thirdly, there is the creation of the perpetual teaching power, the authority by which truth was to be imparted: "make disciples all nations." He placed it in them as in one Body, here fulfilling what St. Augustine afterwards expressed, that He "seated the doctrine of Verity in the Chair of Unity." They, invested with one Spirit, His own Spirit of Truth, should go forth and make disciples all nations to one Body of Truth. It is the creation of a power new as the Incarnation, as it is unique, because springing from it, founded and continued in it. He Himself is the one Teacher whose voice they express: He who came on earth for three and thirty years speaks for evermore in those whom He sends as one Body, which calls no man teacher, because it is the Body of Christ, *the* Teacher: so that this function of magisterial teaching is the great distinctive office of His Church, coming from above, and invested with the authority of the God-man, by which it draws to it disciples, whose consent is not the ground but the result of its authority. Fourthly, there is the creation of the sacraments, as containing the grace which is needed for the reception of this Truth, and they are summed up in the first, which is the beginning of the new life, illumination, and perfection, and which is given in the covenant name of God, as the Christian God, and is the mark of the triune Creator, Redeemer, and Sanctifier, impressed on his own people of acquisition. Thus Grace is for ever associated with Truth as the means whereby alone on earth Truth shall prevail and be received, and that only as the teaching of that Body whose Head is full of Grace and Truth. Fifthly, there is marked the manner of the teaching, the nature of the magisterial office created as that of a living body of men: "teaching them to observe all things whatsoever I have commanded you." The fund from which this teaching is drawn is that whole communication of truth from the Incarnate Word Himself, given to them by word of mouth, of which we have spoken above as the great Tradition or Delivery; and out of which a part is incorporated in the written word, while the whole dwells ever in the Body created to receive it, from which it is to be imparted by perpetual oral teaching. The teaching, therefore, rests upon the perpetual presence of the Body representing Christ, and as in the days of His flesh He teaches through it, and has fixed part of His tradition in it by writing, not to the exclusion of the rest, but as the charter of a sovereign, the title-deeds of an empire, to be perpetually applied, interpreted, and developed in that whole system of institutions, by that whole race of teachers, in the life of that one Body, which He was creating. And lastly, to this perpetual living line of teachers, to this perpetual living doctrine, to this perpetual living framework of grace, He has promised His own presence without fail to the end. In this triple succession He is seen, lives, and rules, and this is His Kingdom, His Temple, His Body, His Bride, His Family, to whom He says, " Behold, I am with you all days, even to the end of the world."

From these words of our Lord, as from the whole previous argument, we gather that while the Truth which Christ imparted to His Apostles was one and complete, its development in its various relations was designedly left as the proper work of such a Body as He created. He Himself spoke as God in human flesh, uttering, that is, creative words, which gathered up in a sentence a germ of truth capable of a long series of applications, and requiring them in order to be understood. And the aptitude to make these applications, so that the truth proclaimed by Him and committed to His Apostles should penetrate through and leaven the whole human society, He gave to His mystical Body. Let us take an instance of this. The Pharisees approached Him one day to entangle Him by their words, and proposed to Him a dilemma from which they thought that He could not escape save by ruining His influence with one great party, or by encountering the danger of being charged with seditious teaching by another. They put to Him the question whether it was lawful to give tribute to Cæsar or not. Whereupon He asked them to show Him the tribute-money, and pointing to the image of the emperor upon it, uttered those famous words, "Render therefore to Cæsar the things which are Cæsar's, and to God the things which are God's." Now these words were laid up in the treasury of His Church, and by them she has had to determine the relation between the civil and the spiritual powers in the society created by Him who spake them. Here is a vast development from a small seed: but it is a seed cast by the world's Creator and the Body's Head. And His teaching is full of such seeds, as the history of His Church is one great process of developing and harmonising and conveying to man the truth thus cast into the fallows of her soil. It is not new truth, for He gave the germ, and no power in man could have developed it without the germ, any more than it could produce the oak without the acorn. It is the same truth, as He taught it, but with that process passed upon it which He intended when He gave it in such a form, and when He made a living Body, to be called by His name, to propagate His teaching, to collect His members into one, and to fill the earth with the knowledge which He brought.

Such a work, therefore, the root and authorisation of which we have been attempting to delineate in this lecture, stretches over the whole field which Truth and Grace occupy, and over all the relations of men which are summed up in what they are to believe and what they are to do. These ramifications are all but endless. But to all these extends that giving

of the Holy Ghost in his fourfold character of the
Spirit of Unity, Verity, Charity, and Sanctity, which
is the result of the Incarnation, and which makes the
Church. What we have said here has a special relation to Truth, and to Christian morals as resting upon
Christian dogma. But it is impossible to separate
Truth from Grace, in their actual operation as powers:
faith and charity in the Christian are linked together,
as the intellect and the will are one soul. What we
have said is but an introduction to a sketch of the
great evolution of dogmatic truth through eighteen
centuries: but in recording its rise, the secret of its
growth, and the source of its strength, it was impossible not to bring out the great fact that Christianity
was nothing less than a divine life produced in the
world over against the existing heathenism, and laying
hold of the whole soul of man, in which, as we have
just said, intellect and will are inseparable. It did
not consist in anything which individuals believed,
however true; but in a society of which Truth and
Grace were the joint spring, and it was produced in
the midst of a world which had to a great extent
forfeited both Truth and Grace, while both returned
to it as the gift of Christ assuming man's nature.
This error and distraction of heathenism, and this
great unity of Christian life grounded in faith and
charity which rose up against it, were profoundly felt
by all the Fathers, being eye-witnesses of the old
world and the new. Their writings express it again
and again, with the vividness which only eye-witnesses,
who are likewise actors and sufferers, feel. In nothing,
perhaps, do they so differ from modern writers as in
the energy with which they appreciate the supernatural
character of the Christian, and the wonderful being

and endowment of that Christian Body which impressed this character on its members. One cause, we may suppose, of this was the sight of heathenism before them with all its impurities and its impotence to produce good. So they were not even tempted to that naturalism which is the besetting sin of our age and these countries. It would have seemed to them not only an ingratitude but an absurdity to refer to the inborn force of humanity a change equally of the intellect and of the will which they saw to belong only to the power of Christ revealed in His Church. We will cite one such passage as a conclusion to this discussion, and because it represents the whole train of thought which we have been drawing out.[1]

"Of this sacrament, this sacrifice, this priest, this God, before, having been made of a woman, He entered on His mission, all sacred and mystical, angelic and miraculous appearances to our fathers, as well as their own deeds, were resemblances, in order that every creature might in a manner by its acts speak of that One destined to come, in whom should be the salvation of all that were to be restored from death. For as we had started away from the one true supreme God by the injustice of impiety, and fallen out of harmony with Him, and become unstable as water, and wasted ourselves on a multitude of vanities, rent in pieces, and hanging in tatters to every piece, need was there that by the will and command of a compassionating God this multitude of objects itself should utter a cry in unison, calling for One to come; and that thus called upon this One should come, and that the multitude should attest together that the One had come: and so we, discharged from the burden of this

[1] St. Aug. *de Trin.* iv. 11, 12, tom. viii. 817.

multitude, should come to One; and dead in our soul by many sins, and from our sin doomed to death in the flesh, should love that One, who, being without sin, died for us in the flesh: and believing on Him when risen, and with Him rising again in the Spirit through faith, should be justified, being in the One Just made one: and should not despair of rising again in our very flesh, beholding our Head being One going before His many members; in whom now, cleansed by faith, and hereafter restored by vision, and reconciled by the Mediator to God, we might inhere in the One, enjoy the One, and continue One for ever.

"Thus the Son of God, Himself at once the Word of God and Son of man, Mediator of God and men, equal to the Father by the unity of the godhead, and partaker of us through the assumption of the manhood, interceding with the Father for us through that which was man, yet not concealing that as God He was One with the Father, thus speaks: 'Neither pray I for these alone, but for those also who shall believe through their word on Me; that all may be one, as Thou, Father, art in Me, and I in Thee, that they also may be One in Us, that the world may believe that Thou hast sent Me. And the glory which Thou gavest Me, I have given them, that they may be One as we also are One.' He said not, that I and they may be One thing, although in that He is the Head of the Church, and the Church His Body, He might say, I and they not One thing, but One person, because the Head and the Body is One Christ. But marking His Godhead as consubstantial with the Father (whence in another place He says, I and the Father are One thing), He wills that His own should be One thing in their own kind, that is, in the consubstantial parity of the same nature, but in Him, because in themselves they could not, as severed from each other by diversity of pleasures, desires, and impurities of sin. From these they are cleansed through the Mediator, so as to be One Thing in Him, not merely by the same nature in which all from mortal men become equal to the angels, but likewise by the same will breathing in perfect harmony together into the same beatitude, welded, as it were, by the fire of charity into One Spirit. For this is the force of His words, That they may be One, as We also are One: that as the Father and the Son are One not only in equality of substance, but also in will, so these also between whom and God the Son is Mediator, may be One Thing not merely by being of the same nature, but also by the same society of affection. And the very point that He is Mediator, by whom we are reconciled to God, He indicates in the words, 'I in them and Thou in Me, that they may be consummated into One.' Thus as through the mediator of death we had receded from our Creator, stained and alienated, so through the Mediator of life we might be purified and reconciled, wherein consist our true peace and stable union with Him."

LECTURE X

THE FIRST AGE OF THE MARTYR CHURCH

"Magnum hæreditatis mysterium! Templum Dei factus est uterus nescientis virum. Non est pollutus ex ea carnem assumens. Omnes gentes venient dicentes, Gloria tibi, Domine."
Antiphon on Vespers of Circumcision.

THE world which Augustus and Tiberius ruled was not conscious of the fact that there was an order of truth, and of morality based upon that truth, the maintenance of which was to be purchased, and cheaply purchased, with the loss of life, or of all that made life valuable. This world was indeed familiar with the thought and with the practice of sacrificing life for one object—an object which collected all the natural affections and interests of a man together, and presented them to him in the most attractive form, his country. Greek and Roman history, and indeed the history of all nations up to that time, had been full of instances in which privations and sufferings were endured, and, if necessary, life itself given up for wife and children, for the dear affections of house and home, for friends, for freedom, for fatherland. Man, civilised and uncivilised, was alike capable of this, and capable of it in profusion. Rome had many a Regulus and Sparta many a Leonidas in the humblest ranks of their citizens: Gaul had thousands as noble as Vercingetorix, and Spain not one but many Numantias. Human nature had never been wanting in the courage to die for the visible goods of human life. But to labour, to combat, to endure pain, sorrow, privations, to suffer in every form for the invisible goods of a future life, to recognise, that is, an inviolable order of religion and morality, so far superior to all that a man can grasp and hold in his possession, to wife, children, goods, friends, freedom, and fatherland, and to life adorned and crowned with these, that any or all of these, and life itself, are to be sacrificed for its preservation; this may be said to be a thought of which the whole heathen world ruled by Augustus and Tiberius was unconscious.[1] For other reasons also it was familiar enough with the sacrifice of life, since the continual practice of war and the permanent institution of slavery had made human life the cheapest of all things in its eyes. And further, to die rather than to live dishonoured was still the rule of the nobler among the millions who yielded to the sway of Augustus. But to die for the maintenance of moral truth, that is, for faith,—this was known indeed to the Jews, who had already their "cloud of witnesses" to it; but it was unknown to heathendom, which has in all its ranks and times but one man[2] to offer whose death approaches to such a sacrifice, and therefore shines with incomparable lustre among all deeds of purely human heroism. But the death of Socrates found in this no imitators, he created here no line of followers; and he stands alone in

---

[1] Tertullian, *Apol.* 50. "O gloriam licitam, quia humanam, cui nec præsumptio perdita nec persuasio desperata deputatur in contemptu mortis et atrocitatis omnimodæ, cui tantum pro patria, pro imperio, pro amicitia pati permissum est, quantum pro Deo non licet." See again the instances he collects *ad Martyres*, 4; and Eusebius, *Hist.* 5, prooem., draws the same contrast.

[2] Celsus only alleges the suffering of Socrates as a parallel to that of the martyrs. Origen *c. Cels.* i. 3.

this greatness, an exception to an otherwise invariable rule.

However, in our two preceding lectures we have been describing something much more than the exhibition of this order of truth; that is, we have set forth the union of it with a Person, who both exhibits it in Himself, and is the source of it to others. And the difference between these two things is very great. Many at different times have said, "I teach the truth." One only has said, "I am the Truth:" and to say it is the most emphatic indirect assumption of Godhead which can be conceived. And with it that One also joined a similar expression, containing the same assumption of Godhead, and which equally was never approached by any other teacher. "I am the Life." The union of the Truth at once and of the Life with His Person, which is thus become the root of both to human nature, was the subject of the last two lectures. Now, as we have said, that there was an order of truth sacred and inviolable above all things, was borne witness to by the Hebrew martyrs, and therefore was not new to the chosen race of Israel, though it was new to heathendom, at the time at which our Lord appeared. But the union of the Truth and of the Life with the Person of One appearing visibly in the world as man, was as new to the Hebrews as to the heathen, was an absolute novelty to human nature. And so the Christian Faith also, as a system of belief and action, that is, as embracing the mind and the will of man, as giving both Truth and Life, is entirely new in this respect; that in this double action it is in its origin and in its whole course and maintenance bound up with a Person. Thus all which it teaches is not naked truth, unlocalised as it were, and impersonal, but is the development of relations in which the disciples of Christ stand to Him; for instance, as King, as God, as Head, as Bridegroom, as Father. As these, He is at once the Truth and the Life. Thus it is that the Christian Faith flows out of the Person of Christ the God-man; and, as its Truth is centered in that Person, so also its continuous Life depends on Him.

And further, as the connection of doctrine, or truth, and of life, that is, action, with a Person is the point from which all this movement springs, in which respect we have said it was absolutely new, so the term to which it reaches is the creation of something in both these things correlative to that Person, the creation of a Kingdom, a Temple, a Body, a Mother, a Race, in which respect also the term is as new as that from which it springs. That He is the Truth and the Life is shown in this creation, which has a distinctive character, as He has, an unique existence, and an organic unity with Him.

The subject on which we are now employed is to describe as an historic fact how the duty of maintaining, propagating, and dying for the truth and conduct thus identified with the Person of Christ, was carried out through many generations and under difficulties which seemed to preclude the possibility of its success; and to show the means by which this great creation, starting from the day of Pentecost, made a home and established itself in the Roman empire, by which, after a conflict of nearly three hundred years, it was finally recognised.

The worship of the one true God had been fixed in the children of Abraham, Isaac, and Jacob, as the faith which made them a nation, that is, as the dogma on

FIRST AGE OF THE MARTYR CHURCH 149

which their national existence was so based, that through maintaining it they were to continue a people. The Jewish polity lived in and by this belief, and, as a nation, was its prophet. Certainly, this was the noblest form which nationalism has ever assumed. Yet it was nationalism still ;· and the proselyte who would enter into the full worship of the God of Abraham and all its privileges had to become a Jew. But now, instead of this bond another was substituted, signifying that the King of the Jews who had appeared was come as the saviour of *man*, not of this or of that nation. The bond is therefore placed at the point which constituted the salvation of the whole race, that is in the Person of the God-man, and by this the corporation was put beyond the bounds of a nationality, and made co-extensive with the world. The Christian creed was formed round the Person, the actions, and the sufferings of Christ. Now here, precisely in what constituted the character, the greatness, and the glory of the Christian faith, was seated the principle and the beginning of the persecution which it encountered from the Roman empire. In that empire every species of idolatry [1] had a right of homestead as the national or tribe religion of any one of its constituent parts; and the worship of even one God, exclusive as that Jewish worship was of the whole heathen pantheon, was allowed by the laws of Rome to the Jews, because he was considered their national god. But the Chris-

---

[1] With an appeal to this fact Athenagoras begins his apology to the Emperors Marcus Aurelius and Commodus, about A.D. 177. ἑνὶ λόγῳ κατὰ ἔθνη καὶ δήμους θυσίας κατάγουσιν ἃς ἂν ἐθέλωσιν ἄνθρωποί καὶ μυστήρια, οἱ δὲ Αἰγύπτιοι καὶ αἰλούρους καὶ κροκοδείλους καὶ ὄφεις καὶ ἀσπίδας καὶ κύνας θεοὺς νομίζουσι. καὶ τούτοις πᾶσιν ἐπετρέπετε καὶ ὑμεῖς καὶ οἱ νόμοι . . . ἡμῖν δὲ (καὶ μὴ παρακρουσθῆτε, ὡς οἱ πολλοί, ἐξ ἀκοῆς) τῷ ὀνόματι ἀπεχθάνεσθε. Ch. i. See also Kellner's *Hellenismus und Christenthum*, p. 79; and Champagny, *Les Antonins*, ii. 189.

tians had no such justification in Roman eyes for their exclusive worship. They were not a nation nor a province of the empire; they had not, therefore, that title for their worship which constituted the charter of toleration to all besides, including the Jew, who worshipped the same God. For the Christians worshipped Him, not as their ancestral God, but as the Father of that Son who had taken human flesh, and become the Saviour of men. Their worship of the one true God was not only exclusive, but in and through the fact of the Incarnation claimed the homage of all men to it. It knew of no bond of brotherhood but in Him who had deigned to call men His brethren. Thus its special character and pre-eminent glory were the cause of its persecution, and from the moment that it came before the notice of the Roman governor not as a Jewish sect but as a distinct belief, it was considered as not a lawful religion. Thus too it was that the selfsame point which kindled Jewish hatred entailed Roman persecution. The Christian faith was a mortal offence to the Jew because it extended what had been his special privileges to all the Gentiles. He abhorred the substitution of the Person of the God-man for the race of Abraham after the flesh; as the Roman at once despised and hated a worship which not only adhered to one God, but dethroned from his political supremacy the Capitoline Jupiter, and whose title rested not on tradition and national inheritance, but on a fact touching the whole race of man, and therefore claiming the allegiance of the whole race—the assumption of human nature by a Divine Person. Thus the doctrine in which lay the whole creative force, the truth and the life of Christianity, was that which from the first caused the dislike of the Jew and the persecution of the Gentile—the kingship of Christ, involving the headship of a universal religion, and a power which was not that of Cæsar.

We have, then, now to treat of a period of 280 years, homogeneous in its character from the beginning to the end, which is, that it is the carrying out by a people ever increasing in number and strength of that good confession made before Pontius Pilate—that witness at its proper time of which St. Paul[1] in its first stage said that he was the herald and apostle. The course and life of Christians during these ten generations is to be the prolongation of this testimony, the embodiment of this confession. It is as soldiers, imitators, followers of one Chief, that all appear on the scene in their respective order.[2] It is by a direct virtue drawn from the cross of that Chief that they move onward to their own passion. They endure and they conquer simply as under His command, and because He endured and conquered before them. Their oath of military fidelity is the bond of their discipline; they prevail because they are His, and because they are one in Him:

> "And they stand in glittering ring
> Round their warrior God and King—
> Who before and for them bled—
> With their robes of ruby red,
> And their swords of cherub flame."

The whole process and cause of Christians during this

---

[1] 1 Tim. vi. 13; ii. 6.
[2] "Æmulos nos ergo Sibi esse voluit, ac primus virtute cœlesti injustorum justus obtemperavit arbitrio; dans scilicet secuturis viam, ut pius Dominus exemplum famulis Se præbendo, ne onerosus præceptor a quodam putaretur. Pertulit ante illa quæ aliis perferenda mandavit." *Epist. Ecc. Smyr.* i. Ruinart, p. 31.

long period, the ground of their accusation, the conduct and principles of the judges, and their judgment, are summed up as in a parable in that scene which passed before Pilate, while the subsequent day of Pentecost is in the same manner an image of the final result won in these three hundred years. For as the crucifixion of the Truth in the Person of Christ is followed by the descent of the Holy Ghost forming the Church, so the persecution and crucifixion of the truth in ten generations of His people is followed by the empire's public recognition of His eternal kingdom—of that Body of Christ seen visibly in a council of its prelates assembling freely from all lands.

Take first the seventy years which form the Apostolic age. What do we find as the result when St. John, the last Apostle, is taken away? In a large number of cities throughout the Roman empire a community has been planted after the pattern of that which we have described as arising at Jerusalem, and by the same means, the power of oral teaching. Every such community has at its head its bishop, or angel, who sums up and represents in his own person the people over which he presides. This is exactly the picture presented to us at the close of this period by St. John in the Apocalypse, when he is directed by our Lord personally appearing to him to write seven letters to as many bishops of cities on the seaboard of the province of Asia. Each, with his people, is addressed as a unit. One, "I know thy works, and thy labour, and thy endurance, and how thou canst not bear those which are evil:" a second, "Fear not what thou art about to suffer; behold, the devil shall cast some of you into prison:" a third, "I have against thee some few things, that thou hast there some who hold the doctrine of Balaam."[1] Each has around him his council of priests, his ministering deacons, his faithful people. The last Apostle is still living; but in all these communities many exist, both of teachers and taught, who have learned Christian doctrine, either from the mouth of an Apostle or the comrade of an Apostle—a Mark, a Luke, a Silvanus, a Clemens. Thus they live mainly upon oral teaching: the voice which went forth from the day of Pentecost is sounding freshly in their ears. Doctrine is in the stage of simple tradition and authority. The writings of the New Testament are completed, but being addressed to various parts of the Church, are best known to those for whom they were written. They are not yet collected and made the common patrimony of the whole Church. S. John leaves the earth without performing any such function; without setting the seal of his apostolical authority upon the New Testament as a whole; nay, the authorship of some of his own writings, as we now receive them, will be partially contested after his death before their final reception. Of the absolute number of these Christian communities, and of the multitude they severally embrace, we have no account; we can form no estimate, save to infer that the whole number of the faithful, at the end of this period, was very small in comparison with the mass out of which they had been drawn. Still it was a germ with a living force of expansion, planted in every considerable spot of the empire; and wherever it was planted, a Christian people, in the full sense of the word, existed, having a complete spiritual life of its own, possessing the sacraments which insured the beginning and the continuance of that life, an order of

[1] Apoc. ii. 2, 10, 14.

worship based on the great central fact which made them a people, and a ministry charged with the power to teach and to convey on to their successors the doctrines delivered to them.

But in the meantime how had the empire treated it? In these seventy years it has traversed the last seven years of the Emperor Tiberius, and the whole principates of Caligula, Claudius, and Nero; the revolutionary crisis in which Galba, Otho, and Vitellius reigned for an instant, and then the settled time of Vespasian, Titus, Domitian, and Nerva. Now, during this period its treatment by the empire has been a singular reproduction of what passed in the hall of Pilate. For the Jewish religion was one allowed by Roman law. The profession of it entailed no penalty. Now the first heralds of the Gospel, as Jews, preached their message boldly and publicly, and in doing so it does not seem that Roman law would have interfered with them.[1] At this stage it looked upon Christians as a sect of Jews. As no authority of the empire had interfered with the public ministry of our Lord, so it would seem to have left the ministry of His disciples in the first instance free. It is from another quarter that opposition arises. The Jew in his jealous anger at the promulgation of a Messiah and a spiritual kingdom which is not after Jewish taste, both because it is a kingdom not of this world, and because it raises the Gentile to co-inheritance with the race of Abraham, drags the Christian missionary before the tribunal of the Roman magistrate and imputes to him "sedition." Then many a Gallio, many

---

[1] This is what Tertullian calls "sub umbraculo insignissimæ religionis, certe licitæ," *Apolog.* 21; and *ad Nationes*, i. 11, "Nos quoque ut Judaicæ religionis propinquos."

a Felix, many a Festus have as it were unwillingly
to enter into and decide these questions of the Jewish
law. It would seem that converts to the Christian
faith in these its earliest days might long have escaped
the notice of the magistrate, as belonging to a Jewish
sect, but for this enmity of the Jews themselves. But
as the teachers of the new faith everywhere addressed
themselves first to their countrymen, so everywhere
they found these countrymen alive to their progress
and bitterly set against it.[1] This state of things is
pretty well expressed by that answer of the Roman
Jews to St. Paul when he excuses himself before them
for having been compelled to appeal to the Emperor
Nero: "as concerning this sect, we know that it is
spoken against everywhere."[2] This, however, was
Jewish, not Roman, contradiction. So far as everywhere Jewish hatred and jealousy could malign and
counterwork the progress of the Christian Faith, and
bring suffering on its teachers, it had been done.
But nevertheless with this exception it would seem
that for thirty-five years after the day of Pentecost
that faith had been freely and publicly taught throughout the empire. It was through the malignity of his
own countrymen, stirring up a dangerous conspiracy
against him, that S. Paul felt himself compelled to
appeal to the emperor, and the result of his appeal
was that he was set free. But in the year 64 another
state of things had arisen. The ruin of a large part
of Rome by fire had brought a great odium upon
Nero. Now his wife Poppæa is said to have been a
Jewish proselyte, he himself to have been surrounded

---

[1] See Justin Martyr, *Dial. c. Tryph.* 17, who speaks of the Jews as sending everywhere deputies in order to defame Christians.
[2] Acts xxviii. 22.

by Jewish influences, and nothing is more probable than that Jewish hatred, which had tracked the Christians everywhere, pursued them especially here, and suggested them to him both as authors of the conflagration, and as convenient scapegoats whereon to divert the odium against himself which had arisen from it. Thus he took the opportunity of exposing to shame and torment, as victims of the popular dislike, and in popular opinion guilty of "hatred of the human race," or of being hated by them, "a vast multitude"[1] of Christians, who, says the heathen historian, were put to the most exquisite suffering, being wrapt in the skins of wild beasts, and torn to pieces by dogs, or crucified, or clothed in garments of pitch and set on fire to illuminate the night. Thus it is, as decorations of Nero's games, in his gardens of the Vatican, where the obelisk from Heliopolis, once the ornament of his circus, now bears witness to the victory of Christ, that Christians first come before us in the pages of Roman historians, just at the middle of the period we are now describing, thirty-five years after the Ascension.

It may be considered part of this first persecution that the two great Apostles—Peter, who had founded the Roman Church, and Paul, who after its first foundation had helped to build it up—were condemned in the last year of Nero, and by his deputies[2] during his absence, to suffer as Christians, the one the death of a Roman citizen by the sword, and the other that of a slave by crucifixion. Thus the two great brethren by enduring together the martyr's death, the highest mark of Christian charity, sealed their joint founda-

---

[1] Tacitus, *Ann.* xv. 44.
[2] Ὁ Παῦλος, μαρτυρήσας ἐπὶ τῶν ἡγουμένων, οὕτως ἀπηλλάγη τοῦ κόσμου. St. Clem. Rom. *ad Cor.* 5.

tion of Christian Rome, that like as the Rome which had gained the conquest of the world by the strong hand of violence, had been planted in the blood of one brother shed by another, so the Rome which was to be the centre of Christ's kingdom, and in the words of St. Ignatius " preside over charity," should have for her founders brethren in supernatural love, pouring forth their blood together for the seat of that Christian unity which binds the earth in one.

But this persecution by Nero is not transitory in its consequences. The emperor had judged that Christians as such professed a religion not allowed by the Roman laws, and were guilty therein of a capital crime. This crime, if technically expressed, would amount to sacrilege and treason;[1] for they could not acknowledge the Roman gods as gods, nor the emperor as Pontifex Maximus; nor could they swear by his genius, which was the oath expressing fidelity to the Roman constitution in its civil and religious aspect. This was that "hatred of the human race," that is, in other words, of the Roman empire, of which in the eyes of Tacitus and Pliny, of Nero now and of Trajan afterwards, they were guilty as Christians. But the singular thing is this, that the Jew, who was the first to drag them before the Roman tribunal, who was their omnipresent, ever-ready antagonist and traducer, though he worshipped one only God, though he abhorred the whole Roman polytheism, though he swore not by the genius of the emperor, was exempt from punishment: his religion was recognised by Roman law and the senate its interpreter,

[1] Tertull. *Apol.* 10. "Sacrilegii et majestatis rei convenimur: summa hæc causa, immo tota est." Lassaulx says, "die beiden Hauptanklagen, die Religion-verachtung, die Majestäts-beleidigung." *Fall des Hellenismus,* p. 11.

because it was the national and time-honoured religion of a constituent part of the empire. On the same ground the vilest Egyptian, Asiatic, African idol was allowed the worship of those who claimed it as their ancestral god. The Christian Faith was the sole exception to this universal tolerance, because it was not the religion of a subject nation, because it was new, because, in fine, it rested on principles which, if carried out, would sweep away the whole fabric of polytheism on which the Roman State rested. And the act of Nero had its great importance in that it formally distinguished the Christian from the Jewish religion, and took away from it by a legal decision of the State's highest authority the claim to be considered "licit."

Nero then bestows the crown of martyrdom on St. Peter and St. Paul, and on what Tacitus calls, even within Rome alone, a vast multitude. But he does more than this. On the first appearance of Christians before the supreme authority he so applies an existing law to their case as to establish their liability under it to capital punishment, and this liability rests upon them henceforth down to the time of Constantine. It is by no means always carried out; it is often suspended, sometimes for many years together, according to the character of the ruling prince, or the maxims of his government, or the state itself of the empire. But it is henceforth the legal position of Christians. It is a danger which besets their condition, and may be called into action at any moment, in any city of the empire, from any motive of private enmity, cupidity, or passion. It is the legal Roman equivalent and interpretation of their Master's words, "You shall be hated of all men for My name's sake."[1]

[1] Matt. x. 22; xxiv. 9.

How often, and in how many instances, it was carried out in this period of seventy years we have no means of telling; but another emperor is named as a persecutor. Domitian not only put to death as Christian his cousin, the Consul Flavius Clemens, but, as it would seem, a great many others at Rome, in the latter years of his principate.[1] Domitian and Nero are mentioned as persecutors by Melito when addressing Marcus Aurelius, and by Tertullian,[2] in the time of Severus, though it was the object of both to make the emperors appear to have been not unfavourable to Christians. But, independent of any general act which would constitute an emperor a persecutor,[3] this liability to punishment,[4] in virtue of which the confessor or martyr was brought before the local magistrates, was that under which individual Christians, in most peaceful times, and in the reign of emperors generally just and moderate, endured their sufferings. The Emperor Tiberius is said by Tertullian to have brought before the senate a proposition to allow the Christian Faith as a lawful religion. Had this been done, the whole course of Christian history in these

[1] St. Clemens Rom., writing just after Domitian's time, associates as sufferers with St. Peter and St. Paul in his own time πολὺ πλῆθος ἐκλεκτῶν, οἵτινες πολλὰς αἰκίας καὶ βασάνους διὰ ζῆλον παθόντες ὑποδείγμα κάλλιστον ἐγένοντο ἐν ἡμῖν. Ad. Cor. 6.
[2] Euseb. Hist. iv. 25; Tertull. Apol. 5.
[3] In Tertullian's words, "debellator Christianorum," Apol. 5.
[4] Thus a late Protestant writer, Schmidt (Geschichte der Denk- und Glaubensfreiheit, p. 165), remarks of the condition of Christians, "Vollkommen gewiss ist, dass unter Domitian eine neue Drangperiode für die Christen begann, die sich in Verfolgungen, in Hinrichtungen, und Verbannungen äusserte. (Dio. 67, 14, und die Ausleger.) Damals soll auch der Apostel Johannes nach Pathmos verwiesen worden sein. Erst Nerva lüftete wiederum diesen Druck, indem er den Verhafteten die Freiheit gab, und die Verbannten zurückberief. (Dio. 68, 1.) Es war dies aber doch nur als eine Amnestie, als ein Gnadenact anzusehen, nicht als eine Anerkennung der Unsträflichkeit, wie das schwankende Verhalten des nicht minder hochherzigen und freisinnigen Trajan zur Genüge darthut."

three centuries would have been changed. As it was, every one, in becoming a Christian, accepted the chance that he might thereby be called upon to forfeit the possession of wife, children, goods, every civil right, and life itself.

The end of the reign of the first Antonine, in the year 161, furnishes us with a second fitting epoch at which we may estimate the growth and position in the empire of the Christian Faith.

During the sixty years which elapse from the death of St. John to the accession of Marcus, the Roman empire is ruled by three sovereigns, who have each left a fair name and a considerable renown behind them, and who, compared with most of those who preceded or who followed them, may almost be termed great. Trajan by his military successes raised to the highest point the credit of the Roman arms, by his moderation in civil government effaced the remembrance of Domitian's cruelties, and gave the Romans perhaps as much liberty as they could bear. His successor Hadrian, joining great energy, administrative ability, and moderation of his own to the fear and respect for the Roman name, which the powerful arm of Trajan had spread around, was able at once to exercise his army with unwearied discipline, and to maintain the empire at its full tide of power in honourable peace, while Antoninus crowned the forty years of equable and generally just government— bestowed on the Roman world by Trajan and Hadrian —with a further happy period of more than half that length, wherein the glory of the empire may be said to have culminated. Imperial Rome never saw again such a day of power, or such a prospect of security, as when Antoninus celebrated the secular games at the completion of nine hundred years; and for ages afterwards his name carried respect, and men looked back on his reign as on an ideal period of happiness for those whom he ruled.

One of the most competent observers of our time has marked the last ten years of the reign of Pius as the period at which the independent development of Græco-Roman heathenism terminated, when it had exhausted all the forms of its own inward life, since the Neoplatonic philosophy which is the only striking product of intelligence that arises afterwards, is manifestly due to the antagonism with Christianity, and is no pure offspring of the heathen spirit.[1] From this time forth Christian influences become unmistakable in their action upon heathen thought and society. This, then, affords another reason why we should endeavour to trace the progress and extension which the Church had reached at this point.

Now a contemporary of Antoninus declares that in his time, that is, about the year 150, there was no race of men, either barbarians or Greeks, none even of Scythian nomads roaming in waggons, or of pastoral tribes dwelling in tents, among whom prayers and thanksgivings were not offered to the Father and Creator of the universe in the name of the crucified Jesus.[2] Thus, in a hundred and twenty years the Church had outstripped the limits of the empire. The germ which in the time of St. John was rooted in the chief cities, had spread out thence and increased, taking more and more possession of the soil in all directions. Still we must consider the Chris-

---

[1] Döllinger, *Heidenthum und Judenthum*, Vorwort, iv.
[2] Justin, *Dialog. with Tryphon*, 117. Tertullian, fifty years later, *adv. Judæos*, 7, goes beyond this.

tian Church in each place of its occupation as a small minority of the people: nor is there any reason to doubt the statement made by Celsus, that at the period when he wrote, the middle of the second century, the Christian faith counted few of the educated, distinguished, and rich among its adherents;[1] for Origen, in replying to him, alleges no specific example to the contrary. Yet, here too we must consider the justice of Origen's remark,[2] that these classes are everywhere few in proportion to the poor and ignorant, and that Christianity being the daystar arising on every soul, took of all classes alike. So much, then, as to the Church's material extension: now as to its internal growth.

As this period opens, comrades of the Apostles still abound in the churches. We know of several instances wherein such persons hold eminent rank. At Rome, St. Clement is the third successor of St. Peter; and St. Irenæus,[3] recording him as such eighty years afterwards, specially notes that he had seen and lived with Apostles, and had their preaching still sounding in his ears, and their tradition before his eyes; at Antioch, St. Ignatius, second after the same St. Peter; in the See of Jerusalem, St. Simeon, the brother of James, still survives; at Smyrna, St. John's disciple Polycarp is bishop. Many more such St. Irenæus declares that there were. This would prepare us for the strength with which the principle of authority and tradition was held, and show how

[1] Kellner, *Hellenismus und Christenthum*, p. 85.
[2] Origen *cont. Cels.* i. 27.
[3] Lib. iii. 3. Ἔτι ἔναυλον τὸ κήρυγμα τῶν ἀποστόλων καὶ τὴν παράδοσιν πρὸ ὀφθαλμῶν ἔχων, οὐ μόνος, ἔτι γὰρ πολλοὶ ἐπελείποντο τότε ἀπὸ τῶν ἀποστόλων δεδιδαγμένοι : where τὸ κήρυγμα and ἡ παράδοσις τῶν ἀποστόλων indicate the whole body of truth which they communicated to the Church, whether written or unwritten.

completely the sense of a spiritual government, of
cohesion, and continuity of moral life, and of a common doctrine and teaching, the foundation of these,
prevailed. But we are not left to inferences, we have
the clearest statements on this point about fifteen
years after St. John's death. It has been remarked
above how in the Apocalypse our Lord Himself,
addressing the seven churches, gathers them up in
their bishops, and speaks of them each collectively
as of one person. In the year 116, as is supposed,
Ignatius still after forty-eight years bishop of one
of the three great mother churches, all of them Sees
of Peter, and types and models of church government,
whence missions went forth, and the layers of apostolic
teaching were propagated, in his seven extant epistles
conveys the same idea as that presented by those
divine words which St. John had heard in vision, and
was commanded to record, but with much greater
detail. As he is being led to martyrdom, in the
long transit between Antioch and Rome, he pours
forth the earnestness of one under sentence of death,
glowing at the prospect of shedding his blood for
Christ, and being for ever united with Him. These
letters remain as a sample of numberless conversations
held with the deputations which came to meet him
on his way, mingling their tears at his approaching
passion with their exultation in his triumph. They
are of one tissue throughout. Ignatius dwells with
incessant repetition upon union with God and with
Christ through obedience to the hierarchy of bishops,
priests, and deacons, by maintenance of one faith, in
one body of the Church, which is wherever Christ
is.[1] Let us take one instance from his letter to the

[1] St. Ign. *ad Smyrn.* 1 and 8.

Ephesians. After saying that he had "received their whole multitude in the person of Onesimus, their bishop," he continues: "It is, then, fitting that you should by all means glorify Jesus Christ who has glorified you; that by a uniform obedience you may be perfectly joined together in the same mind and in the same judgment, and may all speak alike concerning everything, and that being subject to the bishop and the presbytery, you may be altogether sanctified. I am not giving you commands, as if I were any one; for, though I am in bonds for His name, I am not yet perfected in Jesus Christ. For now I begin to learn, and I speak to you as my fellow-disciples, for I had need to be encouraged by you in faith, exhortation, endurance, long-suffering. But since charity suffers me not to be silent to you, I have taken on me to exhort you to run together all with the mind of God. For Jesus Christ, your inseparable life, is the mind of the Father, as also the bishops, placed in their several limits, are the mind of Jesus Christ. Therefore you should run together with the bishop's mind, as indeed you do. So then in your concord and harmonious charity Jesus Christ is sung. And each several one of you makes up the chorus; so that all being harmonious in concord, you take up the melody in unity, and sing with one voice through Jesus Christ to the Father, that He may hear you, and perceive by your good works that you are members of His Son. It is good for you then to be in blameless unity, that you may always have fellowship with God." And then he adds: "For if I in a short time have had such familiarity with your bishop, and that not human, but spiritual, how much more should I think you happy, who are so fused with him as the Church with Jesus Christ, and as Jesus Christ with the Father, that all things may be accordant in unity."[1]

This is an incidental passage out of a very short letter, in which the speaker is addressing practical exhortations to the people of a great church, founded by St. Paul about sixty years before, dwelt in by St. John up to about fifteen years of the time at which he was speaking. We should not in such a writing expect St. Ignatius to speak with the scientific correctness of a theologian, nor is he completely exhibiting his subject in a treatise; yet here, as it were at the first moment after the Apostles have left the earth, we have a picture of the Church as a world-wide institution, held together by a divine unity, which has its seat in the Person of Christ as the mind of the Father. It is a composite unity which is contemplated in the image of a harp with its strings pouring forth one song—the song of Christ—to the Father. It is a unity wide as the earth; for the bishops, placed in their several limits, constitute the mind of Christ, who is Himself the Father's mind. It is the unity of the diocese, for it is summed up in the bishop: but it is the unity likewise of the whole Church, for the bishops are linked together in One whose mind they collectively represent, and that One is He from whose Person their authority radiates; in whom, as he says in this same letter, "the old kingdom was being destroyed, God appearing in the form of a man, unto the newness of eternal life."[2] Again, it is not merely an outward unity of government, but an inward unity of the truth held in common, and also held as given by authority: not truth, as a result of the curiosity of

[1] St. Ignat. *ad Ephes.* i.-iv.   [2] *Ad Ephes.* xix.

the human intellect, rather truth, as a participation in the mind of Christ. Thus the Catholic unity of government is at the same time a unity of belief, which two unities are not, in fact, separable, for their principle is one in the Person of Christ, in respect of whom submission to the Ruler is one and the same thing with belief in the truth revealed by Him, who is King no less than Word, Word no less than King.

We have, then, here the principle of authority and tradition as seated in the hierarchy, and at the same time the whole order and unity of the Church as girdling the world by its chain of the Episcopate, and as possessing the truth and exhibiting it in its quality of an institution. It is before us and at work in its succession of men, in its sacraments which they administer,[1] in its truth which is imparted by the one and delivered by the other. It is no vague congeries of opinions held by individuals with the diversity of individuals, but a body strongly organised, and possessing an imperishable life, the life of its Author. And we have all this mentioned as fulfilled at the distance of one life from our Lord's ascension, while indeed his kinsman and elder in age, St. Simeon, is still bishop of Jerusalem, and mentioned by one of whom a beautiful though insufficiently-grounded legend says that he was that child whom our Lord had called and placed before His disciples as the model of those who should enter into His kingdom. He was at least so near in time to Christ that this could be said of him. He is

---

[1] Another point on which St. Ignatius dwells repeatedly is the receiving the flesh of Christ in the Eucharist: thus he says of the heterodox, *ad Smyrn.* 6: " They abstain from the Eucharist and prayer, because they do not confess that the Eucharist is that flesh of our Saviour Jesus Christ which suffered for our sins, which in His goodness the Father raised."

the bishop of Antioch; he is on his way to be thrown to the beasts in the Colosseum at Rome;[1] he is welcomed on his way by church after church, and he sees and describes the bishops, in their several boundaries through the earth, as each maintaining the mind of Christ in the unity of His Body.

Such is the Church merely stated as a fact towards the beginning of the second century.

And the trial which in these sixty years the Church was going through was well calculated to test her constitution. It is against the spread of false doctrine that St. Ignatius in these epistles so constantly appeals to the unity of the faithful among each other.[2] He warns them to use only Christian nourishment, and to abstain from strange food, which is heresy.[3] The Church was then continually receiving into her bosom converts at all ages of life, some from the Jews, many more from the Gentiles; among these, therefore, minds brought up in Jewish prejudices, and others which had run havoc in eastern superstitions and systems of philosophy. In the course of these sixty years she probably multiplied many times over in number; and the multiplication was rather by the accession of adults than by the education of children born of Christian parents. The Church was composed of a small minority of the general population scattered at wide intervals over an immense empire; and, so far from being assisted by the civil power, was under con-

---

[1] He says, ad Rom. ii.: "Ὅτι τὸν ἐπίσκοπον Συρίας ὁ Θεὸς κατηξίωσεν εὑρεθῆναι εἰς δύσιν ἀπὸ ἀνατολῆς μεταπεμψάμενος. Merivale, Hist. c. lxv. p. 150, note 1, says, "We are at a loss to account for the bishop being sent to suffer martyrdom at Rome." This passage in the epistle confirms the acts of martyrdom. It was the wish of Trajan to make a great example, and the Bishop of Rome, St. Alexander, was at this time in prison, and shortly afterwards martyred.

[2] See Epist. ad Magnes. 13.   [3] Ad Trall. 6.

stant persecution from it. Whatever force her spiritual government possessed could be exercised only by the voluntary submission of her members. Let us weigh the fact that, under these circumstances, a number of heresies arose. Some were of Jewish, some of Gentile parentage. But we are not here concerned either with their cause or with their matter: we dwell at present only on the fact of their existence. In number they were many; in character most diverse; they arose and flourished in different places. Hardly anywhere was the Church free from them. Let us ask only one question here: By what power were they resisted? The human mind had then the fullest liberty of action in Christians. It was by a free choice—a choice accompanied with danger, and persisted in through suffering—that men became Christians. The liberty which men exercised in becoming Christians they could use further against Christian doctrine, by innovating; by mixing it up with other doctrines, with which, perhaps, their minds had been familiar before their conversion; by developing it after their own fashion. The desire of fame, the self-will of genius, the mere luxury of thought, would offer a continual temptation to such a course. Many, from one motive or another, fell into it. The question which we repeat is, What power prevented the one Church from breaking up under this process of free thought into fragments? These heresies began even while the Apostles were teaching. St. Peter, St. Paul, and St. John speak strongly against them. They swarm in the two generations succeeding the death of St. John. How is it that, at the accession of Marcus Aurelius, Christians having passed the limits of the empire, and being found so far as the wandering tribes of the north, there is still one Church, surrounded, indeed, by a multitude of sects, differing from her and from each other, but herself distinguished and unmistakable among them all? We think the epistles of St. Ignatius furnish us with a reply to this question. As we have seen above, he views the Church in each place as a community closely bound together under a spiritual government which is summed up in the bishop, while the bishops in their several dioceses are as closely linked to each other, and all form one society, wherein is Jesus Christ. And these two truths are not separated from each other, but the unity of the part is deduced from the unity of the whole, and is subordinate to it. See, first, with what force he states the unity of the diocese.[1] "Avoid divisions, as the beginning of evils. Follow all of you the bishop as Jesus Christ the Father, and the presbytery as the Apostles, and reverence the deacons as God's command. Let no one without the bishop do aught of what appertains to the Church. Let that be deemed a sure Eucharist which is under the bishop, or under him who has the bishop's authority for it. Wherever the bishop appears, there let the multitude (of the faithful) be." But this strict unity of the diocese is derived from that of the whole Church; for he adds as the reason of the foregoing, "just as wherever Jesus Christ is, there is the Catholic Church."[2] This is the first time when the word "catholic" is known to be used, and it is applied to

---

[1] *Ad Smyrn.* viii.
[2] Compare with this expression of St. Ignatius that of the Church of Polycarp, fifty years later, describing how after his martyrdom, σὺν τοῖς Ἀποστόλοις καὶ πᾶσι δικαίοις ἀγαλλιώμενος, δοξάζει τὸν Θεὸν καὶ Πατέρα, καὶ εὐλογεῖ τὸν Κύριον ἡμῶν καὶ κυβερνήτην τῶν [ψυχῶν τε καὶ] σωμάτων ἡμῶν, καὶ ποιμένα τῆς κατὰ τὴν οἰκουμένην καθολικῆς ἐκκλησίας. *Acta Polycarpi*, xix.; Ruinart, p. 45.

the Church as its distinctive character, to convey the two attributes of unity and universality, in connection with the Person of Christ, exactly as it has been used, an unique term for an unique object, from that day to this. St. Ignatius further views the Church in each place as having one faith; and not only so, but the same faith in every place; one faith at Antioch, one at Rome, one at every city between them, beyond them, around them. Here, then, is a double unity, inward and outward. As the double unity of body and spirit makes the man, so the double unity of government and of faith makes the Church. As neither mind nor body alone makes the man, so neither faith nor government alone makes the Church, but the coherence of both. The Incarnation is the joining a human soul and body with the Person of the Divine Word; after which pattern the Church, which is His special creation, is the joining of one faith and one government in a moral unity. It is by this force, by the same hierarchy everywhere guarding the same faith, by the principle of authority and tradition planted in this one living organisation throughout the earth, that the attacks of heresy are everywhere resisted. What St. Paul[1] lays down in dogma, history exhibits in fact. A hundred years after his words are written, the Church has stretched her limits beyond the empire, has multiplied incessantly, has been attacked by a crowd of heresies striving to adulterate her doctrine, and has cast them out of her by this double unity of her faith and her government, and so is one Body and one Spirit. Her victory lies not in being without heresies, but in standing among them as a contrast and a condemnation.

[1] Ephes. iv. 4-16.

FIRST AGE OF THE MARTYR CHURCH 171

The solidity of internal organisation, and the definiteness of the One Faith which animated it, kept pace with the material increase of numbers. At the expiration of this period it is probable that among all the contemporaries and immediate disciples of the Apostles one only of high rank remained, that Polycarp, joint-hearer with Ignatius of St. John, and to whom in his passage the martyr addressed a letter as well as to his Church; whose own letter written at the time of the martyr's combat, and commemorating the wonderful patience therein shown forth, is yet extant. But in the meantime in every Church the transmission of authoritative teaching passed to those who had grown up themselves in the bishop's council—his presbytery, which Ignatius loved to represent as being to each bishop what the Council of Apostles was to their Lord. And as the death of Apostles themselves had caused no break in this living chain, so the gradual departure of their immediate disciples was made up by the careful handing-on of the same deposit, lodged securely in its receptacle, the succession of men, which carried on the teaching office of the Church.[1]

In the meantime, what was the attitude of the empire to the Christian Faith under Trajan, Hadrian, and Antoninus Pius? Domitian's reign had ended in active persecution, to which Nerva had put a stop on his accession.[2] But though Domitian's edicts had been

---

[1] See Eusebius, *Hist.* iii. 37, who speaks exactly in this sense; and an important passage in Döllinger, *Kallistus und Hippolytus*, 338–343, on the force of the word πρεσβύτερος, as Ecclesiæ Doctor, one particularly charged with the magisterium veritatis. See also Hagemann, *die Römische Kirche*, pp. 607, 608.

[2] Tillemont, *Ecc. Hist.* ii. 132.

reversed, like those of Nero, one of the most ancient laws of the Roman empire forbade the worship of any god not approved by the Senate.[1] This, as we have said above, was the sword perpetually suspended over the heads of Christians, without any fresh action on the part of the emperors. By virtue of this, even when it was forbidden to accuse them, yet if they were brought before justice it was forbidden to absolve them.[2] And even senators,[3] if accused, were not exempt from this severity. We find Trajan acting upon this law in the year 111, when Pliny, being governor of Bithynia, brings expressly the case of the Christians before him. And the terms in which he does this show at once the temper of the Roman magistrate in such cases and the state of the law.

"I have never been present," he says, "at the trials of Christians, and therefore do not know either the nature of their crime, or the degree of the punishment, or how far examination should go. And I have been in great hesitation whether age made any difference, or the tender should not be distinguished from the strong; whether they should be pardoned upon repentance, or, when once a man had been a Christian, ceasing to be so should not profit him; or whether the mere profession without any crime, or whether the crimes involved in the profession should be punished. In the meantime, with regard to those brought before me as Christians, my practice has been this:

---

[1] Tertull., *Apol.* 5, and Euseb., *Hist.* v. 21, assert the existence of this law. [2] Tillemont, *E. H.* ii. 182, 183.
[3] See the singular instance given by Euseb. v. 21, in the reign of Commodus. An informer accuses Apollonius of being a Christian, at a time when the imperial laws made such an accusation a capital offence. The accuser is put to death; but Apollonius, who is supposed to have been a senator, having made a brilliant defence before the Senate, suffers martyrdom.

I asked them if they were Christians. If they admitted it, I put the question a second and a third time, threatening them with death. If they persevered, I ordered them to be led away to execution.[1] For whatever it was which they were confessing, I had no doubt that stubbornness and inflexible obstinacy deserved punishment. There were others of a like infatuation, but as being Roman citizens I directed them to be sent to the city. Presently the crime spreading, from being under prosecution, as is usual, several incidents happened. An anonymous delation was sent in to me, containing the names of many who say that they are not Christians, nor ever were. As at my instance they invoked the gods, and made supplication with frankincense and wine to your image, which I had ordered for that purpose to be brought, together with the statues of the gods, and as moreover they reviled Christ, none of which things, it is said, real Christians can be induced to do, I thought they might be let go. Others, being accused by a witness, admitted that they were Christians, and presently said that they had been, some three years before, some many years, and some even twenty, but were no longer. All venerated your image and the statues of the gods, and reviled Christ. But they alleged that

---

[1] Duci jussi (confer Acts xii. 19, ἐκέλευσεν ἀπαχθῆναι). The extreme brevity with which the most urbane, kind-hearted, and accomplished of Roman gentlemen, as Mr. Merivale conceives him, describes himself as having ordered a number of men and women to be put to death for the profession of Christianity, is remarkable and significant. Compare it with the bearing of his friend Trajan to St. Ignatius below. As soon as the saint's confession of "bearing the Crucified in his heart" is specific, Trajan without a word of remark orders his execution. The "duci jussi" of Pliny and Trajan's manner in sentencing perfectly correspond and bear witness to each other's authenticity. So later the like tone used by Junius Rusticus, prefect of the city under Marcus Aurelius, to Justin Martyr, as will be seen further on.

the utmost of their fault or error was this: They were accustomed to meet before dawn on a stated day, and addressed themselves in a certain form to Christ as to a god, binding themselves by oath not to any crime, but not to commit theft, robbery, adultery, the breaking of their word, or the refusal to restore a deposit. After this they were wont to separate, and then reassemble to take a common and harmless meal. This, however, they had ceased to do from the publication of my edict forbidding, according to your command, private assemblies. I therefore thought it the more necessary to examine into the truth by putting to the torture two female slaves, who were said to be deaconesses among them. I found, however, nothing but a perverse and immoderate superstition, and so, adjourning the inquiry, I took refuge in consulting you. For the matter seemed to me worthy of consultation, especially on account of the number of those involved in danger. For many of every age, every rank, both sexes, have been already, and will be endangered, since the contagion of this superstition has spread not only through cities but through villages and country. And it seems capable of being arrested and corrected. At all events there is proof that the almost deserted temples have begun to be frequented, and the long intermitted rites renewed, and victims for sacrifice are found ready, whereof hitherto there were very few purchasers. Hence it is easy to form an opinion what a number of persons may be reclaimed if pardon be allowed."[1]

To which the emperor replies: "You have pursued the right course, my dear Secundus, in examining the causes of those delated to you as Christians. For no

[1] Pliny, *Ep.* x. 97, chiefly Melmoth's translation.

universal rule can be laid down in a certain formula. They are not to be searched after; but if brought before you and convicted, they must be punished. Yet with this condition, that whoever denies himself to be a Christian, and makes it plain in fact, that is, by supplicating our gods, though he has been in past time suspected, shall obtain pardon for his repentance. But anonymous delations must not be admitted for any accusation. This is at once the very worst precedent, and unworthy of our time."

A great difficulty in tracing the progress of the Christian Faith in these three centuries is that we possess nothing like a consecutive secular or religious history of them. We only catch glimpses of what passes at intervals. Incidents are recorded which, like a flash of lightning, suddenly reveal the landscape and the actors. Such an incident is this letter of Pliny to Trajan, and his reply. We have here the governor of a province before whom Christians are brought as criminals. We find that if they acknowledge their faith and persist in professing it, he sentences them to death. But embarrassed by their numbers, and perplexed also by the fact, that, save the profession of their faith, there appeared nothing criminal in their conduct, he refers the matter to the emperor. The emperor, no Nero or Domitian, but one renowned for his justice and moderation, praises what the governor has done; pronounces that Christians as such are guilty of a capital crime, and that Pliny was right in so interpreting the existing law; that, however, it is not desirable to seek them out; that even when brought before justice they are to be released if they deny their faith, but that if they persist in it, they are to be punished with death.

Here, then, is the law—an original law of Rome before the Christian Faith began—under which the martyrs suffered at different times, throughout every province and city, without anything which could be called a general persecution on the part of the emperor directed to the destruction of the whole religion. This perpetual liability to punishment might be called into action anywhere in the empire for various causes. The first in time, and one of the most constant, was the enmity of the Jews; then the dislike of the heathens to Christians and their ways, which was further sharpened by local calamities or distress irritating the mind of the population, or by the jealousy of the heathen priests and worshippers at the desertion of their temples. Then, again, there was the ascription to Christian godlessness, as it was called, that is their refusal to acknowledge the Roman gods, of famines, pestilences, and whatever troubled the popular mind. To these we must add a copious harvest of private grudges, and a host of calumnies, which seem now almost grotesque, but then found wide belief. But it was the existence of such a law as this, acted on by Pliny before he referred to the emperor, and confirmed by Trajan, that gave force and effect to all these causes of persecution. And it would appear that when Christians were brought before the magistrates, as guilty of the Christian Faith, it was not in the magistrates' power to decline hearing the case, any more than any other accusation of sacrilege or treason, for it had been determined that Christians were not a mere Jewish sect, and therefore could not in security worship one God, as the Jews did. It was a ruled point that their worship was unauthorised.

The practice of Trajan himself was in accordance with his answer to Pliny.

The very ancient and genuine Acts of the Martyrdom of St. Ignatius state that having struggled with difficulty through the persecution of Domitian, he had carefully governed his church of Antioch, grieving only that he had not yet reached the rank of a perfect disciple by the sacrifice of his life, for he considered that the confession which is made by martyrdom brings into closer union with the Lord. Trajan then having come to the East, full of exultation at the victories which he had gained, and considering that the subjugation of the Christians was all that was wanting to the perfect obedience of his empire, began to threaten them with the alternative of sacrifice or death. Then Ignatius fearing for his church caused himself to be brought before the emperor, and being in the presence was thus addressed by him : " Who are you, evil spirit, who are zealous to transgress our commands, besides persuading others to come to an evil end ? " Ignatius replied, " No one calls the bearer of God an evil spirit, for the demons fly away from the servants of God. But if you mean that I am a trouble to these, and so call me evil to them, I admit it, for having Christ my Heavenly King, I continually dissolve their plots." Trajan said, " Who is a bearer of God ? " Ignatius replied, " He who has Christ in his breast." Trajan said, " We then appear to you not to have gods in our minds, whom we use to help us against our enemies." Ignatius answered, "You in your error call gods the demons of the nations, for there is one God who made the heaven, the earth, and the sea, and all that is in them ; and one Christ Jesus, the only-begotten Son of God, of whose friendship may I partake." Trajan said, "You mean Him who was crucified under Pontius Pilate?" Ignatius answered, "Him who crucifies my sin, with its inventor, and condemns all the error and the malice of the demons under the feet of those who carry Him in their heart." Trajan said, "You then carry the Crucified in your heart?" Ignatius replied, "Yes; for it is written, I will dwell in them, and walk in them." Trajan gave sentence: "It is our command that Ignatius, who says that he carries the Crucified One about in him, be taken in chains by soldiers to the great Rome to become the food of wild beasts, for the pleasure of the people." The holy martyr, when he heard this sentence, cried out with joy, "I thank thee, O Lord, who hast thought me worthy to be honoured with perfect charity towards Thee, and to be bound in iron chains together with Thy Apostle Paul."[1]

So, with great eagerness and joy, through desire of his passion, having commended his church to God, he set out on that long journey, "fighting, as he says, with wild beasts all the way from Syria to Rome, over land and sea, by day and by night," a captive under sentence of death, in the hands of soldiers, but receiving at each city a deputation from the bishop and people, who came forth to honour him as their champion. And he has but one anxiety, expressed again and again in that fervent letter to the Roman Christians, that they should not by their prayers intercept his martyrdom. "I entreat you not to be untimely kind to me. Suffer me to be the food of the beasts, since by them I may enjoy God. I am God's grain: let me be ground by their teeth, that I may be found the pure bread of Christ:"[2] and then, presently, "I do not command

---

[1] *Acts of St. Ignatius*, Ruinart, pp. 8, 9   [2] *Ad Rom.* iv.

you, as Peter and Paul;" thus giving an incidental but most powerful witness of the special relation which those Apostles bore to the Roman Church.

And it may be remarked that while he has words of honour, praise, and affection for the other five churches which he addresses, yet in speaking of Rome his heart overflows with emotion. Upon this church he pours out epithet upon epithet, as "the beloved and enlightened in the will of Him who has willed all things which are according to the charity of Jesus Christ our God," whose people are "united to every command of His in flesh and spirit, filled undividedly with the grace of God, and thoroughly cleansed from every spot of foreign doctrine." She is not only the Church "which presides in the fortress of Roman power," but likewise, "worthy of God, and of all honour and blessing and praise, worthy to receive that which she wishes, chaste, bearing the name of Christ and the name of the Father, and presiding over charity." What is the meaning of this last phrase? As she presides in the fortress of Roman power, so she presides over charity. May we thus interpret the mind of the martyr? God in His Triune Being is Charity; the Holy Spirit, the ineffable embrace of the Father and His Image, their Love, or Delight, or Joy, or Blessedness, or whatever human name we may dare to give to what is most divine, is charity: by charity God became man; charity is the individual Christian's state; charity makes men one in the Body of the God-man; charity is the condition of angels and men in the great kingdom to come, the God-formed kingdom. Thus charity is the distinctive mark of the Christian religion, that from which it springs, that which it is, that which it points to, and in which it will be consummated. When, then, St. Ignatius said of the Roman Church, using the same word in one sentence,[1] that as she presided over the country of the Romans, so she presided over charity, does he not with equal delicacy and emphasis indicate her primacy? she presides over that in which the Unity of the Church consists, in which its truth, its grace, and its holiness coinhere.

The desire of the martyr was accomplished: he reached Rome on the last day of the great games, and was thrown in the Colosseum before the beasts, which, according to his repeated prayers, so entirely devoured him that only the greater bones remained. These, says the contemporary account, "a priceless treasure," were carried back to Antioch. Somewhat less than three hundred years afterwards St. Chrysostom, preaching on his day in his city, thus speaks of him : " It was a divine benefaction to bring him back again to us, and to distribute the martyr to the cities: —Rome received his dripping blood, but you are honoured with his relics.—From that time he enriches your city, and like a perpetual treasure, drawn upon every day and never failing, gives his bounty to all. So this happy Ignatius, blessing all that come to him, sends them home full of confidence, bold resolution, and fortitude. Not, then, to-day only but every day go to him, reaping spiritual fruits from him. For, indeed, he who comes hither with faith may reap great goods. Not the bodies only, but the very coffins of the saints are full of spiritual grace. For if in the case of Eliseus this happened, and the dead man who touched his bier broke through the bonds of death, how much more now, when grace is more abundant,

---

[1] 'Εκκλησίᾳ—ἥτις καὶ προκάθηται ἐν τόπῳ χωρίου 'Ρωμαίων—προκαθημένη τῆς ἀγάπης.

and the energy of the Spirit fuller?—So, I beseech
you, if any one be in despondency, in sickness, in the
depth of sin, in any circumstance of life, to come here
with faith, and he will put off all these."[1]

Before St. Ignatius reached that completion of his
faith to which he aspired, he was cheered with the
account that his sacrifice had produced its effect, and
peace had been restored to his church, with the completeness of its body.[2]

Now in all this—in Pliny's conduct as governor, in
his reference to Trajan, in the emperor's reply, in his
treatment of St. Ignatius, and in the restoration of
peace afterwards—there is, we conceive, a very exact
sample of what the position of Christians was in
Trajan's time. His answer ruled the question of
Roman law for the following two hundred years. It
declared the profession of Christianity to be illicit and
a capital offence; but to call this law into action, or
to leave it suspended as a threat over the heads of
Christians, was a matter of expedience. When the
latter took place, the churches were said to be at
peace; when the former, a persecution was said to
rage; but at any time and place an individual might
suffer; while on the other hand a persecution directed
to root out the whole Christian name was not yet
thought of.

And this state of things seems to continue through
Hadrian's principate. In his first year, Alexander,

---

[1] St. Chrysostom, *Hom. on St. Ignatius*, tom. ii. 600.
[2] St. Ignatius in the 11th sec. of his epistle to the Smyrnæans requests them to send a messenger to congratulate the church of Antioch,
ὅτι εἰρηνεύουσιν, καὶ ἀπέλαβον τὸ ἴδιον μέγαθος, ἀποκατεστάθη αὐτοῖς τὸ
ἴδιον σωματεῖον. The word σωματεῖον, or corpusculum, indicates the
completeness of a diocesan church with its bishop, the whole Church
being σῶμα Χριστοῦ, as St. Ignatius had said in sec. 1 of the same
epistle, ἐν ἑνὶ σώματι τῆς ἐκκλησίας αὐτοῦ.

fifth successor of St. Peter at Rome, having been imprisoned under Trajan, suffers martyrdom. It would seem as if the same hand had struck down about the same time the heads of the two great churches of Rome and Antioch, the first and the third in rank, and perhaps ordered the execution of the bishop of Antioch at Rome, with that of the Roman bishop, in order to give greater force to the example.[1] Many other martyrs at Rome and in the north of Italy are found at this time. It is not at all necessary to suppose the personal action of Hadrian in these. After this he was engaged during fifteen years in those splendid progresses, in which he examined personally every part of his vast empire, from its northern frontier between Carlisle and Newcastle to the Euphrates. While he was so engaged, the governors of the various provinces would apply the existing law in the cases brought before them. He would have had to interfere, and that with the whole weight of the imperial arm, if he wished to check the course of the law. We have, however, recorded the most interesting fact, that when he was at Athens in the year 126, Christians for the first time approached a Roman emperor with a public defence of their doctrines, and a persecution is said to have been stopped by the apologies which Quadratus and Aristides presented to him. Perhaps the rescript to Minucius Fundanus, proconsul of the province of Asia, which Justin has preserved, was a result of this. It runs thus: "I have received the letter written to me by your predecessor, the noble

[1] There is some doubt about the time of St. Ignatius's martyrdom. We suppose it to be at the end of Trajan's reign. St. Alexander I. is reckoned a martyr, and placed in the canon of the Mass next after St. Ignatius, which seems to indicate a connection between their deaths.

Serenius Granianus. And indeed it seems to me that that affair should not be passed by without a diligent examination, in order that Christians may not be disturbed, nor an occasion of false accusation be opened to informers. If, then, the provincials can present themselves openly with their petitions against Christians, so as to answer before the tribunal, let them do that, and not betake themselves to mere requests and outcries. It would be much more just that you should take cognisance of the matter, if any one be willing to accuse. If, then, any one denounce them, and prove that they are doing anything illegal, sentence them according to the gravity of the crime. But, by Hercules, if it be a mere false accusation, punish the informer according to its importance."

Here would seem to be a considerable modification of Trajan's rescript. The profession of Christianity is not taken by itself as a capital offence. Proof must be given that something illegal has been committed. So far it approaches to an act of toleration. It plainly discourages anonymous and malicious attacks. But on the other hand it was not difficult to show that Christians did commit something illegal. Any real accuser bringing them before the tribunal could prove by their own testimony that they declared the gods worshipped by the Romans to be demons, while they refused to swear by the emperor's genius. Thus, favourable as this decree was to them, it fell far short of declaring their religion to be allowable.

And the same emperor who could thus write, whose curiosity made him acquainted with all the religious sects of his empire, whose temper, as an exceedingly accomplished man, having the widest experience of men and things, and ruling an empire of the most diverse races with the most various religions, led him to an eclectic indifference, and so far toleration of all, yet showed by his personal conduct at a later period of his life how he would treat the profession of the Christian Faith if it thwarted a ruling desire. When, after fifteen years of incessant travel, study, and observation, he returned to Rome, and had enclosed at Tivoli a space of eight miles in circumference, adorned with copies of the most beautiful temples in his wide dominion, he offered sacrifices and consulted the gods as to the duration of his work; but he received for answer that the gods who inhabited their images were tormented by the prayers which the widow Symphorosa and her seven sons offered daily to their God.[1] If she and her children would sacrifice, they promised to grant all his demands. Upon this Hadrian ordered Symphorosa and her seven sons to be brought before him, and endeavoured by kind words to bring them to sacrifice. She replied, "It was for not consenting to what you ask that my husband Gætulius and his brother Amantius, both tribunes in your army, suffered various tortures, and, like generous champions, overcame your demons by a glorious death. If their death was shameful before men, it was honourable in the sight of the angels, and now they are crowned with immortal light. They live in heaven, and follow everywhere the King who reigns there, covered with glory by the trophies they

[1] So the persecution of Diocletian is said to have arisen from Apollo declaring that the just who were upon the earth prevented him from uttering true oracles ; and a like answer was received by Julian the Apostate at Antioch, where the relics of St. Babylas had been translated by Gallus to Daphne, near a celebrated temple of Apollo. Here Julian, offering in vain a great number of sacrifices to the demon, was at length informed that the body of the saint condemned him to silence, and ordered the Christians to remove it. St. Chrys. tom. ii. 560.

gained in dying for Him." Hadrian, stung by this reply, could not contain himself, but said: "Either sacrifice this instant to the immortal gods, or I will myself sacrifice you with your children to these gods whom you despise." "And how should I be so happy," said Symphorosa, "as to be worthy with my children to be sacrificed to my God?" "I tell you," said Hadrian, "I will have you sacrifice to my gods." "Your gods," replied she, "cannot receive me in sacrifice. I am not a victim for them; but if you order me to be burnt for the name of Christ my God, know that the fire which consumes me will only increase their punishment." "Choose, I tell you," said the emperor; "sacrifice or die." "You think, doubtless, to frighten me," rejoined Symphorosa; "but I desire to be at rest with my husband, whom you put to death for the name of Christ." Then the emperor ordered her to be taken before the temple of Hercules, to be struck in the face, and hung up by her hair. But finding that these torments only served to strengthen her in the faith, he had her thrown into the Anio. Her brother Eugenius, being one of the chief men at Tibur, drew her body from the water, and buried her in the suburbs of the town.

The next day Hadrian ordered the seven sons of Symphorosa to be brought before him. And, seeing that neither his threats nor his promises, nor the exhibition of the most fearful punishments, could shake their constancy, nor induce them to sacrifice to idols, he caused seven poles to be planted round the temple of Hercules, on which they were raised by pulleys. Then Crescentius, the eldest, had his throat cut; Julian, the second, was run through the breast; Nemesius was struck in the heart; Primitivus in the stomach; Justin in the back; Stactæus in the side; while the youngest, Eugenius, was cleft to the middle.

The day following the death of these brethren Hadrian came to the temple and ordered their bodies to be removed, and to be cast into a deep hole. The priests and sacrificers of the temple called this spot the place of the Seven Executed. Their blood stopped the persecution, which was only rekindled eighteen months afterwards.[1]

As the rescript to Minucius Fundanus did not prevent the emperor from thus acting, neither was it an obstacle to such an incident as this occurring in any part of the empire.

That it was so likewise in the principate of his successor, of all down to this period the most tranquil and the least persecuting, we have strong and clear evidence in the earliest of the extant apologies, that of Justin Martyr, presented to the emperor Antoninus Pius about the year 150. He who would breathe the atmosphere in which the early Christians lived will find it in this work of a distinguished convert from heathen philosophy, which is the more interesting as being composed at a moment when the empire seems to have reached its highest point, and the ruler of it was its most moderate spirit. We may cite a few passages bearing on the condition of Christians.

"To the Emperor Titus Ælius Adrianus Antoninus Pius Augustus Cæsar, and to his son Verissimus the Philosopher, and to Lucius the Philosopher, son of Cæsar by birth, and of Pius by adoption, the lover of learning, and to the sacred Senate, and to all the Roman people, in behalf of those out of every race of men who are unjustly hated and persecuted, I, that

[1] *Acts of St. Symphorosa*, from Dom Ruinart, pp. 23, 24.

am one of such myself, Justin, son of Priscus, and grandson of Baccheius, natives of Flavia Neapolis, of Palestine, in Syria, offer this address and supplication.

"Reason dictates that those who are really pious and philosophers should love and honour truth alone, declining to follow the opinions of the ancients if they be corrupt. For right reason not only forbids us to assent to those who are unjust either in practice or in principle, but commands the lover of truth to choose that which is just in word and deed in every way, even before his own life, and with death threatening him. Now you hear yourselves called on all sides Pious, Philosophers, Guardians of Justice, and Lovers of Learning; but, whether you be such in truth, the event will show. For we have come before you, not to flatter you in this address, nor to gain your favour, but to demand of you to pass judgment according to strict and well-weighed reason, not influenced by prejudice, nor by the desire of pleasing superstitious men, nor by inconsiderate passion, nor by the long prevalence of an evil report, in giving a sentence which would turn against yourselves. For, as to us, we are fully persuaded that we can suffer no injury from any one, unless we be found guilty of some wickedness, or proved to be bad men; and, as to you, kill us you may, but hurt us you cannot.[1]

"We ask, then, that the actions of those who are accused before you may be examined, that he who is convicted may be punished as an evil-doer, but not as a Christian. And, if any one appears to be innocent, that he may be dismissed as a Christian who has done no evil. For we do not require you to punish our accusers: they are sufficiently recompensed by their

[1] Justin. 1 *Apol.* 1, 2.

own malice, and their ignorance of what is good. Moreover, bear in mind that it is for your sakes that we thus speak, since it is in our power to deny when we are questioned. But we choose not to live by falsehood.[1]

"And you, when you hear that we are expecting a kingdom, rashly conceive that we mean a human one, whereas we speak of that with God, as is evident even from those who are under examination by you confessing that they are Christians, whilst they know that death is the penalty of the confession. For if we expected a human kingdom, we should deny in order to obtain our expectations; but, since our hopes are not of the present, we do not regard those who kill us, knowing that death is an inevitable debt to all.[2]

"We adore God only, but in all other matters joyfully serve you, confessing that you are kings and rulers, and praying that you may be found to possess, together with your royal power, a sound and discerning mind. If, however, notwithstanding that we thus pray and openly lay everything before you, you treat us with contempt, we shall receive no injury; believing, or rather, being convinced, that every one, if his deeds shall so deserve, shall receive the punishment of eternal fire, and that an account will be required of him in proportion to the powers which he has received from God, as Christ has declared in those words, 'To whomsoever God has given much, of him shall be much required.'[3]

"Though death be the penalty to those who teach or even who confess the name of Christ, we everywhere accept it, and teach it. And if you as enemies meet these words, you can do no more, as we have already

[1] Sec. 7. [2] Sec. 11. [3] Sec. 17.

said, than kill us, which brings no hurt to us, but to you, and to all who hate unjustly, and do not repent, the chastisement of eternal fire."[1]

And his concluding words are: "If now what we have said appears to be reasonable and true, honour it accordingly; but if folly, despise it as foolish; yet pass not sentence of death against those as enemies, who have done no evil. For we tell you beforehand that you will not escape the future judgment of God, if you continue in injustice, and we shall cry, Let the will of God be done."[2]

Such then is the testimony of a Christian as to the way in which the confessors of his religion were treated; and it is corroborated by that of the heathen philosopher Celsus, who writes his books against Christianity about this time, and imputes the secrecy practised by Christians in their teaching and their actions to their attempts to escape the punishment of death hanging over their heads.[3] And again having put into the mouth of Christians the remark, that if they blaspheme or strike a statue of Jupiter or Apollo, these gods cannot defend themselves, he subjoins: "Do you not, then, see that your own demon is not merely blasphemed but expelled from every land and sea, while you, his consecrated image,[4] are chained, and led away to prison, and crucified; and the demon, or as you call him, the Son of God, gives you no protection." And in another place, comparing Christians with Jews, to whom God had made so many promises:

[1] Sec. 45.
[2] Sec. 68. Chevallier's translation, sometimes altered.
[3] Origen c. Cels. i. 3. Περὶ τοῦ κρύφα Χριστιανοὺς τὰ ἀρέσκοντα αὐτοῖς ποιεῖν καὶ διδάσκειν εἰπών, καὶ ὅτι οὐ μάτην τοῦτο ποιοῦσιν, ἅτε διωθούμενοι τὴν ἐπηρτημένην αὐτοῖς δίκην τοῦ θανάτου.
[4] Σὲ τὸν καθωσιωμένον ὥσπερ ἄγαλμα αὐτῷ δήσας ἀπάγει καὶ ἀνασκολοπίζει. viii. 38, 39.

"See," he says, "what good has He done to them and to you? To them, instead of being lords of all the earth, not a clod of soil or a hearth remains;[1] while of you, if any one still wanders about in hiding, yet justice pursues him with the doom of death."

However, we know that at this time at least the bold words of Justin drew down no punishment from Antoninus, and a rescript of this emperor, dated about two years after the presentation of this first apology, has been preserved, which is more favourable to Christians than that of Hadrian. It is addressed to that province of Asia which contained so many flourishing Christian churches, and which accordingly was so bitter against them. They had written to complain of the Christians, and to accuse them as the cause of the earthquakes which had happened. The emperor replies: "It was my belief that the gods would take care that such men as you describe should not escape. For much rather would they, if they could, punish such as will not worship them. Now these men you are annoying, and accusing their opinion as atheistical, and charging them with sundry other things which we cannot prove. Yet it would be serviceable to them to seem to meet their death for such an accusation; and they surpass you in giving up their lives rather than comply with what you call upon them to do. But as to the earthquakes which have happened or are happening now, it is not reasonable that you should mention them, you who lose heart when they take place, comparing your conduct with theirs, who have more confidence than you towards God. And you indeed in such a time seem to have no knowledge of

---

[1] viii. 69; by this we should judge that the work of Celsus appeared not long after the punishment of the Jews by Hadrian.

the gods, and neglect the temples, and know nothing of worshipping God; whence it is that you are jealous of those who do worship him, and that you persecute them to death. Respecting such men various other rulers of provinces wrote to my divine father, and his reply was, not to trouble such men, except they appear to be contriving something against the Roman empire. Many too have referred to me about such, and my reply was in agreement to my father's decision. Now if any one has an accusation to bring against such a one as such, let the accused be released from the charge, even though· he appear to be such, and let the accuser be punished."[1]

Here we reach the highest point of toleration which Christians received in the first 130 years. Instead of Trajan's somewhat reluctant order to punish Christians as Christians, when once convicted, instead of Hadrian's decision that something contrary to Roman law must be proved against them, Antoninus, while quoting the latter, goes far beyond it, and lays down that as Christians they were blameless, and were only to be punished in case some hostility to the Roman empire could be proved in their conduct. Moreover, their accuser was to be punished. And this rescript being repeated to several places, amounted to an assurance that Christians should be left in tranquillity during the principate of Pius.

Putting ourselves into the position of a Roman emperor at this middle of the second century, let us endeavour to form a notion of what Christianity would appear to him. In the first place, he who had all the threads of Roman organisation gathered in his hand, would certainly recognise it as a sect spread through-

[1] Attached to Justin's first Apology.

out the empire, the Jewish origin of which was known to him, and the author as one crucified by order of a Roman governor under Tiberius.[1] Yet he would hardly distinguish accurately the Church from the different heresies which everywhere sprang up around it, holding more or less of its doctrines and mixing them up with corruptions and abuses.[2] And it would scarcely appear to him as a power in the State, either from its numbers or the influence of the people belonging to it; yet on the other hand it would appear as something not inconsiderable in either of these respects. Moreover, we may suppose it would come before him as a *belief*, and not as an *institution*. It had as yet no public churches.[3] A heathen would say of Christians at this time that they had no temples, altars, or statues;[4] no ceremonial worship, for he could not, as a heathen, get admittance to Christian rites, which moreover were carried on in private houses, and carefully concealed. The emperor would be well aware that Christians had rulers of their own;[5] it was as such that Trajan had fixed upon the bishop third in rank among Christian communities for punishment the most severe and degrading, to be thrown as food for wild beasts, for the pleasure of the people. But nevertheless, the internal constitution of the Church would lie hidden from him: the link which bound together the bishops of the various local communities,

---

[1] See Trajan's remark to St. Ignatius: "You mean Him that was crucified under Pontius Pilate."

[2] See the curious letter of Hadrian about the Alexandrians, in which the Christians spoken of are probably heretics.

[3] They are first mentioned at Rome in the reign of Alexander Severus.

[4] See Origen *c. Cels.* vii. 62.

[5] See Trajan's question, "Who art thou who art zealous to transgress our commands, besides persuading others to come to an evil end?"

and so formed the Catholicism of the Church, would be quite invisible to all outside. Jealous as Trajan was of secret societies, so that he could hardly tolerate a guild of firemen in a provincial town, he had no suspicion of a society which had become even in his time conterminous with his empire, and was bound together not only by the profession of one faith, but by the living links of one government. Nor, fifty years later, could Antoninus have had any such knowledge. The persecution which we have seen arose from simpler causes; the faith of Christians in one God who had made heaven and earth, and in one Son of God who had become Man and redeemed them, and with this, and indeed as part of this, their summary rejection, their utter intolerance of all the heathen gods; this it was that had drawn down the Roman sword upon them in answer to the popular cry,[1] "Away with the godless!" And again, their standing aloof from heathen life, their refusal to take part in heathen festivals, their withdrawal as far as possible from all public concerns: this was part of the hatred of the human race imputed to them, which made them objects of suspicion first, and then, when any special excitement arose, of persecution. These peculiarities also, and the secrecy with which their worship was necessarily conducted because it was not allowed, had led to calumnies concerning them, imputing the grossest immorality as well as cruelty.

The apologies of Quadratus, Aristides, and Justin, were probably the first connected revelation of the Christian doctrines which the emperor could have; but these would be very far from conveying to him the character of the Church as an institution. They

[1] Αἶρε τοὺς ἀθέους.

were intended to obviate the persecutions arising from the causes above described, to show the purity of Christian morality, the reasonableness of Christian belief, the fidelity of Christian sentiment to the imperial rule as established by a Divine Providence. They were not in the least intended to lay before him the Christian Church as a whole. Thus Justin, replying to the accusation that they were expecting a kingdom, says, "You rashly conceive that we mean a human one, whereas we speak of that with God." We may then, it seems, conclude with certainty that Antoninus was only partially aware of what Christianity was. That discipline of the secret, which was itself the result of persecution—of the Christian Faith having to make itself a place in a world utterly opposed to it,— became at once its protection, and the cause of further persecution; of persecution, in so far as it put Christians under general suspicion, but of protection, inasmuch as it covered with a veil that complete moral revolution to which the Christian Faith was tending from the first, and towards which it was continually advancing. Could Trajan have foreseen what was apparent under Constantine, his treatment of Christians would have had no forbearance or hesitation in it, his blows no intermission or doubtfulness. As it is, up to the time we are now considering, there are no traces of a general persecution against the Christian name organised by the emperor as head of the State. There are numberless local and individual persecutions starting up in this city and in that, and arising from the fundamental contrariety of Christian belief to the existing heathen worship and the ordinary heathen life. Such we have and no more. And so a great host of martyrs in single combat won their crown.

But the emperor did not set himself to destroy a unity which he did not see.

Now as to the character in Christians which their condition in these hundred and thirty years tended to produce, we can form a clear conclusion. Of the relative proportion of actual martyrs to the whole mass of believers, we can indeed have no accurate notion; but it is plain that all were liable to suffering as Christians in every various degree up to that ultimate point of witnessing by death. Thus the acceptance of the Christian Faith itself involved at least the spirit of confession, if not that of martyrdom. A man lived for years, perhaps a whole generation, with the prospect of suffering, which it may be never came, or came as the crown of a long period in which heroic virtues had been called forth. Thus St. Ignatius had been more than forty years bishop of Antioch, and had carried his church hardly through the bad times of Domitian, when he gained at last what he deemed perfect union with his Lord, by being ground under the teeth of lions, as "the pure bread of God." What is here expressed with so sublime a confidence by one actual martyr, must have made the tissue of Christian life in general. Those early disciples of the cross put in the cross their victory. The habitual danger which hung about their life must have scared away the timid, the insincere, the half-hearted. Yet alternations of peace rapidly succeeded times of suffering. Throughout these hundred and thirty years there is no long-continued even local persecution. Breathing-times of comparative tranquillity come, wherein Christians can grow, propagate, and mature for the conflict which may at any time arise. Thus while the opposition made to the infant faith is quite sufficient to have destroyed an untrue religion, born of earth or human device, to have scattered and eradicated its professors, it was precisely what would favour the real advance of a faith rooted upon a suffering God, and in which suffering with Him was made the means of union with Him.

And here we halt at the accession of Marcus Aurelius, as a middle point between the day of Pentecost and the time of Constantine.

LECTURE XI

THE SECOND AGE OF THE MARTYR CHURCH

"Magnus ab integro sæculorum nascitur ordo.
Jam nova progenies cœlo demittitur alto.
Ingredere, O magnos, aderit jam tempus, honores,
Cara Dei soboles, magnum Jovis incrementum."

I. THERE is a moment in the history of the Roman empire when it comes before us with the most imposing grandeur. The imperial rule has been definitively accepted by that proud old aristocracy under which the city of the seven hills was built up from a robber fortress to be the centre of a world-wide confederation; while on their side the nations all round the Mediterranean bow with an almost voluntary homage before the sceptre of their queen. If the north be still untameable, it has learnt to dread the talons of the Roman eagle, and cowers murmuring in its forests and morasses; if the Parthian still shoot as he flies from the western Cæsar's hosts, he has at least expiated in the ruin of Ctesiphon the capture of Crassus and the dishonour of Mark Antony. But far more than this. On the Cæsar in his undisputed greatness has dawned the real sublimity of the task which Providence had assigned to him; to mould, that is, under one rule of equal beneficence the many tongues and many nations which a course of conquest, often the most unjust, had brought to own his sway. And this point of time is when after the great warrior Trajan comes Hadrian the man of culture; in whom seems implanted the most restless curiosity, carrying him with the speed of a soldier and the power of a prince over every climate from Carlisle to Alexandria, from Morocco to Armenia, in order that he may see in each the good of which so many varying races of men are capable, and use them all for his grand design. To him Rome is still the head; but he has learnt to esteem at their due value the members of her great body. The first fifteen years of his reign are almost entirely spent away from Rome, in those truly imperial progresses wherein the master of this mighty realm, when he would relieve himself of his helmet, walks like the simple legionary,[1] bareheaded in front of his soldiers, under the suns of the south, examining, wherever he comes, the whole civil and military organisation, promoting the capable and censuring the unworthy, scattering benefits with unsparing hand. York has known him as a protecting genius; Athens blends his name with that of her own Theseus as a second founder; wayward Alexandria exalts him, at least for the time, as a granter of privileges; the extreme north and utmost south acknowledge alike the unsparing zeal and majestic presence of their ruler. At that moment Rome is still Roman. While the Augustan discipline still animates her legions, the sense of the subordination of the military power to the civil spirit of a free State is not wholly lost; her proconsuls and præfects have passed out of those plundering magnates, who replenished in the tyranny of a year or two from a drained province the treasures they had squandered in a life of corruption at Rome, into the

---

[1] The Roman legionary, if he wished to lay aside his helmet, was only allowed to go bareheaded.

orderly and yet dignified magistrates accountable to the Republic's life-president[1] for their high delegated power. Perhaps the world had never yet seen anything at once so great and so beneficent as the government of Hadrian. But one thing was wanting to the many-tongued and many-tempered peoples ruled by him, that they should of their own will accept the worship of one God, and so the matchless empire receive the only true principle of coherence and permanence in the common possession of one religon. And the thoughtful student of history can hardly restrain himself from indulging his fancy as to what might then have been the result, and into how great a structure provinces worthy of being kingdoms might then have grown by the process of an unbroken civilisation instinct with the principles of the pure Christian Faith. Then the northern flood of barbarism and the eastern tempest of a false religion, which together were to break up the fabric of a thousand years, might have been beaten back from its boundaries, and from them the messengers of light have so penetrated the world in all directions that the advance of the truth should not have been impeded by any great civil destruction, but the nations of Europe have developed themselves from their Roman cradle by a continuous growth, in which there had been no ages of conquest, violence, and confusion, no relapse into chaos, no struggle back into an intricate and yet imperfect order, but the serene advance from dawn to day.

So, however, it was not to be. The time of proba-

---

[1] Champagny remarks, that the emperors were never in the mind of the Romans *sovereigns* in the modern acceptation of the word, but *life-presidents* with absolute power.

tion in the reigns of Hadrian and Antoninus Pius, wherein a sort of toleration had seemed to be allowed to Christians, passed away, and the beginning of a far different destiny broke upon the empire. With the accession of Marcus Aurelius the great old enemies, the North and the East, awoke from their trance in fresh vigour. A Parthian war of four years, a German war of twelve, with pestilence, earthquakes, and famines through a large part of the empire, try to the utmost the vigour and temper of one of the most upright sovereigns known to heathenism. Marcus Aurelius meets both enemies with equal courage and ability, but he dies prematurely, and leaves the rule, carried so temperately by four great sovereigns successively adopted to empire at mature age, in the untried hands of the heir of his blood, a youth of nineteen, born in the purple. In this at least the great Roman was wanting both to Stoic greatness and to Roman duty. And it was a fatal error. During thirteen years this son of the most virtuous heathen shows himself the most vicious of tyrants. At a single bound Rome passes from a ruler more just than Trajan to a ruler more abandoned than Nero; and in the palace of Marcus Aurelius endures an emperor who has a double harem of three hundred victims;[1] who spares the blood of no senator, and respects the worth of no officer.

When a revolution, similar to that which swept away Domitian, has removed Commodus, the Roman world is not so fortunate as to find a second Trajan to take his place. Three great officers who command in Syria, Illyricum, and Britain, contend for the prize, and when victory has determined in favour of Septi-

[1] Champagny, *Les Antonins*, iii. 311.

mius Severus, he rules for eighteen years with a force and capacity which may indeed be compared with Trajan's, but with a deceit and remorseless severity all his own. At one time forty senators are slaughtered for the crime of having looked with favour upon that pretender to the empire who did not succeed. Nor is this a passing cruelty, but the fixed spirit of his reign. The sway of the sword is openly proclaimed. That the army is everything is not only acted on, but laid down as a guiding principle of state to his children. The unbroken discipline of her legionaries had hitherto indeed proved the salvation of the State; but this Septimius fatally tampers with, and in so doing sows the seeds of future anarchy and dissolution.

His death in 211 places the empire in the hands of a youth of twenty-three, all but born in the purple, like Commodus, and his rival in tyranny and dissoluteness of every kind. Caracalla is endured for six years, and being killed by a plot in the camp, is succeeded by his murderer Macrinus. He again, after a year, gives place to a Syrian boy of fourteen, who took at his accession the honoured name of Marcus Aurelius Antoninus, but is known to posterity as Heliogabalus. Once more during a space of four years the crimes of Commodus and Caracalla are repeated, or even exceeded. Indeed in these years from 218 to 222 the story of shame and degradation reaches its lowest point. But the soldiers of the prætorian camp themselves rise against Heliogabalus, massacre him with his mother, and place on the throne his cousin Alexander Severus, at the age of fourteen. Now Alexander has for his mother Mammæa, if not a Christian, at least a hearer of Origen, who gives her son from his earliest youth a virtuous education, who surrounds him on the perilous height of the Roman throne with the arms of her affection and her practical wisdom. Alexander rules for thirteen years, a period equal to that of Commodus, and little less than that of Nero. Younger than both at his accession and his death, his reign offers the most striking contrast to theirs. Of all heathen rulers he stands forth as the most blameless. It is a reign which, after the obscene domination of Commodus, Caracalla, and Heliogabalus, with the savagery between them of Septimius Severus immediately preceding it, seems like a romance of goodness. Simple and admirable in his private life, he rivals Marcus Aurelius in his zeal for the administration of justice, for the choice of good governors, for devotion to the public service; and, happier than Marcus Aurelius, on his name rests no stain of persecution. "He suffered the Christians to be,"[1] are the emphatic words of his biographer; concerning which it has been well remarked that little as this seems to say, it had been said of no one of his predecessors, though several had not persecuted the Church.[2] And therefore this expression must mean that he left them in an entire liberty as to religion. It is indeed the exact contradiction of what, thirty years before, Tertullian had stated respecting the law in the time of Septimius Severus; for one of his complaints in pleading for Christians was, "your harsh sentence 'that we are not allowed to exist,' is an open appeal to brute force."[3]

---

[1] "Christianos esse passus est." Lampridius.
[2] Tillemont, *Hist. Ecc.* iii. 250.
[3] *Apolog.* iv. "Jampridem, cum dure definitis dicendo, non licet esse vos, et hoc sine ullo retractatu humaniore describitis, vim profitemini et iniquam ex arce dominationem, si ideo negatis licere quia vultis, non quia debuit non licere."

Alexander Severus, the darling of his people, perished by the hands of some treacherous soldiers suborned by his successor Maximin; and with him ends this period of seventy-four years, which we will consider together, in order to estimate the progress of the Christian Faith. A time of more remarkable contrasts in rulers cannot be found. It begins with Marcus Aurelius, and it ends with Alexander Severus, the two most virtuous of heathen princes; between them it contains Commodus, Caracalla, and Heliogabalus, the three generally reputed the most vicious; while the definitive course which the history of the empire took is given to it by another, Septimius Severus, of great abilities and mixed character, who gained the empire as a successful soldier, and was true to his origin in that he established the ultimate victory of pure force over every restriction of a civil constitution: an African unsparing of blood, who sat on the throne of Augustus, and worked out the problem of government which the founder of the empire had started by preparing the result of Diocletian.

The rule of Commodus and his successors fully revealed the fatal truth, that the five princes who from the accession of Nerva had governed as if they were really responsible to the senate, had only been a fortunate chance; that this time of prosperity rested upon no legal limitation of rights between those things wont to exist only in severance,[1] the sovereign's power and the subject's freedom; that it was no result of a constitution which had grown up under a mutual sense of benefit arising from authority exercised conscien-

---

[1] "Res olim dissociabiles, principatum et libertatem." Tacit. *Agric.* 3.

tiously, and obedience cordially rendered. The age which Tacitus[1] at its commencement had called "most blessed" was indeed over, and as soon as the second Antonine left the scene, a state of things ensued in which tyranny and cruelty were as unchecked as under Nero or Domitian at their worst. It became evident that all had depended on the sovereign's personal character. From Marcus to Commodus the leap was instantaneous; and so, again, afterwards the short-lived serenity and order of Alexander's rule passed at his death into a confusion lasting for more than forty years, which threatened to break up the very existence of the empire.

But in Rome from the accession of Commodus in 180 to the death of Heliogabalus in 222 we find a profound corruption of morals, an excess of cruelty, and a disregard of civil rights, which could scarcely be exceeded. Tacitus, at the beginning of Trajan's reign, burst forth into indignation at the thought that it had cost Rusticus and Senecio their lives, in Domitian's time, to have praised Thrasea and Helvidius Priscus, and that their very writings had been publicly burned, as if that fire could extinguish the voice of the Roman people, the liberty of the senate, and the conscience of mankind. "Truly great," he cried, "was the specimen of patient endurance which we exhibited."[2] What words, then, would he have found to express the degradation of servile spirit in that self-same city a hundred years later, when Plautianus, the favourite minister of Septimius Severus, at the marriage of his daughter with Caracalla, caused a hundred persons of good family, some of them already fathers,

---

[1] "Primo statim beatissimi sæculi ortu." *Ibid.*
[2] *Agricola,* 2.

secretly to be made eunuchs, in order that they might serve as chamberlains to the imperial bride.[1] Or to take another example; as Quintillus, one of the chiefs of the senate, both by birth and by the employments which he had held, a man of advanced years and living retired in the country, was seized in order to be put to death, he declared that his only surprise was that he had been suffered to live so long, and that he had made every preparation for his burial. A third incident will show both the sort of crimes for which men were punished, the protection given by the law to the individual, and the spirit and temper of the senate. It had condemned Apronianus, proconsul of Asia, without giving him a hearing, because his nurse had dreamt that he was one day to reign, concerning which he was reported to have consulted a magician. Now, in reading the informations laid against him, it was found that a witness deposed that during the consultation some senator who was bald had stretched out his head to listen. Upon this all the bald senators, even those who had never gone to the house of Apronianus, began to tremble, while the rest put their hands to their heads to make sure that they had still their hair. However, a certain Marcellinus fell under special suspicion, whereupon he demanded that the witness should be brought in, who could not fail to recognise him if guilty. The witness looked round upon them all for a long time without saying a word, until upon a sign that a certain senator made him, he declared it was Marcellinus, who forthwith was hurried out of the senate to be beheaded, before Severus was even informed of it. As he went to execution he

---

[1] See Döllinger, *Hippolytus und Kallistus*, p. 187, who quotes from Dio Cassius, l. 75, p. 1267, Reimar. This was A.D. 203.

met four of his children, to whom he said that his greatest grief was to leave them living after him in so miserable a time.[1] It was not without reason that Tertullian at this very moment encouraged the martyrs to be constant, with the reflection that there was no one who might not, for the cause of man, be made to suffer whatever nature would most shrink from suffering in the cause of God. "The times we live in are proofs," he cried, "of this. How many and how great are the instances we have seen, in which no height of birth, no degree of rank, no personal dignity, no time of life, have saved men from coming to the most unexpected end, for some man's cause, either at his own hands, if they stood against him, or if for him, by the hands of his adversaries."[2]

It was a time at which the extremes of reckless cruelty, of profuse luxury, of shameless dissoluteness, met together; in which women were forbidden by an express law to expose themselves on the arena as gladiators; in which, when the Emperor Severus would legislate against adultery, a memorial was handed to him with the names of three thousand persons whom his law would touch.[3] Such was the character of the time which followed at once on the empire's golden age; the time in which the Church of God was lengthening her cords and strengthening her stakes, and building up her divine polity amid the worthlessness of the world's greatest empire, and the instability of all earthly things.

II. In the last review which we took of her material progress we said that to the eye of Pius Antoninus

---

[1] Tillemont, *Life of Severus*, iii. 75, from Dio : A.D. 206.
[2] Tertullian, *ad Martyres*, 4 : about A.D. 196.
[3] Dio, quoted by Döllinger, *ut supra*.

she would not yet appear from her multitude as a power in the State. But before the end of the seventy-four years which we are here considering as one period, it was otherwise. Already in the reign of Commodus, Eusebius states that the word of salvation was bringing to the worship of the one God men out of every race, so that in Rome itself many distinguished for wealth and rank embraced it with their whole families.[1] A few years later, when Tertullian writes his apology, he makes the heathen complain "that the State is overrun with us, that Christians are found in the country, in forts, in islands; that every sex and age and condition and rank come over to them."[2] And again, "We are of yesterday, and have already filled every place you have, your cities, islands, forts, boroughs, councils, your very camps, tribes, corporations, the palace, senate, and forum. Your temples only we leave you. For what war should we not be equal, we who are so ready to be slaughtered, if our religion did not command us rather to suffer death than to inflict it?" Elsewhere he speaks of Christians as "so great a multitude of men as to be almost the majority in every city." Now make whatsoever allowance we will for Tertullian's vehemence, such statements, laid before adversaries, if they had not a great amount of truth in them, would bring ridicule on his cause rather than strengthen it. Tertullian besides wrote at the time of the general persecution set on foot by Septimius Severus against the Christian Faith, which itself was a proof of what importance it had assumed. We may perhaps put the first twenty years of the third century as the

---

[1] Euseb. *Hist.* v. 21.
[2] Tertullian, *Apol.* i. 37; *ad Scap.* 2.

point at which, having passed through the period when it was embraced by individuals with a several choice, it was become the faith of families, and one step only remained, that it should become the faith of nations.[1]

Let us consider a moment the mode of its increase. It was twofold. The plant of which a root was fixed by the Apostles and their successors in each of the cities of the empire grew, gathering to itself in every place the better minds of heathenism, and exercising from the beginning a marked attraction upon the more religious sex and upon the most down-trodden portion of society; women were ever won to it by the purity which its doctrines inculcated, slaves by its tender charity: it gave a moral emancipation to both. If we possessed a continuous and detailed history of the Christian Faith in any one city, say Rome, or Alexandria, or Antioch, or Ephesus, or Carthage, or Corinth, for the first three centuries, what a wonderful exhibition of spiritual power and material weakness it would offer! By fixing the mind on Christianity as merely one object, as an abstraction, we lose in large part the sense of the moral force to which its propagation bears witness. It was in each city a community,[2] which had its centre and representative in its Bishop, which had its worship, discipline, and rule of life presided over by him; its presbytery, diaconate, and deaconesses; its sisterhoods and works of charity, spiritual and temporal: a complete government and a complete society held together by purely spiritual

---

[1] De Rossi, *Archeol. Christiana*, 1866, p. 33, makes this estimate.
[2] From a passage in the account of the Martyrs of Lyons, A.D. 177 (Euseb. *Hist.* v. 1, p. 201, l. 3), it appears that the word "Church" was only given to a mother or cathedral church by writers of that time.

bonds, which the State sometimes ignored, not unfrequently persecuted, but never favoured. Such was the grain of mustard-seed, from north to south, from east to west, in presence of the political Roman, the sensitive and lettered Greek, the sensuous African, the volatile and disputatious Alexandrian, the corrupt Antiochene. It had one sort of population to deal with at Rome, quite another in the capital of Egypt, a third at Ephesus, which belonged to the great goddess Diana, and the statue which had fallen down from heaven, a fourth at Carthage, where the hot Numidian blood came in contact with the civilisation of Rome, a fifth at Corinth, the mistress of all art and luxury. And so on. Now in each and all of these cities and a hundred others the divine plant met with various soils and temperatures; but in them all it grew. It had its distinct experiences, encountering many a withering heat and many a stormy blast, and watered full oft with blood, but in them all the seed, dropped so imperceptibly that the mightiest and most jealous of empires was unconscious of what was cast into its bosom, became a tree. It was an organic growth of vital power. Christianity, during the ten ages of persecution, is the upspringing of several hundred such communities, distinct as we see here, and as described above by St. Ignatius, but at the same time co-inherent, as we saw in the beginning, and as we shall find presently. As, then, all the cities of the Roman empire had a secular political and social life, and a municipal government of their own, so had the Christian Faith in each of them a corresponding life of spiritual government and inward thought; and if we had the materials to construct the history of this Faith in any one, it would give us a wonderful insight into the course of that prodigious victory over the world which the whole result presents. We cannot do so. The data for it do not exist, and because they do not, we allude here to this first mode of growth made by the Christian Faith.

Its second mode was thus. The Apostolical Churches, as they severally grew, scattered from their bosoms a seed as prolific as their own. They sent out those who founded communities such as their own. Thus the Christian plant was communicated from Rome to all the west. With every decade of years it crept silently over the vast regions of Gaul and Spain, advancing farther west and north. This extension was not a chance springing up of Christians in different localities. It always took place by the founding[1] of sees, with the apostolic authority, after the apostolic model. If the Roman colonia had its rites of inauguration, and was a transcript of the great city, its senate and its forum, so much more the Christian city had its prototype and derived its authority from the great citadel of the Faith, wherein Peter's prerogative was stored up,[2] and whence it had a derivation wider in extent and more ample in character than that of Rome, the natural city. But we will take from another quarter what is as perfect a specimen of this extension as any that can be found. In the great city of Alexandria, the centre of intellectual and commercial life to all the

---

[1] Thus St. Irenæus (iii. 3, 3) speaks of St. Peter and St. Paul as θεμελιώσαντες καὶ οἰκοδομήσαντες the Church of Rome, and of the Church of Ephesus (*ibid.* iv.) as τεθεμελιωμένη ὑπὸ Παύλου.

[2] This St. Innocent states to St. Augustine and the African bishops in 417 as a fact well known to them: "Scientes quid Apostolicæ Sedi, cum omnes hoc loco positi ipsum sequi desideremus Apostolum, debeatur, *a quo ipse episcopatus et tota auctoritas nominis hujus emersit.*" Constant, *Epist. Rom. Pontif.* 888.

East and the whole Geeek name, St. Peter set up the chair of his disciple Mark. There the evangelist taught and there in due time suffered. Dragged by an infuriated populace through the streets he thus gave up his soul. But the plant which he so watered with his blood was of extraordinary vigour. It not only grew amid the intensest intellectual rivalry of Greek and Jew in the capital, but likewise in course of time occupied the whole civil government which obeyed the præfect of Egypt. From Alexandria, Egypt and the Pentapolis of Cyrene derived their Christian faith and government; and so powerful was this bond that the bishop of the capital exercised control over all the bishops of the civil diocese, as it was then termed. He was in power a patriarch long before he had that name, or even the name of archbishop. How great and strict this rule was we may judge from an incident preserved by Photius,[1] which occurred in the very last year of the period we are considering, in 235. Heraclas, bishop of Alexandria, a former pupil of Origen, had inflicted upon that great writer a second expulsion from the Church for his erroneous teaching. Origen on his way to Syria came to the city of Thmuis, where Bishop Ammonius allowed him, in spite of the abovementioned censure of Heraclas, to preach. When Heraclas heard this, he came to Thmuis and deposed Ammonius, and appointed in his stead Philippus as bishop. Afterwards, on the earnest request of the people of the city, he restored Ammonius to the office of bishop, and ordained that he and Philippus should be bishops together. The latter, however, voluntarily gave way to Ammonius, and succeeded him at his

[1] Photius, συναγωγαί καὶ ἀποδείξεις, quoted by Döllinger, *Hippolytus und Kallistus*, pp. 264, 265.

death. Such, ninety years before the Nicene Council, which recognised and approved these powers of the bishop of Alexandria, as being after the model of those exercised by the bishop of Rome,[1] was his authority by the natural force of the hierarchic principle which built up the Church. And so little were these Christian communities, which we have seen so complete in their own organic growth, independent of the bond which held the whole Church together, and of which the authority of the Egyptian primate was itself a derivation.

These, then, were the two modes in which the Christian Faith pursued and attained its orderly increase; as a seed it grew to a plant in each city, and as a plant it ramified, or as Tertullian says, carried "the vine-layer of the faith"[2] from city to city, from province to province. In the meantime the last disciples of the Apostles, those who from the especial veneration with which they were regarded as teachers of the Faith and "second links in the chain of tradition," were termed Presbyters,[3] had died out. St. Polycarp, at the time of his martyrdom in 167, was probably the sole remaining one, though his pupil St. Irenæus had known others. When the latter, upon

---

[1] Can. 6, Concil. Nic. τὰ ἀρχαῖα ἔθη κρατείτω, τὰ ἐν Αἰγύπτῳ καὶ Λιβύῃ καὶ Πενταπόλει, ὥστε τὸν ᾽Αλεξανδρείας ἐπίσκοπον πάντων τούτων ἔχειν τὴν ἐξουσίαν, ἐπειδὴ καὶ τῷ ἐν ῾Ρώμῃ ἐπισκόπῳ τοῦτο σύνηθές ἐστιν. See Hagemann, *die Römische Kirche*, 596-8.

[2] "Traducem fidei et semina doctrinæ." *De Præscrip*. 20.

[3] See Döllinger, *Hipp. u. Kall*, pp. 338-343, for the meaning of this word in the time of St. Irenæus, as carrying with it a special magisterium fidei. "Presbyteros" was added as a title of honour to the name of Bishop. In St. Irenæus the same persons have as Bishops the succession of the Apostles, as Presbyteri "the charisma of the truth." Papias marks the Asiatic Presbyteri as those who had heard of St. John; and Clement of Alex. speaks of Presbyteri who, occupied with the office of teaching, and deeming it diverse from that of composition, did not write. *Eclogæ* xxvii. p. 996.

the martyrdom of St. Pothinus in 177, is raised to the government of the See of Lyons, we may consider that no one survived in possession of that great personal authority which belonged to those who had themselves been taught by Apostles; and so at the third generation from the last of these the Church throughout the world stood without any such support, simply upon that basis of the tradition and teaching of the truth, and of the succession of rulers, on which the Apostles had placed it, to last for ever. Now in this position it had already, throughout the whole course of the second century, been violently assaulted by a family of heresies, which growing upon one root—a natural philosophy confusing the being of God with the world —burst forth into an astonishing variety of outward forms. Gnosticism completely altered and defaced Christian doctrine under each of the four great heads, the Being of God, the Person of Christ, the nature of man, the office and function of the Church. Into the Godhead it introduced a dualism, recognising with the absolute good an absolute evil represented by matter: it denied the reality of the Incarnation; it made the body a principle of evil in man's nature: but we will here limit ourselves to the characteristic and formal principle of the system from which it derived its name, to Gnosis as the means of acquiring divine truth. Now the Christian religion taught that revealed truth was to be attained by the individual through receiving, upon the ground of the divine veracity, those mysterious doctrines superior but not contrary to reason which it unfolded; and that the communication of such doctrines might continue unimpaired and unchanging, it taught that our Lord had established a never-failing authority charged with the execution of this office, and assisted by the perpetual presence of His Spirit with it to the end. But the Gnostics admitted only in the case of the imperfect or natural man that faith was the means for acquiring religious truth ; to the spiritual, the proper Gnostic, gnosis should take the place of faith : for to many a heathen, accustomed to unlimited philosophical speculation, the absolute subjection of the intellect to divine authority, required by the principle of faith, was repugnant. Now this gnosis was in their mind not knowledge grounded upon faith, but either philosophic science, or a supposed intuition of truth, which was not only to replace faith, but the whole moral life, inasmuch as the completion and sanctification of man were to be wrought by it. And thus instead of an external authority the individual reason was set up as the highest standard of religious truth, the issue of which could only be rationalism in belief and sectarianism in practice.

This formal principle of Gnosticism when duly carried out would deny the idea of the Church, its divine institution, its properties and prerogatives. For the Gnostic mode of attaining divine truth, as above stated, contains in it such a denial. Besides this, the Gnostic doctrine that matter was the seat of evil, destroyed the belief that Christ had assumed a body : the Gnostic doctrine that the supreme God could enter into no communion with man made their Æon Christ no member of human society, but a phantom which had enlightened the man Jesus, and then returned back to the "Light-realm." Not being really the Son of God, he could have no Church which was his body : not really redeeming, for sin to the Gnostic had only a physical, not a moral cause, he was but a teacher, and therefore had created no institution to convey grace; which, moreover, was superfluous, for whatever elements of good human nature had were derived from creation and not from redemption. Nor was such an universal institution wanted, since not all men but only the spiritual were capable of being drawn up to the Light-realm. The Gnostic therefore required neither hierarchy nor priesthood, since the soul of this system was the gnosis of the individual. For this a body enjoying infallibility through the assistance of the Holy Ghost was not needed. It was enough for enthusiasts and dreamers to pursue their speculations without any limit to free inquiry, save what themselves chose to impose as the interpretation of such scriptures as they acknowledged, or as the exhibition of a private tradition with which they held themselves to be favoured.

Lastly, the idea of Sacraments, as conveying grace under a covering of sense, would be superfluous to the Gnostic, inasmuch as the spiritual elements in man belong to him by nature, and are not communicated by a Redeemer, and would be repulsive to him because matter is a product of the evil principle, and cannot be the channel of grace from out the Light-realm.[1]

My purpose here has only been to say just so much of Gnosticism as may show how the whole Christian truth was attacked by it, and especially the existence and functions of the Church.

And this may indeed be termed the first heresy in that it struck its roots right up into apostolic times. Irenæus, Eusebius, and Epiphanius account Simon Magus to be its father, and the father of all heresy.

---

[1] I am indebted for the above sketch of Gnosticism mainly to Schwane, *Dogmengeschichte der vornicänischen Zeit*, pp. 648–51.

As such it is not without significance that he encountered the first of the Apostles in Samaria, endeavouring to purchase from him the gifts of grace and miraculous power, and that he likewise afterwards encountered him at Rome. To this the first manifestation of Gnosticism succeed heretical doctrines concerning the Person of our Lord, which sprung out of Judaism; but no sooner are these overcome than Gnosticism in its later forms spreads from Syria and Alexandria over the whole empire, everywhere confronting the Church, seducing her members, and tempting especially speculative minds within her. A mixture itself of Platonic, Philonic, Pythagorean, and Parsic philosophy, affecting to gather the best out of all philosophies and religions, in which it exactly represented the eclectic spirit of its age, arraying itself in the most fantastic garb of imagination, but at the bottom no dubious product of the old heathen pantheism, it set itself to the work, while it assumed Christian names, of confusing and distracting Christian truth. From the beginning of the second century it was the great enemy which beset the Church. It may, then, well represent to us the principle of heresy itself, and as such let us consider on what principles it was met by the Church's teachers.

Now to form a correct notion of the danger to which the Christian people at this time was exposed, we must have before us that it was contained in several hundred communities, each of them forming a complete spiritual society and government. These had arisen under the pressure of such hostility on the part of the empire that it is only in the time of the last emperor during this period, Alexander Severus, that churches are known to have publicly existed at

Rome.[1] For a very long time all meetings of Christians and all celebration of their worship were secret. It is obvious what an absolute freedom of choice on the part of all those who became Christians this fact involved. Nor did that freedom cease when they had been initiated into the new religion. Their fidelity to the Christian faith was all through their subsequent life solicited by the danger in which as Christians they stood. Only a continuous freedom of choice on their part could maintain it. And not only did every temporal interest turn against it, but in the case at least of the more intellectual converts the activity of thought implied in their voluntary acceptance of a new belief served as a material on which the seductions of false teachers might afterwards act, unless it was controlled by an ever-living faith, and penetrated by an active charity. The more these Christian communities multiplied, the more it was to be expected that some of them would yield to the assaults of false teachers. It is in just such a state of things that a great dogmatic treatise was written against Gnosticism by one who stood at only a single remove from the Apostle John, being the disciple of his disciple Polycarp. Irenæus, by birth a native of lesser Asia, enjoyed when young the instructions and intimate friendship of the bishop of Smyrna. In his old age he delighted to remember how Polycarp had described his intercourse with John, and with those who had seen the Lord: how he repeated their discourse, and what he had heard from them respecting the teaching and the miracles of that Word of life whom they had seen with their

[1] Tillemont, *Hist. des Emp.* iii. 281, deduces it from a passage of Origen on St. Matt. tom. iii. p. 857 c.

own eyes. "These things," says Irenæus, "through the mercy of God I then diligently listened to, writing them down not on paper, but on my heart, and by His grace I ruminate upon them perpetually."[1] Later in life he left Smyrna, and settled in Lyons, of which Church he was a presbyter when the terrible persecution of 177 broke out there. Elected thereupon to succeed a martyr as bishop, he crowned an episcopate of twenty-five years with a similar martyrdom. He wrote, as he says, during the episcopate of Eleutherius, who was the twelfth bishop of Rome from Peter, and sat from 177 to 192. After describing at length the Gnostic errors concerning the divine nature, he sets forth in contrast the unity of the truth as declared by the Church in the following words:

"The Church, though she be spread abroad through the whole world unto the ends of the earth, has received from the Apostles and their disciples faith in one God;" and he proceeds to recite her creed, in substance the same as that now held: then he adds, dwelling with emphasis on the very point which I have been noting, the sprinkling about, that is, of distinct communities so widely dispersed, which yet are one in their belief:

"This proclamation and this faith the Church having received, though she be disseminated through the whole world, carefully guards, as the inhabitant of one house, and equally believes these things as having one soul and the same heart, and in exact agreement these things she proclaims and teaches and hands down, as having one mouth. For, though the languages through the world be dissimilar, the power of the tradition is one and the same. Nor have the

[1] *Frag. Epist. ad Florin.* tom. i. p. 340.

churches founded in Germany otherwise believed or otherwise handed down, nor those in Spain, nor in Gaul, nor in the East, nor in Egypt, nor those in the middle of the world. But as the sun, God's creature, in all the world is one and the same, so too the proclamation of the truth shines everywhere, and lights all men that are willing to come to the knowledge of the truth. Nor will he among the Church's rulers who is most powerful in word say other than this, for no one is above his teacher;[1] nor will he that is weak in word diminish the tradition, for the Faith being one and the same, neither he that can say much on it has gathered too much, nor he that can say little is deficient."

Against the Gnostic claim to possess a private tradition, in virtue of which each of them "depraving the rule of the truth was not ashamed to preach himself," he sets forth the one original tradition which the Apostles,[2] only "when they had first been invested with the power of the Holy Ghost coming down on them, and endued with perfect knowledge," delivered to the churches founded by them. "And this tradition of the Apostles, manifested in the whole world, may be seen in every church by all who have the will to see what is true, and we can give the chain of those who by the Apostles were appointed bishops in the churches, and their successors down to our time, who have neither taught nor known any such delirious dream as these imagine. For, had the Apostles known any reserved mysteries, which they taught to the perfect separately and secretly from the rest, assuredly

---

[1] He seems to refer to Matt. x. 24: οὐκ ἔστι μαθητὴς ὑπὲρ τὸν διδάσκαλον.
[2] St. Irenæus, lib. iii. c. 2 ; lib. iii. c. 1.

they would have delivered them to those especially to whom they entrusted the churches themselves. For very perfect and irreprehensible in all respects did they wish those to be whom they left for their own successors,[1] delivering over to them their own office of teaching, by correct conduct on whose part great advantage would accrue, as from their fall the utmost calamity. But since it were very long, in a volume like this, to enumerate the succession of all the churches, we take the church the greatest, the most ancient, and known to all, founded and established at Rome by the two most glorious Apostles Peter and Paul, and pointing out the tradition which it has received from the Apostles, and the faith which it has announced to men, reaching down to us by the succession of its bishops, we confound all those who form societies other than they ought, in any way, whether for the sake of self-fancied doctrines, or through blindness and an evil mind. For, with this church, on account of its superior principate, it is necessary that every church agree, that is, the faithful everywhere (every church) in which by the (faithful) everywhere, the apostolic tradition is preserved.

"The blessed Apostles, then, having founded and built up the Church, committed to Linus the administration of its episcopate. . . . Anencletus succeeds him, from whom in the third place from the Apostles Clemens inherits the episcopate. . . . He is succeeded by Evaristus; Evaristus by Alexander, who is followed by Xystus, sixth from the Apostles. Then Telesphorus, who was gloriously martyred; next Hyginus; then Pius; after whom Anicetus. Soter followed Anicetus;

---

[1] "Quos et successores relinquebant, suum ipsorum locum magisterii tradentes."

and now, in the twelfth degree from the Apostles, Eleutherius holds the place of bishop. By this order and succession the tradition from the Apostles in the Church and the teaching of the truth have come down to us. And this proof is most complete that it is one and the same life-giving Faith which has been preserved in the Church from the Apostles up to this time, and handed down in truth. . . . With such proofs, then, before us, we ought not still to search among others for the truth, which it is easy to take from the Church, since the Apostles most fully committed unto this, as unto a rich storehouse, all which is of the truth, so that every one, whoever will, may draw from it the draught of life. For this is the gate of life: all the rest are thieves and robbers. They must therefore be avoided; but whatever is of the Church we must love with the utmost diligence, and lay hold of the tradition of the truth. For how? if on any small matter question arose, ought we not to recur to the most ancient churches in which the Apostles lived, and take from them on the matter in hand what is certain and plain. And suppose the Apostles had not even left us writings, ought we not to follow that order of tradition which they delivered to those to whom they entrusted the churches? To this order many barbarous nations of believers in Christ assent, having salvation written upon their hearts by the Holy Spirit without paper and ink, and diligently guarding the old tradition."[1]

This capital point of the ever-living teaching office he further dwells on:

"The Faith received in the Church we guard in it, which being always from the Spirit of God, like an

[1] St. Irenæus, lib. iii. c. 3, 4.

admirable deposit in a good vessel, is young itself, and makes young the vessel in which it is. For this office on the part of God [1] is entrusted to the Church, as the breath of life was given to the body, in order that all the members receiving may be quickened, and in this is placed the communication of Christ, that is, the Holy Spirit, the earnest of incorruption, the confirmation of our faith, and the ladder by which we ascend to God. For, says he, in the Church God has placed Apostles, Prophets, Teachers, and all the remaining operation of the Spirit; of whom all those are not partakers who do not run to the Church, but deprive themselves of life by an evil opinion and a still worse conduct. For where the Church is, there also is the Spirit of God: and where the Spirit of God is, there is the Church and all grace: but the Spirit is Truth. Wherefore they who are not partakers of Him are neither nourished unto life from the breasts of the mother, nor receive that most pure fountain which proceeds from the Body of Christ, but dig out for themselves broken cisterns from earthly ditches, and from the filth drink foul water, avoiding the Faith of the Church lest they be brought back, and rejecting the Spirit that they may not be taught. So estranged from the truth they deservedly wallow in every error, tossed about by it, having different opinions on the same subjects at different times, and never holding one firm mind, choosing rather to be sophists of words than disciples of the truth; for they are not founded upon the one rock, but on the sand, which has in it a multitude of pebbles." [2]

And he elsewhere contrasts the certainty within, and the uncertainty without, this teaching power:

[1] "Hoc enim Ecclesiæ creditum est Dei munus." [2] Lib. iii. c. 24.

"The said heretics, then, being blind to the truth, cannot help walking out of the track into one path after another, and hence it is that the vestiges of their doctrine are scattered about without any rule or sequence. Whereas the road of those who are of the Church goes round the whole world, because it possesses a firm tradition from the Apostles, and gives us to see that all have one and the same faith, where all enjoin one and the same God the Father, believe one disposition of the Son of God's incarnation, know the same gift of the Spirit, meditate on the same precepts, guard the same regimen of ecclesiastical rule, await the same advent of the Lord, and support the same salvation of the whole man, body and soul alike. Now the Church's preaching is true and firm, in whom one and the same way of salvation is shown through the whole world. For to her is entrusted the light of God; and hence the wisdom of God, by which He saves all men, 'is sung at her entrance, acts with confidence in her streets, is proclaimed on her walls, and speaks ever in the gates of the city.' For everywhere the Church proclaims the truth: she is the seven-branched candlestick bearing Christ's light."[1]

It has been necessary to give at considerable length the very words of St. Irenæus, because they are stronger and more perspicuous than any summary of them can be, and because they exhibit a complete answer not to this particular heresy only, but to all heresy for ever. Such an answer, coming from one who stood at the second generation from St. John, is of the highest value. Thus he meets the Gnostic principle that divine truth is acquired by the individual through some process of his own mind, which in this particular

[1] Lib. v. c. 20.

case is termed gnosis, but which may bear many other names, by appealing to an external standard, the Rule of Faith in the Church from the beginning, which by its unity points to its origin and lineage from the Apostles and Christ. And this serves to bring out the central idea which rules his whole mind, that "where the Church is, there also is the Spirit of God; and where the Spirit of God is, there is the Church and all grace: but the Spirit is Truth." The deposit of which he spoke is not a dead mass, or lump of ore, requiring only safe custody, but a living Spirit dwelling in the Church, the source within her of unity, truth, and grace, using her teaching office, which is set up in her episcopate, for the drawing out and propagation of the deposit from the double fountain of Tradition and Scripture, for these her teachers as such have a divine gift of truth.[1] It is thus that he expands without altering the doctrine of his teacher Polycarp's fellow-disciple, "Where Jesus Christ is, there is the Catholic Church."[2] And from it he proceeds to what follows necessarily on such a conception, that this Church must have a visible point of unity. As then he appeals to the churches founded by Apostles as the principal centres of living tradition, so before yet one of these churches had fallen into possession of heretics,[3] before yet there was any disagreement between them, he singles out one for its superior principate, on account of which it was necessary for every church to agree with it, which he grounds on its descent from St. Peter and St. Paul, giving every

---

[1] "Qui cum episcopatus successione charisma veritatis certum secundum placitum Patris acceperunt," iv. 26, 2; and 5, "Ubi igitur charismata Domini posita sunt, ibi discere oportet veritatem, apud quos est ea quæ est ab apostolis ecclesiæ successio."

[2] St. Ignatius, quoted above, p. 169.   [3] Schwane, p. 661.

link in the chain of succession during the hundred and ten years which had elapsed between their martyrdom and his own episcopate. He sees an especial prerogative lodged in that church as the means of securing the whole Church's organic unity; and this prerogative is, that it is among churches what St. Peter and St. Paul were among Apostles;[1] as the first general western council expressed it, "in it the Apostles sit daily, and their blood without intermission bears witness to the glory of God."[2]

Thus the conception expressed by Irenæus, with the greatest emphasis and continual repetition, in order to refute heresy, is that all truth and grace are stored up in the one body of the Church; to which his doctrine of the Roman Primacy is as the keystone to the arch. For everything in his view depends on the unity, the intrinsic harmony, of the truth which he is describing as lodged in the episcopate: the means therefore of securing that unity are part of its conception. Accordingly, to see in its due force his statement that every church must agree with the Roman Church, it must not be severed from the context and taken by itself, but viewed in connection with the argument as part of which it stands. If the Church is to speak one truth with one mouth, which is his main idea, she must have an organic provision for such a result, which he places in the necessary agreement of all churches with one: and this is his second idea, subsidiary to the first, and completing it.

Irenæus by birth and education represents in all

---

[1] Hagemann, p. 622.
[2] Letter of the Synod of Arles to Pope Sylvester: "Quoniam recedere a partibus istis minime potuisti, in quibus et Apostoli quotidie sedent, et cruor ipsorum sine intermissione Dei gloriam testatur." Mansi, *Concilia*, ii. 469.

this the witness of the Asiatic churches; as bishop of Lyons, the churches of Gaul.

A few years after Irenæus, Tertullian in a professed treatise against heresy lays down exactly the same principles. With him, too, the main idea is the possession of all truth and grace by the one Body which Christ formed and the Apostles established. This he thus exhibits:

"We must not appeal to the Scriptures, nor try the issue on points on which the victory is either none, or doubtful, or too little doubtful. For though the debate on the Scriptures should not so turn out as to place each party on an equal footing, the order of things requires that that question should be first proposed which is the only one now to be discussed, To whom does the Faith itself belong? Whose are the Scriptures? From whom and through whom, when and to whom, was that discipline by which men become Christians delivered? For wherever the truth of that which is the Christian discipline at once and faith be shown to be, there will be the truth of the Scriptures, of their exposition, and of all Christian traditions. Our Lord Jesus Christ (may He suffer me so to speak for the present), whoever He is, of whatever God the Son, of whatever substance God and Man, of whatever reward the promiser, Himself declared so long as He was on earth, whether to the people openly, or to the disciples apart, what He was, what He had been, what will of the Father He administered, what duty of man He laid down. Of whom He had attached to His own side twelve in chief, the destined teachers of the nations. One of these having fallen off from Him, He bade the other eleven, on His departure to the Father after the resurrection, go and teach the nations, who were to be baptized into the Father, into the Son, and into the Holy Ghost. The Apostles then forthwith, the meaning of their title being the Sent, assuming by lot Matthias as a twelfth into the place of Judas, by the authority of the prophecy in the psalm of David, when they had obtained the promised power of the Holy Ghost for miracles and utterance, first through Judea bore witness to the Faith in Christ Jesus, and established churches, thence proceeding into the world promulgated the same doctrine of the same Faith to the nations, and thereupon founded churches in every city, from which the other churches thenceforth borrowed the vine-layer of the Faith and the seeds of the doctrine, and are daily borrowing them that they may become churches. And for this cause they are themselves also counted apostolical, as being the offspring of apostolical churches. The whole kind must be classed under its original. And thus these churches so many and so great are that one first from the Apostles, whence they all spring. Thus all are the first, and all apostolical, while all being the one prove unity: whilst there is between them communication of peace, and the title of brotherhood, and the token of hospitality.[1] And no other principle rules these rights than the one tradition of the same sacrament."[2]

Here is the summing up of what Irenæus had said with the force, brevity, and incisiveness which characterise Tertullian. Further on he rejects any appeal on the part of heretics to Scripture:

"If the truth be in our possession, as many as

[1] Tertull. *de Præsc.* 19, 20.
[2] The word here stands evidently for the whole body of Christian truth, rites, and discipline, the communication of which was a sacramentum.

walk by the rule which the Church has handed down from the Apostles, the Apostles from Christ, and Christ from God, the reasonableness of our proposition is manifest, which lays down that heretics are not to be allowed to enter an appeal to scriptures, since without scriptures we prove them to have no concern with scriptures. For if they are heretics, they cannot be Christians, inasmuch as they do not hold from Christ what they follow by their own choice, and in consequence admit the name of heretics.[1] Therefore not being Christians, they have no right to Christian writings. To whom we may well say, Who are you? when did you come? and whence? What are you, who are not mine, doing in my property? By what right dost thou, Marcion, cut down my wood? By what licence dost thou, Valentinus, turn the course of my waters? By what power remove my landmarks? This is my possession: how are you sowing it and feeding on it at your pleasure? It is mine, I repeat: I had it of old; I had it first: I have the unquestioned title-deeds from the first proprietors. I am the heir of the Apostles. According to their will, according to their trust, according to the oath I took from them, I hold it. You, assuredly, they have ever disinherited and renounced, as aliens, as enemies. But why are heretics aliens and enemies to Apostles, save from difference of doctrine, which each at his own pleasure has either brought forward or received against Apostles?"[2]

Thus Tertullian adds the witness of the African church to that of the Asiatic and Gallic churches in Irenæus.

---

[1] That is, he opposes the word *choosers* to the word *Christians;* the one signifying those who believe what they *choose*, the other those who believe what Christ taught.

[2] *De Præscrip.* 37.

We have noted the great church of Alexandria as a most complete instance of the growth whereby from the mother See the hierarchy took possession of a land. But the principle of such growth was the ecclesiastical rule, and its strength the energy with which that rule was preserved. This rule was twofold: the rule of discipline, or outward regimen, what we now call a constitution; and the rule of Faith. What the church of Alexandria was in discipline has been seen above: and now just at this time we have, in the first great teacher of this church who has come down to us, the most decisive exhibition of this rule as a defence against this same Gnostic heresy. "As," says Clement, "a man like those under the enchantment of Circe should become a beast, so whoever has kicked against the tradition of the Church, and started aside into the opinions of human heresies, has ceased to be a man of God, and faithful to the Lord." . . . "There are three states of the soul, ignorance, opinion, knowledge. Those who are in ignorance are the Gentiles; those in knowledge, the true Church; those in opinion, the adherents of heresies." . . . "We have learnt that bodily pleasure is one thing, which we give to the Gentiles; strife a second, which we adjudge to heresies; joy a third, which is the property of the Church." Again, he speaks of those who "not using the divine words well, but perversely, neither enter themselves into the kingdom of heaven, nor suffer those whom they have deceived to attain the truth. They have not indeed the key to the entrance, but rather a false key, whereby they do not enter as we do through the Lord's tradition, drawing back the veil, but cutting out a side way, and secretly digging through the Church's wall, they transgress the truth, and initiate into rites of error the soul of the irreligious. For that they have made their human associations later than the Catholic Church, it needs not many words to show." Then, after referring to the origin and propagation "of the Lord's teaching,"[1] exactly after the mode of Irenæus and Tertullian, he concludes, " So it is clear from the most ancient and true Church, that these heresies coming in subsequently to it, and others still later, are innovations from it, as coins of adulterate stamp. From what has been said, then, I consider it manifest that the true Church, the really ancient Church, is one, in which are enrolled all who are just according to (God's) purpose. For inasmuch as there is one God and one Lord, therefore that which is most highly precious is praised for being alone, since it is an imitation of the one Principle. The one Church, then, which they try by force to cut up into many heresies, falls under the same category as the nature of the One. So then we assert that the ancient and Catholic Church is one alone in its foundation, in its idea, in its origin, and in its excellence, collecting by the will of the one God, through the one Lord, into the unity of one Faith, according to the peculiar covenants, or rather to the one covenant at different times, the preordained whom God predestined, having known before the foundation of the world that they would be just. But the excellence of the Church, as the principle of the whole construction, is in unity, surpassing all other things, and having nothing similar or equal to itself."[2]

[1] ἡ τοῦ κυρίου κατὰ τὴν παρουσίαν διδασκαλία.
[2] Clem. Alex. *Strom.* vii. 16, pp. 890-894 ; 17, pp. 897-900. The sections 15-17, pp. 886-900, treat of the spirit and conduct of heresy.

One other writer remains, the larger part of whose life falls within this period, greater in renown than either of the foregoing; and into whatever particular errors Origen may have fallen, he did not swerve from their doctrine as to the mode of meeting error itself. "Since," says he, "there are many who think that they hold the tenets of Christ, while some of them hold different tenets from those who went before them, let the ecclesiastical preaching as handed down by the order of succession from the Apostles, and maintained even to the present time in the churches, be preserved: that alone is to be believed as truth which in nothing is discordant from the ecclesiastical and apostolical tradition."[1] And the ground for such a principle he has given elsewhere:

"The divine words assert that the whole Church of God is the Body of Christ, animated by the Son of God, while the limbs of this Body as a whole are particular believers: since as the soul quickens and moves the body, whose nature it is not to have the movement of life from itself, so the Word moving to what is fitting, and working in, the whole body, the Church, moves likewise each member of the Church, who does nothing without the Word."[2]

The four great writers, then, of this period, Irenæus, Tertullian, Clement, and Origen, none of them indeed from Rome, but representing the churches of Asia, Gaul, Africa, and Egypt, exactly concur in the principle by which they refuted heresy, the propagation, that is, of the rule of Faith in its purity and integrity, by those who possessed the succession of

---

[1] *De Principiis*, pref. p. 47. See also on Matt. tom. iii. 864, a passage equally decisive.
[2] *Cont. Cels.* vi. 48, tom. i. 670.

the Apostles and their office of teaching, in which lay a divine gift of the truth.

But to those who proceeded from this basis it was a further labour to set forth the true knowledge against the false. And we may trace the following results of heresy, quite unintended by itself, in its operation on the Church.

1. In the first place, St. Augustine continually remarks that the more accurate enucleation of true doctrine usually proceeded from the attacks of heresy; and this happened so continually that it seems to him a special instance of that law of Divine Providence which educes good from evil. "If the truth," says he, "had not lying adversaries, it would be examined with less carefulness," and so "a question started by an opponent becomes to the disciple an occasion of learning."[1] And he observes that "we have found by experience that every heresy has brought into the Church its own questions, against which the divine Scripture was defended with greater care than if no such necessity had existed."[2] Thus the doctrine of the Trinity owed its perfect treatment to the Arian assault on it; the doctrine of penance to that of Novatian; the doctrine of baptism to those who wished to introduce the practice of rebaptizing; even the unity of Christ was brought out with greater clearness by the attempt to rend it, and the doctrine of one Catholic Church diffused through the whole world cleared from its objectors by showing that the mixture of evil men in it does not prejudice the good.[3] And he illustrates his meaning by a very picturesque image: "When

[1] *De Civ. Dei*, xvi. 2.   [2] *De dono persev.* 53.
[3] Enarr. in Ps. 54, tom. iv. 513.

heretics calumniate, the young of the flock are disturbed; in their disturbance they inquire; so the young lamb butts its mother's udder till it gets sufficient nutriment for its thirst."[1] For the doctors of the Church being called upon for an answer supply the truth which before was latent. And there is no more signal instance of the great writer's remark than himself; for the attacks of the most various heresies led him during forty years of unwearied mental activity into almost every question of theology.

The Gnostic heresy, then, presents us with the first instance of a law which will run all through the Church's history. Peter, the first Apostle, meets and refutes Simon Magus, the first propagator of falsehood, who receives divine sacraments and then claims against the giver to be "the great power of God." This fact is likewise the symbol of a long line of action, wherein it is part of the divine plan to make the perpetual restlessness of error subserve the complete exhibition of truth. The Gnostics denied the divine monarchy; at once mutilated and misinterpreted Scripture; claimed to themselves a secret tradition of truth. We owe to them in consequence the treatises of Irenæus, Tertullian, and Clement, and a written exhibition of the Church's divine order, succession, and unity, as well as a specific mention of the tie which held that unity together; and the mention of this tie at so early a period might otherwise have been wanting to us. But these three writers do but represent to us partially an universal result. The danger which from Gnostic influence beset all the chief centres of ecclesiastical teaching marks the transition from the first state of simple faith to that of

[1] Serm. 51, tom. v. 288.

human learning, inquiry, and thought, turned upon the objects of Christian belief. The Gnostics had a merit which they little imagined for themselves. They formed the first doctors of post-apostolic times. Irenæus, Tertullian, and Clement are a great advance upon the more simple and external exhibition of Christianity which we find in the apologists. In them the Church is preparing to encounter the deepest questions moved against her by Greek philosophy. They are her first champions in that contest with Hellenic culture which was a real combat of mind, not a mere massacre of unresisting victims, and which lasted for five hundred years.

2. Secondly, when the Gnostic attack began, the canon of the New Testament was still unfixed. Nothing can be more certain than that the Apostles did not set forth any official collection of their writings, and that no such collection existed shortly after their death. This fact most plainly shows that the Christian religion at their departure did not rest for its maintenance upon writings. Not only had our Lord written no word Himself, but He left no command to His Apostles to write. His command was to propagate His Gospel and to found His kingdom by oral teaching; and His promise was that the Holy Ghost should accompany, follow upon, and continue with, this their action. What we find is, that they did this, and that the writings which besides they left, being from the first kept and venerated by the several churches to which they were addressed, gradually became known through the whole body of the Church. With the lapse of time they would become more and more valuable. Moreover, when the Gnostics set themselves to interpolate and corrupt them, and to

fabricate false writings, the need of a genuine collection became more and more urgent. It is from the three writers above mentioned, towards the end of the second century, that we learn that such a collection existed, in forming which these principles were followed: only to admit writings which tradition attested to spring from an Apostle or a witness of our Lord's life,[1] among whom Paul was specially counted: secondly, only such writings as were attested by some church of apostolical foundation: and thirdly, only such writings the doctrine contained in which did not differ from the rule of faith orally handed down in the churches of apostolic origin, or in the one Catholic Church, excluding all such as were at variance with the doctrine hitherto received. Thus in the settlement of the canon authority as well as tradition intervened; an authority which felt itself in secure possession of the same Holy Spirit who had inspired the Apostles, and of the same doctrine which they had taught.[2]

With the reception of a book into the canon of Scripture was joined a belief in its inspiration, which rested on what was a part of oral tradition, that is, that the Apostles as well in their oral as in their written teaching had enjoyed the infallible guidance of the Holy Spirit. It is evident that such a tradition reposes, in the last instance, upon the authority of the Church.[3]

If by means of the Gnostic attacks the canon of the New Testament, as we now possess it, was not absolutely completed, it had at least advanced a very great

---

[1] St. Mark's Gospel would be referred to St. Peter, and St. Luke's writings to St. Paul.
[2] See Schwane, pp. 779, 780.   [3] Schwane, pp. 783, 784.

way towards that completion, which we have finally attested as of long standing in a Council held at Carthage in 397.[1]

3. Another result of the Gnostic attack was the setting forth the tradition of the Faith, seated and maintained in the apostolic churches, as the rule for interpreting Scripture. The Gnostics in two ways impeached this rule, by claiming a private tradition of their own, and by interpreting such Scripture as they chose to acknowledge after their own pleasure. Irenæus, Tertullian, and Clement found an adequate answer to both errors by showing that the Faith which the Apostles had set forth in their writings could not contradict the Faith which they had established in the Church. These were two sources of the same doctrine; but it is by the permanent connection and interpenetration of the two that the truth is maintained; and that which holds both together, that which utters and propagates the truth which they jointly contain, is the Teaching office, the mouth of the Church. Hence the force of the appeal in Irenæus to the succession of the episcopate, and to the divine gift of truth which the Apostles had handed down therein with their teaching office. Hence Tertullian's exclusion of heretics from the right to possess Scriptures which belong only to the Church. Hence Clement's description of the only true Gnostic, as "one who has grown old in the study of the Scriptures, while he preserves the apostolic and ecclesiastical standard of doctrine."[2] For neither in founding churches, nor in teaching orally, nor in writing, did the Apostles exhaust or resign the authority committed to them.[3]

[1] "Quia a patribus ista accepimus in ecclesia legenda," n. 47.
[2] *Stromata*, vii. c. 16, p. 896.
[3] See Kleutgen, *Theologie der Vorzeit*, iii. 957; Schwane, vol. i. 3.

The authority itself, which was the source of all this their action, after all that they had founded, taught, or written, continued complete and entire in them, and was transmitted on to their successors, for the maintenance of the work assigned to it. It is this perpetual living power which Irenæus so strongly testifies,[1] to which he attaches the gift of the Spirit, not Scripture, nor tradition, but that which carries both Scripture and tradition through the ages, which is "as the breath of life to the body, which is always from the Spirit of God, wherein is placed the communication of Christ, which is always young, and makes young the vessel in which it is."[2] The writings which the Holy Ghost has inspired, and the tradition of the Faith which he has established, would be subject, the one to misinterpretation, the other to alteration and corruption, without that particular presence of His, in which consists the divine gift of truth, the teaching office, "the making disciples all nations."

4. And the action of heresy, which was so effective in bringing out the function of the teaching church, was not without force in extending and corroborating the function of the ruling church. The first synods of which we have mention are those assembled in Asia Minor towards the end of the second century against the diffusion of Montanism.[3] But what through the loss of records has been mentioned only in this one case must have taken place generally, since it is obvious that as soon as erroneous doctrines spread from one diocese to another, they would call forth joint action against them. Since then heresies have

---

[1] L. iv. 26. 2, p. 262. "Quapropter *iis qui in Ecclesia sunt* presbyteris obaudire oportet," &c.
[2] L. iii. 24, p. 223.   [3] Schwane, p. 683.

been the frequent, almost the exclusive, cause of councils. The parallel is fruitful in thought, which is suggested between the action of error in eliciting the more precise expression of the truth which it abhors, and its action in strengthening the governing power of the body which it assaults. In the one case and in the other the result is that which it least desires and intends; heresy, disbelieving and disobeying, is made to perfect the faith and build up the hierarchy.

Now to sum up our sketch of the internal history of the Christian Faith in the seventy-four years which elapse from the accession of Marcus Aurelius to the death of Alexander Severus. At the first-named date we find that it had spread beyond the confines of the Roman empire, and taken incipient possession of all the great centres of human intercourse by founding its hierarchy in them. At the second date it has subdued the powerful and widespread family of heresies which threatened to distort and corrupt its doctrines, and has done this by the vigour of its teaching office, which combined in one expression the yet fresh apostolic tradition stored up in its churches, and the doctrine of its sacred Scriptures; while it has well-nigh determined the number and genuineness of these, severing them off from all other writings. The episcopate in which its teaching office resides appears not as a number of bishops, each independent and severed, and merely governing his diocese upon a similar rule, but with a bond recognised among them, the superior principate of the Roman See. That is, as the teaching office itself is in them all the voice of living teachers, so its highest expression is the voice of the living Peter in his see. And this bond as discerned and recognised by the Asiatic disciple of

St. Polycarp, the bishop of the chief city of Gaul, is so strong that he uses for it rather the term denoting physical necessity than moral fitness:[1] as if he would say: As Christ has made the Church, it must agree from one end to the other in doctrine and communion with the doctrine and communion of the Church in which Peter, to whom He has committed His sheep, speaks and rules. And so powerful is the derivation of this authority that he who sits in the place of Mark, whom Peter sent, punishes by degradation a bishop who disregards his sentence in the case of a great writer, the brightest genius of the Church in that day. And when we look at the spiritual state of the world at the commencement of the third century, we find that Christianity, having formed and made its place in human society, is penetrating through it more and more in every direction. It is then that we discern the first beginnings of that great spiritual creation, in which Reason has been applied to Faith under the guidance of Authority, which the Christian Church, alone being in possession of these three constituents, could alone produce, and has carried on from that day to this. Alexandria was at this time the seat of a Jewish religious philosophy; it had just become the seat likewise of a heathen religious philosophy; there was within its church a great catechetical school, in which the Faith as taught by the apostolical and ecclesiastical tradition according to the Scriptures

---

[1] Observed by Hagemann, p. 618, referring to the words of St. Irenæus, "ad hanc enim Ecclesiam propter potiorem principalitatem *necesse est* omnem convenire Ecclesiam," &c. It must be remembered that the proper word for the power which held together the whole Roman empire was Principatus, the very word used by St. Augustine to express the *original* authority of the Roman See: "Romauæ Ecclesiæ, in qua *semper* apostolicæ cathedræ viguit *principatus.*" *Ep.* 43.

was communicated. It was to be expected that its teachers, such men as Pantænus, Clement, and Origen, would be led on from the more elementary work of imparting the rudiments of the Faith to the scientific consideration of its deeper mysteries; and even the sight of what was going on around them among Jews and Greeks would invite them to attempt the construction of a Christian religious philosophy.

Moreover, Gnosticism, of which Alexandria was the chief focus, had raised the question of the unity and nature of the Godhead, and professed a false gnosis as the perfection of religion. By this also thoughtful minds were led to consider the true relation of knowledge to faith, and hence to attempt the first rudiments of a Theology, the Science of Faith.

To refute heathenism both as a Philosophy and as a Religion, and to set forth Christianity as the absolute truth, was the very function of such men as Clement and Origen; and the former in his work entitled "The Pedagogue" exhibits the conduct of life according to the principles and doctrines of Christianity; while his *Stromata*, or Tapestries, exhibit the building up of science on the foundation of faith.[1] We can hardly realise now the difficulties which beset his great pupil Origen, when, carrying on the master's thought, he endeavoured to found a theology. The fact that he was among the first to venture on such a deep, is the best excuse that can be made for those speculative errors into which he fell.

III. And now we turn to the conduct of the empire towards this religion which has grown up in its bosom.

[1] See Kuhn, *Einleitung in die katholische Dogmatik*, i. 345, 346.

At once with the accession of Marcus Aurelius a temper of greater severity to Christians is shown. The sort of toleration expressed in the rescript of Pius to the province of Asia is withdrawn. No new law about them is enacted, for none is needed, but the old law is let loose. The almost sublime clemency of Marcus towards his revolted general Cassius, his reign of nineteen years unstained with senatorial blood, and the campaigns prolonged from year to year of one who loved his philosophic studies above all things, and yet at the call of imperial duty gave up night and day to the rudest toils of a weary conflict with barbarous tribes on the frontier, have won for him immortal honour: his regard for his subjects in general has sometimes given him in Christian estimation the place of predilection among all princes ancient and modern.[1] It is well, then, to consider his bearing towards Christians. Now among his teachers was that Junius Rusticus, grandson of the man who perished for the sake of liberty in Domitian's time, and in his day no doubt a perfect specimen of the Roman gentleman and noble, a blending of all that was best in Cicero, Lælius, and Cato, whom Marcus made Prefect of Rome, and to whom when bearing that office he addressed a rescript containing the words, "To Junius Rusticus, Prefect of the city, our friend." And what this friend of Marcus thought on the most important subjects we may judge from the sentiments of another friend and fellow-teacher of the emperor, Maximus of Tyre, who has left written, "How God rules a mighty and stable kingdom having for its limits not river or lake or

---

[1] Guizot ranks Marcus Aurelius with St. Louis, as the only rulers who preferred conscience to gain in all their conduct.

shore or ocean, but the heaven above and the earth beneath, in which He, impassive as law, bestows on those who obey Him the security of which He is the fountain: and the gods his children need not images any more than good men statues. But just as our vocal speech requires not in itself any particular characters, yet human weakness has invented the alphabetical signs whereby to give expression to its remembrance, so the nature of the gods needs not images, but man, removed from them as far as heaven from earth, has devised these signs, by which to give them names. There may be those strong enough to do without these helps, but they are rare, and as schoolmasters guide their scholars to write by first pencilling letters for them, so legislators have invented these images as signs of the divine honour, and helps to human memory. But God is the father and framer of all things, older than heaven, superior to time and all fleeting nature, legislator ineffable, unexpressed by voice, unseen by eye; and we who cannot grasp His essence rest upon words and names, and forms of gold, ivory, and silver, in our longing to conceive Him, giving to His nature what is fair among ourselves. But fix Him only in the mind; I care not whether the Greek is kindled into remembrance of Him by the art of Phidias, or the Egyptian by the worship of animals, that fire is his symbol to these, and water to those; only let them understand, let them love, let them remember Him alone."[1]

I doubt not that Junius Rusticus was familiar with such thoughts as these, and as a matter of philosophic reflection assented to them. And now let us study

[1] Maximus Tyrius, diss. 17, 12; Reiske, and diss. ii. 2. 10.

the scene which was enacted in his presence and by his command.[1]

"At a time when the defenders of idolatry had proposed edicts in every city and region to compel Christians to sacrifice, Justin and his companions were seized and brought before the Prefect of Rome, Rusticus. When they stood before his tribunal, the Prefect Rusticus said: 'Well, be obedient to the gods and the emperor's edicts.' Justin answered: 'No man can ever be blamed or condemned who obeys the precepts of our Saviour Jesus Christ.' Then the Prefect Rusticus asked: 'In what sect's learning or discipline are you versed?' Justin replied: 'I endeavoured to learn every sort of sect, and tried every kind of instruction; but at last I adhered to the Christian discipline, though that is not acceptable to those who are led by the error of a false opinion.' Rusticus said: 'Wretch, is that the sect in which you take delight?' 'Assuredly,' said Justin; 'since together with a right belief I follow the example of Christians.' 'What belief is that, I pray?' said the Prefect. Justin replied: 'The right belief which we as Christians join with piety is this, to hold that there is one God, the Maker and Creator of all things which are seen and which are not seen by the body's eyes, and to confess one Lord Jesus Christ the Son of God, foretold of old by the prophets, who will also come to judge the human race, and who is the herald of salvation and the teacher of those who learn of Him well. I indeed as a man am feeble, and far too little to say anything great of His infinite Godhead: this I confess to be the office of prophets, who many ages ago

---

[1] *Acta Martyrum sincera*, Ruinart, pp. 58–60.

by inspiration foretold the advent upon earth of the same whom I have called the Son of God.

"The Prefect inquired where the Christians met. Justin answered: 'Each where he will and can. Do you suppose that we are accustomed all to meet in the same place? By no means, since the God of the Christians is not circumscribed by place, but being invisible fills heaven and earth, and is everywhere adored, and His glory praised by the faithful.' The Prefect said: 'Come, tell me where you meet and assemble your disciples.' Justin answered: 'For myself I have hitherto lodged near the house of a certain Martin, by the Timiotine bath. It is the second time I have come to Rome, and I know no other place than the one mentioned. And if any one chose to come to me, I communicated to him the doctrine of truth.' 'You are, then, a Christian?' said Rusticus. 'Assuredly,' said Justin, 'I am.'

"Then the Prefect asked Charito: 'Are you too a Christian?' Charito replied: 'By God's help I am a Christian.' The Prefect asked the woman Charitana whether she too followed the Faith of Christ. She replied: 'I also by the gift of God am a Christian.' Then Rusticus said to Evelpistus: 'And who are you?' He replied: 'I am Cæsar's slave, but a Christian to whom Christ has given liberty, and by His favour and grace made partaker of the same hope with those whom you see.' The Prefect then asked Hierax whether he too was a Christian; and he replied: 'Certainly I am a Christian, since I worship and adore the same God.' The Prefect inquired: 'Was it Justin who made you Christians?' 'I,' said Hierax, 'both was and will be a Christian.' Pæon likewise stood before him and said: 'I too am a Christian.' 'Who taught you?' said the Prefect. He replied: 'I received this good confession from my parents.' Then Evelpistus said: 'I also was accustomed to hear with great delight Justin's discourses, but it was from my parents that I learnt to be a Christian.' Then the Prefect: 'And where are your parents?' 'In Cappadocia,' said Evelpistus. The Prefect likewise asked Hierax where his parents were, and Hierax replied: 'Our true Father is Christ, and our mother the Faith, by which we believe on Him. But my earthly parents are dead. It was, however, from Iconium in Phrygia that I was brought hither.' The Prefect asked Liberianus whether he too was a Christian and without piety towards the gods. He said: 'I also am a Christian, for I worship and adore the only true God.'

"Then the Prefect turned to Justin and said: 'You fellow, who are said to be eloquent, and think you hold the true discipline. If you are beaten from head to foot, is it your persuasion that you will go up to heaven?' Justin answered: 'I hope if I suffer what you say, that I shall have what those have who have kept the commands of Christ. For I know that to all who live thus the divine grace is preserved until the whole world have its consummation.' The Prefect Rusticus replied: 'It is, then, your opinion that you will go up to heaven to receive some reward?' 'I do not opine,' said Justin, 'but I know,' and am so certain of this that I am incapable of doubt.' Rusticus said: 'Let us come at length to what is before us and urgent. Agree together and with one mind sacrifice to the gods.' Justin replied: 'No one of right mind deserts piety to fall into error and impiety.' The Prefect Rusticus said: 'Unless you be willing to obey our commands, you will suffer torments without mercy.' Justin answered: 'What we most desire is to suffer torments for our Lord Jesus Christ and to be saved: for this will procure for us salvation and confidence before that terrible tribunal of the same our Lord and Saviour, at which by divine command the whole world shall attend.' The same likewise said all the other martyrs, adding: 'What thou wilt do, do quickly; for we are Christians and sacrifice not to idols.'

"The Prefect hearing this pronounced the following sentence: 'Let those who have refused to sacrifice to the gods, and to obey the emperor's edict, be beaten with rods, and led away to capital punishment, as the laws enjoin.' And so the holy martyrs praising God were led to the accustomed place, and after being beaten were struck with the axe, and consummated their martyrdom in the confession of the Saviour. After which certain of the faithful took away their bodies, and laid them in a suitable place, by the help of the grace of our Lord Jesus Christ, to whom be glory for ever and ever."

As the pillars of Trajan and Antonine faithfully record the deeds of those whose names they bear, and stand before posterity as a visible history, so, I conceive, the judgment of Ignatius by Trajan, and that of Justin by Rusticus, under the eye as it were of Marcus Aurelius and in his name, embody to us perfectly the mind and conduct of those great emperors towards Christians. The marble of Phidias could present no more perfect sculpture, the pencil of Apelles no more breathing picture, than the simple transcription of the judicial record given above. In the mind of Marcus the jealousy of the old Roman for his country's worship joined with the philosopher's dislike of Christian principles to move him from that more equable temper which dictated the later moderation of his immediate

predecessor. It scarcely needed the spirit which ruled
at Rome to kindle passionate outbreaks against Christians in the various cities of the empire. We have
just seen the impassive majesty of Roman law declaring at the chief seat of power that to be a Christian
is a capital crime. If we go at the same time to
Smyrna, there the voices of a furious populace are demanding that an aged man venerable through the whole
region for his innocent life and his virtues, be cast to
the lions, because he is "the teacher of impiety, the
father of the Christians, the destroyer of our gods, who
has instructed many not to sacrifice to them or adore
them." No grander scene among all the deeds of
men is preserved to us, as described by his own church
at the time, than the martyrdom of Polycarp, as after
eighty-six years of Christian service he stood bound at
the stake before the raging multitude in the theatre,
and uttered his last prayer: "I thank thee, O God of
angels and powers, and all the generation of the just
who live before thee, that thou hast thought me worthy
of this day and hour to receive a portion in the number
of thy martyrs, in the chalice of thy Christ." Ten
years later, in the great city of Lyons a similar spectacle was offered on a far larger scale. The Bishop
Pothinus, more than ninety years old, is carried before
the tribunal, "the magistrates of the city following
him, and all the multitude pursuing him with cries as
if he were Christ." But the triumph of the bishop is
accompanied by that of many among his flock, of whom
while all were admirable, yet the slave Blandina, poor
and contemptible in appearance, surpassed the rest.
"She was exposed to the beasts raised as it were upon
a cross, and so praying most contentedly to God, she
inspired the utmost ardour in her fellow-combatants,

who with the eyes of the body saw in this their sister's person Him who had been crucified for them in order to persuade those who should believe in Him that whoever suffers for the glory of Christ shall obtain companionship with the living God."[1] Since the wild beasts refused to touch her, Blandina and the survivors among her fellow-sufferers were remanded to prison, in order that the pleasure of the emperor might be taken, one of them being a Roman citizen. For this persecution had arisen without any command of his, and the punishments were inflicted in virtue of the ordinary law. After an interval, as it would seem, of two months, a rescript was received from Marcus Aurelius which ordered that those who confessed should be punished ignominiously, those who denied, be dismissed. "And so at the time of our great fair, when a vast multitude from the various provinces flock thither, the governor ordered the most blessed martyrs to be brought before his tribunal, exhibiting them to the people as in theatric pomp; and after a last interrogation those who were Roman citizens were beheaded, and the rest given to the wild beasts."[2] But Blandina, after being every day brought to behold the sufferings of her companions, "the last of all, like a noble mother who had kindled her children to the combat, and sent them forward as conquerors to the king,—was eager to follow them, rejoicing and exulting over her departure, as if invited to a nuptial banquet, not cast before wild beasts. At length, after scourging and tearing and burning, she was put in a net and exposed to the bull. Tossed again and again by him, yet feeling now nothing which was done to her, both from the intensity of hope with which she grasped the rewards of faith, and from her

[1] Ruinart, p. 67.   [2] *Ib.* p. 68.

intimate intercourse in prayer with Christ, in the end she had her throat cut, as a victim, while the heathen themselves confessed that never had they seen a woman who had borne so much and so long."[1]

These three scenes of martyrdom at Rome, at Smyrna, and at Lyons, will give a notion of the grounds upon which Eusebius asserts that in the reign of Marcus Aurelius innumerable martyrs suffered[2] throughout the world through popular persecutions. Respecting the following reign of Commodus he says, on the contrary, that the Church enjoyed peace, for while the law which considered Christianity an illicit religion had not been revoked, it was made capital to inform against any one as Christian; and yet if the information took place, and the crime was proved, the punishment of death ensued, as in the case of the senator Apollonius recorded by him.[3] This state of things would seem to have lasted about seventeen years, until the year 197, when Severus, some time after his accession, became unfavourable to Christians. And it brings us to Tertullian, whose writings are full of testimonies to the sufferings endured by Christians for their Faith. For some time these sufferings would seem to fall under the same sort of intermittent popular persecution, which we have seen prevailing in the time of Marcus: but in the year 202 Severus published an edict forbidding any to become Jews or Christians. And forthwith a persecution broke out so severe and terrible, that many thought the time of Antichrist was come. It was no longer the mere action of an original law against all unauthorised

---

[1] Ruinart, p. 69.
[2] *Hist.* v. i. μυριάδας μαρτύρων διαπρέψαι στοχασμῷ λαβεῖν ἔνεστιν.
[3] *Ib.* v. 21.

religions, but an assault led on by the emperor himself, who turned directly the imperial power against Christianity as a whole. It raged especially at Alexandria, where the master of the catechetical school writes: "We have before our eyes every day abundant instances of martyrs, tortured by fire, impaled, beheaded: they are superior to pleasure; they conquer suffering; they overcome the world."[1] Then it was that Origen, a youth of seventeen, desired to share the martyrdom of his father Leonides, and that seven whom he had himself instructed, gained this crown. Then it was that the slave Potamiæna, in the bloom of youth and beauty, not only rejected every blandishment of corruption, but suffered the extremest torture of fire to preserve her innocence and faith, and gained at Alexandria such a name as St. Lawrence afterwards gained at Rome. So at Carthage Perpetua and Felicitas, young mothers, with their companions repeated the example of those whom we have seen suffering at Lyons; in which city a second persecution as vehement as the first breaking out, numbered Irenæus with his predecessor Pothinus, his people in this case as in the other accompanying the pastor's sacrifice with their own. This state of suffering continued during the life of Severus for nine years; and splendid examples of Christian championship were shown in all the churches.[2] It is only with the accession of Caracalla that peace is restored, and then ensues a period of comparative repose: that is, while the ordinary law against the Christian Faith as an illicit religion still continues, it is understood that the emperor does not wish it to be put in action. In such intervals that

---

[1] Clem. Alex. *Strom.* ii. c. 20, p. 494.
[2] Euseb. *Hist.* vi. 1.

Faith, strengthened by the conflicts it had undergone, and admired by those before whose eyes it had enabled its adherents to brave and endure every sort of suffering, sprung up and shot out with redoubled vigour, and the seed which the blood of the martyrs had shed abroad found time to grow.

The summary of the seventy-four years is this. From 161 to 180 there are nineteen years of irregular but severe persecution, followed by seventeen, from 180 to 197, wherein the denouncing of Christians is forbidden, though if brought to trial, they are punishable with death. Five years succeed, from 197 to 202, in which the favour of Severus seems lost, and the state of intermittent persecution takes effect. Then breaks out a general persecution, set on foot by the emperor himself, and we may judge if he who slaughtered his senate spared Christians. This lasts for nine years until his death in 211, whereon a time of peace returns, which is most complete during the reign of Alexander, but continues more or less from 211 to the end of his reign in 235.

On a review of the whole period it is evident that the Church has passed from its state of concealment into almost full light. The fiery trial which it met at the beginning of the third century from the hand of Severus is the best proof that can be given how greatly it had increased, how it could no longer be ignored or despised; how its organisation which was hidden from Trajan was at least partially revealed to Severus, and how he saw and attempted to meet the danger which the earlier emperor would have tried to stamp out, had he divined it. But it is evident also that in proportion as the Christian Faith had grown, the heathen empire had been shaken in its foundations.

Its period of just government was over; its imperial power was to fall henceforth into the hands of adventurers, with whom it would be more and more the symbol of force alone, and not of law: henceforth they would seldom even in blood be Roman, and more seldom still in principles. Marcus was well-nigh the last zealot for the Jupiter of the Capitol: within a generation after him Heliogabalus will think of a fusion of all religions in his god the sun, and Alexander Severus of a religious syncretism wherein Orpheus, Abraham, and Christ testify together to the divine unity.[1] Nor is this a fancy of the prince alone. All the thinking minds of his time have become ashamed of Olympus and its gods. The cross has wounded them to death. A new philosophy—the last fortress into which retreating heathenism throws itself —while it breaks up Roman life, prepares the way for the Christian Faith which it strenuously combats. The Emperor Severus, fixing the eye of a statesman and a soldier on that Faith, contemplates its grasp upon society, and decrees from the height of the throne a general assault upon it; while his wife encourages a writer[2] to draw an ideal heathen portrait as a counterpart to the character of Christ, tacitly subtracting from the gospels an imitation which is to supply the place of the reality. The time was not far distant when Origen would already discern and prophesy the complete triumph of the religion thus assailed; and if Celsus had objected, that were all to do as Christians did, the emperor would be deserted, and his power fall into the hands of the most savage and lawless bar-

---

[1] Champagny, *les Antonins*, iii. 326, 338.
[2] Philostratus in his *Life of Apollonius of Tyana*, written at the request of the Empress Julia Domna. See Kellner, *Hellenismus und Christenthum*, c. v. s. 4, 81-4.

barians, would reply: "If all did as I do, men would honour the emperor as a divine command, and the barbarians drawing nigh to the word of God would become most law-loving and most civilised; their worship would be dissolved, and that of the Christians alone prevail, as one day it will alone prevail, by means of that Word gathering to itself more and more souls."[1]

But before such a goal be reached, many a martyr's crown has yet to be won, and more than barbarian lawlessness and cruelty have to be overcome.

[1] Orig. c. *Cels.* viii. 68, tom. i. p. 793.

LECTURE XII

THE THIRD AGE OF THE MARTYR CHURCH

"Rex pacificus magnificatus est, cujus vultum desiderat universa terra."

I. THE third century is that during which the Christian Church was making its way into every relation of life, and taking possession of human society. During this period it advances into full light, and becomes a manifest power. In the second century Celsus had attacked it as disclosed only to the yearning hearts of slaves, and fostered by the devotion of the weaker sex. At the distance of three generations Origen answered him, but the religion which he defended already stood avowed alike before the inquiring gaze of philosophers, the corrupt crowds of cities, and the jealous fear of rulers. Even in Rome, the sceptred head of idolatry, whose nobles the great political traditions of their city, and whose populace their sensual life, having its root in a false worship, made the most difficult to convert, the hated faith is known to have had public churches by the time of Alexander Severus, two hundred years after its first rise.[1] And much more everywhere else it had planted its foot openly on the soil of the empire. It is time, then, to view the Church as an institution offering the

[1] Churches in private houses, under cover of that great liberty which invested with a sort of sacred independence the Roman household, it had from the beginning: the church of St. Pudentiana in the house of the senator Pudens still guards the altar on which St. Peter offered.

strongest contrast to the empire itself, to the barbarism which surrounded the empire, and to the sectarianism which was everywhere aspiring to counterwork and supplant that entire body of truth on some portion of which nevertheless it was all the time feeding.

1. And first the empire during this century presents itself to us in a most unwonted aspect.

Septimius Severus having destroyed the rivals who competed with him for what was now become the great object of a successful general's ambition, based his power avowedly on the sword. The secret of empire which he transmitted to his children was to foster and indulge the army, and to disregard all else. The senate, the representative of legal power, he despised and decimated. He died in 211, not before his eldest son had already lifted his hand against him, and the four princes of his house all perished by the sword, one by the hand of a brother, the other three by revolted soldiers. In the seventy-three years which elapse from his death to the accession of Diocletian, twenty-five emperors are acknowledged at Rome, of whom twenty-three come to an end by violent deaths, almost always by insurrections of soldiers, under instigation of ambitious officers. Besides these, eight associates of the empire, and nineteen generals who during the reign of Gallienus assume the purple in various provinces, are all slain. During eighty-two years Trajan, Hadrian, Antoninus, and Marcus, all at a mature time of life, adopted by the actual ruler to succeed, had governed a stable empire: but now it passes within a shorter period of time, the term of a single human life, nay a term in one case embraced by a single reign,[1] into

[1] The reign of Louis XIV.

twenty-five different hands. And indeed it seemed after the capture of the Emperor Valerian by the Persians, as if that great confederacy, which had just celebrated the thousandth anniversary of the imperial city's foundation, was about to break up and be resolved into its component parts. At one moment two great princesses, Victoria and Zenobia, worthy even by the avowal of Romans to wear the Roman diadem, were on the point of establishing the one an empire of the Gauls in the West, the other an empire of the East, embracing just those countries which Antony had ruled with Cleopatra at his side. A succession of great generals, all from the province of Illyricum, at last saves the empire and reasserts its unity. But the forty-nine years following the murder of Alexander Severus are filled by the struggles of twenty sovereigns and nineteen pretenders to sovereignty, scarcely any of whom reign so much as five years. Many of them are rulers of great ability and remarkable energy. Claudius, Aurelian, Probus, and Carus, and perhaps Decius, required but happier circumstances to be emperors whose fame would have matched that of Trajan or Hadrian: but their short tenure of power, occupied with the vast effort to restore unity and beat back the barbarian, prevented their doing more than preserve the imperial power and the empire itself. This whole time, then, in civil society was one of fluctuation, anxiety, disaster, alarms from beyond the frontiers and anarchy within them. The Roman peace seemed departing, and the majesty of the empire irreparably violated. Men could not tell what the morrow would bring forth. The fairest cities of the Roman world, Alexandria and Antioch, narrowly escaped perishing through internal discord or hostile surprise. Greece and Asia Minor, after reposing for centuries under the safeguard of the Roman name, found themselves swept through and desolated by barbarian hordes. Italy itself was in imminent danger of the same lot. Towards the end of this period, the senate by the election of Tacitus seems to make what may be termed its final effort to assert itself as the depository of legitimate power, the representative of civil society: and this time of confusion issues in a rejection of any such claim, and the establishment of unlimited despotism in the empire as reconstituted by Diocletian. To these straits, then, the first great and haughty enemy of the Christian Church was reduced, so that the power which a century before could look down with proud indifference on the sufferings of Christians now seemed to tremble for its own existence. And in such a condition of human society the great advance of the Church was carried on.

2. But beyond the empire to the north, advancing upon it like the multitudinous waves of the ocean on an exposed coast, lay the ever-battling legions of the northern tribes in their three great divisions of the Teutonic, Slavic, and Finnish races. If Roman society suffered throes of distress, its condition was peace compared with the instability which may be said to have been the very life of these tribes. Once at least in every century they gather themselves up for a concentrated effort against the empire whose rich civilisation lies stretched out before them as a continual prey. After the failure of Arminius to construct a German kingdom, and of Marobod to construct a Suevian, in the time of Augustus, Decebalus, in the time of Trajan, makes another effort in behalf of his

Dacians. But here the great Roman general forces barbarism to retreat, and plants a fresh citadel in its very stronghold by establishing a province north of the Danube. Then there is comparative tranquillity for sixty years. It seems as if these two generations were offered by Divine Providence to the empire yet in its unbroken strength as a time for its pacific conversion, which if it had accepted, the eruption of the northern nations might for ever have been kept back by the unity which religious conviction would have bestowed on civilisation, and the fresh and living force which it would have imparted to society not yet exhausted by despotic power. But with Marcus Aurelius the empire turns definitively away. A new religious revolution under Odin in Scandinavia had wakened up with redoubled force the destroying energy of barbarism. The Goths had migrated from Sweden to the Black Sea; all the tribes in the interval had been displaced and dashed upon each other by this removal. The war of the Marcomans occupied during eighteen years, from 162 to 180, the whole forces of the empire; Rome was obliged even to arm its slaves, and Italy feared an invasion more terrible than that of the Cimbri, which it cost Marcus Aurelius his life to avert.

Again, during the captivity of Valerian, another grand assault of the northern tribes takes place. The Franks attack western, the Alamans eastern Gaul; they pass the Alps and advance to Ravenna, while Alamans and Sarmatians throw themselves upon Pannonia, and the Goths seize upon Thrace and Greece. The emperors Claudius, Aurelian, and Probus are the saviours of Rome from this new flood. Of the last of these it is recorded that he dealt successively with

Franks, Burgundians, Alamans, Vandals, the Bastarnæ, and the whole barbarian brood: and seventy cities raised from their ruins, and fortifications repaired upon a line of fifteen hundred miles, were the fruits of his victories.[1]

So much for the north: while on the east the Persian empire, hereditary foe of the Roman name, had found a new and more vigorous master in the race of the Sassanidæ, who took the religion of Zoroaster to reanimate the national spirit. Ardeschir claimed once more the whole realm which Cyrus and Darius had ruled. Henceforth the Romans had a neighbour more than ever threatening their eastern frontier, and never to be wholly subdued, until the empire of Mohammed arose to detach a great part of their dominion, and to move with redoubled force upon what remained.

To the south of the Roman provinces in Africa were tribes at least as savage as those of the north. Thus the whole empire was enringed with enemies: on the east an opposing civilisation and religion; on the north and south barbarian tribes in perpetual confusion and conflict with each other. Such was the great realm of disorder which surged and heaved to the north and south of the empire; and such the second great enemy which in future times was to occupy the Christian Church, and at present offered the strongest contrast to that moral polity of peace and good-will, of loyal submission, patient endurance, and heroic fortitude, which was spreading daily in the empire.

3. But there was yet another enemy within the empire itself, which from the beginning tracked the

[1] Am. Thierry, *Tableau de l'Empire Romain*, p. 412.

footsteps of the Church, grew with its increase, and everywhere attempted to dissolve its organisation and weaken its influence. The whole second century is occupied with the rise and tangled growth of the Gnostic sects. But these were not alone. From the very time of the Apostles we find the evidence of a number of sects, rising and falling, preying on and devouring each other, none without some portion of Christian truth, on which it feeds, blended with Jewish, Greek, Oriental, Egyptian, Libyan notions, prejudices, and errors; domiciled in various parts of the empire in accordance with the national or local character which they represent. They reproduce with a Christian colour the sects and the sect-life of the Greek schools of philosophy. As the wheat has its proper weed, which springs up in the midst of it and counterfeits it, so error, everywhere gathering round some portion of truth, forms itself into an antagonistic life. The force and truth of the Christian Church were shown not in the absence of these rivals, but in its triumph over their variety, in its remaining one whilst they diverged endlessly from that unchanging original type, in its continuous and uniform growth whilst they rose and fell, domineered in certain times and places, and then disappeared. In this its course the Church had to master very great difficulties, which were inherent in the manner of its rise. It had to remain one society in spite of the isolation and self-government of its local portions. It possessed in each place but a feeble minority of members compared with the mass of unbelievers. Against its assimilating power was ranged the force of national feelings which underlay the Roman authority throughout the whole empire. It had to deal entirely by moral means with the full liberty of error to which its adherents were exposed. Lastly, it had to do all this amid the continual strain of threatened or actual persecution, a state which at its best was one of insecurity, and which any local trouble, the ill-will of a mob, the greed or ambition or fear of provincial rulers, not to speak of the imperial state-policy, might turn into the pressure of severe suffering.

In the face of such difficulties, if the Christian Church continued one in its doctrine, organisation, and manner of life, such unity was assuredly the proof of a divine power residing in it.

I shall now proceed to show by the testimony of eye-witnesses that such unity was its distinguishing characteristic.

Now there was not a race or a religion in all this Roman empire, endless as the races and religions comprehended in it were, out of which individuals were not drawn into the bosom of the one great Christian society; and yet within this there was a perfect union of all hearts and minds in the conviction that the multitude so collected was one people apart from all other peoples. And this conviction is itself the great marvel. How was it wrought? For it was an utterly new thing upon the earth. The union of race, language, and locality, with which sameness of religion was usually interwoven, had been hitherto the bond of such nations as had as yet existed. The great city itself had sprung up and flourished by the strict union of these four things. After its career of foreign conquest had substituted for the government of a city the great Roman confederation, it had indeed, like the preceding world-empires, in fact disregarded all these, being supported by a force independent of them all. But that force was material power. The great statue was of iron. It was a novelty unheard of as yet among the Gentiles and unimagined by poet or philosopher, to create a polity which, disregarding sameness of race, of language, and of locality, should exist and maintain itself throughout the whole earth solely by the force of faith and charity.

Such was the idea of Christians about themselves from the beginning. The idea preceded the fact. The prophets foretold it; the Apostles proclaimed it:[1] let us observe the fulfilment of the prophecy and the proclamation. We will take our stand in the middle of the third century, when seven full generations have passed since the day of Pentecost. In this time a people has been formed. Already a hundred and fifty years before, an eye-witness among themselves had observed the nature of this people. "Christians are not distinguished from other men either by country, or by language, or by customs: for they have no cities peculiar to themselves, nor any language different from others, nor singularity in their mode of life. . . . But they dwell both in Greek and in barbarous cities, as the lot of each may be, following local customs as to raiment and food, and the rest of their life, but exhibiting withal a polity of their own, marvellous and truly incredible. They dwell in their own country, but it is as sojourners; they share in everything as citizens, yet suffer everything as strangers. Every foreign land is to them a country, and every country a foreign land. . . . In a word, what the soul is in the body, that Christians are in the world. The soul is diffused through all the limbs of the body,

[1] Zach. ii. 11, Is. ii. 2, Mich. iv. 1, compared with Titus ii. 14 and 1 Pet. ii. 9.

THIRD AGE OF THE MARTYR CHURCH 263

and Christians through all the cities of the world. . . . The soul is shut within the body, of which it is the bond, and Christians are like a garrison in the world, which they hold together."[1]

Here a writer, calling himself a disciple of Apostles, describes to us, at the beginning of the second century, what the apostolic age of seventy years had wrought. He puts his finger just upon the marvel which we are contemplating. Fifty years later, at the moment the empire was culminating under the serene rule of Antoninus, a convert from heathenism, a philosopher who had spent his life in examining all the sects and races of the empire, and who afterwards became a martyr, said of Christians that being "quarried out of the side of Christ, they were the true Israelitic race," "altogether being called the body, for both people and church, being many in number, are called by one name as one thing;" they are in fact "as one man before the Maker of all things, through the name of His first-born Son," the High-priest gathering up first in the prophetical vision and then in the real fact "the true high-priestly race"[2] in His own Person. Thus Justin pointed out this conception of the Christian people to the Jew of his time as both foretold in prophecy and exhibited in fact. The longer that such a people as this endured, the greater would be the marvel.

A hundred years after this, Origen uses the same language and points to the same marvel. He had in the year 249, at the entreaty of a friend and pupil, set himself in the maturity of life, and of a renown

[1] *Ep. ad Diognetum*, 5, 6.
[2] St. Justin Martyr, *Tryphon*, sec. 135, 42, 116; where he refers to and explains the vision of the high-priest Jesus in the prophet Zacharias iii. 1.

which filled the Church as no man's before had filled it, to answer the attack of a heathen philosopher, Celsus, upon Christianity. He was writing just at the end of the longest period of peace which is found during those three centuries. From the death of the Emperor Septimius Severus in 211 to that of the Emperor Philip in this year 249, there had been, with the exception of a short attack from Maximin, to which his death put a stop, no general persecution of Christians. Thus thirty-eight years had passed of such tranquillity as it was ever in those times the lot of Christians to obtain. The mother of one emperor had been Origen's disciple, and the emperor actually reigning was a Christian, however unworthy of such a profession. Now in this work Origen speaks of the superiority of the Christian churches in each several place, as, for instance, at Athens, Corinth, Alexandria, to the heathen assemblies, and of the Christian rulers to the heathen. He puts it as a mark of divine power that God sending His Son, "a God come in human soul and body,"[1] should have established everywhere churches offering the contrast of their polity to the assemblies of the superstitious, the impure, and the unjust. He considers that Christians do a greater benefit to their country than all other men by teaching them piety to the one God, and "gathering up into a certain divine and heavenly city those who have lived well in the smallest cities."[2] "We," he says, "knowing that there is in each city another fabric of a country, founded by the word of God, call those who are powerful in word and of a virtuous life to the government of churches: we do not accept the

---

[1] ὡς υἱὸν Θεοῦ, Θεὸν ἐληλυθότα ἐν ἀνθρωπίνῃ ψυχῇ καὶ σώματι. *Cont. Cels.* iii. 29.   [2] *Ibid.* viii. 74.

covetous to such a place, but force it against their will upon those who in their moderation would decline taking on them this general care of the Church of God."¹ And the compulsion thus exercised is that "of the great King, whom we are persuaded to be the Son of God, God the Word." But this other form of country which he saw in each city is "the whole Church of God, which the divine Scriptures assert to be the Body of Christ, animated by the Son of God, while the limbs of this Body are particular believers; for as the soul quickens and moves the body, whose nature it is not to have the movement of life from itself, so the Word moving to what is fitting, and energising in the whole Body, the Church, moves likewise each member of it, who does nothing without the Word."² And he completes this view in another beautiful passage wherein he describes Christ as the high-priest Aaron, who has received upon His single body the whole chrism, from whom it flows down upon His beard, the symbol of the complete man, and on to the utmost skirt of His raiment. Every one who partakes of Him, partakes likewise of His chrism, because Christ is the Head of the Church, and the Church and Christ one Body.³ We have here in Origen's thought one and the same divine power, proceeding forth from the Incarnation, which forms first the Body of the Lord, and then gathers into this Body every individual as a copy of the Christ. The heathen scoffer had objected: "Why send forth one spirit into one corner of the earth? It was needed to breathe that spirit into many bodies, and to send them forth into all the world." "Nay," replied Origen,

---

[1] *Cont. Cels.* viii. 75. [2] *Ibid.* vi. 48, p. 670.
[3] *Cont. Cels.* vi. 79, p. 692.

"the whole Church of God—animated by the Son of God as the soul quickens and moves the body—was enough. It needed not that there should be many bodies and many souls, like that of Jesus, in the way you suppose, for the one Word as the sun of righteousness rising from Judea was sufficient to send forth rays that should reach every soul that would receive Him." He has done far more than you suggest: every member of that one Body has received according to his measure a due portion of anointment: after the model of the Christ, they too are Christs; "so that beginning in the body He should dawn in power and in spirit upon the universe of souls which would no longer be destitute of God."

In Origen's mind, then, the greatness of the King lies specifically in this, that out of confusion He draws unity, out of those who were no people He forms a people, out of nations and tribes at enmity He moulds an indivisible kingdom, and from His own Body a Body which shall embrace a universe of souls, instinct with one life, and that His own. This was Origen's view of the work and triumph of Christ, as he saw it before him, at the eve of the great Decian persecution in 249.

Origen was writing this at a moment of great interest. It was the last year which preceded those two generations, in the course of which five great persecutions should be directed by the emperors against the Church. He was then a man of sixty-four. The son of a martyr, he had when a youth of eighteen beheld his father imprisoned for the faith, and had encouraged him to suffer the loss of all his goods, and death itself, without regarding that large family which must be left in penury, of whom Origen was the eldest.

He was burning himself to share his father's sufferings. In the persecution of which this was the opening Eusebius tells us that seven of his disciples were martyrs: and, lastly, he was to undergo such cruelties himself in the persecution of Decius, then on the eve of breaking out, that he is believed to have died of their results. Now it is in this work that he speaks of the remarkable providence of God in preserving Christians, who by their religion were bound not to defend themselves, against the attacks of their enemies, for God, he says, had fought for them, and from time to time had stopped those who had risen up with the purpose of destroying them. Few and easily numbered were those who hitherto had suffered death for the Christian Faith, samples chosen by God as champions to encourage the rest, while He prevented their whole nation from being rooted out: for it was His purpose that this nation should be firmly rooted and consolidated, and the whole world be filled with its saving doctrine and discipline.[1] Thus it was by His will alone that He scattered every plot directed against them, so that neither emperors, nor local governors, nor the people should be able to indulge their wrath beyond a certain point. Origen, when he thus wrote, could look back on a period of thirty-eight years, during which, with the exception of the severe but

---

[1] Κωλύοντος τοῦ Θεοῦ τὸ πᾶν ἐκπολεμηθῆναι αὐτῶν ἔθνος. συστῆναι γὰρ αὐτὸ ἐβούλετο καὶ πληρωθῆναι πᾶσαν τὴν γῆν τῆς σωτηρίου ταύτης καὶ εὐσεβεστάτης διδασκαλίας. *Cont. Cels.* iii. 8. It must be remembered that Celsus in the passage to which this is an answer had asserted that the Christians had arisen out of the Jews through a sedition; which makes the train of thought pertinent. For Origen is contrasting the losses which occur through exterminating wars, such as a sedition, or civil war, excites, with the losses to the Christian body through martyrdom. The comparison therefore lies between the whole number of Christians viewed *en masse* and the martyrs. Lasaulx remarks that this was written before the Decian persecution.

passing storm raised by the Emperor Maximin, peace had reigned: years which he had himself employed in unwearied labours of teaching, writing, and converting; in which he had directed and advised an emperor's mother, and seen a Christian emperor; in which he had witnessed a wonderful increase of the Christian people, and indeed of this increase his words above cited convey a faithful picture. He knew not the fearful trials which were to be encountered before that triumph of the truth which he already anticipated should be attained: or that God was about to accept from the grey-haired man the sacrifice which the impetuous youth had affronted without success. For scarcely has he written this book when he has to fly for his life before the edict of Decius, who will attempt to destroy the Christian religion, and to whose anger Pope St. Fabian falls a victim. Amid great peril after long delay the next Pope Cornelius is chosen. And now for the first time a new danger from within assaults the Church. Novatian, a Roman presbyter of great repute, attempts after the due election and consecration of Cornelius to usurp his place, and to divide the one flock of Christ. Under circumstances so wholly altered from those in which Origen above was writing, we come to our next witness, the man in all the Western Church the most renowned, as Origen was in the Eastern.

For it was on the occasion of the first antipope, an effort, that is, within the See of Peter itself to arm the episcopal power at its very source against itself, to set an altar up against the legitimate altar, and to divide the sacraments of the Church from the Bride whose dowry they are, that St. Cyprian wrote his treatise on the Unity of the Church. "It was for the

purpose of reminding his brethren that unity is the
first element of the Christian state, and that those who
break off from the principle of unity, which is lodged
in the Episcopate, even though they be confessors and
martyrs, have no portion in the hopes of the gospel."[1]
This definite purpose, so unlike that state of leisure
and tranquillity in which Origen answered by thought
and learning a speculative attack, will account for the
very remarkable precision and force of St. Cyprian's
language.

"The enemy," he says, "detected and downfallen
by the advent of Christ, now that light is come to the
nations—seeing his idols left—has made heresies and
schisms, wherewith to subvert faith, to corrupt truth,
and to rend unity." But this will all be in vain if
men will look to the Head, and keep to the doctrine
of the Master. For the truth may be quickly stated.[2]
"The Lord saith unto Peter : ' I say unto thee that thou
art Peter, and upon this rock I will build My Church,
and the gates of hell shall not prevail against it.
And I will give unto thee the keys of the kingdom of
heaven, and whatsoever thou shalt bind on earth shall
be bound also in heaven, and whatsoever thou shalt
loose on earth shall be loosed in heaven.' To him
again, after His resurrection, He says : ' Feed My sheep.
Upon him, being one, He builds His Church ; and
though He gives to all the Apostles an equal power,
and says : ' As my Father sent Me, even so send I you ;
receive ye the Holy Ghost : whosesoever sins ye remit,
they shall be remitted to him, and whosesoever sins ye
retain, they shall be retained ;—yet in order to manifest

---

[1] Preface to the Oxford edition of St. Cyprian's treatise on the Unity
of the Church.
[2] *De Unitate*, iii. &c.

unity, He has by His own authority so placed the source of the same unity as to begin from one. Certainly the other Apostles also were what Peter was, endued with an equal fellowship both of honour and power; but a commencement is made from unity, that the Church may be set before us as one: which one Church in the Canticle of Canticles doth the Holy Spirit design and name in the Person of our Lord: 'My dove, my spotless one is but one; she is the only one of her mother, elect of her that bare her.'

"He who holds not this unity of the Church, does he think that he holds the faith? He who strives against and resists the Church, is he assured that he is in the Church? For the blessed Apostle Paul teaches this same thing, and manifests the sacrament of unity thus speaking: 'There is one Body and one Spirit, even as ye are called in one Hope of your calling; one Lord, one Faith, one Baptism, one God.' This unity firmly should we hold and maintain, especially we bishops, presiding in the Church, in order that we may approve the Episcopate itself to be one and undivided. Let no one deceive the brotherhood by falsehood; no one corrupt the truth of our faith by a faithless treachery. The Episcopate is one, of which a part is held by each without division of the whole. The Church is likewise one, though she be spread abroad, and multiplies with the increase of her progeny: even as the sun has rays many, yet one light, and the tree boughs many, yet its strength is one, seated in the deep-lodged root; and as, when many streams flow down from one source, though a multiplicity of waters seems to be diffused from the bountifulness of the overflowing abundance, unity is preserved in the source itself. Part a ray of the sun from its orb, and its unity forbids this division of light; break a branch from the tree, once broken it can bud no more; cut the stream from its fountain, the remnant will be dried up. Thus the Church, flooded with the light of the Lord, puts forth her rays through the whole world, with yet one light, which is spread upon all places, while its unity of body is not infringed. She stretches forth her branches over the universal earth, in the riches of plenty, and pours abroad her bountiful and onward streams; yet is there one head, one source, one mother, abundant in the results of her fruitfulness.

"It is of her womb that we are born; our nourishing is from her milk, our quickening from her breath. The Spouse of Christ cannot become adulterate; she is undefiled and chaste; owning but one home, and guarding with virtuous modesty the sanctity of one chamber. She it is who keeps us for God, and appoints unto the kingdom the sons she has borne. Whosoever parts company with the Church and joins himself to an adulteress, is estranged from the promises of the Church. He who leaves the Church of Christ, attains not to Christ's rewards. He is an alien, an outcast, an enemy. He can no longer have God for a Father who has not the Church for a mother. If any man was able to escape who remained without the ark of Noah, then will that man escape who is out of doors beyond the Church. The Lord warns us and says: 'He who is not with Me is against Me, and he who gathereth not with Me, scattereth.' He who breaks the peace and concord of Christ, sets himself against Christ. He who gathers elsewhere but in the Church, scatters the Church of Christ. The Lord says: 'I and the Father are one;' and again of the Father, the Son, and the Holy Ghost it is written: 'And these three are one.' And does any one think that oneness, thus proceeding from the divine immutability, and cohering in heavenly sacraments, admits of being sundered in the Church, and split by the divorce of antagonist wills? He who holds not this unity holds not the law of God, holds not the faith of Father and Son, holds not the truth unto salvation.

"This sacrament of unity, this bond of concord inseparably cohering, is signified in the place in the Gospel where the coat of our Lord Jesus Christ is in nowise parted or cut, but is received a whole garment, by them who cast lots who should rather wear it, and is possessed as an inviolate and individual robe. The divine Scripture thus speaks: 'But for the coat, because it was not sewed, but woven from the top throughout, they said one to another, Let us not rend it, but cast lots whose it shall be.' It has with it a unity descending from above, as coming, that is, from heaven and from the Father; which it was not for the receiver and owner in anywise to sunder, but which he received once for all and indivisibly as one unbroken whole. He cannot own Christ's garment who splits and divides Christ's Church. On the other hand, when on Solomon's death his kingdom and people were split in parts, Ahijah the prophet, meeting King Jeroboam in the field, rent his garment into twelve pieces, saying: 'Take thee ten pieces; for thus saith the Lord: Behold, I will rend the kingdom out of the hand of Solomon, and will give ten tribes to thee; and two tribes shall be to him for My servant David's sake, and for Jerusalem, the city which I have chosen, to place My name there.' When the twelve tribes of Israel were torn asunder, the prophet Ahijah rent his garment. But because Christ's people cannot be rent, His coat, woven and conjoined throughout, was not divided by those to whom it fell. Individual, conjoined, co-entwined, it shows the coherent concord of our people who put on Christ. In the sacrament and sign of His garment, He has declared the unity of His Church.

"Who, then, is the criminal and traitor, who so inflamed by the madness of discord, as to think aught can rend, or to venture on rending God's unity, the Lord's garment, Christ's Church? He Himself warns us in His Gospel and teaches, saying: 'And there shall be one Fold and one Shepherd.' . . . Think you that any can stand and live who withdraws from the Church, and forms for himself new homes and different domiciles? . . . Believers have no house but the Church only. This house, this hostelry of unanimity, the Holy Spirit designs and betokens in the Psalms, thus speaking: 'God who makes men to dwell with one mind in a house.' In the house of God, in the Church of Christ, men dwell with one mind, and persevere in concord and simplicity." To this he adds: "There is one God, and one Christ, and His Church one, and the Faith one, and one the people joined into the solid unity of a body by the cement of concord. Unity cannot be sundered, nor can one body be divided by a dissolution of its structure, nor be severed into pieces with torn and lacerated vitals. Parted from the womb, nothing can live and breathe in its separated state: it loses its principle of health;" for "charity will ever exist in the kingdom; she will abide evermore in the unity of a brotherhood which entwines itself around her."

And he is more specific still; for this "one Church is founded by the Lord Christ upon Peter, having its source and its principle in unity," "on whose person

He built the Church, and in whom He began and exhibited the source of unity."[1]

Certainly if any idea has ever been put forth clearly and definitely, it would seem to be the idea of organic unity here delineated by Cyprian, as necessary not merely to the well-being but to the essence of the Church. Nor does one see what words he could have found more expressly to reject the notion that the individual bishop in his diocese was the unit on the aggregation of which the Church was built, and to assert in contradiction that the Church was built on the Primacy of Peter as its generative, formative, controlling, and unifying power. According to him the whole order and government of the Church are bound up in the Lord's words to Peter: while as to the Church herself three ideas are in his mind so compacted together, so running into and pervading each other, that they cannot be severed; and these ideas are Unity, Grace, and Truth. The symbols of the Sun, the Tree, and the Fountain, the Lord's Coat, the one Flock tethered in one Fold under one Shepherd, the one House as opposed to sundry self-chosen domiciles, the Mother embracing her whole progeny in her womb, illustrate and enforce each other, and all contain the three ideas, of which Grace and Truth are as the warp and woof in which the substance of the one web consists. For Unity, Truth, and Grace, viewed as attributes of the Church, are blended together in the light and warmth of the sun, in the sap which vivifies every branch of the tree, and gives it fruitfulness from the root, in the fountain of water, under which image our Lord has so often summed up his whole gift to man, in the flock which the Shepherd has chosen, and

[1] Epist. 70 and 73.

for which He cares, in the house where the master
dwells and collects his family, in the one robe which
encompassed and contained the virtue of the Wearer,
in the prolific womb which gives birth to the whole
sacred race. The force of all these images lies in
their unicity: plurality would not modify, but destroy
them. Yet even these symbols are surpassed by that
argument from the divine Unity which he sets forth
as the type and cause of the Church's unity. From
created likenesses—the fairest and choicest which the
world presents—he passes to the uncreated nature,
and from the divine immutability, wherewith these
three, the Father, the Son, and the Holy Ghost, the
divine Exemplar of Unity, Truth, and Grace, are one,
deduces the Unity of the Church their dwelling-place.

Cyprian, then, cannot sever the Church of his heart,
the Church for which he lived and died, from Unity,
or from Truth, or from Grace: and this Church is to
him founded on the Primacy of Peter, and developed
from his person. The one Episcopate, whose golden
chain he looks upon as surrounding the earth in its
embrace, "of which a part is held by each without
division of the whole," wherein therefore joint possession is dependent on unity, would have no existence
without the bond of the Primacy, from which it was
developed and which keeps it one. Take away this,
and the office of each bishop is crystallised into a
separate mass, having no coherence or impact with its
like: bishops so conceived would hold indeed a similar
office, but being detached from each other would not
hold joint possession of one Episcopate. Separate
crystals do not make one body; nor a heap of pebbles
a rock. But it was a Rock on which Christ built and
builds His Church, that Rock being His own Person,

from which He communicated this virtue, wherein the cohesion and impact of the whole Episcopate lies, to the See of him whom He constituted His Vicar. Finally, Cyprian contrasts pointedly the people of Christ *which cannot be rent* with the twelve tribes of Israel, which were torn asunder: as if he would beforehand repudiate that parallel between the Synagogue and the Church, in the question of unity, which has before now been resorted to as a refuge by minds in distress, who failed to see the tokens of the Bride of Christ in the community to which they belonged.

In Origen and in Cyprian we put ourselves back into the middle of the third century. In the words of the latter we see portrayed to the life that idea which had filled the hearts of Christians through seven generations of labours and sorrows from the day of Pentecost down to his time. But whence arose this perfect union of all hearts and minds in the early Christians, who were penetrated with the conviction that the Church was the home of truth and grace? We may answer this question thus: No catechumen was received into the fold without a clear and distinct belief in that article of the earliest creed, and part of the baptismal profession, "the Holy Catholic Church." A new word was made to express a new idea, the glorious and unique work of that ever-blessed Trinity whom the creed recited: the Home and House in which the Triune God, whom the Christian glorified, by indwelling made the fountain of that grace and that truth which God had become Man in order to communicate. The catechumen's baptism into the one Body was the foundation of all the hope in which his life consisted;[1] the integrity, duration, sanctity of that

---

[1] τῇ γὰρ ἐλπίδι ἐσώθημεν.

Body being component parts of the hope. And with regard at least to all Gentile converts this precise and definite catechetical instruction was reinforced by the new sense which at their conversion was impressed on them of the heathenism out of which they were then taken. In how many of them was the remembrance of their past life connected with the guilt of deeds and habits which their new Christian conscience taught them to regard as fearful sins. Nay, the notion of sin itself—as a transgression of the eternal law and an offence against the personal Majesty of God—was a Christian acquisition to the corrupted heathen. Thus the passage into the one Body and the divine Kingdom was contemporaneous in their case with a total change of the moral life. It is Cyprian, again, who has given us a vivid account of this change, which took place at a time of mature manhood in his own life, and which will serve as a graphic sketch of what had happened to the great mass of adult converts besides himself.

Let us suppose a man forty-five years of age speaking: "For me, while I yet lay in darkness and bewildering night, and was tossed to and fro on the billows of this troublesome world, ignorant of my true life, an outcast from light and truth, I used to think that second birth, which divine mercy promised for my salvation, a hard saying according to the life I then led: as if a man could be so quickened to a new life in the laver of healing water as to put off his natural self, and keep his former tabernacle, yet be changed in heart and soul. How is it possible, said I, for so great a conversion to be accomplished, so that both the obstinate defilement of our natural substance, and old and ingrained habits, should suddenly and rapidly be put off; evils whose roots are deeply seated within? When does he learn frugality, to whom fine feasts and rich banquets have become a habit? Or he who in gay sumptuous robes glisters with gold and purple, when does he reduce himself to ordinary and simple raiment? Another whose bent is to public distinctions and honours cannot bear to become a private and unnoticed man; while one who is thronged by a phalanx of dependents, and retinued by the overflowing attendance of an obsequious host, thinks it punishment to be alone. The temptation still unrelaxed, need is it that, as before, wine should entice, pride inflate, anger inflame, covetousness disquiet, cruelty stimulate, ambition delight, and lust lead headlong.

"Such were my frequent musings; for whereas I was encumbered with the many sins of my past life, which it seemed impossible to be rid of, so I had used myself to give way to my clinging infirmities, and, from despair of better things, to humour the evils of my heart, as slaves born in my house and my proper offspring. But after that life-giving water succoured me, washing away the stain of former years, and pouring into my cleansed and hallowed breast the light which comes from heaven, after that I drank in the heavenly Spirit, and was created into a new man by a second birth, then marvellously what before was doubtful became plain to me, what was hidden was revealed, what was dark began to shine, what was difficult now had a way and means, what had seemed impossible now could be achieved, what was in me of the guilty flesh now confessed that it was earthy, what was quickened in me by the Holy Ghost now had a growth according to God. Thou knowest well, thou canst recollect as well as I, what was then taken from me, and what was given by that death of sin, that quickening power of holiness. Thou knowest, I name it not; over my own praises it were unwelcome to boast, though that is ground never for boasting but for gratitude, which is not ascribed to man's virtue but is confessed to be God's bounty; so that to sin no more has come of faith, as heretofore to sin had come of human error. From God, I say, from God is all we can be; from Him we live, from Him we grow, and by that strength which is from Him accepted and ingathered we learn beforehand, even in this present state, the foretokens of what is yet to be. Let only fear be a guard upon innocency, that that Lord who by the influence of His heavenly mercy has graciously shone into our hearts, may be detained by righteous obedience in the hostelry of a mind that pleases Him; that the security imparted to us may not beget slothfulness, nor the former enemy steal upon us anew."[1]

Add to this that Christians were marked out as one Body by the Jewish and heathen persecution which tracked them everywhere. But the sects were not persecuted. The various schools of the Gnostics all agreed in this, that it was not necessary or desirable to suffer martyrdom for the faith. Their view was, that they could believe with their minds whatever they pleased, though an enemy might force them by threats of suffering to utter with the mouth what they abhorred; and with this convenient distinction they escaped imprisonment, poverty, bereavement, and death. But the Christian was bound—when the fitting circumstances came—to repeat the confession of his Lord before Pilate. Joined therefore to his

[1] Ep. I, Oxford translation.

baptismal belief, and to the utter change of life involved in his conversion, was the bond of common suffering which held together Christians as one Body throughout the world: whence an old martyr bishop said: "The Church, for that love which she bears to God, in every place and at every time sends forward a multitude of martyrs to the Father, whereas all the rest not only have no such thing among themselves to show, but deem not even such a witness necessary."[1]

Moreover, as a fourth cause, the historic origin of their name and belief led them up to that day of Pentecost when the descent of the Spirit of God constituted the formation of that body in belonging to which was all their hope and trust; with the existence of which their faith was identified; in the communion of which their charity was engendered. As the birth and the life and the passion of Christ were that subject-matter on which their whole faith grew, so the creation of their existence as a people was a definite act in which the Redeemer showed Himself the Father of His Race, creating them as His children and generating them by His Spirit. The loving thought of Christians in every age ran along this line to its source. Nature herself presents us with an image of what this idea of the Church was to them. As the great river whose water is the symbol of blessing and the bearer of fertility leaps down a giant birth from its parent lake, ever blazing under the splendour of a tropical sun, yet ever fed by sources springing from snow-crowned mountains, and changes in its course the desert into earth's fruitfulest region, so the river of God, welling forth on the day of Pentecost from the central abyss of the divine love,

[1] S. Irenæus, lib. iv. 33 g.

bore down to all the nations the one water of salvation, and wheresoever it spread, the desert retreated, and the earth brought forth corn and wine in abundance. And the idea of this divine stream was from the beginning as deep as it was clear in every Christian heart. It is one of a very few doctrines, such as the unity of the Godhead, whereof indeed it is the image and the result, of which there is not only an implicit belief but a definite consciousness from the first. For the thought of the kingdom is inseparable from that of the king: and he could be no Divine Sovereign whose realm was not one and indivisible: and that this realm should break in pieces and consume all other kingdoms,[1] but itself stand for ever, was the trust on which the whole Christian life of endurance and hope was built.

The Christian society through its whole structure was marked with the seal of that great act on which it grew, the assumption of human nature by a divine Person. Its whole government, its whole worship, and the whole moral and spiritual being of its people radiate from that Person as King, as Priest, and as Prophet. Take first the character of the individual Christian. It is in all its gradations, in that marvellous range of the same being which stretches from the highest saint matured in acting and suffering to the most imperfect penitent received into the bosom of the one mother, a copy, more or less resembling, of our Lord Himself. He, the divine Image, is the original from which every Christian lineament is traced, and every one of His race repeats Him in some degree. Every virtue is such as a transcript of some portion of

---

[1] Dan. ii. 44. Compare Apoc. i. 9. ὁ ἀδελφὸς ὑμῶν καὶ συγκοινωνὸς ἐν τῇ θλίψει καὶ ἐν τῇ βασιλείᾳ καὶ ὑπομονῇ Ἰησοῦ Χριστοῦ.

His character; and the whole life of the individual resolves itself into an imitation of Him. Thus He is the Prophet not only declaring the whole divine will to men, but leading them in it by His own example. The divine Painter is but representing in every one of His children a copy in some sort of that life, which He set forth in full in the thirty-three years: a thought which we have seen Origen expressing in the chrism which descended from the head of Aaron to the utmost skirt of his raiment.

But likewise in His Priesthood a parallel derivation ensues. First He multiplies Himself in His Apostles: they again in the Bishops whom they create; while each of these communicates himself in his priests. A triple transfusion suffices to form the whole hierarchical order. Nothing can be conceived more simple, yet nothing more efficient supposing that He is what He proclaimed Himself to be. The victim which He appoints to be offered by this priesthood is Himself, and His Body so offered is the food, the life, and the bond of the whole spiritual Body thus created. That Person with which He took the manhood is the centre of all this worship, of which the manhood so taken is the instrument. Thus it is that His second office of Priest, bound up so entirely with Himself, is yet communicated through His divine manhood to the whole Body which He forms. And this order remains through all ages, as intimately connected with his Person now, as eighteen centuries ago, and as it will be when all the centuries to come are evolved.

One office remains; His office of King. And here, again, the jurisdiction which He created for His kingdom springs from His Person, and that not only in its origin but in its perpetual derivation. He was Himself[1] the Apostle: as such He first multiplied Himself in the Twelve, whom from Himself He named Apostles. His public life on earth is an image of the whole mission or government which He would set up after His ascension. He lives with the Twelve: He teaches them: He is their Instructor, Father, and Friend. When His Apostles afterwards created Bishops, this form of our Lord's life on earth was exactly reproduced in the earliest dioceses. Thus St. Mark went forth from the side of Peter, and the mode of his living and the family which he drew around him at Alexandria was after this pattern. He, the Bishop, is the image of Christ, and his twelve presbyters of the Apostles. This model is continually set forth by St. Ignatius as a divine command and institution, he being himself the occupant of the great Mother See of the East, the third See of Peter, and that wherein he first sat.[2] Thus the canonical life was formed by the exactest imitation of our Lord's public life, and its reproduction throughout the various dioceses formed the Church. Such was the life which St. Augustine afterwards practised and reduced to rule; and those who planted the Christian Faith throughout the north, Apostles to new and barbarous races, had this model before them. The diocese was first a family, in which the Bishop as a father presided over his priests, and sent them forth to their work. The Eucharist which he consecrated was from the beginning dispensed from

---

[1] Κατανοήσατε τὸν ἀπόστολον καὶ ἀρχιερέα τῆς ὁμολογίας ἡμῶν Χριστὸν Ἰησοῦν. Heb. iii. 1.

[2] Thus St. Gregory the Great wrote to Eulogius, Patriarch of Alexandria, that the three original patriarchal Sees were all Sees of Peter: " Cum multi sint Apostoli, pro ipso tamen principatu sola Apostolorum Principis Sedes in auctoritate convaluit, quæ in tribus locis unius est." *Epist.* lib. vii. 40. The patriarchal authority is a derivation from the Primacy, which is the well-head.

his church to all his flock. The diocese, then, in its earliest form was an image of our Lord's intercourse with the Twelve, wherein the Bishop represents Him, and the priesthood His Apostles.

But the whole Church in its Episcopate or mass of dioceses no less represented His public life. For as He was the Head, the Living Teacher and Guide of His Apostles, and as He came to establish one Kingdom, and one only,[1] wherein the Twelve represented the whole Episcopate, and contained in themselves its powers, so the Primacy which He visibly exercised among them, He delegated, when He left them, to one of their number. Peter, when he received that commission to feed His sheep, took the place on earth of the great Shepherd, and in him the flock remains one.

Thus the double power which expresses the divinely-established government of the Church, the Primacy and the Episcopate, is as close a transcript of the Lord's life on earth with His Apostles as the diocese taken by itself. In His intercourse with His Apostles He is the germ of the Bishop with his priests; in His Vicariate bestowed upon Peter He repeats or rather continues His visible Headship on earth.

But spiritual jurisdiction is the expression of Christ's sovereignty on earth, and in the order just described it is linked with His Person as strictly as the worship exercised by means of His Priesthood, and the spiritual character which every one of His children bears. Surely no kingdom has ever been so contained in its king, no family in its father, no worship in its object, as the Christian kingdom, family, and worship, which together is the Church. Is it, then, any wonder that all Christian hearts from the

---

[1] Κηρύσσων τὸ εὐαγγέλιον τῆς βασιλείας. Matt. iv. 23.

first were filled with the blessing of belonging to such a creation as this, in which to them their Redeemer lived and reigned, penetrated them with His own life, and gathered them in His kingdom? Are not the words of St. Cyprian just what we should expect those to utter who overflowed with this conviction? At the same time that Cyprian was so writing, Dionysius, the Archbishop of Alexandria, addressed Novatian the antipope in these words: "It was better to suffer any extremity in order not to divide the Church of God. And martyrdom endured to prevent schism were not less glorious than that endured to refuse idolatry, but in my opinion more so. For in the one case a man suffers martyrdom for his own single soul, but in the other for the whole Church."[1]

But let us trace the chronological sequence in history of that great institution, the real as well as logical coherence of which has just been set forth. The Church was a fact long before its theory became the subject of reflection. It came forth from the mind of the Divine Architect and established itself among men through His power; and it is only when this was done that the creative thought according to which it grew could be delineated.

The fact, then, exactly agrees with the theory, and history here interprets dogma.

It is during the great forty days that our Lord founded the Primacy, when He made St. John and the rest of the Apostles sheep of Peter's fold. The period of thirty-eight years which follows is the carrying into effect His design in the first stage. The Church grows around Peter. First in Jerusalem he forms a mass of disciples; then for a certain number

[1] St. Dionys. Alex. Ep. 2. Gallandi, iii. 512.

of years at Antioch. In the second year of Claudius, the thirteenth after the Ascension, he lays the foundations of the Roman Church. In the sixtieth year of our era he sends forth St. Mark to found the Christian society in Alexandria. Thus he takes possession of the three great cities of the empire, of east, west, and south. In the meantime the labours of St. Paul and the other Apostles, in conjunction with those of Peter and in subordination to them, plant the Christian root in a great number of cities. As St. Paul toils all round the northern circuit of the empire, through Asia Minor, Macedonia, Illyricum, to Spain, his work has a manifest reference to the work of Peter in the metropolis of the east, of the south, and of the west. In the latter he joins his elder brother, and the two Princes of the Apostles offer up their lives together on the same day in that city which was to be the perpetual citadel of the Christian Faith, the immovable Rock of a divine Capitol. Thus was it Peter, "from whom the very Episcopate, and all the authority of this title sprung,"[1] and what Pope Boniface wrote in 422 is a simple fact of history: that "the formation of the universal Church at its birth took its beginning from the honour of blessed Peter, in whose person its regimen and sum consists. For from his fountain the stream of ecclesiastical discipline flowed forth into all churches, as the culture of religion progressively advanced."[2] Thus the whole initial movement was from above downwards, and St. Cyprian was not only enunciating dogma but speaking history when he wrote that the Lord built the Church upon Peter. In

---

[1] Answer of Pope Innocent I. to the Council of Carthage in 416, among the letters of St. Augustine.
[2] Constant. *Epist. Rom. Pontif.* p. 1037.

one generation the structure rose above the ground, and during all that time St. Peter's hand directed the work.

Just at the end of this time, on the point of being thrown into prison, whence he only emerged to martyrdom, Paul was at Rome with Peter, and he describes in imperishable words the work which had been already accomplished. Again it is not only dogma but history, not only that which was always to be, but that which already was, which he set forth as it were with his dying voice: the one Body, and the one Spirit, the one Lord, one Faith, and one Baptism, as there is one God. That Body in which Apostles, Prophets, Evangelists, Pastors and Teachers were fixed, that the visible structure might grow up to its final stature, in whose accordant unity was the perpetual safeguard against error. When Paul so wrote,[1] the Body was formed, and its headship was incontestably with Peter. He had no need to remind them of the man with whom he was labouring, of whose work the whole Church from Rome to Antioch and Alexandria was the fruit. But he places the maintenance of truth, and the perpetual fountain of grace, in the unity of the Church, which was before those to whom he wrote an accomplished fact.

Two generations pass and the aged St. Ignatius, on his way to martyrdom, attests the same fact. "Where Jesus Christ is," he says, "there is the Catholic Church." The King is in His Kingdom; the Master in His House; the Lord in His Temple. The bishops throughout the world inseparably linked together are His mind: and the presidency of charity, which is the inner life of all this spiritual empire, is at Rome. St.

[1] Ephes. iv., written during St. Paul's imprisonment at Rome.

Ignatius and the author of the letter to Diognetus write just after the expiration of the apostolic period; and they both regard Christians as one mass throughout the world, living under a divine form of spiritual government. No one who studies their words can doubt that the one Body and the one Spirit were as visible to their eyes and as dear to their heart as to St. Paul.

We pass two generations further and St. Irenæus repeats the same testimony. The interval has been filled by incessant attacks of heresies, and the Bishop of Lyons dwells upon the fact that the Church speaks with one voice through all the regions of the earth as being one House of God, and that the seat of this its unity is in the great See founded by the Princes of the Apostles at Rome. He reproduces at great length the statements of St. Paul that the safeguard of truth lies in the one apostolic ministry, for which he runs up to the fountain-head in Rome. It is in the living voice and the teaching office of the Church that he sees a perpetual preservative against whatever error may arise. Thus it has been up to his time, and thus it will ever be.

Another period of seventy years runs on, and we come to the just-cited testimony of Cyprian, who therefore said nothing new, nor anything exaggerated; but when the truth was assailed in its very citadel, he spoke out and described wherein its strength lay. He gathers up and gives expression to the two hundred and twenty years between the day of Pentecost and his own time. Here are the creative words of our Apostle and High-priest explained and attested and exhibited as having passed into fact by four witnesses, first St. Paul, then Ignatius, thirdly St. Irenæus, fourthly St. Cyprian. Between all the five there is no shadow of divergence, between the Master who designed the building and the servants who described its erection; between the Prophet who foretold and the historians who recorded. The one said, "Upon this rock I will build My Church;" the others pointed out that the work was accomplished.

The original and fundamental conception of all this work is expressed by St. Matthew and St. Mark when they speak of our Lord at His first going forth as "proclaiming the gospel of the kingdom." His three years' ministry is the germ and type of the perpetual mission which He founded. It was to be from first to last a work of personal ministry, beginning from above, not spreading from below; its power and virtue descending from Him through those whom He chose, the people being the work of the Prince, their government a delegation from Him, as their moral condition lay in following Him, and their life and support in feeding on Him. And He declared that the original conception should be carried out to the end, and that "the gospel of the kingdom" should be proclaimed through the whole world as a witness to all nations, until the consummation should come.[1]

The chief events of the third century brought out more and more the unity of the Church and the Primacy of St. Peter's See as the power within the Church by which that unity is produced and maintained.

With this century the great persecutions begin. That of Septimius Severus arose in the year 202.

[1] This text is continually used by St. Augustine against the Donatists, as containing an express divine prophecy that the one Catholic Church should continue to the end of the world. The Gospel *of* the Kingdom, and the Gospel *without* the Kingdom, are ideas far as the poles apart.

Now a persecution which assaulted the mass of Christians was the occasion of fall and apostasy to some, of martyrdom to others. Hence the question became urgent how those should be treated by the Christian society who through fear of suffering had failed to maintain the confession of their faith. It was necessary to lay down more distinctly rules as to what crimes should be admitted to penance, and what that penance should be. The practice here involved doctrine; it raised immediately the question of the power which the society itself had to grant pardon, and to receive the guilty back into its bosom. And here the authority of the chief Bishop was at once called out. We find as a matter of fact Pope Zephyrinus in the first years of this century determining the rules of penance, and a small party of rigid disciplinarians, among whom Tertullian was conspicuous, who considered his rules as too indulgent. It is in the vehement pamphlet with which Tertullian assails the Pope that we have one of the earliest expressions of the great authority claimed by him. "I hear," he exclaims, "that an edict has been set forth, and a peremptory one. The Pontifex Maximus, in sooth, that is, the Bishop of Bishops, issues his edict: 'I pardon to those who have discharged their penance the sins both of adultery and of fornication.'"[1] Twenty years later Pope Callistus carried the indulgence yet further, receiving to penance those who had committed murder or idolatry.[2] Once more, after a period of thirty years, the breaking out of the Decian persecution raised afresh the question of admitting great

---

[1] *De Pudicitia*, § 1. See Hagemann, p. 54.
[2] He is so represented by Hippolytus, *Philosophumen*, lib. ix. p. 209. See Hagemann, p. 59.

sinners to penance, and the actual discipline of the Roman Church, as established under Zephyrinus and Callistus, is set forth in a letter to Cyprian by Novatian, then one of the most esteemed presbyters of that church. By the discipline which these facts attest it is determined that the Church has lodged in her the power of pardoning any sin whatsoever according to the rules of the penance which she imposes. And it is the Roman Church which herein takes the guidance. She maintained the ancient faith, severity, and discipline, yet tempered with that consideration which the full possession of the truth alone bestows.[1] Thus she received back without hesitation those who returned from heresy or schism, as well as those who had fallen in the conflict with persecution.

For another question of great importance which her guidance determined was that concerning the rebaptization of heretics; and in this she went against the judgment of Cyprian with his council, of Firmilian, and of other bishops. It had been the custom that those who had received baptism among heretics, provided it was with the proper rite, should, when they sought admission into the Church, be received only by an imposition of hands, not by the iteration of baptism. And though Cyprian and a great majority of African bishops, through their horror of schism and heresy, wished to modify this rule, and to insist that baptism given outside the Church was invalid, Pope Stephen

---

[1] "Nec hoc nobis nunc nuper consilium cogitatum est, nec hæc apud nos adversus improbos modo supervenerunt repentina subsidia : sed antiqua hæc apud nos severitas, antiqua fides, disciplina legitur antiqua ; quoniam nec tantas de nobis laudes Apostolus protulisset dicendo : Quia fides vestra prædicatur in toto mundo, nisi jam exinde vigor iste radices fidei de temporibus illis mutuatus fuisset : quarum laudum et gloriæ degenerem fuisse maximum crimen est." *Epist. Cleri Rom. ad Cyprian.* 31.

resisted, and maintained the ancient rule, with the decision that nothing save what had been handed down should be done.

It is evident that the question of penance and that of rebaptization touched the whole Christian society, and here accordingly we find the superior Principate of the Roman Church exert itself. In fact, the right decision as to both these questions involved the right conception of the Church herself, her constitution, power, and prerogatives. The rigorism [1] with which some had endeavoured to exclude certain sinners from the faculty of receiving penance, and the view which led them to confine the validity itself of baptism to its reception within the one Church, led when fully developed in the following century to the obstinate schism and heresy of the Donatists. These dangerous tendencies were resisted, when they first appeared, by the Roman See, and we owe to such resistance the application by Tertullian to the Pope of the title of "Pontifex Maximus" and "Bishop of Bishops," about the year 202, as the expression of the power which he then claimed and exercised.

Another question likewise touching the whole Christian society, which the Roman Pontiff had already decided against the practice of the influential and ancient churches of Asia Minor, was the time of holding Easter. Pope Victor insisted that the practice of the Roman Church must be followed, which kept the day of the Crucifixion invariably on the Friday, and that of the Resurrection on the Sunday, and not the Jewish practice of the Asiatics, which took the 14th and the 16th days of the month Nisan, on whatever days of the week they might fall, for that purpose.

[1] Hagemann, p. 77.

And here in the peremptory tone of Pope Victor, and in the threat of excommunication which he issued, the consciousness was shown that the right to determine lay with him, while subsequent times justified his judgment and followed it. Nor was it of little importance that the greatest festival of the Church should be celebrated by all her children both on the same day and in the same spirit.

We have then now traced up to the end of the third century the inner growth and constituent principles of that great institution, which out of every language, tribe, and religion in the empire or beyond it had formed and welded together one people, the bearer of that Truth and that Grace which the Son of God in assuming manhood had conveyed to the world. It remains rapidly to review the relations of the empire with this people during seventy-eight years, from the death of Alexander Severus in 235 to the edict of toleration in 313.

II. The seizure of the empire by Maximin was accompanied by a violent attack upon Christians, whom Alexander was held to have favoured. It is on this occasion that we learn from Origen[1] that churches were burnt, and thus their existence as public buildings is attested. The clergy were especially threatened, and amongst them Ambrosius, the friend of Origen, and Origen himself. But Maximin, after reigning three years with extraordinary cruelty, was slain by his own soldiers. And then during eleven years a period of comparative tranquillity for Christians ensued.

It is with the accession of Decius that the severest trials of the Church commence. In the sixty-four years which elapse from this to the edict of toleration,

[1] In Matt. tom. iii. 857 c.

the force of the empire is five times directed by its rulers against the Christian name. The cause of this is disclosed to us by St. Cyprian, mentioning incidentally the very words of that emperor whose name is associated with the bitterest hatred to Christians. He praises Pope Cornelius,[1] who, when Pope "Fabian's place, that is," he says, "the place of Peter and the rank of the sacerdotal chair, was vacant," "sat fearless in that chair at Rome at the moment when the tyrant who hated God's priests uttered every horrible threat, and with much more patience and endurance heard the rise of a rival prince than the appointment of God's priest at Rome." But why should Decius regard with such dislike the nomination of a Roman Bishop? Why, but that the emperors had now come clearly to discern the organisation of the Church as a visible kingdom of Christ, at the head of which the Roman Bishop stood. That kingdom, the whole moral and religious doctrine of which, together with the life founded upon it, they felt to be in contradiction with the heathen life and the maxims of polity on which from time immemorial the empire had been based, that kingdom Decius saw to be summed up and represented in him who held, to use the words of Cyprian, "Peter's place." With that religious association which Decius saw extending round him on every side, and gradually drawing into its bosom the best of the two sexes, there was no way of dealing but either to yield to those new maxims which it set forth, or to destroy it. In proportion as the

---

[1] "Cum Fabiani locus, id est, cum locus Petri et gradus cathedræ sacerdotalis vacaret." *Epist.* lii. p. 68. "Sedisse intrepidum Romæ in sacerdotali cathedra eo tempore cum tyrannus infestus sacerdotibus Dei fanda atque infanda comminaretur, cum multo patientius et tolerabilius audiret levari adversus se æmulum principem quam constitui Romæ Dei sacerdotem." *Ibid.* p. 69.

emperors were zealous for the worship of the Roman gods, and instinct with the old discipline of the state, they inclined to the latter alternative, and none more decisively than Decius, who prided himself on following the spirit of Trajan. The persecution which he set on foot reached and slew Pope Fabian, and caused the election of a successor to be deferred for sixteen months. When at the end of that time Cornelius was chosen, Cyprian praises him "as to be reckoned among the glorious confessors and martyrs, who sat so long awaiting his butchers, ready either to slay him with the sword, or crucify him, or burn him, or tear open and maim his body with any unheard-of kind of punishment."[1] Decius indeed was slain by the Goths in battle after less than two years' reign, but the persecution was renewed by Gallus, and again by Valerian, so that in ten years no less than five Pontiffs, holding that place of Peter, Fabian, Cornelius, Lucius, Stephen, and Sistus, offered up their lives for the faith. Then it was that the ten years' noble episcopate of St. Cyprian after many minor sufferings ended in martyrdom: and then too the deacon Laurence wore out in the agony of fire all the malignity of the enemy, and gained his almost matchless crown.[2]

---

[1] *Epist.* lii. p. 69.
[2] Compare with the savageness of the Prefect of Rome in torturing St. Laurence the following incident which occurred five years later. Valerian had been captured by the Persian monarch, and his son the Emperor Gallienus bore the reproach with great tranquillity. In the great festival which he held at Rome about 263, to commemorate the victory of Odenatus over Sapor, some revellers mixed themselves with the pretended Persian captives, and examined their faces closely. When asked what they meant, they replied, "We are looking for the emperor's father." The jest so stung Gallienus that he had them burnt alive. Weiss, *Lehrbuch der Weltgeschichte*, ii. 224. It was for showing him the Church's spiritual treasures, the poor, the helpless, and the suffering, instead of the coveted gold and silver, that the Prefect burned St. Laurence alive.

The state of things which immediately preceded this grand attack of the empire on the Church is thus described by Cyprian in the interval which followed the persecution of Decius and preceded that of Gallus; and the words of one who not only taught but died for his teaching carry with them no common force. "As long repose had corrupted the discipline which had come down to us from God, the divine judgment awakened our faith from a declining, and if I may so speak an almost slumbering state; and whereas we deserved yet more for our sins, the most merciful Lord has so moderated all, that what has passed has seemed rather a trial of what we were than an actual infliction. Every one was applying himself to the increase of wealth, and forgetting both what was the conduct of believers under the Apostles, and what ought to be their conduct in every age, they with insatiable eagerness for gain devoted themselves to the multiplying of possessions. The priests were wanting in religious devotedness; the ministers in entireness of faith; there was no mercy in works, no discipline in manners. Men wore their beards disfigured, and women stained their complexion with a dye. The eyes were changed from what God made them, and a lying colour was passed upon the hair. The hearts of the simple were misled by treacherous artifices, and brethren became entangled in seductive snares; ties of marriage were formed with unbelievers; members of Christ abandoned to the heathen. Not only rash swearing was heard, but even false; persons in high place were swollen with contemptuousness; poisoned reproaches fell from their mouths; and men were sundered by unabating quarrels. Numerous bishops, who ought to be an encouragement and example to others, despising their sacred calling, engaged themselves in secular vocations, relinquished their chair, deserted their people, strayed among foreign provinces, hunted the markets for mercantile profits, tried to amass large sums of money while they had brethren starving within the Church, took possession of estates by fraudulent proceedings, and multiplied their gains by accumulated usuries."[1]

Such was the end of the long peace which succeeded the persecution of Septimius Severus, and yet it was followed at once by that ten years' conflict which, if stained with apostasies at first, soon became rife in martyrdoms. And as the former relaxation seems to prove that the third century among Christians was no ideal time in which moral corruptions and abuses did not largely exist, so the improvement which trial and suffering at once produced, calling forth some of the greatest triumphs which the Faith has ever known, seems to indicate that the divine power of the Church lies not in forming a community free from imperfections, or even secured from scandals, but in building up a portion of her children to sanctity. At all times the wheat and the chaff lie together on her threshing-floor, and the flail of suffering winnows them. But those who seek for a time when all professing believers were saints, will find it neither when the Apostles taught nor afterwards.

The Emperor Valerian, after being during four years more kindly disposed to Christians than any preceding emperor, and after filling his palace with them, was instigated by an Egyptian magician into becoming a most bitter persecutor.[2] This was ended

---

[1] *De Lapsis*, iv. pp. 182, 183, Oxford translation.
[2] Euseb. *Hist.* l. vii. c. 10.

in less than three years through his capture by the Persian monarch, when his son Gallienus restored the sacred places to the Christians, and ordered the bishops not to be disturbed.[1] The empire during the following eight years seemed through the supineness of Gallienus to be on the point of dissolution; it is the time when nineteen commanders in various provinces assume the purple, and successively perish. At last Gallienus is put out of the way by a council of officers, and the empire is restored by Claudius and by Aurelian. The latter, after being for some years fair to Christians, ends by persecuting them. But he too is speedily removed by death. It is remarkable that all these persecutions, by Maximin, by Decius, by Gallus, by Valerian, and by Aurelian, are of short duration: none of them continue more than three years. After Aurelian's death in 275 a whole generation ensues in which Christians by the ordinary operation of the empire's laws, according to which their religion was illicit, were liable to suffer much in individual cases. Thus it is in a time not reckoned persecuting, shortly after Maximianus had been made his colleague in the empire by Diocletian, that one of the most merciless acts of tyrannical cruelty took place, which gave an occasion for several thousand men at once to offer up their lives. Unresisting victims, yet brave soldiers with arms in their hands, they endured two decimations, and when remonstrance had proved in vain, piled their arms, and let themselves be massacred to the last man rather than violate their conscience. The place where they suffered took the name of their heroic captain, Maurice; the churches of that Alpine valley to this day bear witness by his figure over their

[1] Euseb. *Hist.* l. vii. c. 13.

altars to that most illustrious act of Christian sacrifice:
and beside the place of their repose rises still a monastery which for thirteen hundred and fifty years has guarded the sepulture of a legion of martyrs, and is become one of the most ancient Christian houses of prayer.

It cannot be doubted that in the last twenty-five years of the third century the number of Christians was being largely increased, and moreover they were daily gaining the higher ranks of society. Diocletian had reigned for eighteen years, and seemed effectually to have stopped that incessant succession of soldiers gaining the throne by assassination and yielding it in turn to their assassins, which for fifty years threatened to destroy the state. At such a moment it was that Diocletian, belying all the past conduct of his life, let loose against the Christian Church the last, the fiercest, and the longest of the heathen persecutions.

It was in truth scarcely less than the rending in pieces the whole social framework when a proclamation of the Emperors Diocletian and Maximian, in the year 303, declared that the Christian Faith should cease to exist. How entirely that faith had now penetrated all ranks was shown in Diocletian's own household, wherein his most trusted[1] chamberlains, beloved as his children, were cruelly tortured because they refused to worship the heathen gods, while his wife Prisca and his daughter Valeria purchased immunity for the present by compliance. We have the emperor described by an eye-witness of those times as himself sitting in judgment,[2] and putting men to the

---

[1] See the martyrdom of the favourite chamberlain Peter, who, says Eusebius (*Hist.* viii. 6), was violently scourged, and then slowly roasted alive.

[2] "Diocletianus . . . excarnificare omnes suos protenus cœpit. Sede-

torture of fire. The same power was delegated to the governors throughout the provinces. "It was," says Eusebius, "the nineteenth year of Diocletian's reign, in the month of March, when the festival of the Lord's Passion was drawing near, that imperial edicts were everywhere published, ordering the churches to be levelled, the Scriptures to be burnt, those of rank to be deprived of it, the common people, if they remained faithful, to be reduced to slavery. This was the first edict against us; another soon came enjoining that all those who ruled the churches should first be imprisoned, and then by every means compelled to sacrifice."[1] Lactantius adds that every action at law was to proceed against Christians, while they should not be allowed to claim the law for any wrong inflicted, or spoliation suffered, or dishonour done to their wives.[2] Many in consequence of these edicts suffered willingly terrible torments: many others at first gave way. What these torments were Eusebius describes: some were beaten; some torn with hooks.[3] "It is impossible to say how many and how great martyrs of Christ might be seen in every city and country." A man of the highest rank in Nicomedia, from an impulse of zeal when the edict first appeared, tore it down: he was seized, and not merely tortured but slowly roasted alive,[4] which he bore with

---

bat ipse atque innocentes igne torrebat. . . . Omnis sexus et ætatis homines ad exustionem rapti; nec singuli, quoniam tanta erat multitudo, sed gregatim circumdato igni amburebantur," &c. Lactant. 14, 15.

[1] Eusebius, *Hist*. viii. 2.
[2] Lactantius, *de Morte Persecutorum*, 13.
[3] Euseb. viii. 4.
[4] "Statim productus non modo extortus sed etiam legitime coctus cum admirabili patientia, postremo exustus est." Lact. *de Mort. Pers.* 13; Euseb. viii. 5.

unflinching patience, preserving joyousness and tranquillity to his last breath. The emperors polluted the provinces subject to them, by the slaughter of men and women who worshipped God, as if it had been in a civil war, with the exception of Constantius,[1] who ruled the Gauls and Britain, and preserved his soul pure from this stain. But it was so much worse than a war in which the conquered have only to suffer servitude or at most death, whereas in this case what was committed against those who refused to do wrong passes all description. They used against them every imaginable torture, and thought it little to slay those whom they hated, unless by cruelty having first exposed their bodies to mockery. If they could persuade, by terror, any to violate the faith to which they were bound, and to agree to the fatal sacrifice, these they praised and with their honours destroyed, but on the others they exhausted the whole ingenuity of their butchery, calling them desperate as disregarding their own body.[2] For two years the whole Roman world ruled by Diocletian, Maximian, and Galerius was exposed to this misery: when on the retirement of Diocletian and Maximian in 305 Galerius became the chief emperor, the persecution continued in all its intensity, save in the territory subject to Constantius. "It is impossible to describe the individual scenes which took place throughout the world. The several governors having received their commission carried it out according to their own ferocity. Some through excess of fear did more than their orders; some were inspired by personal enmity; some by natural cruelty; some sought to advance

---

[1] Euseb. *de Vita Constant.* l. i. 13.
[2] Lactant. *Divin. Institut.* l. v. 9; Gallandi, tom. iv. 313, 314.

themselves; some were precipitate in the work of destruction, as one in Phrygia,"[1] where, says Eusebius, the soldiers surrounded a Christian town and burnt it with all its inhabitants, "men, women, and children, calling upon the name of Christ, the God of all."[2] "And in devising various kinds of tortures they aim at gaining a victory. They are well aware that it is a struggle between champions. I myself saw in Bithynia a governor beside himself in joy, as if he had subdued some barbarous nation, because one who for two years had with great virtue resisted was seen to fail. They inflict therefore exquisite pains, only avoiding to put the tortured to death, as if it were only death that made them blessed, and not likewise those torments which in proportion to their severity produce a greater glory by the virtue which they exhibit."[3]

Eusebius declares that such cruelties were perpetrated not for a short time, but during several years; that ten, twenty, thirty, sixty, and as many as a hundred men, women, and children would be slain in a day by various tortures. "When I was in Egypt myself I saw a crowd in one day, some beheaded, some burnt; with my own eyes I beheld the marvellous ardour, the truly divine virtue and alacrity of those who believed in Christ. Scarcely was sentence passed against the first, when a fresh number hastened before the tribunal, professing themselves Christians: with joy, gaiety, and smiles they received the award of death, singing hymns, and returning thanks to their last breath."[4]

Among those distinguished for their learning in all

---

[1] Lactant. *Divin. Institut.* l. v. 11.
[2] Euseb. *Hist.* viii. 11.
[3] Lactantius, as above.
[4] *Hist.* viii. 9.

Grecian studies, and for the universal honour in which they had been held, Eusebius mentions especially a bishop of Thmuis named Phileas. While he lay in prison under sentence of death, which was afterwards executed by beheading, he wrote a letter to his people, detailing the scenes in which he bore a part. This letter the historian has happily preserved for us. "Inasmuch," he says, "as the Holy Scriptures presented us with so many fair ensamples and lessons, the blessed martyrs who are with me felt no hesitation. They fixed their mind's eye steadily upon the God of all, formed the conception of death suffered for piety's sake, and clung firmly to that to which they were called. For they knew that our Lord Jesus Christ had become man for our sakes in order to cut up all sin by the root, and to supply us with food on that journey by which we enter into eternal life. For He thought it not robbery to be equal with God, but emptied Himself by taking the form of a slave, and being found in fashion as a man humbled Himself to death, and that death the cross. Hence it was that the martyrs, bearing Christ within them, in their zeal for the greater gifts endured every suffering and all the various inventions of torture not once, but some of them a second time, and all the threats of their guards, which did not stop with words in their zeal to overcome them, without their resolution being broken, because perfect charity casts out fear. What words can I find to enumerate their virtue and their endurance in each particular trial? Since they were left exposed to any one's outrage, some being struck with clubs, others with rods, others with scourges, some with lashes, some with ropes. The sight of the tortures presented every variety, but great suffering throughout. These with hands bound behind them were distended on the wood, and had every limb stretched by machinery; and thus their tormentors by command attacked the whole body, tearing them not on the sides alone as murderers are treated, but on the stomach, the knees, and the cheeks. Others were hung by one hand from the portico, and this tension of the sinews and limbs caused a more terrible pain than any. Others were bound to pillars face to face, the feet not reaching the ground, but the weight of the body tightening the bonds, and this they suffered not during the time of examination only, or while the governor was engaged with them, but almost the whole day. For when he went to others, he left his officers watching over these, to see if the extremity of torture should cause any to give way: and he charged them to be bound without mercy, but when at their last gasp to be let down and dragged along the ground. For he said that no account at all was to be taken of us, but we were to be both reputed and treated as non-existent. This last was a second torture which they superadded to their blows. There were those also who after their tortures were put in the stocks with their feet distended to the fourth hole, where they must needs lie down, not being able to hold themselves up through their wounds gaping over the whole body. Others flung on the pavement lay there through the repeated violence of their racking, the many signs of suffering over their body presenting a more fearful spectacle to those who looked on than the racking itself. Thus treated, some died under the torture, putting their adversary to shame by their endurance; some shut up in prison half-dead, after a few days expired through the extremity of their pains; the rest having treatment applied became still more resolute through the time spent in prison. And so when the choice was presented to them either to touch the abominable sacrifice, and depart unmolested, gaining by this course an execrable deliverance, or, not sacrificing, to receive sentence of death, without any doubt they joyfully went to death. For they knew what the sacred writings enjoin: 'He that sacrifices to other gods shall be rooted out,' and 'Thou shalt have no other gods but Me.'"[1]

This may suffice as a specimen of what was done during a course of years throughout the dominion of Galerius, Maximin, and Maxentius. It is in this persecution especially that the virgin martyrs suffered the extremity of the heathen malignity in the threatened loss of that purity which they valued more than life. And here a fellow-Christian at Alexandria, disguising himself as a soldier, was to St. Theodora the guardian which her angel himself became to St. Agnes at Rome. In this persecution also St. Vincent repeats in Spain the trial and the triumph of St. Laurence at Rome. The authentic account of his martyrdom shows the utmost point to which the most ingenious and the most ferocious cruelty could reach on the one side, and the most enduring patience on the other. But the numberless details concerning the sufferings of this time preserved to us show that it was indeed a conflict prolonged during eight years, in which the Roman State put forth the utmost strength which unlimited power guided by unhesitating cruelty could exert to destroy the Christian Church and name.

At the end of this time the conflict was terminated by the Emperor Galerius, the chief mover of the whole persecution, being struck by a mortal disease, in which,

[1] Euseb. *Hist.* viii. 10.

reduced to impotence by his sufferings, he withdrew his edicts against the Christian Faith. One after another the persecuting emperors are taken away by death. Constantine, inheriting his father's justice towards Christians and preserving them in his own territory from these outrages, gradually appears as their champion. It is when advancing to Rome against Maxentius that he sees in the Cross the token of victory over all enemies: enrolling it on his banner he rules with Licinius the Roman world, and by a decree issued at Milan in 313 assures to all Christians the free exercise of their religion.

In the year 64 Nero had declared, by initiating a persecution against Christians, that their religion was illicit, and fell under the ban of the old Roman laws which forbade the exercise of any worship not approved by the senate. From that time down to the edict of Constantine no Christian could stand before a Roman tribunal plainly avowing his faith in one God and one Christ without incurring the liability of capital punishment. In this period of two hundred and forty-eight years it is true that there were intervals of comparative peace when the emperors did not themselves call into action the laws against Christians. During the whole second century there would seem to be no emperor who set himself to destroy the Christian name and people as a whole. In the time of Commodus it was even forbidden to accuse a Christian of his religion; yet even then, if the accusation was made and proved, it was a capital offence, followed, and that too in the case of a senator after defence before the senate, by the infliction of the penalty. Alexander Severus is the first of whom it is said that "he suffered the Christians to be;" Philip also favoured them; so again

Valerian at first; Gallienus gave back their churches; Diocletian trusted them and filled his palace with them: but no one of these emperors ventured to declare the Christian religion to be according to the laws of Rome a "licit" religion, and no one therefore enabled Christians to avow it without danger of suffering. The most favourable suspended the action of the laws either by positive edict, or by letting it be understood that they did not wish Christians to be disturbed. A change either of the ruler, or of the ruler's inclination, as was seen in the cases of Valerian, Aurelian, and Diocletian, induced at once that full state of penality under which Christianity was as much forbidden as homicide or treason, and in virtue of which Roman magistrates could as little refuse to judge the crime of being a Christian as those other crimes. Thus it is that we find martyrdoms assigned to times at which there is not known to have been any general persecution: and in unnumbered cases Christians won their crown through private enmity or local tumults, when any one of the thousand motives which awaken ill-will was sufficient to cause an appeal to that great and unchanged enemy, the Law of Rome, which proscribed them. To Constantine belongs the glory of having removed this enemy. He made the profession of Christianity no longer a crime. He accomplished that which Justin and Tertullian and every Christian apologist had asked for in vain, that every Christian in the Roman empire might profess and practise the Christian Faith without suffering punishment for it.

LECTURE XIII

THE CHRISTIAN CHURCH AND THE GREEK PHILOSOPHY

PART I

"*Socrates.* It is, then, necessary to wait until we learn how we ought to be disposed towards gods and men.
"*Alcibiades.* But when, Socrates, will that time arrive ? and who shall teach us it ? For it seems to me that I should with the greatest pleasure see that man.
"*Socrates.* It is he who cares for thee."[1]   *Second Alcib.* § 22.

IN the three preceding lectures we have witnessed a great spectacle, a spectacle in all history unique and without a rival, the encounter, that is, with the forces of the great world-empire of a voluntary society which bears in its bosom and propagates a body of truth, and this encounter carried on without respite during ten generations of men. The elements of this conflict are, on the one side, power, throned in civilisation, and defended by that sword before which nothing hitherto had stood; on the other, a belief testified by suffering and patience, but which moreover appears only as the possession of a society which is itself dropped as a seed into the earth's bosom and silently fills its expanse. Attention must now be called to another aspect of the same encounter. Rome, as we have said, pre-eminently wielded power; not the power

---

[1] Σωκ. Ἀναγκαῖον οὖν ἐστὶ περιμένειν ἕως ἄν τις μάθῃ ὡς δεῖ πρὸς θεοὺς καὶ πρὸς ἀνθρώπους διακεῖσθαι.
Ἀλκ. Πότε οὖν παρέσται ὁ χρόνος οὗτος, ὦ Σώκρατες; καὶ τίς ὁ παιδεύσων; ἥδιστα γὰρ ἄν μοι δοκῶ ἰδεῖν τοῦτον τὸν ἄνθρωπον τίς ἐστιν.
Σωκ. Οὗτός ἐστιν ᾧ μέλει περὶ σοῦ.

of her legions only, immense as that was, but the power of her laws, and the power of that many-sided and as it seemed triumphant all-embracing civilisation, of which she was the golden head. The mind, however, the thought of the world which she ruled, belonged to the great Hellenic race: and it remains to consider what contest this mind waged with the truth which the Christian Church sustained and suffered for. The sword hews away limbs; the fire destroys bodies; and the martyrs offered freely their limbs and their bodies to sword and flame. But the martyrs were inspired with a mind; they carried Christ in them; and a mind too was opposed to theirs; the mind which animated that ancient civilisation; the mind which had erected such shrines as Diana of Ephesus and the Parthenon at Athens; the mind which dictated the laws of Solon and Lycurgus; the mind which taught in the Academus, the Lyceum, the Portico, and the Garden; the mind which built Alexandria for the world's emporium and university, and raised Antioch to be the gorgeous throne of eastern magnificence. We have to consider how this heathen mind encountered the Christian; in short, how, "after that in the wisdom of God the world by wisdom knew not God, it pleased Him through the folly of Christian preaching to save those that believed."[1] Let us trace the encounter of heathen wisdom—that is, Philosophy —with Christian wisdom, that is, the truth of a God incarnate and crucified, with all its consequences, as upborne by the Christian Church and planted among men.

Now the system of polytheistic worship which was then in possession of the Græco-Roman world had

[1] 1 Cor. i. 21.

been subjected for many ages to all the analytic power of human reason as exercised by the most gifted of races which have hitherto embodied their genius in a corresponding civilisation. The philosophy of Greece is in fact such an analysis, and the rise of this philosophy is carried back by the ablest inquirers to the time of Thales and Pythagoras in the sixth century before Christ. In the beautiful climate of Ionia and Southern Italy there arose at this time men who attempted by the efforts of their own reason to form a physical and a moral theory of the world which surrounded them. Philosophy is not merely thought, but methodical thinking, thinking consciously directed upon the knowledge of things in their connection with each other. Nor is it content merely with the collecting of observations and the knowledge so derived, but proceeds to gather the individual instances into a whole, to draw to a centre what was scattered, and to form a view of the world resting upon clear conceptions and at unity with itself.[1] This was the nature of that work which Thales and Pythagoras commenced. Let us give a glance at the race which bore them, and of which they were representative men.

This race had dwelt for some ages in Greece, and from thence occupied by emigration the shores of Asia Minor, Sicily, and Southern Italy, with a part of Africa. Pythagoras, the father of Italian philosophy, had migrated from Samos to Crotona, having visited

---

[1] Zeller, *die Philosophie der Griechen*, 2te Aufl. vol. i. pp. 6 and 35, "Philosophy," says Grote, *Plato*, vol. i. v. "is, or aims at becoming, reasoned truth: an aggregate of matters believed or disbelieved after conscious process of examination gone through by the mind and capable of being explained to others:" who quotes Cicero's "Philosophia ex rationum collatione consistit."

THE CHURCH AND THE GREEK PHILOSOPHY 311

Egypt, examined and gathered from all the stores of its knowledge. A century later Herodotus, the father of Greek history, migrated likewise from his country Halicarnassus, and after spending many years in extensive travels through Egypt and Western Asia settled at Thurii. In the succeeding century Plato travelled in like manner with similar purposes. He was familiar with Sicily as with his own Attica, not to speak of Egypt or Phœnicia. These three great men, Pythagoras, Herodotus, and Plato, are specimens herein of the cultured Greek, the gentleman, as we should call him. Thus though Greece proper was a very small country, the whole region from middle Italy, including Sicily, and the rich coast-land of Northern Africa from Carthage to Egypt, with again Phœnicia and Syria, and the continent to the depth of perhaps a hundred miles round the three sides of Asia Minor watered by the sea, were in a larger sense the Greek's country, a field of Grecian thought, and enterprise, and observation, a sphere in which his mind was enlarged, and his judgment of men and things matured.[1] Generally speaking these regions were singularly favoured as to richness of soil and convenience of situation. Herodotus himself has marked the climate of Ionia as the most beautiful and best-tempered of the earth; and with a far wider knowledge of its regions we should not venture to dispute the justness of his remark. Some modern writers are wont to dwell on the effect which climate exercises upon man's mind. However this may be, it is certain that the race whose energies were diffused over this

---

[1] Thus Herodotus says of Solon, τῆς θεωρίης ἐκδημήσας εἵνεκεν, i. 30,; and presently, ξεῖνε 'Αθηναῖε, παρ' ἡμέας γὰρ περὶ σέο λόγος ἀπῖκται πολλός, καὶ σοφίης εἵνεκεν τῆς σῆς καὶ πλάνης, ὡς φιλοσοφέων γῆν πολλὴν θεωρίης εἵνεκεν ἐπελήλυθας.

region was most highly gifted with natural endowments. When out of the world which Christianity has mainly formed, and from the bosom of nations which have grown through the struggle of a thousand years, and with perpetual competition among each other, into a rich civilisation, we look back on that ancient and simpler world, we find in Hellenism the most perfect expression of the natural man, as a plastic, artistic, poetical, philosophical, and generally intellectual race, wherein matter was most completely permeated by mind. The language which they used even yet presents a very perfect image of such a race, as not being formed from the corruption of other idioms, but a mother tongue, the most brilliant of the Aryan sisters. In its union of strength with beauty, of pleasing sound with accurate sense, in its power to convey the most subtle distinctions of philosophic thought, or the most radiant images of sensuous loveliness, the gravest enunciations of law, or the tenderest dreams of romance, it was well calculated to be the organ of a people wherein bodily form and immaterial intellect alike culminated. The language which we use ourselves is full of nerve and vigour, with a certain northern force and a habit of appropriating the material stores of other languages by incorporating their words, which suits well the descendants of sea-kings, who have provinces all over the world; but it is without inflexions, deprived of cases and genders, defective in marking time, whereas the Greek in all these is most rich and flexible: the one resembles the torso of a Hercules without its limbs, the other an Apollo as he touches the earth in his perfect symmetry. Then compare its sound with that of the old Hellenic tongue, and we seem to hear the poet's "stridor ferri tractæque catenæ," beside the voice of a lute; while as to texture, it is like the train of a railway matched with the golden network, fine as the spider's web, indissoluble as adamant, which the poet feigns to have been wrought by Vulcan: the English imprisons thought in a rude and cumbrous iron, while the Greek exhibits it in a rich and ductile gold. As was the language, so was the people. Fond of society and intercourse, skilful, crafty, commercial, enterprising, with a most human and genial intellect, with a keen and critical judgment, and a vivid imagination. When such a race turned itself to a scientific consideration of the world, it might well produce what we are now to pass in review, the Greek philosophy.

And here it is well to lay down first the standing-point of the Greek mind. The Hellenic religion was a natural religion, inasmuch as according to it man had no need to raise himself above the surrounding world and his own nature in order to connect himself with the Deity. As he was originally constituted, he felt himself related to it: no inward change in his mode of thought, no struggle with his natural impulses and inclinations, was required of him for this purpose. All that to him was humanly natural seemed to him to have its justification in regard to the Deity likewise; and so the most godlike man was he who worked out most completely his powers as man, and the essence of religious duty consisted in that man should do for the honour of the Deity what is in accordance with his own nature.[1]

But this natural religion of the Greeks differed from that of others in that neither outward nature as such, nor the sensuous being of man as such, but

[1] Zeller, i. 39, quoted.

human nature in its beauty, as illumined by mind, is its point of excellence. The Greek did not, like the Eastern, lose his independence before the powers of nature, nor revel like the northern savage in boundless liberty, but in the full consciousness of his freedom saw its highest fulfilment in obedience to the general order as the law of his own nature. And as the purely Grecian deities are the ideals of human activity, he thus stands to them in a calm and free relation, such as no other nation of antiquity felt, because they are the mirror of his own being, but his being exalted, so that he is drawn to them without purchasing this at the cost of the pain and toil of an inward struggle.[1]

How the features of his own land served to image out to his fancy the Greek's religious attitude a poet has told us in exquisite verses, worthy of the beauty which they describe; the apotheosis of nature.

> "Where are the Islands of the Blest?
>   They stud the Ægean sea;
> And where the deep Elysian rest?
>   It haunts the vale where Peneus strong
>   Pours his incessant stream along,
>   While craggy ridge and mountain bare
>   Cut keenly through the liquid air,
>   And in their own pure tints arrayed,
>   Scorn earth's green robes which change and fade,
>   And stand in beauty undecayed,
>   Guards of the bold and free."[2]

It seems to me essential to bear in mind throughout our whole inquiry this standing-point of the Greek mind, because through all the succession of schools

---

[1] Zeller, i. p. 38.
[2] Newman, *Verses on Various Occasions;* Heathen Greece, p. 158.

and the fluctuation of doctrines, it remains, so to say, the groundwork on which they are embroidered. It is the very texture of Hellenic thought upon which first Pythagoras, then Plato, Aristotle, Epicurus, Zeno, Cleanthes, Panætius, and even Plotinus and Porphyrius spin their web. They vary the decoration, but the substance remains unaltered. This standing-point rules the conception of virtue, and therefore of the whole moral world. It reaches also to the final end of man, and determines it.

Moreover as the intellectual power of man seems to have culminated in the Hellenic race, so it would seem that a state of things existed among that people which left the human reason practically more to its own unaided resources than we find to have been the case elsewhere. No doubt the Greek mind had lived and brooded for ages upon the remains of original revelation, nor can any learning now completely unravel the interwoven threads of tradition and reason so as to distinguish their separate work. However, it is certain that in the sixth century before Christ the Greeks were without a hierarchy, and without a definite theology: not indeed without individual priesthoods, traditionary rites, and an existing worship, as well as certain mysteries which professed to communicate a higher and more recondite doctrine than that exposed to the vulgar gaze. But in the absence of any hierarchy holding this priesthood together, and teaching anything like a specific doctrine about divine and human things, a very large range indeed was given to the mind, acting upon this shadowy religious belief, and reacted upon by it, to form their philosophy. The Greeks did not, any more than antiquity in general, use the acts of religious service for instruction by religious discourse.[1] In other words, there was no such thing as preaching among them. A domain therefore was open to the philosopher on which he might stand without directly impeaching the ancestral worship, while he examined its grounds, and perhaps sapped its foundations. He was therein taking up a position which their priests, the civil functionaries of religious rites scarcely any longer retaining a spiritual meaning or a moral cogency, had not occupied.

Thus it was that in the midst of a people who worshipped traditionally a multitude of gods and goddesses, such as we have them exhibited in the Homeric and Hesiodic poems, the chief, perhaps the only, and the yet unwritten literature of that day, beings with a personal character and will, who were supposed to divide the government of the world between them, with a more or less recognised sovereignty of one chief, arose men who set themselves by the light of reason to think steadily and continuously how that world in which they were living had become what it was. Such a movement of mind indicated in itself dissatisfaction with the existing religion, wherein the gods were considered the causes of things, and their wills the rulers of them, though in the background even here loomed the idea of fate, the representative, as it were, of brute matter, from which the Greek mind could never disengage itself. Yet we do not find that these philosophers set themselves openly to attack the existing religion; rather

[1] Zeller, i. p. 43. "Aber es liegt überhaupt nicht in der Weise des Alterthums, die gottesdienstlichen Handlungen zur Belehrung durch Religionsvorträge zu benützen. Ein Julian mochte in Nachahmung christlicher Sitte dazu den Versuch machen, aus der klassischen Zeit selbst ist uns kein Beispiel hievon überliefert."

leaving it in possession, and themselves usually complying with its forms, they pursued their own train of thought, as it were by its side, not choosing to look whither it would lead them.

Such very much appears the position of inquirers in the first period of Greek philosophy, which is generally made to extend from its rise under Thales to the time of the Sophists and Socrates. Their thoughts were mainly occupied with the appearances of the physical world: they speculated how it could have arisen. Thus Thales, we are told, imagined its first principle to be water; Anaximander, boundless matter; Anaximenes, air; the Pythagoreans said, all is number; the Eleatic school, all is the one unchangeable being.[1] On the contrary Heracleitus conceived the one Being as ever in motion, involved in perpetual change: in accordance with which he nowhere finds true knowledge, and thinks the mass of men have no understanding for eternal truth.[2] Empedocles of Agrigentum sets forth the four elements, earth, water, air, and fire, as the material principles or roots of things, attaching to these two ideal principles as moving forces, Love as the unitive, and Hatred as the severing.[3] Anaxagoras, over and above mechanical causes, to which he limited himself in the explanation of everything in particular, recognises a divine spirit, which as the finest of all things is simple, unmixed, passionless reason, which came upon chaos, forming and ordering the world out of it.[4] Democritus of Abdera takes for his principles the Full and the Empty, identifying these with

[1] Zeller, i. p. 141.   [2] *Ibid.* i. pp. 449-452.
[3] Ueberweg, *Grundriss der Geschichte der Philosophie*, drit. Aufl. i. p. 65.   [4] *Ibid.* i. 68.

Being and Non-being, or Something and Nothing. His Full consists of indivisible atoms.[1]

The remarkable thing about all these systems, if we may so call them, is, that while the existing popular religion teemed over, so to say, with the idea of a number of personal agents directing human things, these philosophers nearly all concurred in the attempt to find some one agent, and that material, from which all should spring. As yet even the radical distinction of matter and spirit was not clear to their minds:[2] the soul of the individual man was to them merely a particle of the vital power which disclosed itself through the universe, the purest portion, but a portion still, of primal matter. In their conception of the constituent cause, while they advanced towards unity they receded from personality. Even the world-forming Intelligence of Anaxagoras, who first distinctly declares that spirit is not mixed with matter, works only as a power of nature, and is portrayed to us in a semi-sensuous form, as a finer matter.[3]

After Greek philosophy had run out during about a hundred and fifty years in this sort of vague and imaginative speculation upon the physical world, it underwent a great change, which marks the transition to its second period. These successive opinions of philosophers led a class of men who arose at Athens about the middle age of Socrates to the conclusion, that it would be more profitable to turn the course of human thought from such cosmological reveries

---

[1] Ueberweg, i. 72.
[2] Döllinger, *Heidenthum und Judenthum*, p. 272, and Zeller, i. p. 139, who states this of the Eleatics, Heracleitus, Democritus, and even the Pythagoreans, who, though they put Number instead of Matter, yet conceived incorporeal principles as material, and so considered from the same point of view the soul and the body, the ethical and the physical, in man.   [3] Zeller, *ibid.*

THE CHURCH AND THE GREEK PHILOSOPHY 319

to the question of the perception itself of truth by man. He who accomplished this was Socrates, who turned his reflection by preference upon man himself as the subject who thinks and wills.[1] And herein his character had an influence over Greek philosophy which is strikingly marked through the whole of its second period. This period embraces the Sophists, Socrates himself, Plato and Aristotle, and the Stoics and Epicureans; finally those Sceptic and Eclectic schools which rose naturally from the criticism detecting what is untenable in preceding systems. During the six hundred years which elapse from the teaching career of Socrates to the death of Marcus Antoninus we may say that one great line of inquiry occupied among philosophers the human mind; it was man himself, as the subject of logical thought and moral will.[2] The chief endeavour was to form a science of ethics, and a science of reasoning, to which physical and mathematical studies, though at times warmly pursued and never wholly neglected, were yet subordinate.[3]

Who is this man of singular ugliness, with a face like a Silenus, with a body enduring hunger and

---

[1] Ueberweg, i. 75. "Die Sophistik bildet den Uebergang von der kosmologischen zu der auf das denkende und wollende Subject gerichteten Philosophie," p. 76. "Sokrates . . . theilt mit den Sophisten die allgemeine Tendenz der Reflexion auf das Subject, tritt aber zu ihnen dadurch in Gegensatz, das seine Reflexion sich nicht bloss auf die elementaren Functionen des Subjects, die Wahrnehmung und Meinung und das sinnliche und egoistische Begehren, sondern auch auf die höchsten gestigen, zur Objectivität in wesentlicher Beziehung stehenden Functionen, nämlich auf das Wissen und die Tugend richtet."
[2] *Ibid.* i. 76.
[3] Thus Zeller throughout his great work perpetually deplores that through this long period, and with increasing force after Aristotle's time, pure science, *die reine Wissenschaft*, was not studied for its own sake, but was subordinate to a moral purpose, the question, that is, of man's greatest good, and his happiness.

impervious to heat and cold, who for thirty years frequents from morning to night the agora, the streets, the porticoes of Athens; who can drain the wine-cup through the night, and with reason unimpaired discuss philosophy through the following day; never alone, ready to converse with all in whom he discerned the germ of inquiry; who neither courts the high nor despises the low, but beside whom may be found the reckless beauty of Alcibiades and the staid gravity of Nicias, the admiring gaze of Plato even in youth majestic, and the sober homage of plainer Xenophon? Who is this, the man most social of men where the whole population is a club, the club of Athenian citizenship; whose tongue arrests the most volatile and inconstant of peoples; whose reason attracts and by turns draws out or silences the most opposite of characters; whose whole life is publicity; of spirit at once homely and subtle, simple and critical, parent both of philosophic certitude and philosophic scepticism? This is Socrates, the son of Sophroniscus, to whom Greek philosophy will look back as on one that had given its bent and directed its course during a thousand years, until the last of its defenders [1] will fight a hopeless battle with triumphant Christianity, as the gods of Greece vanish, never more to return, and the lurid star of a false prophet teaching a false monotheism appears above the horizon, and takes the place, which they have left vacant, to be chief foe of the Christian name.

The special principle of Socrates is thus described to us by an historian of Greek philosophy.[2] "It is not merely an already existing mode of thought

---

[1] Simplicius, in the sixth century.
[2] Zeller, i. p. 117.

which was further developed by Socrates, but an essentially new principle and proceeding which were introduced into philosophy. Whilst all preceding philosophy had been directed immediately on the object, so that the question of the essence and grounds of natural appearances is in it the radical question, on which all others depend, Socrates was the first to give utterance to the conviction that nothing can be known respecting anything which meets our thought, before its general essence, its conception, be determined: that accordingly the trial of our own representations by the standard of the conception is philosophical self-cognition, the beginning and the condition of all true knowing: whilst those who preceded him had arrived through the consideration of things only to distinguishing between the representation of things and the knowing of them, he, reversing this, makes all cognition of things dependent on the right view of the nature of knowledge."

Another [1] says: "It is stated in Aristotle's *Metaphysics* [2] that Socrates introduced the method of Induction and Definition, which proceeds from the individual to the determination of the conception. Aristotle marks [3] the domain of ethics as that on which Socrates applied this method. According to him the fundamental view of Socrates was the indivisible unity of theoretical prudence and practical ability on ethical ground. Socrates conceived all the virtues to be prudences, inasmuch as they are sciences.[4] These statements are fully borne out by

---

[1] Ueberweg, i. p. 88.   [2] xiii. 4.   [3] *Metaph.* i. 6.
[4] Σωκράτης φρονήσεις ᾤετο εἶναι πάσας τὰς ἀρετάς· . . . λόγους τὰς ἀρετὰς ᾤετο εἶναι· ἐπιστήμας γὰρ εἶναι πάσας. *Ethic. Nic.* vi. 13.

the portraits of Xenophon and Plato: Aristotle has only given point to their expression. Thus Xenophon says,[1] 'He was ever conversing about human things, inquiring what was piety and what impiety; what honour and what turpitude; what just and what unjust; what sober-mindedness and what madness; what courage and what cowardice; what policy and what politician; what the government of men and who capable of it; and suchlike things; and those who knew these he esteemed men of honour and goodness, those who knew them not to be justly called of servile mind.' 'Never did he cease inquiring with those who frequented him about what everything was.'[2] 'And he did not distinguish between wisdom and temperance, but he asserted that justice and every other virtue was wisdom.'[3] With this view hang together the convictions that virtue can be taught, that all virtue in truth is only one, and that no one is willingly wicked, but only through ignorance.[4] The good is identical with the beautiful and the expedient. Right dealing, grounded upon prudence and practice, is better than good fortune. Self-knowledge, the fulfilment of the Delphic Apollo's injunction, 'Know thyself,' is the condition of practical ability. External goods do not advance. To need nothing is godlike; to need the least possible comes nearest to the divine perfection.[5] Cicero's well-known expression is substantially correct,[6] that Socrates called down philosophy from heaven to earth, introduced it into cities and houses, and required it to study life, morals, goods and evils, which

[1] Xen. *Mem.* i. 1. 16. [2] *Ibid.* iv. 6. 1. [3] *Ibid.* iii. 4. 9.
[4] *Ibid.* iii. 9, iv. 6; *Sympos.* ii. 12. Plat. *Apol.* 25 e; *Protag.* p. 329 b.
[5] *Memor.* i. 6. 10. [6] *Tusc.* v. 4.

constituted a progress from the natural philosophy pursued by his predecessors to ethics whose province is man. But Socrates possessed no complete system of ethical doctrines, but only the mainspring of inquiry; and so it was natural that he could only reach definite ethical statements in conversation with others. Thus his art was Mental Midwifery,[1] as Plato designates it. His confessed non-knowledge, resting on the firm consciousness of the essence of true knowledge, stood higher than the imagined knowledge of those who conversed with him; and to it was attached the Socratic Irony; that apparent recognition which is paid to the superior wisdom and prudence of another until this is dissolved into its nothingness by the dialectic examination which measures what is maintained as a generalisation by the fixed point of the particular case. Thus it was that Socrates exercised the charge of examining men,[2] which he was convinced had been imposed upon him by the Delphic god in the oracle elicited by Chærepho, that he was the wisest of men."

The opinion, practice, and teaching of Socrates concerning the gods and the Godhead are set forth most graphically by his disciple Xenophon in two chapters of his *Memorabilia*. Scarcely could a Christian moralist exhibit more lucidly the argument from design in proof of a Divine Providence which has formed and which rules the world; more than this, which has produced the seasons of the year, the plants, the animals, for the good of man. In the eyes of Socrates the human body itself is a never-failing proof of the divine love of man. He

---

[1] ἡ μαιευτική, Plat. *Theæt.* p. 149.
[2] ἐξέτασις, Plat. *Apol.* p. 20.

details the wisdom with which it is put together, and forces the opponent, who is introduced as not sacrificing, nor praying to the gods, nor believing in divination, to confess: "When I consider this, assuredly these things seem the device of some wise world-maker, the lover of living things."[1] Another he compels by a long enumeration of divine benefits to man to come to a similar conclusion.[2] "Certainly, Socrates, the gods seem to have a great care for men." "Besides," he replies, "when we cannot foresee in the future what is good for us, they help us by revealing through divination what is to come, and instructing us as to the best course." "Nay, Socrates," rejoins the other, "they seem to treat you even more kindly than other men; for without being asked by you, they signify before to you what you should do and what leave undone." "That I say true," answers Socrates, "even you, O Euthydemus, will acknowledge, if you do not wait until you see the forms of the gods, but are contented, when you behold their works, to worship and honour them. And consider that the gods themselves point this out to you: for not only do the rest of them, when they give us good things, not exhibit themselves to our senses in so doing, but he[3] who co-ordinates and holds together the whole universe, in whom are all beautiful and

---

[1] Xen. *Mem.* i. 4. 7. σοφοῦ τινὸς δημιουργοῦ καὶ φιλοζῴου.
[2] *Ibid.* iv. 3.
[3] ὁ τὸν ὅλον κόσμον συντάττων τε καὶ συνέχων, ἐν ᾧ πάντα τὰ καλὰ καὶ ἀγαθά ἐστι, καὶ ἀεὶ μὲν χρωμένοις ἀτριβῆ τε καὶ ὑγιᾶ καὶ ἀγήρατον παρέχων, θᾶττον δὲ νοήματος ἀναμαρτήτως ὑπηρετοῦντα, οὗτος τὰ μέγιστα μὲν πράττων ὁρᾶται, τάδε δὲ οἰκονομῶν ἀόρατος ἡμῖν ἐστι. Compare the famous passage of St. Paul, Rom. i. 19, 20. διότι τὸ γνωστὸν τοῦ Θεοῦ φανερόν ἐστιν ἐν αὐτοῖς· ὁ γὰρ Θεὸς αὐτοῖς ἐφανέρωσε· τὰ γὰρ ἀόρατα αὐτοῦ ἀπὸ κτίσεως κόσμου τοῖς ποιήμασι νοούμενα καθορᾶται, ἥ τε ἀΐδιος αὐτοῦ δύναμις καὶ θειότης εἰς τὸ εἶναι αὐτοὺς ἀναπολογήτους. Socrates draws precisely the conclusion which St. Paul asserts that the premises warrant.

good things, and who provides them for the perpetual use of men free from waste, disease, and old age, so that they help us unfailingly, quicker than thought, is discerned in the greatness of his operations, but while he administers these to us, is himself invisible. And take thought that the sun, who seems to be manifest to all, allows not men to examine him closely, but should any one attempt to look at him shamelessly, takes away his sight. And the ministers of the gods too you will find evading our senses; the lightning shoots from on high, and is master wherever it alights, but is seen neither in its approach, nor in its stroke, nor in its departure. The winds themselves are invisible, but their works are manifest, and we feel them as they come. Nay, and man's soul too, or if there be anything else in man participating the divine, manifestly rules in us as a king, but is not seen. Bearing in thought these things we must not despise the invisible, but learning their power by their results, honour that which is divine."[1] "Indeed, Socrates," says Euthydemus, "for my part I am quite resolved not the least to neglect what is divine; but my trouble is, that it seems to me that no single man can ever be duly thankful for the kindnesses of the gods." "Do not let this trouble you, Euthydemus, for you see the god at Delphi, when any one asks him how to be grateful to the gods, answers, 'By your country's law.' Now it is surely law everywhere to please the gods by sacrifices, as best you can. How then can any one honour the gods better or more piously than by doing what themselves bid? Only we must not be behind our power: for any one who is so behind surely is manifest therein as not honouring the gods. Our

[1] τὸ δαιμόνιον.

duty is to honour them to the utmost of our power, and then to take heart and hope from them the greatest goods: for a man cannot show a sound mind in hoping from others greater goods than from those who have the power to give the greatest aid; nor from those in any other way than by pleasing them. And how can one better please them than by the most unfailing obedience to them?" Now, by saying such things, and himself doing them, he was ever bringing those who were in intercourse with him to piety and a sound mind.

The last words of this man to his judges were: "And now it is time that we depart, I to death, and you to life; but which of us are going unto the better thing is not clear to any one save to God."[1] And when the hemlock was reaching his heart,[2] he uncovered his head, and said with his last utterance, "O Crito, we owe a cock to Æsculapius: pay it, and do not neglect it."

I have cited at length these passages because I think that they exhibit clearly the opinions and convictions of Socrates on the most important of all subjects. We behold here a man of a very religious mind, holding with the utmost tenacity the idea of a Providence, the Benefactor of men and their Judge, since it discriminates between them by reward and punishment: nor is it an impersonal Providence, an abstract Reason, but "a wise world-maker," who loves man and does him good, and whose operations in this very purpose of doing him good indicate unity of design and perfection of execution: and yet in his conception of the Godhead itself he halts between unity and plurality, and beside a statement such as we might

[1] Plato, *Apol.*, at the end.   [2] *Phædo*, p. 118.

read in a Pauline epistle of the one God who orders in harmony the universe and holds it together, we find him passing to the recognition and worship of many gods: beside words to his judges most sublime and most pathetic, concerning the issue of life and of death, we find him with his last breath directing his friend to discharge the sacrifice of a cock which he had promised to Æsculapius. He does not attempt to solve either the rational or the moral antagonism between many gods and one; but practically he throws himself into the worship of his country, referring to the law of each place as that which should determine for every man the question how the gods are to be honoured. And in this I believe that he is typical of the whole race of philosophers at whose head he stands. Like him they spoke of one God, and they offered the cock to Æsculapius. If we seek the highest expressions concerning the divine unity, wisdom, and power which are to be found in their writings, they approach St. Paul: if we consider other expressions, and above all, their practice, it is in the main that other word of Socrates, " Worship according to the law of your country." In the doctrine attributed to him both by Xenophon and Aristotle, that he identified virtue and prudence, and believed that no man is willingly wicked, but only out of ignorance, we have a proof which can scarcely be exceeded in force how entirely the standing-point of Socrates was that above attributed to the Greek mind in general, that of a religion according to nature. It ignores in the most emphatic, because in the most unconscious way, the inclination to evil in man. The relation between God and man is simply that of greater and less. There is a physical affinity and a numerical proportion between that mighty nature which is ruled through all its length and breadth by a pervading reason, and the portion of it contained in man's body and soul.[1]

It is curious to imagine what would have been the effect of the life and the death of Socrates had he lived and died just as he did with one sole exception, that Plato and Xenophon had not been his disciples. Socrates wrote nothing: oral discourse was his sole instrument of teaching. When its last memories had faded away, we might have known as little of him as we really know of Pythagoras. He would still indeed have been the greatest of heathen names because he died for his moral convictions. This might have been all, and it would have been very much. This, however, was not to be. In Xenophon's *Memorabilia* we have an accurate life-portrait of the man, while in the great genius of Plato we have the application of what may be termed Socratic principles to the formation of an ethical, logical, and physical system. The Megaric[2] school of Euclides, and Phædo's school of Elis, took indeed one side of his doctrine, the dialectic, for their special subject of inquiry; the Cynic school of Antisthenes and the Cyrenian school of Aristippus another side, the ethical: but it was Plato who embraced in one comprehensive scheme the whole grasp of his master's thought, as

---

[1] The view here taken would be powerfully confirmed by citing at length the interview of Socrates with the hetæra Theodote, as given by Xen. *Mem.* iii. 11. The unconscious absence from the mind of Socrates of any notion of turpitude in the occupation of Theodote is very striking indeed. One is reminded that Socrates took lessons in rhetoric of that Aspasia, herself the hetæra of Pericles, who is recorded to have educated a school of Theodotes. Thus Plutarch, *Pericles*, 24, says of her, παιδίσκας ἑταιρούσας τρέφουσα. In the Menexímus, p. 235, Socrates claims her as being his διδάσκαλος οὖσα οὐ πάνυ φαύλη περὶ ῥητορικῆς, quoted by Wallon, *de l'Esclavage*, vol. i. p. 190.

[2] Ueberweg, i. 92, 93.

well as the collective approved elements of former systems.

The principle of Socrates concerning the union of knowledge and virtue invited his followers to work out a system of dialectics and ethics.[1] And further the dialectic process of induction and definition, which Aristotle tells us that Socrates introduced, was made by Plato the foundation of his philosophy.[2] Its central point is the doctrine of Ideas. Now the Platonic Idea is the object of the conception. As a single object becomes known by its representation, so the Idea becomes known by its conception. It is not the essence as such which dwells in many similar individual objects, but that essence as represented perfectly in its kind, unalterably, in unity, independence, and self-existence. The Idea points to the general, but is represented by Plato as an original image of the individual projected as it were outside of time and space. Conceive individuals which have a similar being, or belong to the same class, delivered from the limits of time and space, of materiality and individual imperfections, and so reduced to that unity which is the groundwork of their existence, and such unity is the Platonic Idea. The highest Idea is the Idea of the good,[3] which is as it were the sun in the realm of Ideas, viewed as the first cause of being and of knowledge. Plato seems to identify it with the highest Godhead. Thus the method to attain the knowledge of Ideas is dialectics, which comprehend the double path of rising to the general and returning from the general to the particular.

As to the generation [4] of the doctrine of Ideas,

---

[1] Ueberweg, i. 91.   [2] *Ibid.* i. 117.   [3] *Ibid.* i. 118.
[4] *Ibid.* i. 120, from Aristotle, *Metaph.* i. 6 and 9, and xiii. 4.

Aristotle states it as the common product of the doctrine of Heracleitus that everything which meets the senses is subject to change and flux, and of the Socratic view of the conception. From Socrates Plato learnt that when once this is rightly formed, it can be held fast unchangeably: he would not then apply it to anything which meets the senses, but inferred that there must be other beings which are the objects of the knowledge acquired by the conception, and these objects he named Ideas. The filiation,[1] then, between Socrates and Plato is this: Socrates was the first to require that all knowledge and all moral dealing should proceed from the knowing of the conception, and endeavoured to execute this by his inductive process, while with Plato the same conviction formed the starting-point of a philosophical system: so that what with Socrates was simply a rule of scientific procedure was carried out by Plato to an objective intuition, and when Socrates said, "Only the knowing of the conception is true knowledge," Plato added, "Only the being of the conception is true being."

Thus in Plato we have a man of great original mind attempting with this instrument of induction and definition to form a scheme of the universe, which divides under his hand into a triple aspect of ethics, physics, and dialectics.[2] No doubt his main intention was to offer to the cultured and reflective few,—that inner circle to which his teaching and his writings

---

[1] Zeller, i. 119.
[2] Ueberweg, i. 120, remarks: "Die Eintheilung der Philosophie in Ethik, Physik und Dialektik (die Cicero *Acad. pos.* i. 5, 19, Plato zugeschreibt), hat nach Sextus Empir (*adv. Math.* vii. 16) zuerst Plato's Schüler Xenocrates förmlich aufgestellt: Plato aber sei, sagt Sextus mit Recht, δυνάμει ihr Urheber, ἀρχηγός."

were directed,—a philosophy which should serve them as a religion,[1] which should fill up the gaps and remove the anomalies of the existing worship, purifying and restoring it, while it preserved amity with it notwithstanding. Such being his intention, the manner in which he treats the doctrine of the Divine Being is the more remarkable. Instead of basing his philosophy upon it, and showing its relation as a part of his system of physics, ethics, and dialectics, he speaks of it frequently indeed, but always incidentally.[2] It is not so with other doctrines which he has at heart. Three of his finest dialogues are dedicated to setting forth as many aspects of his doctrine as to the soul's immortality; the Phædrus treats of its pre-existence; the Banquet of the influence of immortality on the relations of the present life; the Phædo of death as the means of a happy futurity.[3] But no one collects together and lucidly exhibits his view of the divine nature. This has to be picked out of his writings, a bit here, and another there, and put together by the student. No doubt he felt, as he has said,[4] "with regard to the Maker and the Father of this universe it is hard to find Him out, and when you have found Him impossible to describe Him to all men." He was intimately convinced that the great mass of mankind was quite unsuited to receive the conception of the Divine Being which he had formed. But I believe there to have been another reason of greater force with him for his not having presented as a whole his

---

[1] See Zeller, vol. ii. part 2, p. 599. Döllinger, p. 299, sec. 122; p. 279, sec. 87.
[2] Zeller, ii. part 1, p. 598. "Ueber diese beiden Gegenstände (die Religion und die Kunst) hat sich Plato ziemlich häufig, aber immer nur gelegenheitlich geäussert."
[3] Döllinger, p. 290, sec. 110.   [4] *Timæus*, 28.

conclusions on this central doctrine of all. It was not merely that the fate of his master Socrates was ever before him,[1] but the singular position which he held with regard to the established worship. He wished to correct, not to destroy it; he wished to reduce it to monotheism, and yet to preserve polytheism. The two are bound together in his mind. If then his writings be carefully analysed, and every reference to the Supreme Being put together into a sort of mosaic,[2] we should find the following picture. The everlasting essence of things, with which Philosophy deals, is the highest object. Ideas are those everlasting gods after the pattern of which the world and all things which are in it are formed, and the Godhead, taken absolutely, is not distinct from the highest Idea. Plato sets forth the causality of Ideas and the sway of reason in the world together with the impossibility to explain what is generated save by an Ingenerate, motion save by a soul, and the ordered disposition of the world, working out a purpose, save by reason; and in all which he declares respecting the Godhead, the Idea of Good, of the highest metaphysical and ethical perfection, is his guiding-point. As this highest Idea stands at the head of all Ideas as the cause of all being and knowledge, so the one everlasting invisible God, the Former and Father of all things, stands at the head of all the gods, alike difficult to find and to describe. Just as the above Idea is distinguished by the conception of the Good, so Plato

[1] Thus Grote, *Plato*, i. 230, speaks of "the early caution produced by the fate of Socrates," and believes "such apprehension to have operated as one motive deterring him from publishing any philosophical exposition under his own name, any Πλάτωνος σύγγραμμα," p. 231.

[2] This has been done by Zeller, vol. ii. part 1, pp. 599–602, from whom I take it. He supports his analysis with a great number of references to various works of Plato.

selects goodness as God's most essential attribute. It is on this ground that he maintains the Godhead to be absolutely good and upright, and its operation to be merely good and upright; against the old notion which imputed envy to it, and derived evil from it. Again, in opposition to the fabulous appearances of the gods, it is from the goodness of the Godhead that he deduces its unchangeableness, inasmuch as what is perfect can neither be changed by anything else, nor change itself, and so become worse. He adds, the Godhead will never show itself to men other than it is, since all falsehood is foreign to it; inasmuch as to falsehood in the properest sense, that is, ignorance and self-deception, it is not exposed, and has no need to deceive others. He extols the divine perfection, to which no beauty and no excellence is wanting; the divine power, which embraces everything and can do everything which is possible, that is, which does not involve a moral or a metaphysical contradiction: for instance, it is impossible for God to wish to change Himself, for evil to cease, and from the doctrine respecting the forming of the world and matter it is clear that the divine activity in producing is limited by the nature of the finite.[1] He extols the divine

---

[1] Zeller, vol. ii, part 1, p. 487, remarks of Plato's doctrine: "So far as things are the appearance and the image of the Idea, they must be determined by the Idea; so far as they have in themselves a proper principle in matter, they must be determined likewise by necessity: since, certain as it is that the world is the work of reason, it is as little to be left out of mind that in its formation beside reason another blindly working cause was in play, and that even the Godhead could make its work not absolutely perfect, but only so good as the nature of the finite permitted;" and he refers to many passages of the *Timæus*, of which one will suffice, wherein at the conclusion of a review of the physical causes of things Plato says: ταῦτα δὴ πάντα τότε ταύτῃ πεφυκότα ἐξ ἀνάγκης ὁ τοῦ καλλίστου τε καὶ ἀρίστου δημιουργὸς ἐν τοῖς γιγνομένοις παρελάμβανεν, ἡνίκα τὸν αὐτάρκη τε καὶ τὸν τελεώτατον Θεὸν ἐγέννα, χρώμενος μὲν ταῖς περὶ ταῦτα αἰτίαις ὑπηρετούσαις, τὸ δὲ εὖ τεκταινόμενος

wisdom which disposes all things to its purpose; its omniscience, which nothing escapes; its justice, which leaves no transgression unpunished and no virtue unrewarded; its goodness, which makes the best provision for all. He rejects, as notions taken from man, not merely the Godhead's having a body, but likewise all those tales which impute passions, quarrels, crimes of every kind to the gods. He declares them to be exalted above pleasure and displeasure, to be untouched by any evil; and is full of moral indignation at the thought that they allow themselves to be won over, or rather corrupted, by prayers and offerings. Moreover he shows that everything is ordered and ruled by Divine Providence, which extends over the least as well as the greatest, and as regards men is especially convinced that they are a carefully-tended possession of the Godhead, and that all things must issue in good to those who through virtue gain its good-will. If the unequal and unjust distribution of men's lot is objected, his reply is, that virtue carries its reward and wickedness its punishment immediately in itself; further, that both are sure of a complete retribution in the after-world, while already in this life as a rule in the end the upright goes not without recognition and thanks, nor the transgressor without universal hate and detestation. As to the general fact that there is evil in the world, it seemed to him so inevitable that it was not requisite expressly to defend the Godhead on that score. All these statements carry us back at

ἐν πᾶσι τοῖς γιγνομένοις αὐτός· διὸ δὴ χρὴ δύ' αἰτίας εἴδη διορίζεσθαι, τὸ μὲν ἀναγκαῖον, τὸ δὲ θεῖον, καὶ τὸ μὲν θεῖον ἐν ἅπασι ζητεῖν κτήσεως ἕνεκα εὐδαίμονος βίου, καθ' ὅσον ἡμῶν ἡ φύσις ἐνδέχεται, τὸ δὲ ἀναγκαῖον ἐκείνων χάριν, λογιζομένους ὡς ἄνευ τούτων οὐ δυνατὰ αὐτὰ ἐκεῖνα, ἐφ' οἷς σπουδάζομεν, μόνα κατανοεῖν, οὐδ' αὖ λαβεῖν, οὐδ' ἄλλως πως μετασχεῖν, p. 68. Compare p. 48. μεμιγμένη γὰρ οὖν ἡ τοῦδε τοῦ κόσμου γένεσις ἐξ ἀνάγκης τε καὶ νοῦ συστάσεως ἐγεννήθη· κ. τ. λ.

last to one and the same point. It is the Idea of the Good by applying which Plato produces so exalted a doctrine of God. In the like spirit he will consider only the moral intention in acts of worship. He alone can please the Godhead who is like it, and he alone is like it who is pious, wise, and just. The gods cannot receive the gifts of the wicked; the virtuous alone have a right to invoke them. God is goodness; and he who bears not the image of that goodness in himself stands in no communion with Him.

The doctrine here set forth is the highest ever reached by purely heathen Greek speculation; but we must remember that it is not thus collected into a head by Plato himself, still less is it put into such a relation to his physical, his logical, and his moral system as such a doctrine ought to bear. A man who had reached so lofty a conviction of the divine unity and moral perfection as this must, if he would make it effectual, give to it in his system the place which it really holds in the world. If there be indeed a Maker and Father of the universe by whom all things consist, all that Plato taught should have been subordinated to this its first principle, and the sum of his teaching to men should have been to set him forth. So far is this from the position which Plato really took, that in his ideal Republic no other religion but the traditional Greek religion was to subsist; he changes nothing in the very forms of the polytheistic worship; he refers the decision on many points to the Delphic Apollo.[1] And when in his last book on the Laws[2] he sets forth the notion of a second-best state, one which can be

[1] Döllinger, p. 297, sec. 119, quoted.
[2] So likewise Zeller remarks, vol. ii. part 1, p. 604: "Die Gesetze, welchen die philosophischen Regenten fehlen, behandeln die Volks-religion durchweg als die sittliche Grundlage des Staatswesens."

realised under actual circumstances, wherein he gives a mass of practical directions for the needs of the lower classes, religion in its purely polytheistic dress is the soul of his teaching, the groundwork of his structure. Men are to worship first of all the Olympian gods, and the gods who are the patrons of the city; then the gods of the earth; then demons and heroes; and all these in the traditional way by offerings, prayers, and vows. All good in public life is their gift; everything is to be consecrated to them; to violate their shrines is the greatest of crimes. In fact, after all, but few of mankind are capable of understanding or receiving the philosophic God. However imperfect[1] the popular belief in the gods may be, and however unsatisfactory to him the allegorical interpretations of it then so much in vogue, yet is it in Plato's conviction indispensable to all those who have not had a scientific education. Men must first be taught with lies, and then with the truth: the popular fables and the worship grounded on them is therefore for all the *first*, and for most the *only* form of religion.[2] The philosopher, it is true, sees deeper and despises them in his heart. Thus the monotheist in speculation is a polytheist in practice: as Socrates, the model and exemplar of Greek philosophy, with his dying breath, so Plato, its most inspired teacher with all the voice of his authority, sacrificed the cock to Æsculapius.

But moreover, this supreme God, who has to be disinterred from the recesses of the Platonic teaching, and conciliated with the worship practically paid to a

[1] Zeller, p. 605.
[2] Here Zeller remarks: "Diese Voraussetzung liegt der ganzen Behandlung dieser Gegenstände bei Plato zu Grunde.... Dass die philosophische Erkenntniss immer auf eine kleine Minderheit beschränkt sein müsse ist Plato's entschiedene Ueberzeugung."

host of subordinate gods, is in Plato's conception neither absolutely personal nor free, and he is not the Creator but only the Former of the world. In Plato's theory there is co-eternal with him a first matter, without form or quality, which exists independently of him; which moreover is inhabited and swayed to and fro in disorderly heavings by a sort of soul, the token of that dark Necessity[1] which rises behind the figures of gods and men in Greek poetry. It is indeed the work of the divine reason to come down upon this shapeless mass and its inborn mover, and out of them to construct the world-soul, with which and with his own reason he forms and maintains and vivifies the ordered universe. As he is by this operation the Father of the universe, so this First Matter is "the Mother of all generation," the condition of the existence of corporeal things. But in this original matter lies the origin of evil, which, perpetuated in the corporeal structure of man, can indeed be tamed and schooled, and in a certain degree subdued, but never can be exterminated by the divine reason. The power, the wisdom, and the providence of Plato's God are encountered by this check, which stands eternally over against the Demiurgos in his world-forming activity, which limits his freedom, and impairs his personality, while it excludes the whole idea of creation. Students of this philosophy[2] attempt to associate together his highest Idea, that of the Good, with the supreme God, of whom he speaks with personal attributes, as the just, the wise, the true, the good; but admit that Plato has not attempted to solve the problem how the Idea, which by his hypothesis as it

[1] Döllinger, p. 293.
[2] See Zeller, vol. ii. part 1, pp. 448-457.

is the highest is also the most general, is at the same time the most individual, the one personal God. In fact, it is admitted that he fails—together with all the ancient Greek writers—in the strict conception of personality.[1] As according to him individual beings are what they are only by participation of something higher, it is no wonder that in describing that one Reason, the Idea of the Good, the highest and most general of all, which forms and governs the world, his language oscillates between the personal and the impersonal. But if his philosophical reasons tend one way, it must be allowed that the heart and affections of the man, and the whole moral sense of the teacher, decide another.

The ethical system of Plato appears to be a strict deduction from his physical. As man in his view is a compound of matter, vivified by a portion of the world-soul, which the divine reason takes and unites with a portion of itself, so his virtues correspond to this threefold composition.[2] For man has an immortal portion in his soul, the reason, the godlike, in him; but the divine reason, in joining a portion of the world-soul with matter, invests it with two mortal parts, one the courageous, or manly, the other, sensuous desire, or the female element, having their seat in the body's activity. To these answer respectively the virtues of prudence, of courage, and of temperance, while justice comes in afterwards as a right ordering of the three, or as prudence applied to practice. The

[1] "Wie es sich aber in dieser Beziehung mit der Persönlichkeit verhalte, dies ist eine Frage, welche sich Plato wohl schwerlich bestimmt vorgelegt hat, wie ja dem Alterthum überhaupt der schärfere Begriff der Persönlichkeit fehlt, und die Vernunft nicht selten als allgemeine Weltvernunft in einer zwischen Persönlichem und Unpersönlichem unsicher schwankenden Weise gedacht wird." *Zeller*, p. 454.
[2] Döllinger, p. 286, sec. 103. Zeller, vol. ii. part 1, p. 538.

seat of all irregular desires, of all evil, in fact, is to
Plato in this union of the soul with matter. As this
matter is primordial, evil in its origin does not indeed
spring from God, but it is beyond his power: it springs
from that state of things which existed before the
action of God on chaos:[1] it must stand over against
the good: and of necessity encompasses this mortal
nature and the place of its habitation: and to man it
lies not in the perverted use of free-will, but in his
original composition, wherein his body is its seat. But
in this triple composition of man Plato does not seem
to have clearly apprehended a human personality at
all: he has not even attempted to explain[2] in what
the unity of the soul consists besides these its three
portions, two of which, being tied to the body, drop
off at death.

It is in the practice of Plato as a teacher that we
can most fitly consider the conception which the Greek
philosophers in general had concerning the method of
studying and imparting philosophy altogether. It was
about the fortieth year of his life, and twelve years
after the death of his master Socrates, that Plato,
having already travelled widely, settled at Athens.[3]
Here he purchased a fixed residence at the Academia,
which became from that time a philosophical school
for study, conversation, oral lectures, and friendly
meetings. Here he drew around him an inner circle
of scholars to whom he addressed his unwritten doctrines,[4] especially his doctrine of Ideas, the key to his

[1] *Theætetus*, p. 176. Σωκ. 'Αλλ' οὔτ' ἀπόλεσθαι τὰ κακὰ δυνατόν, ὦ
Θεόδωρε· ὑπεναντίον γάρ τι τῷ ἀγαθῷ ἀεὶ εἶναι ἀνάγκη· οὔτ' ἐν θεοῖς αὐτὰ
ἱδρῦσθαι, τὴν δὲ θνητὴν φύσιν καὶ τόνδε τὸν τόπον περιπολεῖ ἐξ ἀνάγκης.
[2] See Zeller, vol. ii. part 1, pp. 541–544, who points out a string of
difficulties on the subject of personality, free-will, as maintained by
Plato, and his doctrine that no one is willingly wicked.
[3] See Grote's *Plato*, i. pp. 133, 134.   [4] Ueberweg, i. p. 116.

whole system, according as they were able, after preparation, to receive them: and here besides he gave lectures which might be attended not only by that inner circle of choice disciples but by studious persons in general. This residence of Plato served for three hundred years, from 387 before Christ until the siege of Athens by Sylla in 87, as the centre of Plato's philosophy viewed as a teaching power. Now in this Plato had before him the great example of Pythagoras, in the first age of Greek philosophy. Concerning the doctrines of that philosopher we know little with certainty,[1] but all are agreed as to his manner of teaching them. His attempt was to establish a community which should carry in its bosom, propagate, and perpetuate a doctrine in morals, politics, religion, and philosophy. His whole procedure was by oral teaching, for he left not a word written. It was in fact a religious order of life which he first practised in his own person, and then endeavoured to communicate to others. Into this order trial for every one preceded reception.[2] His scholars were for a long period required to practise silent obedience and unconditional submission to the authority of the doctrine delivered to them. Severe daily examination was imposed upon all. The publishing of his doctrine, especially his speculation as to the nature of God, was strictly forbidden. The upright life, the learning which then could only be attained by personal inquiry, the persuasiveness of Pythagoras, were together so effective that he succeeded in establishing such a com-

[1] So Zeller sets forth at length, i. p. 206; and Ueberweg. i. p. 47.
[2] Ueberweg, i. p. 50. Plato calls it ὁδόν τινα βίου, for which Pythagoras αὐτός τε διαφερόντως ἠγαπήθη, καὶ οἱ ὕστερον ἔτι καὶ νῦν Πυθαγόρειον τρόπον ἐπονομάζοντες τοῦ βίου διαφανεῖς πῃ δοκοῦσιν εἶναι. *Polit.* x. p. 600.

munity both in Crotona and in other cities of Southern
Italy. It was persecuted and suffered continual disasters, but still this Pythagorean community, bearing
on its founder's doctrines and manner of life, existed
for several generations after his death, during which
many of the most distinguished Greeks belonged to it.
Such was the poet Æschylus, whose mind was formed
on Pythagorean principles. In Plato's time the
Pythagorean Archytas was at the head of the State
of Tarentum: and Plato himself was largely imbued
with Pythagorean tenets.[1]

Now Plato, it is true, did not imitate the political
part of the Pythagorean scheme. It was only upon
paper that he set forth his ideal republic. But the
same conception as to the manner of communicating
a doctrine lay in his mind as in that of Pythagoras.
He did not look to writing as a primary instrument
of communicating thought. He places it himself in
a relation of dependence upon oral dialectic instruction. It is only to serve as a reminder of what had
been otherwise taught: and, moreover, it is quite subordinate to his first postulate, the earnestness of a life
devoted to inquiry and education.[2] These principles
are set forth with great lucidity in his dialogue
Phædrus, where he introduces by the mouth of
Socrates the Egyptian god Thoth, the inventor of
arithmetic, geometry, astronomy, draughts and dice,
and also of letters. With these inventions in his hand
the god approached the then king of Egypt Thamous,
recommending him to make them known to his subjects. But Thamous was by no means inclined to
receive these inventions unconditionally: he praises
or blames them, as he judges of them, and at last he

[1] Grote, *Plato*, i. p. 221.   [2] Ueberweg, i. 115.

comes to the letters.[1] " 'This discovery,' says Thoth, 'O king, will make the Egyptians wiser, and improve their memory. It is of sovereign effect in both things.' 'Most ingenious Thoth,' replies the king, 'one man is made to give birth to art, and another to judge what good or what harm it will do to those who use it. And now you, being the father of letters, out of natural affection assert of them that which is just the contrary to their real office. For they will breed forgetfulness in the minds of those who learn them, who will slight the faculty of memory, inasmuch as relying on what is written externally in the types of others they do not exercise remembrance by an inward act of their own. The spell you have found is good, not for fixing in the mind, but for reminding. And as to wisdom, you offer to those who learn them not its reality but its appearance. For they will indeed hear much, but as this will be without teaching, they will seem to have many minds but generally no judgment, and be hard to comprehend, having become wiseacres instead of wise men.' 'O Socrates,' says Phædrus, 'you are one who can easily tell stories from Egypt or any other country.' 'My dear Phædrus, it was in the temple of Dodonean Jupiter that they made the first oracular words to proceed from an oak. The men of that day, not being wise as you young men, were satisfied in their simplicity to listen to an oak or a rock, if they only spoke the truth. Perhaps it makes a difference to you who the speaker is, and from what country; for you do not look merely whether it is true or not.' 'Your rebuke,' says Phædrus, 'is just, and what the Theban says about letters seems to me to be right.' 'Well then,' says Socrates, 'the man who thinks to leave an art in writ-

[1] *Phæd.* sec. 135, p. 274.

ing, and he also who receives it as being, when written, something clear and certain, must be very simple, and be really ignorant of Ammon's oracle, when he thinks that written words are something more than a reminder to one who knows the subject of the matters about which they are written.' 'Exactly so, Socrates.' 'For surely, Phædrus, writing shares this troublesome characteristic with painting. The productions of painting stand there as if they were alive, but if you ask them a question, preserve a solemn silence. Just so it is with writing. You may think that they speak with some meaning, but if you ask what that meaning is, there they stand with just the same word in their mouth. When once a thing is written, it is tossed over and over by all who take it in, whether it concerns them or not, and is unable to speak or to be silent with the proper persons. And if it is maltreated or slandered, it wants its father always to help it, for it can neither defend nor help itself.' 'What you say now is also very true indeed.' 'But,' says Socrates, 'can we not find another word, this one's lawful brother, and see the process by which it arises, and how much better and abler than the former it is?' 'What word is this, and how does it arise?' 'The word which is written on the disciple's soul together with true knowledge, which is able to defend itself, and knows how to speak and to be silent with the proper persons.' 'You mean the living and animated word of one who has knowledge, whereof the written word may justly be called the shadow?'[1] 'I mean that indeed. Tell me now; an intelligent gardener, who had seeds that he cared for, and wished to bear fruit,

---

[1] τὸν τοῦ εἰδότος λόγον λέγεις ζῶντα καὶ ἔμψυχον, οὗ ὁ γεγραμμένος εἴδωλον ἄν τι λέγοιτο δικαίως.

would he hurry with them in summer to the gardens of Adonis, plant them, and rejoice to see them springing up with a fair show in a week? or would he do this for amusement, and in festival-time, if he did it at all, but when he took pains would use his gardener's art, sow them at the fitting time, and be too glad if, seven months afterwards, he saw them coming to perfection?' 'Certainly, Socrates, that would be the difference between his sport and his earnest.' 'Shall we, then, say that he who possesses the science of justice, honour, and goodness, has less intelligence than the gardener for his own seeds? Surely not. He will not, then, hurry to write them with a pen in ink with words, which cannot on the one hand help themselves with speech, and on the other hand are incapable to teach the truth sufficiently.' 'I should think he would not.' 'He will not; but as for these written flower-borders, he will sow and write them, when he does write them, for amusement, storing up reminders for himself, should he come to a forgetful old age, and for every one who pursues the same footsteps, and he will take pleasure in seeing them springing up tenderly: so when other men fall to other amusements, lubricating themselves at the banquet, or other such things, he will take his amusement here.' 'In this, Socrates, you would substitute a very seemly amusement for a bad one, when the man who can play with words sports upon the subject of justice and suchlike.' 'So it is, my dear Phædrus, but it is, I take it, earnest in a far higher sense, when one, using the art of dialectics, takes hold of a fitting soul, and plants and sows with true knowledge words able to help both themselves and their planter, not fruitless, but having seed, whence growing up in a succession of minds they will from age to age produce an immortal line,[1] and will make their possessor happy as far as man can be.'"

In these words, put in his master's mouth, Plato, if I mistake not, has given us the whole purpose of his life, and the manner in which he hoped to accomplish it. It was in the Academia that he sought to establish that immortal line of living words, who should speak as the possessors of real knowledge upon justice, truth, and goodness. He is describing a living culture by living teachers, of whom he aspired to be himself the first; and the written dialogues which he has left are in his intention, and so far as they enter at all upon the higher points of his doctrine,[2] reminders of that which he had set forth to chosen auditors by word of mouth, the word which was able, as he says, to explain and defend itself, and to answer a question put to it.

This, then, was the relation existing in the mind of the prince of Greek philosophers between the written and the spoken word as instruments in imparting true knowledge or science. The written word he regarded as subsidiary, as presupposing instruction by question and answer, and still more the moral discipline of a life earnestly given up to the study of the subjects in question. Without this a writing by itself was like a figure in a picture, which makes an impression on the beholder, but when asked if it is the true impression, keeps, as he says, a solemn face, and makes no reply; which is the same to all, the earnest and the indifferent, and cannot treat them according to their merits. He laughs at the notion of such a writing being by itself any more than sport. And let

---

[1] ἔχοντες σπέρμα, ὅθεν ἄλλοι ἐν ἄλλοις ἤθεοι φυόμενοι τοῦτ' ἀεὶ ἀθάνατον παρέχειν ἱκανοί.

[2] See his averseness to write on such doctrines at all set forth in his 7th epistle.

us remember that he who said this has enshrined his own philosophy in the most finished specimens of dramatic dialogues which the Greek mind produced. These are the statements of the man who wrote Greek in his countrymen's opinion as Jupiter would have spoken it. There are, then, in Plato's mind three constituents of teaching: first, the choice of fitting subjects for it, and what is therein implied, the imposition of a moral discipline upon them regulating their life to the end in view; secondly, the master's oral instruction conveying gradually and with authority to minds so prepared the doctrine to be received; and thirdly, the committing such doctrine to writing, which shall serve to *remind* the disciple of what he has been taught. And this was what he carried into effect.[1] He fixed himself at the Academia, over which he presided for forty years: he was succeeded therein by his nephew Speusippus, who held his chair for eight years; Xenocrates followed in the same post during twenty-five years; and the line was continued afterwards by Polemon, Crantor, Crates, Arcesilaus, and others in uninterrupted series. Plato thus established the method of Greek philosophy, and his example herein was followed by Aristotle, Zeno, and Epicurus.

His great disciple Aristotle came to him at the age of seventeen, and studied under him during twenty years. At a later age, when, after completing the education of Alexander, he fixed himself in middle life at Athens, he set up there a second philosophical

[1] Grote observes, *Plato*, i. 216: "Plato was not merely a composer of dialogues. He was lecturer and chief of a school besides. The presidency of that school, commencing about 386 B.C., and continued by him with great celebrity for the last half (nearly forty years) of his life, *was his most important function*. Among his contemporaries he must have exerted greater influence through his school than through his writings."

school at the Lyceum on its eastern side, and on the model of that of Plato. Attached to this museum were a portico, a hall with seats, one seat especially for the lecturing professor, a garden, and a walk, together with a residence, all permanently appropriated to the teacher and the process of instruction.[1] When Aristotle died in the year 322 B.C., his friend Theophrastus presided over his school during five and thirty years, and the line continued on. We learn that there were periodical meetings, convivial and conversational, among the members both of the Academic and Peripatetic schools, and laws for their regulation established by Xenocrates and Aristotle. It was in the shady walks of his garden that this great philosopher taught by word of mouth the choicer circle of his disciples: for the more general hearers he gave lectures sitting.[2] His instructions were divided into two classes, those which he gave on rhetoric, the art of discussion, knowledge of civil matters, and such-like, which were exoteric, and those which touched the finer and more subtle points of philosophy, which were termed acroatic, as addressed to the ears.[3] Again, his dialogues he called "public" or "issued" discourses, things made over to the general public, in distinction from what was not so disclosed, but reserved for the philosopher's own meditation, to be subsequently communicated either by oral lecture or by writing to the private circle of scholars who gave themselves up entirely to his philosophy. These Aristotle called "philosophical" or "teaching" discourses, proceeding, that is, from the principles proper

---

[1] Grote, *Plato*, i. p. 138.
[2] Ueberweg, i. p. 140, from Diogenes.
[3] Aulus Gellius, *N.A.* xx. 5, quoted by Ueberweg.

to each branch of learning, and not from the opinions of the lecturer. These latter were termed "tentative," as belonging to the exoteric. Simplicius, one of the latest writers on Greek philosophy, defines exoteric as "the common, and what concludes by arguments which are matter of opinion;" and Philoponus, as discourses "not of strict proof, and not directed to lawfully-begotten hearers," that is, trained and prepared, "but to the public, and springing from probabilities,"[1] Thus in Aristotle, the largest in grasp of mind, the most observant of facts, the most accurate in definition among Greek writers, the philosopher in fact and "master of those who know,"[2] for all future ages, we find the same three constituents of teaching as in Plato, and in the same order of importance: first, hearers selected for their natural aptitude, and then submitted to a moral discipline and a common life; secondly, the instruction of such hearers by word of mouth, question and answer, discussion and cross-examination; and lastly, the committing of doctrines to writing. With him too his written philosophical discourses were *reminders* of his oral teaching, which they presupposed and required as a key to their full meaning, and especially for the comprehension of their harmony as a system.

The order of teaching which I have thus sketched as being followed in practice by the two most eminent

---

[1] Ἐν κοινῷ γιγνόμενοι λόγοι ... ἐκδεδομένοι λόγοι· οἱ κατὰ φιλοσοφίαν λόγοι, or διδασκαλικοὶ λόγοι, οἱ ἐκ τῶν οἰκείων ἀρχῶν ἑκάστου μαθήματος καὶ οὐκ ἐκ τῶν τοῦ ἀποκρινομένου δοξῶν συλλογιζόμενοι, which last are λόγοι πειραστικοί. Simplicius calls τὰ ἐξωτερικά, τὰ κοινὰ καὶ δι' ἐνδόξων περαινόμενα; Philoponus, λόγοι μὴ ἀποδεικτικοί, μηδὲ πρὸς τοὺς γνησίους τῶν ἀκροατῶν εἰρημένοι, ἀλλὰ πρὸς τοὺς πολλοὺς, ἐκ πιθανῶν ὡρμημένοι. Quoted by Ueberweg, i. p. 146.

[2] Vidi il maestro di color che sanno
Seder tra filosofica famiglia.   Dante, *Inf.* iv. 131.

Greek philosophers belonged to them all. They had no other conception respecting the method of communicating a doctrine efficiently to men. They none of them considered philosophy merely or chiefly as a literature: none of them attributed to a book the power of teaching it. Their conception was, a master and his scholars, and the living together, the moral subordination and discipline which this involved. This school of education or training in knowledge [1] was their primary thought: the committing of their doctrine to writing was both subsequent and secondary. Their writings were intended, as Plato says, to be recollections [2] of their teaching, and failed to convey the real knowledge to those who had not the stamp of this teaching impressed on their minds.

As Plato made a local habitation for himself and his doctrine in the Academia, and Aristotle in the Lyceum, so Zeno, the founder of the third great philosophic school, took up his abode in the Portico at Athens, a court surrounded with pillars, and adorned with the paintings of Polygnotus. Here he began to teach about 308 B.C., and here he continued teaching as some say for fifty-eight years. It is said that the character of Socrates, as drawn by Xenophon and by Plato in his *Apology*, filled him with astonishment and admiration: [3] and the Stoics afterwards drew their doctrine of the wise man, which they endeavoured to image out and realise, from that living example of it,[4] an instance of the connection of doctrine with person which is full of interest and suggestion. Zeno was succeeded in his office of

---

[1] διδασκαλία.   [2] ὑπόμνησις.
[3] Ueberweg, i. p. 188, from Diogenes and Themistius.
[4] *Ibid.* from Noack, *Psyche*, v. i. sec. 13.

teaching by Cleanthes, and Cleanthes by Chrysippus and a long line of teachers, who for several hundred years continued, with variations, the same general doctrine of ethics.

Just in the same way and at the same time Zeno's great rival Epicurus fixed the seat of his school in the Garden at Athens, which thenceforth became for thirty-six years the central point of the teacher's activity. About him gathered a circle of friends whom similarity of principles and the enjoyment of cultivated intercourse bound together with unusual intimacy. It speaks for the special character of his philosophy that from the beginning women and even hetærææ formed a part of this society. But he succeeded during this long period of teaching in impressing upon his school so strong a character that it is recognised without essential change during hundreds of years.[1]

We should do injustice to the character and the work of Plato, Aristotle, Zeno, and Epicurus; the founders of the four great schools of Greek philosophy, if we did not take into account what was in their day no doubt of greater influence than their writings, that is, their function as teachers, their oral teaching itself, and those fundamental principles of philosophic education which lay at the bottom of it. Plato has left us very little of doctrine put out in his own name. He is not a speaker in his dialogues. He puts what he would say in the mouth of others, especially of Socrates. He tells us that he has purposely done this in order that men might not say, "Here is Plato's philosophy:"[2] and the reason of this was that he

---

[1] Zeller, vol. iii. part 1, p. 343.
[2] Ep. vii. p. 341. οὔκουν ἐμόν γε περὶ αὐτῶν ἐστι σύγγραμμα, οὐδὲ μὴ

utterly distrusted his own or any man's power to disclose to others such a system in a set form of words. It is, then, the more remarkable that he has said in his own person what were his most settled convictions as to intercourse by word of mouth, and continuous written discourse, viewed as instruments for attaining and communicating truth. He expresses his absolute disbelief that men can reach true conceptions by their being set forth in the immutable form of writing. It is a far other and more difficult work which has to be accomplished. In a word, not even aptness for learning and memory will give the power to see the truth as to virtue and vice to one who is not kin to the subject; nor, again, this kinship without such aptitude and memory: but when both are joined, then out of living together, after much time,[1] by the continual friction of name, definition, acts of sight and perception, by thought and meditation, the hearing and answering the objections of others, the process of mutual cross-examination discharged without envy or jealousy, and with sincere love of the truth, a sudden flash of fire kindles in the mind, and

ποτε γένηται· ῥητὸν γὰρ οὐδαμῶς ἐστίν ὡς ἄλλα μαθήματα, ἀλλ' ἐκ πολλῆς συνουσίας γιγνομένης περὶ τὸ πρᾶγμα αὐτὸ καὶ τοῦ συζῆν ἐξαίφνης, οἷον ἀπὸ πυρὸς πηδήσαντος ἐξαφθὲν φῶς, ἐν τῇ ψυχῇ γενόμενον αὐτὸ ἑαυτὸ ἤδη τρέφει· and much more to the same effect; after which he says, ὧν ἕνεκα νοῦν ἔχων οὐδεὶς τολμήσει ποτὲ εἰς αὐτὸ τιθέναι τὰ νενοημένα, καὶ ταῦτα εἰς ἀμετακίνητον, ὃ δὴ πάσχει τὰ γεγραμμένα τύποις. So again in his second letter, p. 314. πολλάκις δὲ λεγόμενα καὶ ἀεὶ ἀκουόμενα καὶ πολλὰ ἔτη μόγις, ὥσπερ χρυσός, ἐκκαθαίρεται μετὰ πολλῆς πραγματείας. ... μεγίστη δὲ φυλακὴ τὸ μὴ γράφειν ἀλλ' ἐκμανθάνειν· οὐ γάρ ἐστι τὰ γραφέντα μὴ οὐκ ἐκπεσεῖν. Grote seems to me fully justified in counting these epistles as genuine, against the attacks of some modern German sceptics.

[1] Μετὰ τριβῆς πάσης καὶ χρόνου πολλοῦ, ὅπερ ἐν ἀρχαῖς εἶπον· μόγις δὲ τριβόμενα πρὸς ἄλληλα αὐτῶν ἕκαστα, ὀνόματα, καὶ λόγοι ὄψεις τε καὶ αἰσθήσεις, ἐν εὐμενέσιν ἐλέγχοις ἐλεγχόμενα καὶ ἄνευ φθόνων ἐρωτήσεσι καὶ ἀποκρίσεσι χρωμένων, ἐξέλαμψε φρόνησις περὶ ἕκαστον καὶ νοῦς, συντείνων ὅτι μάλιστ' εἰς δύναμιν ἀνθρωπίνην. Ep. vii. p. 344.

nourishes itself, disclosing the knowledge required. Thus it is that prudence and intelligence on each subject shining out in this beam of light, go forward as far as man may reach. The view here propounded, if reflected upon, will convey to us what the living work first of Pythagoras, and then of Plato, Aristotle, Zeno, Epicurus, and their successors, was. Both the conception indeed and the realisation seem to have been most complete in Pythagoras. The philosophic living together was its basis. Instruction was oral. Learning was effected by the collision of mind with mind, by objection and answer. It was the Socratic principle inherited from these schools that nothing passed muster for knowledge which did not stand the test of cross-examination:[1] but an unchangeable text was utterly unsuited, according to Plato, to debate the question under treatment in such fashion, while on the other hand the mind of the reader was passive in receiving the impression which it conveyed. On neither side therefore did the conditions of knowledge exist, but this was reached under the circumstances of personal intercourse above mentioned, and might be recalled in the written form to the minds of those who had thus first attained it.

Down to the end of Greek philosophy the same conception as to the method of teaching prevailed. Ammonius Sakkas, the founder of Neoplatonism,

---

[1] Grote, *Plato*, i. 229. "When we see by what standard Plato tests the efficacy of any expository process, we shall see yet more clearly how he came to consider written exposition unavailing. The standard which he applies is, that the learner shall be rendered able both to apply to others and himself to endure a Socratic Elenchus or cross-examination as to the logical difficulties involved in all the steps and helps to learning." Without this "Plato will not allow that he has attained true knowledge" ($\dot{\epsilon}\pi\iota\sigma\tau\dot{\eta}\mu\eta$). Compare the system pursued in the mediæval schools and universities.

THE CHURCH AND THE GREEK PHILOSOPHY 353

delivered his doctrine only by word of mouth, which his chief disciples, Erennius, Origines, and Plotinus, engaged not to make public.[1] It was when one of them, Erennius, had broken this promise, that another, Plotinus, after delivering lectures at Rome, wrote down his philosophy; but his scheme was to carry it out by collecting his disciples together in one city, and thus realising Plato's republic.

[1] Ueberweg, i. pp. 242, 243.

LECTURE XIV

THE CHRISTIAN CHURCH AND THE GREEK PHILOSOPHY

PART II

THE mind of the next great teacher who arose in Greece after Plato presented an almost complete contrast to that of the master under whom he had so long studied. Aristotle's power consisted in a parallel development of two forces which do not often co-exist.[1] He joined together a rare degree of consistent philosophic thinking with an equally rare degree of accurate observation. This double faculty is shown in what he effected. He made the sciences of logic, ethics, and psychology: he built up those of natural history and politics with the wealth of knowledge which his experience had accumulated.[2] Thus his analytic and synthetic genius embraced the whole range of human knowledge then existing. As Plato threw his vivid fancy and imagination and his religious temper into everything which concerned the human spirit, so Aristotle fixed his gaze upon nature, which with him in all its manifestations was the ultimate fact. As Plato rose from the single being to his conception of the true, the good, the beautiful, of which the Idea to him was everything, so Aristotle, steadfastly discarding his master's doctrine of Ideas, took his stand on the single being, examining it with the closest observation

---

[1] Zeller, vol. ii. part 2, p. 632. [2] Döllinger, pp. 304, 305.

and the subtlest thought, and the knowledge thus conveyed to him is everything. Plato's conception of God is that of the great world-former, orderer, and ruler: Aristotle's conception of God is that of a pure intelligence, without power, an eternal, ever-active, endless, incorporeal substance, who never steps out of that everlasting rest into action: who is the world's first cause, but is unconscious of it, His action upon the world being likened to the influence of the beloved object upon the lover. Plato's dualism is summed up in the expression, God and Matter; Aristotle's dualism, in God and the World. Plato represents the action of the Deity as the working-up of the original matter into the millions of forms which the world exhibits: but these millions of forms are taken by Aristotle as if they had existed for ever; the World, as it is, and the Deity, are co-eternal.

Aristotle's doctrine of the human soul is that it exists only as that which animates the body, without which its being cannot be known.[1] It is the principle which forms, moves, and develops the body; the substance which only appears in the body formed and penetrated by it, and which works continuously in it, as the life which determines and prevails over its matter. Thus the body is of itself nothing; what it is, it is only through the soul, whose being and nature it expresses, to which it is related as the medium in which the purpose, which is the soul, realises itself. Thus the soul cannot be thought of without the body, nor the body without the soul: both come into their actual state together. In the soul Aristotle distinguishes three parts, the vegetative, the sensitive, and the thinking. This last, the

[1] Döllinger, pp. 309, 310, sec. 137, 138.

peculiar property of man, is further divisible into the
passive and the active, of which the former is linked
to the soul as the soul is to the body, as form is to
matter, multiplies itself with individuals, and is ex-
tinguished with them. But the reason, or pure intelligence, has nothing in common with matter, comes
from without into man, and exists in him as a self-
consisting indestructible being, without multiplying or
dividing itself. Accordingly this intellect or reason
suffers the soul to sink back with the body into the
nothing from which both have been together produced.
It alone continues to subsist as what is ever the same
and unchangeable, since it is nothing but the divine
intelligence in an individual existence, enlightening the
darkness of the human subject in the passive part of
the understanding, and so must be considered as the
first mover in man of his discursive thinking and
knowing, as well as of his willing.[1] As that which
is properly human in the soul, that which has had a
beginning, must also pass away, even the understanding, and only the divine reason is immortal, and as
memory belongs to the sensitive soul, and individual
thinking only takes place by means of the passive
intellect, all consciousness must cease with death.
And again, clearly as Aristotle maintains that man is
the mover and master of his own actions, and has it
in his power to be good or evil, and thence repudiates
the assumption of Socrates and Plato that no one is
willingly evil, yet he cannot find a place for real
freedom of the will between the motion which arises
from sensitive desire, and that which proceeds from
the divine intelligence dwelling in the soul. Necessity arises on both sides, from the things which deter-

[1] Döllinger, p. 310, sec. 139.

mine the passive understanding, and from the divine intelligence.¹ Thus his physical theory, as in the case of Plato noted above,² prevents a clear conception of the human personality. His notion of man in this point corresponds to his notion of God: he does not concern himself with questions respecting the goodness, justice, and freedom of God, inasmuch as his God is not really personal:³ so with regard to man we find in him no elucidation as to the question of moral freedom, nor of the origin and nature of wickedness in man. Wickedness is with Aristotle the impotence to hold the mean between too much and too little: it presents itself therefore only in this world of contingency and change, and has no relation to God, since the first or absolute good has nothing opposed to it. He has not the sense of moral perversion with regard to evil. In accordance with which the end of all moral activity with him is happiness, which consists in the well-being arising from an energy according to nature; as virtue is the observing a proper mean between two extremes. And the highest happiness is contemplative thought, the function of the divine in man, the turning away from everything external to the inner world of the conceptions.

The religious character, which belongs conspicuously to Plato's philosophy, fails, it will be seen, in that of Aristotle. Whereas Plato strove to purify the popular belief, and urged as the highest point of virtue to become like to God by the conjunction of justice and sanctity with prudence,⁴ Aristotle divides morality from

---
¹ Döllinger, p. 311, sec. 140.   ² See p. 339, above.
³ Döllinger, pp. 307 and 311.
⁴ Διὸ καὶ πειρᾶσθαι χρὴ ἐνθένδε ἐκεῖσε φεύγειν ὅτι τάχιστα· φυγὴ δὲ ὁμοίωσις Θεῷ κατὰ τὸ δυνατόν· ὁμοίωσις δὲ δίκαιον καὶ ὅσιον μετὰ φρονήσεως γενέσθαι. κ. τ. λ. *Theætet.* p. 176.

religion as his God is separated off from the world.[1] His scientific inquiries have not that immediate relation to the personal life and the destiny of man in which the religiousness of Platonism most consists. His whole view of the world goes to explain things as far as possible from their natural causes.[2] Thus he admits in the whole direction of the world the ruling of a divine power, of a reason which reaches its purpose; he believes in particular that the gods care for men, take an interest in him who lives in accordance with reason; that happiness is their gift; he contradicts the notion that the godhead is envious, and so could withhold from man knowledge, the best of its gifts; but this divine providence coincides for him entirely with the working of natural causes. In his view the godhead stands in solitary self-contemplation outside the world, the object of admiration and reverence to man. The knowledge of it is the highest task for his intellect. It is the good to which in common with everything that is finite he is struggling; whose perfection calls forth his love: but little as he can expect a return of love from it, so little does he find in it any co-operation distinct from the natural connection of things, and his reason is the only point of immediate contact with it.

Religion[3] itself Aristotle treats as an unconditional moral necessity. The man who doubts whether the gods should be honoured is a subject fit not for instruction but for punishment, just as the man who asks whether he should love his parents. As the natural system of the world cannot be imagined with-

---

[1] Zeller, vol. ii. part 2, p. 623.   [2] *Ibid.* ii. 2, p. 625.
[3] *Ibid.* p. 629.

out God, so neither can man in it be imagined without religion. But he can give us no other ground save political expediency for resting religion upon fables so apparent as the stories of the popular belief. He sometimes himself uses these fables, like other popular opinions, to illustrate some general proposition, as, for instance, Homer's verses on the golden chain show the immobility of the first mover: just as in other cases he likes to pursue his scientific assumptions to their least apparent beginnings, and to take account of sayings and proverbs. But if we except the few general principles of religious belief, he ascribes to these fables no deeper meaning, and as little does he seem to care about purifying their character. For his state he presupposes the existing religion, as in his personal conduct he did not withdraw from its usages, and expressed his attachment to friends and relations in the forms consecrated by it. But no trace is found in him of Plato's desire to reform religion by means of philosophy: and in his politics he allows in the existing worship even what in itself he disapproves, as the case of unseemly words, inscriptions, and statues. Thus the relation of the Aristotelic philosophy to the actual religion is generally a very loose one. It does not disdain indeed to use the points of connection which the other presents, but has no need of it whatever for itself: nor does it seek on its own side to purify and transform religion, the imperfection of which it rather seems to take as something unavoidable. The two are indifferent to each other; philosophy pursues its way without troubling itself about religion, without fearing any interruption from it.

In the seventy-seven years which elapsed from the death of Socrates, 399 B.C., to that of Aristotle, 322

B.C., Greek life had suffered a great change. That dear-loved independence which every state had cultivated, and which concentrated every energy of the mind in civil life had vanished. During the forty years of Plato's work as a teacher it was becoming less and less; Chæronea gave it the death-blow; while Aristotle is the son of a time at which scientific study had already begun to take the place of active political life.[1] But the conquest effected by his great pupil Alexander completed this change. He opened the East to the Greek mind, bringing it into close contact with Asiatic thought, beliefs, and customs. Under his successors Alexandria, Antioch, and Seleucia, Tarsus, Pergamus, and Rhodes became great centres of Greek culture: but Greek self-government was gone. Athens with the rest of the Greek cities had lost its political independence, but it remained the metropolis of Greek philosophy. From the last decade of the fourth century before Christ four great schools, the Platonic, Peripatetic, Stoic, and Epicurean, all seated here, as embodied in the dwelling-place and oral teaching of their masters, stand over against each other. The point most interesting to our present subject is this, that all these schools take up a common ground, one which we consider to belong properly to religion, that is the question wherein the happiness of man consists, and how to attain it.[2] Thus the political circumstances of the land gave the tone to its philosophy. What the time required was something which would compensate men for the lost position of a free citizen and a self-governed fatherland. The cultivated classes looked to philosophy for consolation and support. The answers to this question which the various systems gave were

[1] Zeller, vol. iii. part 1, p. 7.   [2] *Ibid.* p. 14.

THE CHURCH AND THE GREEK PHILOSOPHY 361

very different from each other, but an answer they all attempted. What they have in common is, the drawing-back of man upon himself, his inner mind, his consciousness, as a being who thinks and wills:[1] while on the other hand the mental view was widened from the boundaries of a narrow state to that which touches man in general. The field of morality opened out beyond the range of this or that city, territory, or monarchy. Thus two hundred full years were occupied with the struggles of the Stoic and Epicurean schools, and the sceptical opposition to them of the middle and later Academy. At the very beginning of this time the man who sat first in Aristotle's chair after him, and therefore the head of the most speculative school, Theophrastus, had shocked the students of philosophy by declaring that fortune, not wisdom, was the ruler of the world. But it was precisely against the despondence which such a conviction would work in the mind that the Stoics struggled with their doctrine of apathy, Epicurus with his self-contentment, the Sceptics with their tranquillity of indifference.[2] These all sought to cure those whom the fables of the popular religion were insufficient to satisfy, those who felt the evils and trials of life and knew not whither to turn in their need. But the Stoic and the Epicurean cures stood in the strongest contrast to each other.

Zeno[3] of Cittium in Cyprus, after listening for twenty years to the teaching of various Socratic masters in Athens, founded a school himself, and wished it to be a school of virtuous men rather than of speculative philosophers. It was a system of com-

[1] Zeller, vol. iii. part 1, p. 18.   [2] *Ibid.* p. 12; Döllinger, p. 318.
[3] Döllinger, pp. 319-321.

plete materialism rigorously carried out. He admitted only corporeal causes, and two principles—matter, and a force eternally indwelling in it and shaping it. These two principles, matter and force, were in fact to the Stoic mind only one eternal being viewed in a twofold aspect. Matter for its subsistence needs a principle of unity to form and hold it together: and this, the active element, is inconceivable without matter as the subject in which it dwells, works, and moves. Thus the positive element is matter viewed as being as yet without qualities, while the active element which runs through and quickens everything is God in matter. In real truth God and matter are one thing, or, in other words, the Stoic doctrine is a pantheism which views matter as instinct with life.[1] God is the unity of that force which embraces and interpenetrates the universe, assuming all forms, and as such is a subtle fluid, fire, ether, or breath, in which are contained all forms of existence belonging to the world-body which it animates, and from which they develop themselves in order: it lives and moves in all, and is the common source of all effect and all desire. God, then, is the world-soul, and the world itself no aggregate of independent elements, but a being, organised, living, filled and animated by a single soul, that is to say, by one original fire manifesting itself in various degrees of tension and heat. If in Aristotle's theory the world is a total of single beings, which are only bound together unto a higher aim by a community of effort, in the Stoic system on the contrary these beings all viewed together are members of a surpassingly perfect organisation, and as such, so bound in one, that nothing can happen to the individual

---

[1] The doctrine of Hylozoismus.

being, which does not by sympathy extend its operation to all others. Thus on His physical side, God is the world-fire, the vital all-interpenetrating heat, the sole cause of all life and motion, and the necessity which rules the world: while on His moral side, inasmuch as the first general cause can only be a soul full of reason and wisdom, He is the world-reason, a blessed being, the originator of the moral law, ever occupied with the government of the world, being in fact Himself the world. Thus everything is subject to the law of absolute necessity; everything eternally determined through an endless series of preceding causes, since nothing happens without a cause, and that again is the working of a cause before it. What, then, is called, or seems to be, chance, is merely the working of a cause unknown to us. The will of man is accordingly mere spontaneity. He wills, but what he wills is inevitable: he determines himself, but always in consequence of preceding causes. And since here every cause is something subject to the conditions of matter, something purely inside the world, it becomes unalterable destiny. But inasmuch as the series of causes leads back to the first, and this first cause has not only a physical side, but includes intelligence with it, and so everything in it is foreseen and predetermined, therefore that which considered under the aspect of inevitable necessity is called fate or destiny, viewed as thought may be termed Providence, a divine arrangement.

With such a doctrine it is evident that all morality was reduced to a matter of physics: and yet no sect of Greek philosophers struggled so hard to solve the great problem of moral freedom as the Stoics.[1] But

[1] Döllinger, pp. 322-324.

the iron grasp of their leading tenet was ever too much for them. Man's soul is of the same substance as the world-soul, that is, breath or fire, of which it is a portion: in man it manifests itself as the force from which knowledge and action proceed, as at once intelligence, will, and consciousness. It is, then, closely allied with the Divine Being, but at the same time corporeal, a being which stands in perpetual action and reaction with the human body. It is that heat-matter bound to the blood, which communicates life and motion: it is perishable, though it lasts beyond the body, perhaps to the general conflagration. It has therefore, in the most favourable view, the duration of a world-period, with the out-run of which it must return to the universal ether or godhead: its individual existence and consciousness end.

As to the popular religion,[1] the Stoics admitted that it was filled with pretended deities, false doctrines, and rank superstition; that its wilderness of fables about the gods was simply contemptible: but that it was well to retain the names of gods consecrated in public opinion, who were merely descriptions of particular incorporations of the one world-god.

The Stoics did not represent the component elements of human nature as struggling with each other, like Plato.[2] With them nature and reason is one thing. Their virtue,[3] or highest good, is life in accordance with nature, that is, the concurrence of human conduct with the all-ruling law of nature, or of man's will with God's will. Thus it was that the Stoic sought to reach his doctrine of philosophical impassibility: and to this system the majority of earnest

[1] Döllinger, p. 324. [2] *Ibid.* p. 326.
[3] ὁμολογουμένως τῇ φύσει ζῆν. Ueberweg, i. p. 198.

and thinking minds in the two centuries before Christ inclined.[1]

At the very same time as Zeno, Epicurus set up at Athens a school destined through all its existence to wage a battle with Stoicism, yet aiming by different means at the same end, the freedom of the individual man from anxiety and disturbance.[2] If Zeno's world was an intelligent animal, that of Epicurus was a machine formed and kept in action by chance. He assumed the atomic theory of Democritus, that all bodies — and there are nothing else but corporeal things — have arisen originally from atoms moving themselves in empty space. They are eternal and indestructible, without quality, but not without quantity, and endlessly various in figure. As these from mere weight and impulse would fall like an everlasting rain in empty space without meeting each other, Epicurus devised a third motion, a slight declension from the perpendicular, in virtue of which their agglomeration is produced: and thus it is a work of pure chance that out of these, the countless worlds which frame the universe began to be. Any order or higher guidance of the universe, as directed to a purpose, is not to be thought of, any more than necessary laws, according to which the appearances of nature reproduce themselves. For a law would ultimately lead to a lawgiver, and this might re-awaken fear, and disturb the wise man's repose. He utterly denied the intervention either of one god or of many gods in the forming or the maintenance of the world: the main purpose indeed of his philosophy was to overthrow that religious view which saw in the argument from design a sure

[1] Döllinger, p. 340.   [2] *Ibid.* p. 330.

proof of a Divine Providence.¹ Nothing, he thought, was more perverted than the opinion that nature was directed for the good of man, or generally for any object at all; that we have tongues in order to speak, or ears in order to hear, for in fact just the reverse is true. We speak because we have tongues, and hear because we have ears. The powers of nature have worked purely under the law of necessity. Among their manifold productions some were necessarily composed in accordance with an end: hence resulted for man in particular many means and powers; but such result must not be viewed as intentional, rather as a purely casual consequence of naturally necessary operations. Gods, such as the people believed, he utterly repudiated. Not he who denied such gods, but he who assumed their existence, was godless. He allowed, indeed, that there existed an immense multitude of gods, beings of human form, but endued with subtle, ethereal, transparent, indestructible bodies, who occupied the intermundial spaces, free from care, regardless of human things, enjoying their own blissful repose.² His gods are in fact a company of Epicurean philosophers, possessing everything which they can desire, eternal life, no care, and perpetual opportunity of agreeable entertainment.

The soul of man is a body made out of the finest round and fiery atoms; a body which, like heated air, most rapidly penetrates the whole material frame. The finest portion of the soul, the feeling and thinking spirit, which as a fourth element is added to the fiery, aerial, and vaporous portions, dwells in the breast. In these elements all the soul's passions and

[1] Zeller, vol. iii. part I, p. 370.   [2] Ibid. p. 398.

impulses are rooted. When death destroys the body, the sheltering and protecting home of the soul's atoms, these evaporate at once. It was clear that in such a system the soul could not outlive the body, but Epicurus laid a special stress on this, since thereby only could men be delivered from the greatest impediment to repose and undisturbed enjoyment of life, the torturing fear of the world below, and of punishments after death. It was the crown of his system, to which ethics, physics, and such logic as he admitted were entirely subordinate, to emancipate men from four fears—the fear of death, the fear of natural things, the fear of the gods, the fear of a Divine Providence, which was the same thing as fate.[1] Nevertheless, the followers of Epicurus had no scruple, after the manner of their master, who had spoken of the worship of the gods like a priest, to visit temples and take part in religious ceremonies. These, it is true, were useless, since they had nothing to fear and nothing to hope from the gods, but it was an act of reason, and could do no harm, to honour beings naturally so high and excellent.[2]

Of this school we learn that it gradually became the most numerous of all. Its social force really lay in setting forth as a model the undisturbed security of individual life. It agreed at the bottom with Stoicism that man's wisdom and highest end was to live in accordance with nature. Zeno, it is true, called this living in accordance with nature, virtue, man's highest and only good; Epicurus called it pleasure; but Zeno's virtue consisted essentially in the absence of passions, the pleasure of Epicurus

---

[1] Döllinger, pp. 331–333. Zeller, vol. iii. part 1, p. 392.
[2] Döllinger, p. 335.

in the mind's undisturbedness.¹ The Epicureans were more attached to their master's memory than any other school. They were renowned for their friendship with each other. Epicurus's Garden at Athens meant the highest refinement of Athenian life, the enjoyment of everything that was pleasant in the society of like-minded men.² It was this side of his philosophy which made it popular.

While the schools of Zeno and Epicurus seated at Athens were powerfully influencing Grecian thought, the former especially drawing to it the stronger and more thinking minds, resistance arose to them both in the chair of Plato. First Arcesilaus and then Carneades, who had succeeded to this office, set up in the middle Academy the school of Scepticism. While Stoics and Epicureans alike sought peace of mind through knowledge of the world and its laws, they on the contrary maintained that this same peace of mind could only be attained by renouncing all such knowledge.³ They held that no truth and no certainty were given to man by the representations of his senses, by his feelings, and by his consciousness of these, which do not enable him to know the real being of anything.⁴ Those who held this view would not say downright that what they contradicted was untrue: they were of opinion that it might be true, only there was no certitude of this, and therefore it must be left undetermined. The uncertainty was as great on the one side as on the other. Sextus Empiricus defined the state of skepsis to be "skilfulness in so setting forth appearances and re-

---

[1] Zeller, vol. iii. part 1, p. 427.   ἀπάθια and ἀταραξία.
[2] Ibid. i. p. 107.   [3] Ibid. p. 435.
[4] Döllinger, p. 336, who quotes Sextus, Hypot. i. 8.

THE CHURCH AND THE GREEK PHILOSOPHY 369

flections against each other, as to be brought through the equilibrium of opposing facts and grounds in their favour first to a suspension of judgment, and then to imperturbable tranquillity."

Carneades, whose life occupied the greater part of the second century before Christ, and who is extolled by Cicero as the keenest and most copious of disputants, was the man in whom this school of thought reached its highest point. He had appeared at Rome among a deputation of philosophers in the year 155, when his eloquence and earnestness made a great impression on his Roman hearers. This scepticism of the younger Academy however ran in accordance with the direction which the collective philosophy of the Greeks naturally took, and was carried out with an acuteness and a scientific ability which makes us recognise in it an important member of philosophical development.[1] Carneades subjected the Stoic doctrine as to God in particular to a criticism the range of which went far beyond the dogmas of this school, and in fact tended to represent every conviction as to the existence of the Godhead, and every religious belief, as something impossible and untenable.[2] This, however, as Cicero repeatedly assures us, was not done for the purpose of destroying belief in the gods, but only to point out the weakness and groundlessness of Stoic doctrines. It is chiefly in his assaults on the assertions and assumptions of his adversaries that Carneades is victorious: when he attempts anything positive on his own side, it amounts to this, that a rational man will take probability for his guide, when he cannot be assured of truth: and his chief merit appears to have

[1] Zeller, vol. iii. part 1, p. 477.
[2] Döllinger, p. 338.

been in more accurately determining the degrees of probability.[1]

The contests of these schools bring us down to the middle of the second century before Christ, when Greece fell under the dominion of Rome. From this time forth not only were Greek philosophers of eminence drawn to live themselves at Rome, and so to meet her statesmen and nobles in habits of intercourse, but the higher classes of the great capital commonly completed their education by visiting and studying at Athens, Rhodes, and other centres of Grecian thought. Thus by the fusion of Greece with the empire, while her political importance dwindled away, her influence upon the mind of her subjugators was immensely increased. But the Roman on his side obtained a sort of victory. As a rule he was anything but an original thinker. He was an essentially practical man: he had a steady instinct which led him to distrust first causes and general principles. The Greek schools were to him of value only as they might fit into his daily life, not as coherent systems of thought. The spirit therefore in which he regarded their differences was to select from them what best suited his tastes and feelings. If he had no power to originate, he could choose. But such likewise had been the result among the Greeks themselves of two centuries of conflict, in which the rival systems of Stoicism, Epicureanism, and Scepticism had stood over against each other. They sprung from the same soil; they might even be termed three branches of one stem,[2] inasmuch as their common root was the desire to find for the

---

[1] For a full account of the line of thought followed by Carneades, see Zeller, vol. iii. part 1, pp. 454-477.
[2] Zeller, vol. iii. part 1, p. 436.

individual man something which would give him tranquillity of mind, happiness in fact, independent of his civil circumstances. In this they all took up a practical rather than a theoretical ground, the ground indeed which is now assigned to religion. Utterly opposed, then, as they were in their means, they sought the same end, and it was not in nature that the collision of their various arguments should not at length kindle the spirit of eclecticism. Thus the temper of the Roman statesman and noble, and the course of Greek philosophy itself, combined to produce this spirit, which from the beginning of the first century before Christ pervaded the thinkers of the Græco-Roman world.[1] But eclecticism betokens a weakening of the philosophic mind, that weariness which is unable to take a firm grasp of truth, an absence of the keen aim and high desire which such a grasp betokens. It is a confession that no one system possesses the truth: in which state of things nothing remains for the individual but to choose for himself out of different systems those morsels of truth which approve themselves most to his taste or tact, or, as he would term it, his truth-seeking sincerity.

But it is not too much to say that the whole spirit of later antiquity, so far as it interested itself in the discovery of truth, from the time that Greek philosophy was diffused over the Roman world, leant more or less to eclecticism. Its most able, most distinguished, and most interesting representative is Cicero.[2] He lived at a time when rival criticism had searched

[1] Zeller, vol. iii. part 1, pp. 482, 492.
[2] Ueberweg, i. p. 218; and Zeller, iii. part 1, p. 593, calls him "neben seinem Lehrer Antiochus den eigentlichsten Vertreter des philosophischen Eklekticismus in dem letzten Jahrhundert vor dem Anfang unserer Zeitrechnung."

out and exposed every weak point in the different systems of thought. To found new systems there was no further creative force; his eclectic position was the necessary result. His genius supplied him with no means to overcome it. His philosophical writings are scarcely more than transcripts from various Grecian sources, wherein he uses his skill as a rhetorician and his unfailing wealth of words to set forth with lawyer-like balancing the arguments of different schools. We can yet detect the originals, from which in the short intervals of enforced absence from political life before and after the death of Cæsar he transfused with such rapidity into a Latin shape the products of Greek discussion.[1] Thus his treatise on the Republic and on Laws are in form imitations of Plato's writings with the same title, while for their contents Cicero applies Platonic, Aristotelian, and Stoic doctrines to his own political experiences, making also much use of Polybius. His *Paradoxa* explain Stoic propositions. The groundwork of his *Consolatio* is Crantor's writing upon Grief. The *Lost Hortensius* is drawn from an exhortation of Aristotle to Themison, a prince of a city of Cyprus, or from a similar work of the academician Philo of Larissa; his books *De Finibus* from works of Phædrus, Chrysippus, Carneades, Antiochus, as well as the studies which Cicero himself in his youth made while attending lectures; his *Academica* from the writings and partly also from the lectures of the best-known Academicians; his *Tusculan Disputations* from Plato and Crantor, from Stoics and Peripatetics. The first book on the *Nature of the Gods* from the writing of an Epicurean, which has been discovered in the rolls of Herculaneum, and was first supposed to be a

[1] Ueberweg, i. pp. 221, 222.

treatise of Phædrus, but is now known to be a work of Philodemus: his critique on the Epicurean standingpoint is drawn from the Stoic Posidonius; the second book from Cleanthes and Chrysippus; the third from Carneades and Clitomachus. Of his books on *Divination*, the first is taken from Chrysippus, Posidonius, Diogenes, and Antipater; the second from Carneades, and the Stoic Panætius. His treatise on *Fate* from the writings of Chrysippus, Posidonius, Cleanthes, and Carneades: his *Elder Cato* from Plato, Xenophon, Hippocrates, and Aristo of Chius: his *Lælius* mainly from a writing of Theophrastus on Friendship. His main authority for the first two books on *Offices* is Panætius; and for the third Posidonius; while besides Plato and Aristotle he has made use of Diogenes of Babylon, Antipater of Tyre, and Hecato.

Now in this selection from rival and antagonistic schools — this oscillation between the positive and sceptical tone of thought, this sitting as a judge rather than obeying as a disciple — Cicero very exactly represented the tone and attitude of the cultivated classes in his own time and in the century following his death. Originality of mind in philosophic studies was gone; nor was any system as a whole believed in. The sceptic and eclectic turns of mind are but the reverse sides of the same mental coinage: he who selects from all is convinced by none. Neither his doubts nor his choices satisfied Cicero, or any one of those who followed him in that most important century, the eighth of the Roman city, fifty years of which preceded and fifty followed the coming of Christ. In its philosophical productions no preceding century had been so poor as this. It had only to show the school of the Sextii, which arose at Rome about the beginning of our era, and took a sort of middle standing between Pythagorean, Cynic, and Stoic principles.[1] This school was of small importance, and soon became extinct. With this exception, from Cicero to Seneca no names of distinction appear. There is a gap in philosophical thought. A period so influential on the destinies of man in its events, so celebrated for its polite literature, on which the world has since been feeding, is barren in the highest realm of inquiry. For this reason there is a particular justice in taking Cicero as an exponent of heathen thought and spirit, the living specimen of the kind, inasmuch as he is the last philosophic writer before Christian thought appears in the world, and chose for himself the function of summing up what he thought of value in the ages before him.

We omit therefore nothing in our review if we place ourselves at the end of this century, in the reign of Claudius, and cast a glance backward over that prodigious labour of human reason through which we have hastily travelled, and which had then lasted six hundred years. The problem was, given the universe, what will man's reason in the most gifted, cultivated, inquiring, dialectic race of the ancient world do with it? And more particularly, to what results will reason come as to the power which has formed, or which rules it: as to its chief inhabitant, his nature, and the purpose for which he exists, and the end to which he is ever advancing: as to the duties by which he is bound to this creating, or at least maintaining and ruling power: as to those offices which he owes to his fellow, the individual to the individual, the civil community to the community. It was to these points

[1] Ueberweg, i. 219, 223.

especially that the greatest character in the whole movement—the single heathen who knew how to die for his convictions—turned the thoughts of those who followed him. Again, at the very starting-point of Greek philosophy a man of most virtuous conduct, gifted likewise with great powers of attraction, had sought to realise in a society the philosophic life. And we have seen this conception of the mode of propagating truth to lie at the bottom of Greek teaching, and to have been pursued by Plato, by Aristotle, by Zeno, by Epicurus, to have been the original and even the only form of teaching which they recognised. What was the result in this respect also? In the four hundred and forty years following the death of Socrates had reason produced a consistent doctrine, and a society of which that doctrine should be the law and bond, a fitting body for its soul to tenant, the immortal race of that living word which Plato contemplated? Time there had been enough, and even a superfluity of genius: but there were also two great outward events which might be expected to favour and advance such a result.

The first of these was the subjection of the whole East to the influence of the Greek mind by the conquest of Alexander, the effect of which continued in the kingdoms carried on by his successors. Originally the civil position of the Greek, as the free citizen of a free state, had been all in all to him. His country was his single measure. But during the lifetime of Plato and Aristotle this position had been more and more altering. The philosophy of Zeno and Epicurus was set up by men who had lost it altogether, who were thrown back on themselves, on the intrinsic nature of man, for support. Their inmost thought was how to produce tranquillity of mind and, so far as might be, happiness, for man, in something independent of his civil position. The loss of self-government had opened to them perforce a field far wider than the narrow confines of a provincial citizenship. Henceforth the schools of Plato, Aristotle, Zeno, and Epicurus issued their mental legislation not for the inhabitant of Attica, but for all that fusion of races which occupied the eastern coasts of the Mediterranean, was ruled by Greek potentates, and spoke the Hellenic tongue. Thus the ground taken up by philosophy was at once religious and cosmopolitan; the former because it attempted to deal with the nature of man as man, and to give him inward contentment, the latter because the mind, which used as its organ the Greek language, swayed large and independent empires, embracing various races of men. Then, if ever, it might have been expected that heathenism would make a great spring,[1] would cast aside what was local and accidental in the various customs, races, and beliefs brought under the fusing influence of one spirit, and idealise out of them a religion bearing the stamp and showing the force of that human reason of which Greece was the great representative. But the three centuries which witnessed the birth, the vigorous growth, and the incessant contests of the schools of Zeno and Epicurus, together with the scepticism which from Plato's chair passed judgment on them both, produced no such result, but rather terminated in that balancing of opposite systems, and the selection of fragments from each, which we have seen in Cicero.

The second great event which we have to note is that when the Greek mind had thus been for three

[1] Döllinger, p. 313.

hundred years in possession of society throughout the East, the Roman empire came to bind in unity of government not only all those races which the successors of Alexander had ruled, but the wide regions of the West as well, and their yet uncivilised inhabitants. Here, again, the Greek mind was not dethroned, but married, as it were, to Roman power. Philosophy made a sort of triumphal entry into Rome in spite of Cato and all the conservative force of the old Roman spirit. And if fusion had been the thought, the desire, and the attempt of the Ptolemies and the Seleucidæ, even more certainly was it the only spirit by which Augustus and Tiberius could hope to rule in peace the world made subject to them. And not less than the extinction of Greek autonomy did the loss of self-government accompanying the institution of the empire force the Roman also back upon himself. When Cicero could no longer sway the senate, he studied philosophic systems at Tusculum : and certainly his book of Offices has been more valued by all posterity than his speeches against Catiline or his defence of Milo. A long train of writers from the Fathers downwards have seen in the civil unity of the Roman empire a providential preparation for a great religion. But the field on which that empire arose had already, so far as concerns the thinking classes, long been occupied by the Greek philosophy. The two forces come into operation now together : and seventy years after the battle of Actium, when Augustus and Tiberius had completely established one ruling authority, and when this second outward revolution had had full time to give its impulse to thought, and had set before the eyes of men for two whole generations the vision of an empire which seemed conterminous with civilisation itself, we may fairly ask what philosophy had done towards producing a corresponding unity of doctrine, and a society sustaining and propagating it.

If, then, we take our stand at the moment when Claudius began to reign, and count a century backwards, it is impossible to mention a time when philosophy was more impotent for good, and when the higher classes of the Roman empire were more thoroughly irreligious and unbelieving. To understand the reason of this we must take into account first the negative and then the positive action of philosophy up to that time. As to the former, there can be no doubt that the effect of philosophy in all its schools and through all its shades of thought had been hostile to a simple belief in polytheism and its mythology. Human reason had been turned with pitiless severity on its mass of fables, its discreditable stories, its manifold contradictions. As early as the sixth century before Christ it had used the key of allegory in order to infuse into these some better meaning, and this was carried out into full detail by Metrodorus, a follower of Anaxagoras. Thus if Homer, the mirror in which the Greek saw his religion reflected, described Jupiter as suspending Juno between heaven and earth, Heracleitus was indignant with the atheists who did not see that it meant how the world and the elements were formed.[1] By this process indecent personal agencies melted away into physical effects, or were even sublimated into moral lessons. Men were told that only soft Phæacians could see in the loves of Mars and Venus a consecration of adultery: to the man of sense it meant that valour and beauty were worthy of each other. Through all the following centuries this tone

[1] Döllinger, p. 254.

of mind continued. As to the Stoical philosophers
in particular, this physical allegorising was the perpetual instrument by which they reconciled their stern
system of material Pantheism with all the stage scenery
of the poet's Olympus. Epicurus, on the contrary,
recognised the existence of gods in countless numbers,
but they were beings who lived in the enjoyment of
his philosophy, far removed from the cares of providence and the thought of human things. On the
other hand, Plato's attempt to purify, while he recognised, polytheism, and to sweep away all its fables as
purveyors of evil thoughts and desires, found little
success, though his conception of the Godhead as the
Idea of goodness, remained the highest ever reached
in that long process of thought; and through all this
period the best and purest minds found in him a support against that bewilderment of the reason which
the vulgar religion inflicted on them. But few and
far between were those who followed Plato in this
his highest conception, while the literature of that
last century, in the midst of which Christ appeared,
remains an abiding proof that the critical, scoffing,
negative spirit of philosophy had spread itself over
all the cultured classes. We seek in vain in Julius
Cæsar and Cicero, in Lucretius, Catullus, Virgil, Mani-
lius, Horace, Ovid, in Polybius, Dionysius, Diodorus,
or Strabo, for any real belief in the immortal gods
whose names appear in their writings. The poets
use them for stage-effect, the statesmen as part of the
machinery of government, the historians as names
interwoven with the events which they recount: yet
the life of all these men was filled with the frequenta-
tion of rites and ceremonies, as a matter of law and
custom, having reference to a multitude of gods,

concerning whom they had a contemptuous disbelief, though none of them were without many a dark superstition.

Such was the negative influence of philosophy; but what inward support had it given to minds whose ancestral belief, still entertained by the mass of men all around, was thus eaten out? What substitute had it provided for this discredited polytheism with its ridiculed mythology?

1. First, did the Greek philosophy teach the unity of the Godhead? If by this question be meant, did philosophy ever go forth into the midst of the temples and smoking sacrifices with which every city teemed, and proclaim, These gods which you worship are no gods: there is one Maker and Ruler of the universe, and the homage due to Him alone is usurped by a multitude of pretended deities?—then there is no doubt about the answer, that this is what neither Socrates, nor Plato, nor Aristotle, nor Zeno, nor any other philosopher thought of doing. The philosophic god was never set in the forefront of the battle after this fashion. He dwelt in the most secret shrine of Plato's mind, hard to be discovered, and to be confessed, if at all, in secret. If with Aristotle he was a pure spirit, yet he abode apart from the world, working on it indeed, as the magnet on the iron, but unconscious of it, not ruling it with free-will.[1] And, save so far as this is an exception, the Greek mind from beginning to end never succeeded in absolutely separating God from matter. And as time went on, this original defect showed itself more and more,

---

[1] Döllinger, p. 307. "Er wirkt also zwar auf die Welt, aber ohne sie zu kennen, wie der Magnet auf das Eisen, und seine Action auf die Welt ist keine freiwollende."

until in the Stoic system, which, as to the conception of the power ruling the world, prevailed over all the rest, that which was called God was simply a force pervading all matter.[1] The Stoics could, indeed, as in the hymn of Cleanthes, invest this god of theirs with many beautiful, grand, and attractive attributes. His was almighty power;[2] he was the author of nature; he ruled all things with law; and the world willingly obeyed his will. And this common law passed through all things, so that evil mixed with good resulted in a general order. Thus they could address him as Father and as King, guiding all things with justice; and this being they termed Jupiter. But this is only a poetic[3] exhibition of their genuine thought and meaning, which was, that "all which was real was corporeal; matter and force are the two chief principles; matter in itself is motionless and formless, but capable of assuming every motion and every form. Force is the active, moving, and forming principle; it is indivisibly joined with matter: the operating force in the whole of the world is the Godhead."[4] "By the names World-soul, World-reason, Nature, Universal Law, Providence, Fate, the same thing is indicated, the one Primal Force determining everything with absolute regularity, interpenetrating

---

[1] Dollinger, pp. 340, 572.
[2] Ζεῦ, φύσεως ἀρχηγέ, νόμου μέτα πάντα κυβερνῶν·—
Σοὶ δὴ πᾶς ὅδε κόσμος ἑλισσόμενος περὶ γαῖαν
Πείθεται ᾗ μὲν ἄγῃς, καὶ ἑκὼν ὑπὸ σεῖο κρατεῖται—
'Αλλὰ σὺ καὶ τὰ περισσὰ, ἐπίστασαι ἄρτια θεῖναι,
Καὶ κοσμεῖς τὰ ἄκοσμα, καὶ οὐ φίλα σοὶ φίλα ἐστίν.
Ὧδε γὰρ εἰς ἓν ἅπαντα συνήρμοκας ἐσθλὰ κακοῖσιν,
Ὥσθ' ἕνα γίγνεσθαι πάντων λόγον ἀεὶ ἐόντα.

[3] Cleanthes preferred expressly the poetic form; see the note in Zeller, vol. iii. part 1, p. 289; for poetry and music are better suited to reach the truth of divine contemplation than the bare philosophical expression. [4] Ueberweg, i. p. 195.

the whole world." "And even the opposition between the material and the spiritual description of the Godhead disappears upon closer examination, for on Stoic principles the Godhead can only then be considered as real when considered as body.[1] It was to such a unity that Greek philosophy advanced, receding more and more from that imperfect conception of personality with which it had started. Further, the idea of creation is wanting to Greek philosophy from its beginning to its end. The power which it contemplates is evermore confronted with matter, which it can permeate, fashion, move through a natural alchemy of endless changes, but in face of which it is not free to create or not to create, not even free to prevent the evil which lies therein as a sort of blind necessity. As there was always Force, so was there always Matter. To the conception of a free Creator of spirit and of matter the Greek mind never rose: nor accordingly to that of a free Ruler of the universe: and this is only to say in other words, that the conception of personality—that is, of self-consciousness and moral freedom, as applied to a Being of infinite power, wisdom, and goodness—was imperfect and confused. Plato in his highest flight had seemed to recognise one God, whom to enjoy is the happiness of man; but Plato and all who followed him had endured, had countenanced, had taken part in the polytheistic worship. And again, neither he, nor Aristotle, nor Zeno showed any inclination to suffer for their doctrines. This philosophic god, gradually evolved by the reasoning mind, produced the very smallest effect upon the unphilosophic world. The Stoic argument from final

[1] Zeller, vol. iii. pp. 130, 131 : see the many authorities he produces, pp. 126-131.

causes, which Cicero has preserved for us, and the force of which he has acknowledged in very remarkable words,[1] generated no martyrs. Was it merely from want of earnestness that the philosophers tolerated and practised the polytheism which surrounded them, and avoided all suffering for their opinions by compliance with a worship which they disbelieved? or was it that their standing-ground, in all more or less pantheistic, was identical with that which they impugned?[2] that the gods of Olympus were powers of nature personified, while their god was simply one power inhabiting nature? that they never reached the one personal creating God, and were consequently unable to maintain His absolute distinction from the world together with His relation to it as Creator and Ruler? That which they cherished as a private philosophical good, which they cared so little to exhibit to the world, was in fact incapable of conquering the world, for the human heart cannot live upon an impersonal god, and will not suffer for a conception of the reason. But it was in this conception that philosophic thought had terminated. And here we find the chief cause of its powerlessness to improve and purify the mythology which it attacked, and much more to affect the lives and conduct of

[1] He says of the opposite theory of Epicurus, the construction of the world from the chance falling-together of atoms : "Hoc qui existimat fieri potuisse, non intelligo, cur non idem putet, si innumerabiles unius et viginti formæ literarum, vel aureæ vel quales libet, aliquo conjiciantur, posse ex his in terram excussis annales Ennii, ut deinceps legi possint, effici : quod nescio an ne in uno quidem versu possit tantum valere fortuna." *De Nat. Deor.* ii. 37.

[2] So Zeller remarks, iii. 1, p. 296 : "A Pantheism, such as the Stoic, could take up into itself the most boundless polytheism, a double liberty only being allowed, that of passing on to derived beings the name of deity, from the Being to whom alone originally and in the strict sense it belonged, and that of personifying as God the impersonal, which is an appearance of divine power."

those who professed its tenets. For the old mythology had at least a strong consciousness of personality in its gods. In Homer himself the original tradition, of which his religion was a corruption, still spoke of the father of gods and men as the ruler and judge of the world. In the heathen mind generally such a conception still existed; nor is it too much to say that the common people among the Greeks and Romans were nearer to the truth of one personal God than the philosopher; and the philosopher himself when he listened at any moment of danger and anxiety to the promptings "of the soul naturally Christian" within him, than when he indulged in his esoteric problems.

2. But the conception of personality in God rules the conception of personality in man. As throughout the Greek philosophy the former was weak and imperfect, until in the Stoic system it vanished, so the latter. The physical theory of the Greek overmastered and excluded the conception of free-will in his mind, first as to God and then as to man. As evil existed throughout the world, for which he had no better solution than to place its seat in that matter which was co-existent with the divine reason, and which that reason was powerless wholly to subdue, so in the smaller world of man. In him a portion of the divine reason was united with matter. If Plato, Aristotle, and the Stoics arranged somewhat differently the mode of this composition, yet to all of them alike from the one side and the other the notion of physical necessity came in. The material constituent tended to evil, the reasoning constituent to good: in the man who was made up of the two there was a perpetual jar. There was no room left in their

theory for the conception of the soul as a self-originating cause of action. No sect struggled so hard and so persistently to maintain a doctrine of free-will as the Stoic: but it went down before that central tenet of their system, physical necessity, the inexorable sequence of cause and effect, which made up their "common law," by which the world was ruled. The conception of an all-wise, all-good, and all-powerful personal Creator, in whose nature the eternal law is based, not being clear to their minds, so neither was the conception of sin, as the infringement of that law. The law of physical necessity took the place of the eternal moral law: that which man did he did by virtue of the physical constituents out of which he was composed. The evil which he did was physical rather than moral: and he was not responsible for what he could not prevent. The questions of free-will, of evil viewed as sin, and of responsibility, are inextricably bound up with the doctrine of the human personality; and on all these the philosophic mind was dark and confused.

But if the Greek's physical theory stood in the way of his conceiving clearly the human personality in this life, much more did it impede his conception of that personality as continuing after death. For as the union of a portion of the divine reason with matter constituted man, and as death put an end to that union, the compound being ceased to exist, the portion of the divine reason reverted to its source, but the sensitive soul, as well as the body, was dissolved and came to nothing. There was in his mind no "individual substance of a rational nature" to form the basis of identity, and maintain the conception of personality. In the absence of this, he who had felt, thought, and acted, was no more. He could not therefore receive retribution for his deeds, since there was no personal agent on whom the retribution was to fall.

3. A god who was not personal and did not make man,—man in whom free-will, the mark of personality, was not recognised, so long as he lived, and in whom after death no personal agent continued to exist,—these correspond to each other, and these were the last result of Græco-Roman philosophic thought up to the time of Claudius. But what sort of duty did man, being such, owe to such a god? Cicero's book on Offices had been written upwards of eighty years, but nothing that followed it during that time equalled it in reputation or ability. It was the best product that his Roman thought could draw from all the preceding Grecian schools: and it was accepted for centuries as the standard of heathen morality. Let us, then, first note that in this book [1] there is nothing like a recognition of God as the Creator and Common Father; no call upon the human soul to love him as such, and for his own perfections; no thought that the duty of man consists in becoming like to him, nor his reward in attaining that likeness. The absence of such a thought gives its character to the whole book, and measures its level. The second point to be noted is, that the happiness of man consists not in being like God, and consequently, in union with Him, but in virtue, which is living according to nature. In his reasonable nature every one possesses a sufficient standard of moral action under every circumstance which may arise. Thirdly, throughout the whole of his

---

[1] See Hasler, *Verhältniss der heidnischen und christlichen Ethik*, p. 28; and Zukrigl's commentary on the same, *Tübingen theol. Quartalschrift*, 1867, pp. 475-482.

treatise Cicero makes no use of the doctrine of man's immortality. His happiness, then, is left to consist in virtue—life according to reason, which again is life according to nature—without respect to any future state of existence. Now, if Cicero stood alone in these three points, his book would only represent his own authority, but he is in fact the mouthpiece herein of that whole preceding heathen philosophy which he criticised, and from which he selected. Even Plato himself, by far the highest and best of Greek philosophers in this respect, though he had in single expressions indicated that the happiness of man was to be made like to God, constructed no system of ethics in dependence on that conception, which, if it be true, is of all-constraining influence, and is to the whole moral system what the law of gravity is to the material universe. Plato's ethical system was a strict deduction from his physical theory of the three parts in man, to each of which he assigned its virtue. Far less did Aristotle connect morality with God. The Stoics, indeed, who occupy by far the largest space in Greek philosophy, seem to be an exception. It is said that "their whole view of the world springs from the thought of the Divine Being who generates all finite beings from himself, and includes them all in himself, who penetrates them with his power, rules them with his unchangeable law, and thus merely manifests himself in them all;" so that their system "is fundamentally religious, and scarcely an important statement in it which is not in connection with their doctrine of God;" and so with them "all moral duties rest on a religious ground, all virtuous actions are a fulfilment of the divine will and law;"[1] but then this

[1] Zeller, iii. 1, pp. 288, 289.

God is but a name for the sternest and most absolute system of material necessity: a God without a moral nature, without freedom, without personality; under that name, in fact, force and matter making up one thing are substituted for a living God, who, in virtue of the laws of nature, is swept out of His own universe. So, again, Cicero's statement that man's happiness consists in virtue, which virtue is life according to nature, is the general doctrine of philosophy, which the Stoics in particular had elaborated. If there be any one expression which would sum up in a point the whole heathen conception of what man should do, it would be "Life according to nature." So, again, the exclusion of any thought of immortality, and a consequent retribution, in its bearing on morality, was common to all the schools of Grecian thought, if we except the faltering accents and yearning heart of Plato, and most of all was truly Stoic. The imperfection and unclearness of their view as to the divine personality, and as to the human, in the reasonable being, the image and reflection of the divine, accords but too truly, while it accounts for, this detachment of man from God in the field of moral duty.

4. What, then, remained to man, after such deductions? There remained the earthly city, the human commonwealth. And when, passing beyond the bounds of any particular nation, and man's civil position therein, philosophy grasped the moral life as the relation between man as man,[1] and conceived human society itself as one universal kingdom of gods and men, it made a real progress and reached its highest point. But this was the proper merit of the Stoics.[2]

[1] Zeller, iii. 1, 12.
[2] Καὶ μὴν ἡ πολὺ θαυμαζομένη πολιτεία τοῦ τὴν Στωϊκῶν αἵρεσιν καταβαλλομένου Ζήνωνος εἰς ἓν τοῦτο συντείνει κεφάλαιον, ἵνα μὴ κατὰ πόλεις

Plutarch attributes to Zeno, their founder, this precise idea, that we ought not to live in cities and towns, each divided by peculiar notions of justice, but esteem all men as tribesmen and citizens, who should make up one flock feeding in a common pasture under a common law. The grandest passages of Cicero are those in which he clothes in his Roman diction this Stoic idea, as for instance:[1] "They judge the world to be ruled by the power and will of the gods, and to be a sort of city and polity common to gods and men, and that every one of us is part of this world." The bond of this community is the common possession of reason,[2] "in which consists the primal society of man with God. But they who have reason in common, have also right reason in common. And as this is law, we are as men to be considered as associated with the gods by law also. Now they who have community of law, have likewise community of rights. This latter makes them also to belong to the same polity. But if such pay obedience to the same commands and authorities, then are they even much more obedient to this supernal allotment, this divine mind and all-powerful God. So that this universal world is to be considered one commonwealth of gods and men." "Law is the supreme reason, implanted in nature, which commands all things that are to be done, and prohibits their contraries." "The radical idea of right I derive from nature, under whose guidance we have to draw out the whole of this subject-matter." Thus the great Roman lawyer and statesman,

μηδὲ κατὰ δήμους οἰκῶμεν, ἰδίοις ἕκαστοι διωρισμένοι δικαίοις ἀλλὰ πάντας ἀνθρώπους ἡγώμεθα δημότας καὶ πολίτας, εἷς δὲ βίος ᾖ, καὶ κόσμος, ὥσπερ ἀγέλης συννόμου νόμῳ κοινῷ τρεφομένης. Plutarch, *Alex. M. Virt.* i. 6, p. 329, quoted by Zeller, iii. 1, p. 281.

[1] *De Finibus*, iii. sec. 19. [2] *De Legibus*, i. 7, 6.

robing philosophy in his toga, propounded to his countrymen, full of the greed of universal conquest, with no less lucidity than truth and beauty, the result of Stoic thought, that human society in general rested on the similarity of reason in the individual, that we have no ground for restricting this common possession to one people, or to consider ourselves more nearly related to one than another. All men, apart from what they have done for themselves, stand equally near to each other, since all equally partake of reason. All are members of one body, since the same nature has formed them out of one stuff, for the same destination.[1]

Greek philosophy has undoubtedly the merit of bringing out into clear conception this purely human and natural society. It thus expressed in language the work of Alexander, and still more the work of the Roman empire, as it was to be; and more than this, it herein supplied a point of future contact with Christian morality. The advance from the narrowness of the Greek mind in its proud rejection of all non-Hellenic nations, and no less from the revolting selfishness of Roman conquest, is remarkable. And it is an advance of philosophic thought. As the older thinkers considered the political life of the city to be an immediate demand of human nature, so the Stoics considered the unitedness of man as a whole together, the dilatation of the particular political community to the whole race, in the same light. Its ground was the common possession of reason. The common law which ruled this human commonwealth was to live according to the dictation of reason, that is, according

---

[1] Zeller, iii. 1, p. 278, from Seneca and Marcus Aurelius, who here, however, only enlarge on Cicero's idea, or rather Zeno's.

to nature, in which therefore virtue consists,[1] being one and the same in God and in man, and in them alone.[2] Such virtue branches into four parts, the prudence which discerns and practises the truth: the justice which assigns his own to each; the courage which prevails over all difficulties; the self-restraint and order which preserves temperance in all things. These being bound up together cover the whole moral domain, and embrace all those relations within which human society moves, and, as having their root in the moral nature of man, are a duty to every one.

This human commonwealth enfolds in idea the whole earth. It is the society of man with man. But it closes with this life. It has no respect to anything beyond. It was the Stoics who most completely worked out this system of moral philosophy; who urged the duty of man's obedience to nature, of his voluntary subjection to that one universal law and power which held all things from the highest to the lowest in its grasp; and who likewise most absolutely cut him off from any personal existence in a future state. The virtue in which they placed his happiness was to be complete in itself; it was the work of man without any assistance on the part of God.[3] It made man equal to God. It found its reward in itself. If it was objected that the highest virtue in this life sometimes met with the greatest disasters, sorrows, pains, and bereavements, the system had no reply to this mystery. It did not attempt to assert a recompense beyond the grave.

[1] "Jam vero virtus eadem in homine ac Deo est, neque ullo alio ingenio præterea. Est autem virtus nihil aliud quam in se perfecta, et ad summum perducta natura." *De Legibus*, i. 8.   [2] *De Officiis*, i. 5.
[3] Cic. *de Nat. Deor.* iii. 36. "Virtutem nemo unquam acceptam deo retulit. Nimirum recte. Propter virtutem enim jure laudamur, et in virtute recte gloriamur: quod non contingeret, si id donum a deo, non a nobis, haberemus."

As little did it attempt to account for or to correct the conflict between man's reason and his animal nature. That perpetual approval of the better and choice of the worse part stood before the Stoic as before us all. He admitted that the vast majority of men were bad, and his wise man was an ideal never reached. But he had no answer whatever to the question, why, if vice is so evil in the eye of our reason, it so clings to our nature; why, if so contrary to the good of the mass, it dwells within every individual.[1]

The human city or community of men is the highest point which this moral philosophy contemplates. Each particular commonwealth should be herein the image of the one universal commonwealth which their thought had constructed. But what, then, is the relation of the individual man to the whole of which he is a part? This nature, which is the standard to the whole ideal commonwealth, is, as we have seen so often, in fact a law of the strictest necessity. If virtuous, man follows it willingly; if vicious, he must follow it against his will. There was no real freedom for the individual in the system as philosophy. What was disguised under the name of law, reason, and God, was a relentless necessity before which every one was to bow. But transfer this philosophy to any political community, and consider in what position it placed the individual with regard to the civil government. Human society is considered as supreme: but his own state represents to him that society, and as all things end with this life, no part of man remains withdrawn from that despotism which requires the sacrifice of the part for the good of the whole. Man's conscience had no refuge in the thought of a future life; no reserve

[1] Champagny, *Les Césars*, iii. 333.

which the abuse of human power could not touch. And so we find that in matter of fact there was no issue out of such a difficulty but in the doctrine of self-destruction. They termed it in truth *The Issue*,[1] when disease, or disaster, or pain, or the abuse of human power, rendered it impossible any longer to lead a life in accordance with nature. In this case all the Stoic authorities justified it, praised it, and termed it the Door which Divine Providence had benignantly left ever open.

While therefore it must be acknowledged that the Stoical conception of the whole earth as one city[2] was a true result of Greek thought, and at the same time the highest point it reached, and a positive result of great value, yet it must also be said that it was one rather big with rich promises for the future than of any great present advantage: for it required to be impregnated and filled with another conception of which its framers had lost their hold, the doctrine, that is, of a future retribution, redressing the inequality, the injustice, the undeserved suffering so often falling upon virtue in the present life. When that conception came to complete and exalt the Stoic idea, the need of self-destruction as an issue of the wise man, as soon as he could not live according to nature, ceased, for man himself ceased to be a part of a physical whole governed by necessity. The human city relaxed its right over the individual in presence of a divine city, which embraced indeed man in his present

[1] "'Ἐξαγωγὴ ist bei den Stoïkern der stehende Ausdruck für den Selbstmord." Zeller, vol. iii. part 1, p. 284 n. 2, who quotes Diog. vii. 130. Ἑλλόγως τέ φασιν ἐξάξειν ἑαυτὸν ἀπὸ τοῦ βίου τὸν σοφὸν καὶ ὑπὲρ πατρίδος καὶ ὑπὲρ φίλων, κἂν ἐν σκληροτέρᾳ γένηται ἀλγηδόνι, ἢ πηρώσεσιν, ἢ νόσοις ἀνιάτοις.

[2] "Qui omnem orbem terrarum unam urbem esse ducunt." Cicero, *Paradoxon* 2.

life, but taught him to look for its complete realisation in another.

The human commonwealth, however, extended in idea to the race itself, as possessing reason in common, and individual man therein, as well as the whole aggregate, viewed as being ruled by the cardinal virtues of prudence, justice, fortitude, and temperance, but both the commonwealth and the individual terminating with this life, was the last word of heathen philosophy up to the time of Claudius.

We have seen that from the time the Greek race was absorbed in the Roman empire the systems of philosophy were broken up by the eclectic spirit, which, engendered within already by the ferment of opinions, was strengthened and developed by the accession of the practical Roman mind. Variety of belief is indeed marked as "the essential feature of Greek philosophy" from its outset, and "the antagonist force of suspensive scepticism" as including some of its most powerful intellects from Xenophanes five hundred years before to Sextus Empiricus two hundred years after the Christian era. One of its historians stamps it as "a collection of dissenters, small sects each with its own following, each springing from a special individual as authority, each knowing itself to be only one among many."[1] It is therefore no wonder that if Plato's grand conception of an immortal line of the living word thus came to nought, philosophy proved itself much more incapable of founding a society impregnated with its principles than it had even been of constructing a coherent doctrine which should obtain general reception. And to judge of the actual impotence of philosophy in the

[1] Grote, *Plato*, vol. i. p. 87.

century ending with the principate of Claudius, we must rest a moment on this second fact. Philosophers calling themselves Platonic, Peripatetic, Sceptic, Stoic, Epicurean, or these in various mixtures, were to be found at the various seats of learning, Athens, Rhodes, Alexandria, for instance, or at Rome as the seat of empire, or travelling like wandering stars over her vast territory, but these scattered, nebular, and disjoined luminaries shone with a varying as well as a feeble light, which rather confused than satisfied human reason. They were utterly powerless to transfer their doctrine into any number of human hearts living in accordance therein. The only exception to this statement seems to prove its real truth. By far the most united of the sects was that of the Epicureans, who held with great tenacity to their founder's views and mode of life, which may be summed up in denial of God and Providence, and enjoyment to the utmost of this world's goods; the fair side of it being a general benevolence, courtesy, friendship, in short, a genial appreciation of what we understand by the word civilisation. These antagonists of Stoic principles and of the highest morality which heathen thought had constructed were the most numerous of existing sects, and we are told that hundreds of years after their founder's death they presented the appearance of a well-ordered republic, ruled without uproar or dissension by one spirit, in which they formed a favourable contrast to the Stoics. With the exception of a single fugitive, Metrodorus, never had an Epicurean detached himself from his school.[1]

[1] Döllinger, p. 315, from Numenius, quoted by Eusebius. Ueberweg, i. 205, says of them, that up to the rise of Neoplatonism they were the most numerous of all.

We must give philosophy the credit of this single instance of a capacity to create a social life in accordance with its tenets in a sect whose doctrines were a reproach among the heathens themselves. The failure of Pythagoras, of Plato, of Aristotle, of Zeno, was the success of Epicurus, and at the same time the announcement that the age of Augustus and Tiberius was ready to expire in sensuality and unbelief, and even in exhaustion of the philosophic mind, for no period is so barren of scientific names, which carry any weight, as the fifty years preceding Claudius.[1] We have seen above that all these philosophers aimed at forming a society which should carry out their principles; that this was their original and their only idea of teaching; that with a view to make it permanent they created a chair of teaching, a living authority who was to continue on their doctrine. But the chair of Plato alone presented[2] five Academies with dissentient doctrines; and a Platonic or Stoic city no one had seen. Thus viewing their united action upon the polytheistic idolatry, we may say that while they could discredit its fables in reflecting minds, while they could even raise an altar in their thoughts "to the unknown God," they left society in possession of the temples and observant

[1] See Döllinger, pp. 341 and 572-584; so Champagny, *Les Césars*, iii. 294.

[2] Ueberweg gives them thus: to the first Academy belong Plato's successor Speusippus, who taught 347-339 B.C.; Xenocrates, 339-314; Polemo, 314-270; Crates, a short time. The second Academy was founded by Arcesilaus, who lived 315-241, taking more and more a sceptical direction, which was carried out to the utmost by Carneades, 214-129, in the third: in the fourth, Philo of Larissa, about 80 B.C., returned to the dogmatic direction; and Antiochus of Ascalon, Cicero's friend, founded the fifth, in which he fused Platonic, Aristotelian, and Stoic doctrines together. St. Augustine, *De Civ. Dei* viii. 3, puts his finger on the variations of the Socratici.

of a worship which they pronounced to be immoral, monstrous, and ridiculous. They had destroyed in many the ancestral belief; they had awakened perhaps in some a sense of one great Power ruling the universe; but having taken up the religious ground and professed to satisfy man's desire for happiness, they had been utterly powerless to construct a religion. They failed entirely in the union of three things,[1] a dogma and a morality founded on that dogma, both of which should be exhibited, brought before the eyes and worked into the hearts of men by a corresponding worship. To unite these three things was needed an authority of which above all they were destitute. Their dogma was without the principle of faith; their morality without binding power; but the worship which should blend the two they had not at all. And so they presented no semblance of the society which should carry these three things in its bosom, and they could not in the least satisfy the doubts or the yearnings which they had raised.

But the period beginning with the rise of Greek philosophy and ending with the principate of Claudius will ever remain of the highest interest and importance as showing what human reason, putting forth its highest powers in the race in which it culminated, but at the same time more thoroughly separated from belief, tradition, and authority than anywhere else, did actually achieve. It is in this respect that the heathen philosophers, together with the poets

[1] "Lier ensemble les dogmes, une morale, et un culte, c'est-à-dire donner à la société une foi, une règle, et des pratiques, c'était l'œuvre que le genre humain appelait de ses vœux, et sur laquelle pourtant tous les efforts humains semblaient échouer." A. Thierry, *Tableau de l'Empire Romain*, p. 328.

and historians who precede the publication of the Christian religion in the Roman world, possess a value far beyond any intrinsic merit of their own. It is a study of pathology the results of which are far as yet from being gathered in. It is only by carefully examining what the philosophers taught in theology and morals—for they aspired to be and were both the theologians and the moralists of those ages—that we can at all form an adequate judgment of the real work which the Christian Church has wrought in the world. It is only by using the historians and poets as a mirror of that general society to whose cultured classes the philosophers spoke, that we can estimate what the great mass of mankind then was, and what effect the philosophers produced on them. The difference between their world and their society and ours is the measure of Christian work. The hundred years preceding Claudius, which include in them almost all the greatest names of Roman literature, are the most important of all in this point of view, both as containing the result of scientific thought in the five preceding centuries, and as giving the depth of the moral and intellectual descent. We learn from this whole long period the fulness of the truth conveyed in those words of the angelic doctor at the commencement of his great work: "Even for those things which can be investigated concerning God by the force of human reason, it was necessary for man to be instructed by a divine revelation, because few only, and they after long inquiries, and with the admixture of many errors, would convey to man the truth concerning God as searched out by reason.[1]

[1] St. Thomas, *Summa*, p. 1. 9. 1. a. 1.

What the philosophers from the time of Thales had taken as their special work was to measure and estimate the visible world. And for the last four centuries of this period especially they made the nature and the needs, the supreme good and the happiness, of man their chief concern, in subordination to which they continued their physical inquiries. And surely the judgment which an inspired writer formed of their travail must recur to the mind with great force at the end of the preceding review: "If they knew so much as to be able to estimate the visible world, why did they not more easily discover its Lord?"[1] Why from the goods which they beheld had they not power to know the sole possessor of being, nor when they gave attention to his works, recognised their artificer? Why did they esteem fire or breath, rapid air or circling stars, or the force of water, or the lights of heaven, rulers of the universe? For if the visible beauty of these delighted them so that they conceived them to be gods, how did they not draw the conclusion that the Lord of these was so much better than they? for it was the Author of beauty who created them. If they were struck dumb with the sense of their power and operation, why did they not conceive how much more powerful He who made them was? For from the greatness and the beauty of creatures the parent of them is by the force of reason discerned.[2]

From their capital error in this—which the same writer declares to be inexcusable[3]—proceeded their other errors concerning man, his nature, his supreme

---

[1] Sap. xiii. 9.
[2] Reading with St. Chrys. and St. Gregory ἐκ μεγέθους καὶ καλλονῆς κτισμάτων ἀναλόγως, cognoscibiliter, i.e. by a conclusion of reason.
[3] Μάταιοι μὲν γὰρ πάντες ἄνθρωποι φύσει, οἷς παρῆν Θεοῦ ἀγνωσία· ... πάλιν δὲ οὐδ' αὐτοὶ συγγνωστοί. Sap. xiii. 1, 8.

good, and his final end. It is here sufficient to note that down to the age of Claudius there is no appearance that either of these great errors would be corrected : and still less any appearance of the rise of a great religion which would cause the multitudinous altars of heathenism to disappear before the altar of the unknown God, and would construct a City of God in the midst of that population in the thinking minds of which divergent systems of philosophy had eaten out belief in the babel of false gods, without implanting belief in a personal Creator, the author and the end of man.

INDEX

ACADEMIES, the five, of Plato's school, 396.
Adam, his headship, 49, 51, 53; its result seen in his fall, 55.
Alexander the Great, effects of his conquests on Greek life, 360, 375.
Alexander Severus, his treatment of Christians, 201.
Antoninus Pius, extension of the Church in his reign, 161; treatment of it under him, 186-191; what aspect the Church bore to him, 191-5.
Apollonius, a senator, martyred under Commodus, 249, 172, *note*.
Apostolic age, result of, 152.
Aristotle, his character as a philosopher, 354; his view of the soul, 355; relation of his philosophy to religion, 357; conception of the method of teaching, 346; what he says of Socrates, 321; his account of the generation of the Platonic doctrine of Ideas, 330.
Athanasius, St., 21, 27, 28, 30, 81.
Athenagoras, 149.
Athens, worship at, 5.
Augustine, St., his contrast of Heathenism with Christianity, 142-4; on the moral influence of Polytheism, 17-20, 23, 25, 27; how the Second Divine Person is the Truth, 42; Adam and Christ, 63, 69, 91; the Church Christ's Body, 82; and at once His Temple, House, and City, 72; also the power of the Holy Ghost coming upon men, 80; dowered with Christ's Blood, 119; Christ and the Church one Man, 47, 119; believing Christ, without believing the Church, is decapitating Christ, 87; crime of denying that the Catholic Church will for ever continue in its unity, 87; the Word made flesh that He might become the Head of the Church, 88; the Holy Spirit Vicarius Redemptoris, 95, 98, 102, 103, 115; asserts the perpetual Principatus of the Roman See from the beginning, 239; describes the uses of heresy, 232; admits of no charity but in the unity of the Body, 108, 115; coherence of the natural and mystical Body of Christ in the Eucharist, 85; what the Church will be hereafter, 93.

402   INDEX

Augustus, his idea of the Roman empire, 1 ; prospects of Polytheism at the end of his reign, 38.

Aulus Gellius, 347.

BEUGNOT, *Destruction du Paganisme*, 35, 36.

CAPTIVITY of man to the devil, 23-6, 27-31, 57 ; its full reversal as seen in the Body of Christ, 92.

Carneades, 369.

Catholic, term used of the Church by St. Ignatius about A.D. 115, and by the Church of Polycarp fifty years later, 169.

Celsus, 146, 162, 189, 190, 192.

Champagny, 13, 149, 199, 200, 292, 392, 396.

Christ, declares Himself to be a king, 40 ; His kingdom that of Truth, 41-5 ; the counterpart of Adam as an individual, 63 ; as Head of a race, 63 ; as making one Body with His people, 65 ; parallel in His natural and mystical Body, 79 ; analogies between them, 80 ; coherence of both in the Eucharist, 85 ; His action permanent in His kingdom, 67 ; in His House, 71 ; in His Body, 73 ; in His Bride, 75 ; in the Mother of His race, 76 ; His five distinct loves, 77 ; His Body imperishable, 86 ; crime of imputing falsehood to it, 87 ; force of its corporate unity, 91 ; gifts which He bestows on it, 103 ; connection of Truth with His Person the principle of persecution, 149 ; His Passion repeated in His people, 151 ; His work summed up by St. Augustine, 142-4.

Chrysostom, St., 72, 83, 90, 181, 184.

Church, the, the Kingdom of Truth, 67 ; the House of Christ, 71 ; the Body of Christ, 72 ; the Bride of Christ, 75 ; the Mother of His race, 76 ; the power of the Holy Ghost coming upon men, 80 ; as such, the treasure-house of Truth and Grace, 82, 99-101 ; conveys the fruits of the Incarnation, 83, 118 ; is imperishable and incorruptible, 86 ; possesses Unity, Truth, Charity, and Sanctity as coinherent gifts of the Spirit, 103-6 ; bestows forgiveness of sins, faith, adoption, and sanctification on the individual, 106-8 ; unity of its jurisdiction, 120 ; analogy between it and the relation of soul and body, 110 ; between it and the human commonwealth, 110 ; between it and the natural unity of man's race, 111 ; transmission of truth in it, 122, 137 ; by a triple succession, 129-133 ; development of the Truth its proper work, 139 ; its divine life as opposed to heathenism, 141 ; its witness of Christ's confession in the first ten generations, 151 ; its first persecution by Nero, 156 ; growth in the time of Antoninus Pius, 160 ; picture of it by St. Ignatius, 163 ; its treatment of heresies, 167, 169, 213, 218, 226, 227 ;

bearing of Trajan to it, 171, 177; of Hadrian, 181; of Antoninus Pius, 186; of Marcus Aurelius, 241; of Commodus, 249; of Septimius Severus, 249; its position in the third century, 254; its organic unity as set forth by St. Cyprian, 268-276; power of its idea on Christians, 280; expresses Christ in its moral character, its worship, and its government, 281-5; persecuted by Decius, 293; by Valerian and Aurelian, 297; by Diocletian, 298; obtains freedom from Constantine, 306; how affected by Roman law between A.D. 64 and 313, 306, 307.

Church, a mother or cathedral church only so called, 208,

Churches, public, when first known to exist at Rome, 254.

Cicero, states the work of Socrates, 322; representative of Eclecticism, 371; sources of his philosophical works, 372; what he says of the atomic theory, 383; his book *de Officiis* the standard of heathen morality for centuries after him, 387; his statement of the Stoic idea of the world as one republic of gods and men, 389; his conception of virtue in general, 388, 390; his partition of the cardinal virtues, 391; virtue not a gift of God, but the work of man, 391.

Cleanthes, his hymn quoted, 381.

Clement, Pope St., 156, 159.

Clement of Alexandria, 229, 236, 250.

Commodus, 200, 249.

Cyprian, St., his statement of the Church's organic unity founded on the Primacy given to Peter, 269-73; puts the force of the Episcopate in its unity, 121, 274-6; repudiates a parallel between the twelve tribes of Israel and the Church, on the question of unity, 276; agreement of his witness with that of St. Paul, St. Ignatius, and St. Irenæus, 288; his conversion, described by himself, a type of heathen conversion in general, 277-9; describes the relaxation produced by the long peace of the Church before the Decian persecution, 288-91; his martyrdom, 295; says the Emperor Decius would much rather endure the appointment of a rival emperor than of a Bishop of Rome, 294.

Cyril, St., of Alexandria, 44, 45; on the Fall and the Restoration, 113; to become a Christian is to enter into unity with Christ both physical and spiritual, 113.

DANTE, 348.

Decius, 293.

De Rossi, 208.

Diocletian, 298.

Diognetus, author of letter to, marks the Christians as one body and people, but diffused everywhere, circ. A.D. 100, 262.

Dionysius, St., archbishop of Alexandria, prizes martyrdom for the unity of the Church more highly than for resistance to idolatry, 285

Döllinger, *Heidenthum und Judenthum*, quoted or referred to, 5–13, 20, 161, 318, 331, 335, 337, 338, 354–7, 361, 363–5, 367–9, 376, 378, 380, 381, 395, 396; *Hippolytus und Kallistus*, 205, 211, 212.

Domitian, his persecution, 159.

ECLECTICISM, how it arose in Greek Philosophy, 370; becomes universal, 371.

Epicurus, his conception of the method of teaching, 350; his doctrine, 365.

Episcopate, the, triply defended by Scripture, by institutions, and by continuous personal descent, 135; one and undivided, 270; like the unity of the Godhead, 274; which is effected by the Primacy, 275.

Eucharist, coherence of natural and mystical Body of Christ in, 84; called by St. Ignatius that flesh of our Saviour Christ which suffered for our sins, 166, *note*.

Eusebius, 124, 171, 207, 208, 249, 250, 297, 299–305.

FORGIVENESS of sins, doctrine of, guarded by triple succession of teaching, of men, and of sacraments, 133.

Free-will, no room for it in the physical theory of Greek philosophy, *e.g.* in Plato, 338; in Aristotle, 356; in Stoicism, 363; in all the schools, as to God, 381–4; as to man, 384–6; bearing of this on civil government, 392.

Future life of man as a personal being, why not held by Greek philosophy, 385, 388; absence of it from Cicero's *de Officiis*, 386.

GRACE, Adam created in, 51, 52; loss of this gift in the Fall, 54; grace as restored in Christ, 112; grace in the God-man, 63; as in Adam and as in the God-man compared, 43; as bestowed through the headship of the God-man, 64; as seen in the Body of Christ, the counterpart of the body of Adam, 65; grace, with truth, makes "the power of the Holy Ghost coming upon men," 80, 96; the human fountain of this double power in the created nature of Christ, 100; whence it is transfused into the Church, His Body, 101–4; grace, as given to the Church complete and indefeasible, 105; as given to the individual may be withdrawn, 108; actual bestowal of this grace on the Church, 114–8; grace necessary for the acceptance and maintenance of truth, 128, 138, 140–2, 222; grace, truth, and unity, viewed by St. Cyprian as inseparable, 274.

Greek mind, its standing-point, 313; represents human reason more than any other ancient race, 315; aided by a matchless language, 312; ripens in the most beautiful of climates, 311; pervades the whole East from the time of Alexander, 375; is married to Roman power in the empire, 376; is the great intellectual opponent of the Christian mind and Church, 309; criticises polytheism for six hundred years, 309; its outcome up to the time of St. Peter's founding the Roman Church, 392-400; why its philosophy disbelieved a future life, 385, 388.

Grote, *Plato*, 310, 332, 339, 341, 346, 347, 352, 394.

HADRIAN, grandeur of Rome in his days, 198; treatment of the Church, 181-3; puts to death St. Symphorosa and her sons, 184-6.

Hagemann, *Die römische Kirche in den ersten drei Jahrhunderten*, 171, 212, 225, 239, 290, 292.

Hasler, *Verhältniss der heidnischen und christlichen Ethik*, 386.

Heathenism, what it is, 49, 58, 59; contrasted with Christianity, 65; by St. Augustine, 172-5; its disregard of the value of moral truths, 145-7.

Heresy, subserves the enucleation of doctrine, 232; the determining the Canon of the New Testament, 234; brings out full statements of the principle of tradition, 236; promotes extension and corroboration of the hierarchy, 237; temper of, described by Irenæus, 222; by Tertullian, 227; by Clement of Alexandria, 229, 230; by St. Augustine, 232.

Herodotus, the travelled Greek gentleman, 311.

IDOLATRY, Asiatic, its turpitude, 21; division of gods, how far it could go, 23.

Ignatius, St., Bishop of Antioch, his picture of the Church in his day, 163-7; his martyrdom, 177; his recognition of the Roman Primacy 179; power of his intercession attested by St. Chrysostom, 180; the Eucharist, that flesh of our Saviour Christ which suffered for our sins, 166; "Wherever Jesus Christ is, there is the Catholic Church," 169; completeness of a diocesan church called τὸ ἴδιον σωματεῖον, of the whole church, τὸ ἓν σῶμα τῆς ἐκκλησίας, 181.

Innocent I., Pope St., 210, 286.

Irenæus, St., 95, 218; guilt of those who divide the great and glorious Body of Christ, 114; on the Church's unity of belief, 217-9; gives the descent of the Roman See to his time, 220; affirms its superior principality, 220; sets forth the Church as the treasure-house of truth and grace, 221; distinguishes the perpetual teaching office in her, 222, 236; contrasts her truth with the variation of heresies,

222; summary of his doctrine on the Church, heresy, the Primacy, tradition, 223-6; one of a chain between St. Paul, St. Ignatius, and St. Cyprian, 288; speaks of the number of martyrs, 280; himself martyred with many of his people, 250; speaks of "the tradition of the Apostles" as the whole body of truth which they communicated, 162; speaks of the "founding and building" of Sees, 210.

JUNIUS RUSTICUS, 241.
Jurisdiction, spiritual, its unity, 120; emanates from Christ's Person, 282; is the expression of His sovereignty, 284.
Justin, St., his martyrdom, 242-6; his *Apologia* quoted, 186-9; marks Christians as one people and body, 263; censures Jewish conduct in defaming Christians, 155; describes the extension of Christianity in his time, 161.

KELLNER, *Hellenismus und Christenthum*, 149, 162, 252.
Kleutgen, *die Theologie der Vorzeit*, 51, 52, 236.
Kuhn, *Einleitung in die katholische Dogmatik*, 240.

LACTANTIUS, 300-2.
Lasaulx, *Fall des Hellenismus*, 157, 267.
Laurence, St., his martyrdom, compared with a contemporaneous incident, 295.
Liguori, St. Alphonso, 117.

MAN, various states of, 49; state of pure nature, 50; state of integrity, 50; state of original justice, 51; state of, after the fall, 55; how summed up in Adam, 52, 58: effect of his being a race, 49; force of his social nature, when fallen, 59; when restored, 89-91; his corruption viewed as a fact of modern science, 48.
Marcus Aurelius, treatment of the Church, 241, 246-8.
Martyrdom, said by St. Irenæus to be frequent in the Church, but not deemed necessary by the sects, 280; losses to the Christian body by it contrasted with those of civil war, by Origen, 267; a continuation of Christ's confession before Pilate, 151; its spirit the tissue of early Christian life, 195; identified with "perfect charity" by St. Ignatius, 178; termed "the chalice of Christ" by St. Polycarp, 247.
Maximus of Tyre, a teacher of Marcus Aurelius, his notions of God 241.
Merivale, History of the Romans, 15, 167, 173.
Möhler, 49, 109, 112, 131.

NERO, importance of his act in raising the first persecution, 156.
Newman, Dr., the natural beauty of Greece, 314 ; the martyrs soldiers of Christ, 151.

ORAL teaching, viewed as the only adequate instrument for conveying doctrine by Pythagoras, Plato, Aristotle, and all subsequent Greek philosophers, 339–50; the means by which the Word of God declared that His kingdom should be propagated for ever, 137 ; which, as a fact, is fulfilled in the apostolic age, 122 ; and in all subsequent times, 129.
Origen, his heroic conduct in youth, 250 ; agrees with Irenæus, Clement of Alexandria, and Tertullian, in the principle of tradition, 231 ; states the unity of the Church, 236 ; treats the Church as a polity, and compares it with other polities, 264 ; the Christian people one people, formed on the imitation of Christ, 265 ; dies of ill-treatment under the Decian persecution, 267 ; how Christ leaves His Father and Mother to espouse the Church, 94, *note;* anticipates the universal prevalence of Christianity, 252 ; on the number of martyrs, 267.

PANTHEISM, Stoic, and Polytheism, how they fitted into each other, Zeller, 383, *note.*
Passaglia, -76, 80.
Patriarchal Sees, the three original all Sees of Peter, 283.
Penance, doctrine and practice of, in first half of third century, 290.
Personality, defective conception of, by Plato, in God, 337; in man, 339 ; by Aristotle, in both, 356 ; by Stoicism, in both, 362, 363 ; by all the Greek schools as to God, 380–4 ; as to man, 384–6.
Petavius, 74, 46, 101.
Peter, St., his personal work in building the Church, 285.
Peter and Paul, SS., their martyrdom, 156.
Phileas, Bishop of Thmuis, his account of persecution in Egypt, 303–5.
Philosophy, what it is, 309 ; the pre-Socratic, 317; its second period opened by Socrates, 318 ; its four great schools at Athens, 360; effect of the empire's establishment on it, 377 ; its negative effect, 378 ; its positive effect, 380 ; as to the divine unity and personality, 380–4; as to man's personality, 384–5; as to man's duties to God, 385 ; as to the duties of man to man, 388 ; its conception of the human commonwealth, 390 ; its failure to construct a society ruled by its principles, 393.
Philostratus, 252.
Plato, applies Socratic principles to an ethical, logical, and physical system, 328 ; his doctrine of Ideas, 329; his filiation with

Socrates, 330; his philosophy, and his idea of God, 330-5; with which, however, he retains the iuculcation and practice of the popular religion, 335; his God not absolutely personal, nor free, nor a creator, 336; his ethical system, 338; his conception of the method of teaching, 339; his contrast between oral teaching and writing, as means of imparting doctrine, 341-5; his account in his own person of how real knowledge, ἐπιστήμη, is to be attained, 350; calls the art of Socrates mental midwifery, 323; the highest point of virtue to become like to God, 357.

Pliny, the younger, his report of Christians to Trajan, 172; compared in his conduct to them with Trajan and Junius Rusticus, 172, note.

Plutarch, his statement of Zeno's Politeia, 389.

Polytheism, of the Græco-Roman world, its multiplicity, 3; universality, 10; grasp on daily life, 11; moral influence, 16; absence of moral teaching in it, 19; its internal cause in man, 22; its external cause, 23; its injuriousness to man, 25; illogical character, 26; superhuman power, 27; relation to civilisation, 31; to the empire's constitution, 34; to national feelings, 36; to despotism and slavery, 37; its prospects about A.U.C. 750, 38; is the summing-up of human history before Christ, 48.

Primacy, St. Peter's, defended by specific scriptural proof, unbroken succession, and perpetual recognition, 135; attested by St. Ignatius, 179; by St. Irenæus, 220; by Tertullian, 290; by St. Cyprian, 269-73; necessary to the Church's unity, 120-2; is linked with jurisdiction, and is the expression of Christ's sovereignty, 284; brought out by the questions of penance, rebaptizing heretics, and keeping Easter, 289-93; in it lies the unity of the Episcopate, 275.

Pythagoras, 310; his attempt to construct a philosophic religious community, 340; his conception influences Plato, and all subsequent Greek philosophy, 341.

REAL Presence, defended by the succession of doctrine, of men, and of institutions, 134.

Rebaptization of heretics, 291.

Ruinart, *Acta Sincera Martyrum*, quoted, 151, 169, 178, 186, 243, 248, 249.

SABBATH, the day changed, and the observance modified, by authority of the Church alone, 136.

Schmidt, *Geschichte der Denk- und Glaubensfreiheit*, 159.

Schwane, *Dogmengeschichte der vornicänischen Zeit*, 215, 235, 236, 237.

Scripture, not used as the means for the first foundation of Christianity, 122-4; introduced as subsidiary to oral teaching, 124-6; its great value in this light, 126, 127; relation hence arising of Scripture to the Church, 127; instances of this relation, 133-6; this relation set forth by our Lord for perpetual guidance of His Church, 137-9; the same, urged by Tertullian, 226; by St. Irenæus, 221, 222; by Clement of Alexandria, 229.
Sects, their multitude in early times, 167, 215, 223, 315.
Septimius Severus, maxims of government, 200, 204-6; his persecution, 249.
Socrates, his person, 320; influence on Greek philosophy, 319; the Stoic type of the wise man, 349; Zeller's account of his special principle, 320; that of Ueberweg, 321; his opinion on the gods and the Godhead, 323-6; his last words to his judges, 326; last words of his life, 326; halts between unity and plurality in the Godhead, 326-7; absence from his mind of the sense of impurity, 328, *note*; Plato makes an ethical, logical, and physical system from his principles, 328; the filiation between them, 530; his art termed mental midwifery by Plato, 323; one of his statements compared with that of St. Paul, 324, *note*.
Stoicism, Epicureanism, Scepticism, three branches on one stem, 370.
Suarez, 49-51.
Suicide, termed the Issue in Stoic philosophy, 393.

TACITUS, 156, 203, 204.
Teaching office, created by Christ, 137; witnessed by St. Ignatius, 165; by St. Irenæus, 219, 221, 222, 224; by Tertullian, 226, 227; by Clement of Alexandria, 229; by Origen, 231; alone carries both Tradition and Scripture as a living gift of the Spirit, 237.
Tertullian, 3, 27, 31, 154, 157, 159, 172, 202, 206, 207, 226, 227, 290.
Thierry, Amadée, 259, 397.
Thomas Aquinas, St., 23, 47, 66, 103, 398.
Tillemont, 171, 202, 206, 217.
Tradition, the whole body of Apostolic teaching so called, 123, 124; ἡ παράδοσις, by St. Irenæus, 162; Tertullian, 226-8; Clement of Alexandria, 229; Origen, 231.
Trajan, his treatment of Christians, 175; of St. Ignatius, 176; importance of his answer to Pliny, 181.
Truth, as meaning the whole body of the divine revelation, 115; committed for its propagation to a society, 128, 137; secured in it by a triple succession, 129, 130; its root in the Person of Christ, 42, 100, 148; the gift of His Spirit, 100, 103, 105; development of, 139; in the hall of Pilate, 40; its first transmission by oral teaching only, 122.

UEBERWEG, *Grundriss der Geschichte der Philosophie des Alterthums*, quoted or referred to, 317-9, 321, 328-30, 339-41, 347-9, 353, 364, 371, 372, 374, 381, 395, 396.

VARRO, divides theology into fabulous, natural, and civil, 16.

XENOPHON, 322-6.

ZELLER, *Philosophie der Griechen*, quoted or referred to, 310, 313, 314, 316-20, 330-3, 335-40, 350, 354, 358, 360, 361, 366-71, 382, 383, 387-90, 393.

Zeno, the Stoic, his conception of the method of teaching, 349; his doctrine upon God and the soul, 361-5; his conception of men as one flock feeding in a common pasture under a common law, 389.

Zukrigl, 386.

END OF VOL. II.

BURNS AND OATES, LIMITED, LONDON

No. 1.   1898.

Selection
FROM
Burns & Oates'
Catalogue of Publications.

Latest Publications.

Characteristics from the Writings of Cardinal Wiseman. Edited and with a Preface by the Rev. T. E. BRIDGETT, C.SS.R. Crown 8vo, cloth. 6/-.

Cardinal Wiseman's Meditations on the Sacred Passion of our Lord. With a Preface by H. E. CARDINAL VAUGHAN. Crown 8vo, cloth. 4/-.

THE FOURTH VOLUME OF THE POPULAR EDITION OF

The Formation of Christendom as seen in Church and State. By T. W. ALLIES, K.C.S.G. Crown 8vo, cloth. 5/-.

Genesis and Science. Inspiration of the Mosaic Ideas of Creative Work. By JOHN SMYTH. Crown 8vo, cloth, with Illustrations. 3/6.

Jewels of Prayer and Meditation from Unfamiliar Sources. By PERCY FITZGERALD, M.A., F.S.A. Fancy cloth, gilt. 2/6.

St. Francis de Sales as a Preacher. By the Very Rev. H. B. CANON MACKEY, O.S.B. Wrapper. 1/-.

India: A Sketch of the Madura Mission. By the Rev. H. WHITEHEAD, S.J. Crown 8vo, cloth, with Map and Illustrations. 3/6.

NEW AND POPULAR EDITION.

Life of Don Bosco, Founder of the Salesian Society. Translated from the French of J. M. VILLEFRANCHE by Lady MARTIN. Crown 8vo, 302 pp. Wrapper, 1/- net (postage 3d.).

BURNS & OATES, LIMITED,
Granville Mansions, 28, Orchard Street, London, W.

ALEXIS-LOUIS, PÈRE (O.C.D.).

Five Thrones of Divine Love upon the Earth, The. The Womb of Mary, the Crib, the Cross, the Eucharist, and the Faithful Soul. From the French. Crown 8vo, cloth. 3/6.

"A book of devotion, consisting of a series of short readings or meditations, chiefly on the Incarnation, the Blessed Eucharist, the Crucifixion and the principles which underlie and govern the spiritual life, whether among the Priesthood, the cloistered Religious, or the laity. The sum of the experimental knowledge of a Carmelite priest, it breathes the very inner spirit of St. John of the Cross, and contains the essence of affective theology."—*Monitor.*

ALLIES, T. W. (K.C.S.G.).

A Life's Decision. Second and Cheaper Edition. Crown 8vo, cloth. 5/-.

"Interesting, not only in the way in which all genuine personal narratives are interesting, but also for the many letters from well-known persons that it contains. It is a valuable contribution to the history of the Anglican Church in the eventful years which followed Newman's secession."—*Guardian.*

THE FORMATION OF CHRISTENDOM SERIES.

Vol. I. The Christian Faith and the Individual. Popular Edition. Crown 8vo, cloth. 5/-.

Vol. II. The Christian Faith and Society. Popular Edition. Crown 8vo, cloth. 5/-.

Vol. III. The Christian Faith and Philosophy. Popular Edition. Crown 8vo, cloth. 5/-.

Vol. IV. Church and State. Popular Edition. Crown 8vo, cloth. 5/-.

H. E. CARDINAL VAUGHAN says:—"It is one of the noblest historical works I have ever read. Now that its price has placed it within the reach of all, I earnestly pray that it may become widely known and appreciatively studied. We have nothing like it in the English language."

The Throne of the Fisherman, built by the Carpenter's Son. The Root, the Bond, and the Crown of Christendom. Demy 8vo, cloth. 10/6.

"The most important contribution to ecclesiastical history which has been given to the world for many a long day."—*Tablet.*

The Holy See and the Wandering of the Nations. Demy 8vo, cloth. 10/6.

Peter's Rock in Mohammed's Flood. Being the Seventh Volume of Mr. Allies' great work on the "Formation of Christendom." Demy 8vo, cloth. 10/6.

ALLIES, MARY.

Pius the Seventh, 1800-1823. Crown 8vo, cloth gilt. 5/-.

"Miss Allies has narrated the history of the long and memorable Pontificate of the first Pope of this century with a thoroughness of research and a dignity of style worthy of her illustrious father."—*Irish Monthly.*

Leaves from St. John Chrysostom. With Introduction by T. W. Allies, K.C.S.G. Crown 8vo, cloth. 6/-.

"The selections are well chosen, and Miss Allies' rendering is smooth, idiomatic, and faithful to the original. There is no existing book which is better adapted to make the English reader acquainted with the most eloquent of the Fathers of the Church."—*Dublin Review.*

ALLIES, MARY—*(continued)*.

History of the Church in England, from the Beginning of the Christian Era to the Death of Queen Elizabeth. In Two Vols. Crown 8vo, cloth. Vol. I. From the Beginning of the Christian Era to the Accession of Henry VIII. 6/-. Vol. II. From the Accession of Henry VIII. to the Death of Queen Elizabeth. 3/6.

"Miss Allies has admirably compressed the substance, or such as was necessary to her purpose, of a number of authorities, judiciously selected. . . . . As a narrative the volume is capitally written, as a summary it is skilful, and not its least excellence is its value as an index of the best available sources which deal with the period it covers."—*Birmingham Daily Gazette.*

ARNOLD, THOMAS (M.A., Fellow of the Royal University of Ireland).

Notes on the Sacrifice of the Altar. Crown 12mo, cloth gilt. 1/6.

"A very useful treatise on the Mass. The end of the Holy Sacrifice is first explained. Then the author takes occasion to point out the essential difference between the Anglican service and the Mass. Lastly, Mr. Arnold, following the course of the ritual, brings out clearly the meaning and object of each part of the sacred function. In his illustrative remarks he imparts a good deal of interesting information."—*Catholic Times.*

BAKER, VEN. FATHER AUGUSTIN (O.S.B.).

Holy Wisdom (*Sancta Sophia*). Directions for the Prayer of Contemplation, &c. Edited by Abbot Sweeney, D.D. New and Cheaper Edition. Crown 8vo. Handsomely bound in half leather, xx.-667 pp. 6/-.

"The thanks of the Catholic public are due to Dr. Sweeney for re-editing this famous work. It does not belong to the catalogue of ephemeral publications. It is of a totally different standard. . . . To lovers of prayer and meditation it will be a most acceptable guide and friend."—*Tablet.*

BIBLES, &c.

N.B.—For full particulars of Bindings, &c., see Illustrated Prayer Book Catalogue, sent post free on application.

Holy Bible. POCKET EDITION (size, 5¼ by 3¼ inches). Embossed cloth, red edges, 2/6; and in leather bindings, from 4/6 to 7/6. MEDIUM EDITION (size, 7¼ by 4¾ inches). Cloth, 3/6; and in leather bindings, from 6/- net to 10/6 net (postage 6d.). OCTAVO EDITION (size, 9 by 6 inches). Cloth, 6/-; and in a great variety of leather bindings, from 8/- to 35/- net. Family Editions in quarto and folio. Prices upon application.

New Testament, The. POCKET EDITION. Limp cloth, 6d. (postage 2d.). Cloth, red edges, 1/-. Roan, 1/6. Paste grain, round corners, 3/-. Best calf or morocco, 4/6 each. ROYAL 8vo EDITION (size, 9 by 6 inches). Cloth, 1/- net (postage 3d.). NEW MEDIUM EDITION. LARGE TYPE. Crown 8vo (size, 7½ by 5 inches). 500 pp. Cloth, boards, gilt lettered, 2/-. Paste grain, limp, round corners, red or gold edges, 4/6. German calf, limp, round corners, red under gold edges, 8/6. Morocco, limp, round corners, red under gold edges, 8/6. Also in better bindings for presentation.

BLESSED SACRAMENT, OUR GOD; or, Practical Thoughts on the Mystery of Love, The. By a Child of St. Teresa. Cloth gilt. 1/-.

"It is written in the spirit of reverence and earnestness in simple and forcible language. This little work is calculated to do much good, and we heartily commend it."—*Dublin Review*.

BOWDEN, REV. H. S. (of the Oratory), Edited by.

Dante's Divina Commedia: Its scope and value. From the German of Francis Hettinger, D.D. With an engraving of Dante. Second Edition. 10/6.

Natural Religion. Being Vol. I. of Dr. Hettinger's "Evidences of Christianity." With an Introduction on "Certainty." Third Edition. Crown 8vo, cloth. 7/6.

Revealed Religion. Vol. II. of Dr. Hettinger's "Evidences of Christianity." With an Introduction on the "Assent of Faith." Crown 8vo, cloth. 5/-.

"The two together ('Natural Religion' and 'Revealed Religion') supply a real want in our Catholic literature. Nothing is more common nowadays than for a priest to be asked to recommend a book, written from a Catholic point of view, on the evidence for the Christian religion. And in future he will be able to recommend Father Bowden's 'Hettinger'. . . . It may be confidently affirmed that all who have taken interest in the war against religion raised by its modern adversaries will find in Father Bowden's pages many of their chief difficulties helpfully dealt with."—*Month*.

BRIDGETT, REV. T. E. (C.SS.R.).

Lyra Hieratica: Poems on the Priesthood. Collected from many sources by the Rev. T. E. Bridgett, C.SS.R. Fcap. 8vo, cloth. 2/6 net (postage 3d.).

"The idea of gathering an anthology of Poems on the Priesthood was a happy one, and has been happily carried out. Priests and laity alike owe a debt of gratitude to Father Bridgett for the many beautiful things he has brought together."—*Tablet*.

The True Story of the Catholic Hierarchy deposed by Queen Elizabeth, with fuller Memoirs of its last Two Survivors. By the Rev. T. E. Bridgett, C.SS.R., and the late Rev. T. F. Knox, D.D., of the London Oratory. Crown 8vo, cloth. 7/6.

Wisdom and Wit of Sir Thomas More, The. Crown 8vo, cloth. 6/-.

"Every page in this delightful volume bespeaks the master hand, the clear head, the deep and tender heart. It is lively, eloquent, impressive, genial; without stiffness of parade of learning, but as full as good things as it can hold."—*Catholic Times*.

BROWNLOW, BISHOP.

Memoir of Mother Rose Columba Adams, O.P., first Prioress of St. Dominic's Convent, and Foundress of the Perpetual Adoration at North Adelaide. With Portrait and Plates. Crown 8vo, cloth, 384 pp. 6/6.

"It is a work of the deepest interest and edification. In a handsomely printed and beautifully illustrated volume, Bishop Brownlow tells us the story of a remarkable woman's life and work, drawing on his own recollections of her career, and with the help of her own letters and reminiscences of many friends, giving us a life-like picture of a singularly earnest, devoted, and saintly soul."—*Tablet*.

BUTLER, REV. ALBAN.

People's Edition of the Lives of the Saints. Twelve Pocket Volumes, each Volume containing the Saints of the Month. Superfine paper, neat cloth binding, gilt lettered. 1/6 each; or the complete set (comprising over 6,000 pages), in handsome cloth case to match, 18/-.

DALE, REV. J. D. HILARIUS.

Ceremonial according to the Roman Rite. Translated from the Italian of Joseph Baldeschi. New and Revised Edition. Crown 8vo, cloth. 6/6.

"This work is our standard English directory on the subject. Few functions of any importance are carried on without a glance at it. It is a familiar guide and friend—in short, a classic."—*Catholic Times.*

The Sacristan's Manual; or, Handbook of Church Furniture, Ornament, &c. Fourth and Enlarged Edition. Crown 8vo, cloth. 2/6.

DIGNAM, FATHER (S.J.).

Conferences given by Father Dignam, S.J., with Retreats, Sermons, and Notes of Spiritual Direction. With a Preface by His Eminence Cardinal Mazzella, S.J. Crown 8vo, cloth gilt. 6/- net (postage 4d.).

FABER, FATHER.

All for Jesus; or, The Easy Ways of Divine Love. New Edition. Crown 8vo, cloth, 407 pp. 5/-.

Bethlehem. New Edition. Crown 8vo, cloth, 500 pp. 7/-.

Ethel's Book; or, Tales of the Angels. A New and Cheaper Edition. Beautifully bound in cloth, extra gilt, gilt edges. 2/6.

Growth in Holiness; or, The Progress of the Spiritual Life. New Edition. Crown 8vo, cloth, 464 pp. 6/-.

Hymns. Complete Edition. Crown 8vo, cloth, 427 pp. 6/-.

Notes on Doctrinal and Spiritual Subjects. Fourth Edition. Two Vols. Crown 8vo, cloth, 759 pp. 10/-.

Poems. Complete Edition. Crown 8vo, cloth, 582 pp. 5/-.

Sir Lancelot. A Legend of the Middle Ages. Crown 8vo, cloth, 347 pp. 5/-.

Spiritual Conferences. Eighth Edition. Crown 8vo, cloth, 403 pp. 6/-.

The Blessed Sacrament; or, The Works and Ways of God. New Edition. Crown 8vo, cloth, 548 pp. 7/6.

The Creator and the Creature; or, The Wonders of Divine Love. New Edition. Crown 8vo, cloth, 416 pp. 6/-.

The Easiness of Salvation. Cloth gilt. 1/-.

The Foot of the Cross; or, The Sorrows of Mary. Crown 8vo, cloth, 432 pp. 6/-.

The Precious Blood; or, The Price of our Salvation. Fifth Edition. Crown 8vo, cloth, 308 pp. 5/-.

FABER, FATHER—*(continued)*.

The Life and Letters of Frederick William Faber, D.D. By Rev. John E. Bowden, of the Oratory. Third Edition. Crown 8vo, cloth, 447 pp. 6/-.

Father Faber's May Book. Compiled by an Oblate of Mary Immaculate. A New Month of May, arranged for Daily Reading, from the writings of Father Faber. 18mo, cloth, gilt edges, with Steel Frontispiece. 2/-.

A Brief Sketch of the Early Life of Frederick William Faber, D.D. By his Brother. Limp cloth. 1/-.

FITZGERALD, PERCY.

Jewels of Prayer and Meditation from Unfamiliar Sources. Fancy cloth, gilt. 2/6.

Jewels of the Imitation. A Selection of Passages with a Little Commentary. Cloth, extra gilt. 2/-.

"It is an excellent book for spiritual reading in itself, and it will help its readers to read that holiest of books with more relish and fruit. Mr. Fitzgerald's pithy, up-to-date comments throw a new light on many a wise saying of Thomas à Kempis."—*Irish Monthly.*

Eucharistic Jewels. Second Edition. Fancy cloth, gilt. 2/6.

"Every page is bright with some exquisite passage, and Mr. Fitzgerald's little commentaries, as he carries us along, are not unworthy of the glorious companionship in which he has placed them."—*Freeman's Journal.*

Jewels of the Mass. A Short Account of the Rites and Prayers used in the Holy Sacrifice. Sixth Edition. Fancy cloth gilt. 2/-.

"A treatise on the Mass, in which the author proves himself a sound theologian, an accomplished master of ecclesiastical history bearing on the question, a cultured scholar, and the possessor of a very charming style."—*Nation.*

The Layman's Day ; or, Jewels of Practical Piety. Second Edition. Cloth, extra gilt. 2/-.

"An effort to induce people to consider their every-day life from the point of view of practical common-sense. . . . Admirably done."—*Catholic News.*

FULLERTON, LADY GEORGIANA.

Grantley Manor. An Interesting Story of Catholic Life and Society. New Edition. Cloth gilt, gilt edges, 349 pp. 3/6.

Life of St. Frances of Rome. New Edition. Cloth gilt. 2/-.

Life of Mère Marie de la Providence, Foundress of the Helpers of the Holy Souls. Third Edition. With Preface and Appendix by the Rev. Sydney F. Smith, S.J. Cloth. 1/6 net (postage 3d.).

GIBSON, REV. HENRY.

Catechism made Easy: being a Familiar Explanation of the Catechism of Christian Doctrine. Tenth Edition. Two Vols. Fcap. 8vo, cloth, 800 pp. 7/6.

"Contains a course of fifty-eight instructions on Catholic doctrines, each accompanied by from one to eleven stories, legends, anecdotes, &c., expressly designed to illustrate their meanings and to fix them in the minds of children.

"This work must be of priceless worth to any who are engaged in any form of catechetical instruction. The best book of the kind that we have seen in English."—*Irish Monthly.*

GILLOW, JOSEPH.
Biographical History, and Bibliographical Dictionary of the English Catholics. From the Breach with Rome in 1534 to the Present Time. Vol. I., A-C, 612 pp. Vol. II., D-Grad, 557 pp. Vol. III., Grah-Kem, 688 pp. Vol. IV., Kem-Met, 572 pp. Demy 8vo, cloth. 15/- each.

"The patient research of Mr. Gillow, his conscientious record of minute particulars, and especially his exhaustive bibliographical information in connection with each name are beyond praise."—*British Quarterly Review.*

HAMMERSTEIN, REV. L. VON (S.J.).
Foundations of Faith: The Existence of God Demonstrated. From the German of Fr. Ludwig von Hammerstein, S.J. With an Introduction by the Rev. W. L. Gildea, D.D. Crown 8vo, cloth. 6/-.

"Popular, interesting, forcible, and sound. It is well to have a book like Father von Hammerstein's to put into the hands of serious inquirers; it forms a valuable addition to our apologetic literature."—*Tablet.*

HEDLEY, BISHOP.
The Christian Inheritance. Second Edition. Crown 8vo, cloth gilt, 430 pp. 6/-.

"We do not know any book we could more confidently recommend to intelligent inquirers after truth, perplexed by the prevailing unbelief, than this new volume, in which the Bishop of Newport prints some twenty discourses preached by him on various occasions."—*Tablet.*

Our Divine Saviour, and other Discourses. Second Edition. Crown 8vo, cloth gilt. 6/-.

A Retreat: Consisting of Thirty-three Discourses, with Meditations: for the use of the Clergy, Religious, and Others. Fourth Edition. In handsome half-leather binding. Crown 8vo, 428 pp. 6/-.

"The book is one which, beyond the purpose for which it is directly intended, may be strongly recommended for spiritual reading."—*Month.*

LIGUORI, ST. ALPHONSUS.
A Translation of the Works of St. Alphonsus, edited by the late Bishop Coffin:—

Christian Virtues, and the Means for obtaining them, The. Cloth gilt. 3/-. Or separately, cloth flush—1. The Love of Our Lord Jesus Christ. 1/-. 2. Treatise on Prayer (in many Editions a great part of this work is omitted). 1/-. 3. A Christian's Rule of Life. 1/-.

Eternal Truths. Preparation for Death. 2/6.

The Redemption. Meditations on the Passion. 2/6.

Glories of Mary. New Edition. 3/6.

Reflections on Spiritual Subjects and on the Passion of Jesus Christ. 2/6.

LIVIUS, REV. T. (M.A., C.SS.R.).
St. Peter, Bishop of Rome; or, the Roman Episcopate of the Prince of the Apostles. Demy 8vo, cloth. 12/-.

LIVIUS, REV. T. (M.A., C.SS.R.)—*(continued)*.
   Explanation of the Psalms and Canticles in the Divine Office. By St. Alphonsus Liguori. Translated from the Italian by Thomas Livius, C.SS.R. With a Preface by his Eminence Cardinal Manning. Crown 8vo, cloth, xxx.-512 pp. 7/6.
   Mary in the Epistles; or, The Implicit Teaching of the Apostles concerning the Blessed Virgin. Crown 8vo, cloth. 5/-.
   The Blessed Virgin in the Fathers of the First Six Centuries. Demy 8vo, cloth. 12/-.

McDONALD, REV. WALTER (D.D.).
   Motion: Its Origin and Conservation. An Essay by the Rev. Walter McDonald, D.D., Prefect of the Dunboyne Establishment, St. Patrick's College, Maynooth. Demy 8vo, xii.-458 pp. 7/6 net (postage 4d.).

MADDEN, REV. W. J.
   Disunion and Reunion. Crown 8vo, cloth. 3/-.
   "The volume contains a good deal of practical information in a plain and popular style."—*Catholic Times*.

MANNING, CARDINAL.
   Confidence in God. 32mo, neat cloth gilt. 1/-.
   Lost Sheep Found. A Sermon. Wrapper. 6d. Being an Appeal for the Convents of the Good Shepherd.
   Miscellanies. First Series. Crown 8vo, cloth, 387 pp. 6/-.
   Miscellanies. Second Series. Crown 8vo, cloth, 391 pp. 6/-.
   Religio Viatoris. Crown 8vo, cloth. 1/6.
   Sermons on Ecclesiastical Subjects. Crown 8vo, cloth, 456 pp. 6/-.
   Sin and its Consequences. Crown 8vo, cloth. 4/-.
   The Blessed Sacrament the Centre of Immutable Truth. 32mo, neat cloth gilt. 1/-.
   The Eternal Priesthood. Crown 8vo, cloth. 2/6.
   The Four Great Evils of the Day. Crown 8vo, cloth. 2/6.
   The Fourfold Sovereignty of God. Crown 8vo, cloth. 2/6.
   The Glories of the Sacred Heart. Crown 8vo, cloth. 4/-.
   The Grounds of Faith. Crown 8vo, cloth. 1/6.
   The Holy Ghost the Sanctifier. 32mo, neat cloth gilt. 2/-.
   The Independence of the Holy See. Crown 8vo, cloth. 2/6.
   The Internal Mission of the Holy Ghost. Crown 8vo, cloth, 494 pp. 5/-.
   The Love of Jesus to Penitents. 32mo, neat cloth gilt. 1/-.
   The Office of the Church in Higher Catholic Education. 6d.

MANNING, CARDINAL—(*continued*).
  The Temporal Mission of the Holy Ghost; or, Reason and Revelation. Crown 8vo, cloth. 5/-.
  The True Story of the Vatican Council. Crown 8vo, cloth. 2/6.
  The Workings of the Holy Spirit in the Church of England. New Edition. Crown 8vo, cloth. 1/6.

MARTIN, LADY.
  Life of Don Bosco, Founder of the Salesian Society. Translated from the French of J. M. Villefranche. New Popular Edition. Crown 8vo, 302 pp. Wrapper. 1/- net (postage 3d.).
  "We possess in this volume a popular life of a saintly man whose good works are bearing abundant fruit, and the glory of whose life will continue to stimulate zeal in many lands. Lady Martin's translation is admirable, and the book is extremely cheap at a shilling."—*Catholic Times.*

  Life of Princess Borghese (*née* Gwendalin Talbot). Translated from the French. Crown 8vo, tastefully bound in cloth gilt. 4/-.
  "The life of the charming and saint-like young Englishwoman will come as a welcome surprise to the readers of a later generation, who will find how completely the spirit of Catholic faith and charity was combined in the person of Lady Gwendalin Talbot with the rarest beauty and the most accomplished talents."—*Tablet.*

MEMORIES OF THE CRIMEA. By Sister Mary Aloysius. With Preface by the Very Rev. J. Fahey, D.D., V.G. Crown 8vo, cloth gilt. 2/6.
  "The venerable Sister, upon whom Her Majesty the Queen bestowed the decoration of the Royal Red Cross a few months ago, tells her touching story of heroic self-abnegation with a modest simplicity that is far more impressive than the most elaborate and picturesque style of descriptive writing."—*Daily Telegraph.*

NEWMAN, CARDINAL.
  The Church of the Fathers. Fcap. 8vo, cloth, 361 pp. 4/-.
  An attempt to illustrate the tone and modes of thought, the habits and manners, of the early times of the Church.
  Detailed List of Cardinal Newman's Works on application.

NORTHCOTE, VERY REV. PROVOST (D.D.).
  Mary in the Gospels; or, Lectures on the History of our Blessed Lady as recorded by the Evangelists. Second Edition. Cloth gilt, 344 pp. 3/6.

PERRY, REV. JOHN.
  Practical Sermons, for all the Sundays of the Year. First and Second Series. Sixth Edition. Fcap. 8vo, cloth. 3/6 each.

POPE, REV. T. A. (of the Oratory).
  Life of St. Philip Neri. Translated from the Italian of Cardinal Capecelatro. Second and Revised Edition. Two Volumes. Crown 8vo, cloth. 12/6.
  "Altogether this is a most fascinating work, full of spiritual lore and historic erudition, and with all the intense interest of a remarkable biography. Take it up where you will, it is hard to lay it down. We think it one of the most completely satisfactory lives of a Saint that has been written in modern times."—*Tablet.*

PORTER, ARCHBISHOP (S.J.).

The Banquet of the Angels: Preparation and Thanksgiving for Holy Communion. New Edition. 18mo, blue cloth, gilt. 2/-. Also bound in a variety of handsome leather bindings suitable for First Communion memorial gifts. From 6/6 to 12/6 net.

PRACTICAL MEDITATIONS FOR EVERY DAY IN THE Year, on the Life of our Lord Jesus Christ. Chiefly for the use of Religious. By a Father of the Society of Jesus. With Imprimatur of Cardinal Manning. New Edition, Revised. In two Volumes. Cloth, red edges. 9/-.

These volumes give three different daily points for consideration and application. "A work of great practical utility, and we give it our earnest recommendation."— *Weekly Register.*

PRAYER BOOKS, &c.

N.B.—For full particulars of Prayer Books, see *Illustrated Prayer Book Catalogue*, sent post free on application.

Catholic's Daily Companion. With Epistles and Gospels. Roan, 1/-; and in various leather bindings, 1/6 to 5/-.

Catholic Piety. Containing a Selection of Prayers, Reflections, Meditations, and Instructions adapted to every state in life. By the late Rev. Wm. Gahan, O.S.A. 32mo Edition, with Ordinary of the Mass. Cloth, 6d.; post free, 8d.; roan, 1/-. With Epistles and Gospels, 1/6, 2/-, 2/6, 4/6, &c. Messrs. BURNS & OATES also publish two other Editions of this book.

Catholic's Vade Mecum. A Select Manual of Prayers for Daily Use. Compiled from approved sources. 34th Thousand. With Epistles and Gospels. Calf, 5/6, and also in better bindings.

Children's Pictorial Mass Book. (Abridged.) New Edition. Forty-three Illustrations. 2d.; cloth, 6d.

Daily Exercise. Cloth limp. 6d.

Flowers of Devotion. Being a Collection of Favourite Devotions, for Public and Private use. Compiled from approved sources, and with the Imprimatur of His Eminence Cardinal Vaughan. New Edition. Leather bindings. 1/6 to 5/-.

Spirit of the Sacred Heart, The. A new large-type Prayer Book. Cloth, 3/6; leather, 5/6; German calf or morocco, 8/6.

Garden of the Soul. 700th Thousand. Approved by the Cardinal Archbishop of Westminster, and revised by a Priest of the Archdiocese. New Edition. In which many devotions will be found which now form a necessary part of every Catholic Prayer Book. Cloth, 6d.; post free, 8d.; roan, 1/-. With Epistles and Gospels, cloth, 1/-; and in leather bindings, at 1/6, 2/-, 2/6, 3/-, 3/6, 4/-, 5/-, and upwards.

Messrs. BURNS & OATES have just issued a new Pocket Edition of the "Garden of the Soul," size $3\frac{3}{4}$ by $2\frac{1}{2}$ inches, with red line borders, and Devotions for Mass in large type. This Edition can now be had in various bindings, from 1/- to 5/-. They also publish three other Editions.

PRAYER BOOKS, &c.—(*continued*).

Golden Manual. A Guide to Catholic Devotion, Public and Private, Compiled from approved sources. Fine Paper. Leather, 6/-. With Epistles and Gospels, 7/- and upwards.

Imitation of Christ, Of the. By Thomas à Kempis. NEW POPULAR EDITION FOR DISTRIBUTION. Cloth, red edges, 6d. (postage, 2d.). Leather, red edges, 1/-. SUPERFINE POCKET EDITION. Fancy cloth extra, with red borders, 1/6. And in leather bindings, from 2/6 to 10/-. PRESENTATION EDITION (size, 6¼ by 4¼ inches). With red border on each page. Cloth extra, 3/6. And in leather bindings, from 7/- to 15/-.

Key of Heaven. A Manual of Devout Prayers. 32mo Edition. Cloth, 6d.; post free, 8d.; roan, 1/-. With Epistles and Gospels, 1/6, 2/-, 2/6, 3/-, 4/6, &c. They also publish two Smaller Editions.

Manual of Prayers for Congregational Use. As authorized by the Bishops of England and Wales. With an Appendix containing Prayers for Mass, Confession, and Communion. Cloth, 1/-; leather, 2/6, 5/-, and upwards.

Manual of the Sacred Heart. Compiled and Translated from approved sources. New Edition. Cloth. 2/- upwards.

Missal. New and Complete Pocket Missal, with the Imprimatur of H. E. Cardinal Vaughan, in Latin and English, with all the New Offices, and the propers for Ireland, Scotland, and the Jesuits. (Size, 5¼ by 3¼ inches). Roan or French morocco, 5/-; Rutland roan, limp, 7/-; best calf or morocco, four styles, 8/6 each. Also in better bindings, from 11/- to 30/- net.

Missal for the Laity. Cheap Edition. 6d.; post free, 8d.; and in leather bindings, at 1/6, 2/6, 4/6, and 5/-.

Path to Heaven. Containing Epistles, Gospels, and Hymns, &c. Cloth, 2/- and 2/6; leather, 3/-, 4/-, 4/6, 6/-, and upwards.

Prayers for the People. By the Rev. F. D. Byrne. Imperial 32mo, cloth, extra gilt. 2/-.

QUARTERLY SERIES. Edited by the Jesuit Fathers. 98 Volumes published to date.

SELECTION.

The Life and Letters of St. Francis Xavier. By the Rev. H. J. Coleridge, S.J. Second Edition. Two Volumes. 10/6.

The Life and Letters of St. Teresa. By the Rev. H. J. Coleridge, S.J. Three Volumes. 7/6 each.

Pious Affections towards God and the Saints. Meditations for every Day in the Year, and for the principal Festivals, From the Latin of the Ven. Nicholas Lancicius, S.J. 7/6.

The Life and Teaching of Jesus Christ in Meditations for every Day in the Year. By Fr. Nicholas Avancino, S.J. Two Volumes. 10 6.

QUARTERLY SERIES—(continued).

The Life of St. Alonso Rodriguez. By Francis Goldie, of the Society of Jesus. 7/6.

Letters of St. Augustine. Selected and Arranged by Mary H. Allies. 6/6.

Acts of the English Martyrs, hitherto unpublished. By the Rev. John H. Pollen, S.J. 7/6.

The Life of St. Francis di Geronimo, S.J. By A. M. Clarke. 7/6.

Aquinas Ethicus; or, The Moral Teaching of St. Thomas. By the Rev. Joseph Rickaby, S.J. Second Edition. Two Volumes. 12/-.

The Spirit of St. Ignatius. From the French of the Rev. Fr. Xavier de Franciosi, S.J. 6/-.

Jesus, the All-Beautiful. A Devotional Treatise on the Character and Actions of our Lord. Edited by the Rev. J. G. Macleod, S.J. Second Edition. 6/6.

The Manna of the Soul. By Fr. Paul Segneri. New Edition. In Two Volumes. 12/-.

Life of Ven. Joseph Benedict Cottolengo. From the Italian of Don P. Gastaldi. 4/6.

Life of St. Francis Borgia. By A. M. Clarke. 6/6.

Life of Blessed Antony Baldinucci. By the Rev. F. Goldie, S.J. 6/-.

Distinguished Irishmen of the Sixteenth Century. By Rev. E. Hogan, S.J. 6/-.

Journals kept during Times of Retreat. By the late Fr. John Morris, S.J. Edited by Rev. J. Pollen, S.J. 6/-.

Life of the Rev. Mother Mary of St. Euphrasia Pelletier. By A. M. Clarke. 6/-.

Jesus: His Life, in the very Words of the Four Gospels. A Diatessaron by Henry Beauclerk, S.J. Cloth. 5/-.

First Communion. A Book of Preparation for First Communion. Edited by Fr. Thurston, S.J. Third and Cheaper Edition. With nineteen Illustrations. 3/6.

The Life and Letters of Fr. John Morris, S.J. By Fr. J. H. Pollen, S.J. Cloth. 6/-.

The Story of Mary Aikenhead, Foundress of the Irish Sisters of Charity. By Maria Nethercott. Crown 8vo, cloth. 3/-.

Life of the Blessed Master John of Avila. Secular Priest, called the Apostle of Andalusia. By Father Longaro Degli Oddi, S.J. Edited by J. G. Macleod, S.J. Cloth. 4/-.

Notes on St. Paul; Corinthians, Galatians, Romans. By Joseph Rickaby, S.J. 7/6.

RENDU, A. (LL.D.).
The Jewish Race in Ancient and Roman History.
Translated from the Eleventh Corrected Edition by S. T. Crook.
Crown 8vo, 440 pp. 6/-.
"This should prove a very useful book."—*Dublin Review*.
"The story is well and lucidly told."—*Schoolmaster*.

RICKABY, REV. JOSEPH (S.J.).
Oxford Conferences. Lent and Summer Terms, 1897. Crown 8vo. Wrapper, 1/- net (postage 2d.).

RIVINGTON, REV. LUKE (D.D.).
Rome and England; or, Ecclesiastical Continuity. Crown 8vo, cloth. 3/6.
"Fr. Rivington's method of exposition is admirable—brief and lucid without meagreness, pointed and telling without harshness. . . . . A book to be grateful for; useful alike to the controversialist, the historical student, and the general reader."—*Tablet*.

RUSHE, VERY REV. JAMES P. (O.D.C.) (Father Patrick of St. Joseph).

Carmel in Ireland. A Narrative of the Irish Province of Teresian or Discalced Carmelites. A.D. 1625-1896. Crown 8vo, cloth. 3/6 net (postage 4d.).
". . . . Written in an easy, historical style. The history of the Carmelite Abbeys in Ireland is here told with much graphic power in a series of interesting chapters, which will be valued by very many readers. . . . . The author is most painstaking, and has consulted all available books of reference to make his record complete."—*Irish Times*.

ST. BENEDICT'S SERIES.
The Life and the Rule of our Holy Father, St. Benedict.
Being the Second Book of the Dialogues of St. Gregory the Great, with the Rule of the same Holy Patriarch. In Latin and English. Cloth gilt. 5/-.

St. Benedict and Grottaferrata. Limp cloth, gilt. 1/-.

A Visit to Subiaco, the Cradle of the Benedictine Order.
47 pp., 8vo, wrapper. 6d.

Life of Helen Lucretia Cornaro Piscopia, Benedictine Oblate, and Doctor of the University of Padua. Cloth gilt. 4/6.

Life of the Blessed Joanna Mary Bonomo. With Portrait. Cloth gilt. 3/6.

ST. FRANCIS DE SALES, The Works of. Translated into the English Language by the Very Rev. Canon Mackey, O.S.B., under the Direction of the Right Rev. Bishop Hedley, O.S.B.

Vol. I. Letters to Persons in the World. Third Edition. Crown 8vo, cloth. 6/-.

Vol. II. The Treatise on the Love of God. Fr. Carr's Translation of 1630 has been taken as a basis, but it has been Modernised and thoroughly Revised and Corrected. Second Edition. 6/-.

ST. FRANCIS DE SALES—*(continued).*

Vol. III. The Catholic Controversy. Crown 8vo, cloth. 6/-.

Vol. IV. Letters to Persons in Religion, with Introduction by Bishop Hedley on "St. Francis de Sales and the Religious State." Second Edition. Crown 8vo, cloth. 6/-.

"We earnestly commend these volumes to all readers, and we desire their widest diffusion, as we desire also that the doctrine and spirit of St. Francis may reign in all our hearts, both of pastors and of people."—Cardinal Manning in the *Dublin Review.*

St. Francis de Sales as a Preacher. Wrapper. 1/-.

SALVATORI'S PRACTICAL INSTRUCTIONS FOR NEW
Confessors. Edited by Fr. Anthony Ballerini, S.J., and Translated by Very Rev. William Hutch, D.D. Third Edition. 18mo, cloth gilt, 314 pp. 4/-.

SCHOUPPE, REV. F. X. (S.J.).

Purgatory: Illustrated by the Lives and Legends of the Saints. Second Edition. Crown 8vo, cloth. 6/-.

"Solid, instructive, practical, and interesting as a romance, this book will go far to dispel the vague and erroneous ideas entertained among the faithful on the subject of Purgatory. Its careful perusal will repay the thoughtless Christian, the devout Catholic, and the zealous priest."—*Irish Ecclesiastical Record.*

SMYTH, JOHN.

Genesis and Science. Inspiration of the Mosaic Ideas of Creative Work. Crown 8vo, cloth, with Illustrations. 3/6.

"In the following pages abundant proof is given that the several phenomena recorded in the first chapter of Genesis are scientifically certain. And as the Mosaic days can be shown to embrace, and include, the æons of the geologist, all apparent contradictions vanish. With the Mosaic ideas of creative work thus unfolded in their true light, the inspiration of the first chapter of Genesis becomes manifest."—PREFACE.

SWEENEY, RIGHT REV. ABBOT (O.S.B.).

Sermons for all Sundays and Festivals of the Year. Fourth Edition. Crown 8vo, handsomely bound in half-leather. 10/6.

"For such priests as are in search of matter to aid them in their round of Sunday discourses, and have not read this volume, we can assure them that they will find in these 600 pages a mine of solid and simple Catholic teaching."—*Tablet.*

THOMPSON, EDWARD HEALY (M.A.).

Letters and Writings of Marie Lataste, with Critical and Expository Notes. By two Fathers of the Society of Jesus. Translated from the French. Three Volumes. 8vo, cloth. 5/- each.

Life of Jean-Jacques Olier, Founder of the Seminary of St. Sulpice. New and Enlarged Edition. Post 8vo, xxxvi.-628 pp. 15/-.

The Hidden Life of Jesus. A Lesson and Model to Christians. By Henri-Marie Boudon. Translated from the French by E. Healy Thompson, M.A. Third Edition. Cloth gilt. 3/-.

The Life and Glories of St. Joseph. Grounded on the Dissertations of Canon Vitali, Fr. José Moreno, and other Writers. Second Edition. Crown 8vo, cloth. 6/-.

The Unity of the Episcopate. Crown 8vo, cloth. 4/6.

THOMPSON, EDWARD HEALY (M.A.), Edited by.
LIBRARY OF RELIGIOUS BIOGRAPHY.

Life of St. Aloysius Gonzaga (S.J.). Eleventh Edition. Globe 8vo, cloth, xxiv.-373 pp. 5/-.

Life of Marie Eustelle Harpain; or, The Angel of the Eucharist. Fifth Edition. Cloth, xxi.-388 pp. 5/-.

Life of St. Stanislaus Kostka. Fifth Edition. Cloth. 5/-.

Life of Marie Lataste, Lay Sister of the Congregation of the Sacred Heart. With a Brief Notice of her Sister Quitterie. Second Edition. Cloth. 5/-.

Life of Leon Papin-Dupont, The Holy Man of Tours. Fourth Edition. Cloth. 5/-.

Life of Jean Baptiste Muard, Founder of the Congregation of St. Edme and of the Monastery of La Pierre-qui-Vire. 8vo, cloth, xix.-540 pp. 6/-.

Life of St. Charles Borromeo, Cardinal Archbishop of Milan. Second Edition. Cloth gilt. 3/-.

ULLATHORNE, ARCHBISHOP.

Christian Patience: The Strength and Discipline of the Soul. Sixth and Cheaper Edition. Demy 8vo, cloth, 256 pp. 7/-.

The Endowments of Man considered in their Relations with his Final End. Fifth and Cheaper Edition. Demy 8vo, cloth, 404 pp. 7/-.

The Groundwork of the Christian Virtues. Fifth and Cheaper Edition. Demy 8vo, cloth, 411 pp. 7/-.

Memoir of Bishop Willson, first Bishop of Hobart, Tasmania. With Portrait. Crown 8vo, cloth. 2/6.

The Autobiography of Archbishop Ullathorne. Edited by Augusta Theodosia Drane. Second Edition. Demy 8vo, cloth. 7/6.

"As a plucky Yorkshireman, as a sailor, as a missionary, as a great traveller, as a ravenous reader, and as a great prelate, Dr. Ullathorne was able to write down most fascinating accounts of his experiences. The book is full of shrewd glimpses from a Roman point of view of the man himself, of the position of Roman Catholics in this country, of the condition of the country, of the Colonies, and of the Anglican Church in various parts of the world, in the earlier half of this century."—*Guardian.*

The Letters of Archbishop Ullathorne. Arranged by A. T. Drane. (Sequel to the "Autobiography.") Demy 8vo, cloth, 550 pp. 9/-.

"Compiled with admirable judgment for the purpose of displaying in a thousand various ways the real man who was Archbishop Ullathorne. . . . . This book is very cordially recommended, not only for the intrinsic interest, but also for the sage and prudent counsel which characterizes the intimate correspondence of Archbishop Ullathorne."—*Tablet.*

ULLATHORNE, ARCHBISHOP—(continued).

Characteristics from the Writings of Archbishop Ullathorne, together with a Bibliographical Account of the Archbishop's Works. By the Rev. M. F. Glancey, Crown 8vo, cloth. 6/-.

WALPOLE, F. GOULBURN.

A Short History of the Catholic Church. Crown 8vo, cloth. 3/-.

This work may be described as a Skeleton History of the Church. It is been compiled from notes made by the author for his own instruction, and he hopes that it may prove useful to those who may not have leisure or inclination to study the voluminous standard works upon which it is based.

WHITEHEAD, REV. H. (S.J.).

India: A Sketch of the Madura Mission. Crown 8vo, cloth, with Map and Illustrations. 3/6.

"There are few books of missionary experiences which equal this in interest. This sketch will be deeply appreciated by all who read it."—*Catholic Times*.

WISEMAN, CARDINAL.

Meditations on the Sacred Passion of our Lord. Crown 8vo, cloth. 4/-.

In the Preface H. E. CARDINAL VAUGHAN says:—"The characteristic of these Meditations, as indeed of most of Cardinal Wiseman's writings, is that you will nearly always find in them a 'Hidden Gem.' The beauty and richness of his mind seemed to illustrate and justify every topic he treated by suddenly striking some vein of thought or some point of feeling which, if not new, is at least presented in a new light or reference."

Fabiola. A Tale of the Catacombs. New Cheap Edition. Crown 8vo, cloth, xii.-324 pp. 2/-. Also an Edition on better paper, bound in cloth, richly gilt, gilt edges. 3/6. And an *Edition de luxe* printed on large 4to paper, embellished with thirty-one Full-page Illustrations and a Coloured Portrait of St. Agnes. Handsomely bound. £1 1/-.

A Few Flowers from the Roman Campagna. Small 4to, cloth gilt, printed in red and black. 1/- net (postage 2d.).

New Visits to the Blessed Sacrament. Edited by Cardinal Wiseman. Containing Devotions to the Quarant' Ore and other Occasions of Exposition and Benediction. Cloth, red edges. 2/-.

Characteristics from the Writings of Cardinal Wiseman. Edited, and with a Preface by the Rev. T. E. Bridgett, C.SS.R. Crown 8vo, cloth. 6/-.

New Classified Catalogue of Standard Books (84 pages), comprising every class of book in demand among Catholic Readers, post free on application.

BURNS & OATES, LIMITED,
Granville Mansions, 28, Orchard Street, London, W.

www.ingramcontent.com/pod-product-compliance
Lightning Source LLC
Chambersburg PA
CBHW051722300426
44115CB00007B/420